PARTICIPATORY GRANTMAKING IN PHILANTHROPY

Georgetown Studies in Philanthropy, Nonprofits, and Nongovernmental Organizations

Series Editor
Gregory R. Witkowski, *Kean University*

This series emphasizes critical approaches to understanding formal/informal giving and institutions engaged in the social economy, both domestically and internationally. It brings to light the multiple tools that can advance visions of the social good and, using a critical lens, examines racial and social inequality built into the sector. The series explores how cultural traditions continue to affect us even as new technologies disrupt our practices and shape our work. These books seek to advance knowledge and improve practice, with both scholars and practitioners as intended readers.

Series Editorial Advisory Board
Lucy Bernholz, *Stanford University*
Angela Eikenberry, *University of Nebraska, Omaha*
Chao Guo, *University of Pennsylvania*
Fredrick Harris, *Columbia University*
Michael Moody, *Grand Valley State University*
Bhekinkosi Moyo, *University of the Witswatersrand*

PARTICIPATORY GRANTMAKING IN PHILANTHROPY

HOW DEMOCRATIZING DECISION-MAKING SHIFTS POWER TO COMMUNITIES

CYNTHIA M. GIBSON, CHRIS CARDONA,
JASMINE McGINNIS JOHNSON,
AND DAVID SUÁREZ, EDITORS

GEORGETOWN STUDIES IN PHILANTHROPY, NONPROFITS,
AND NONGOVERNMENTAL ORGANIZATIONS

GEORGETOWN UNIVERSITY PRESS / WASHINGTON, DC

© 2025 Cynthia M. Gibson, Chris Cardona, Jasmine McGinnis Johnson, and David Suárez. All rights reserved. No part of this book may be reproduced or utilized in any form or by any means, electronic or mechanical, including photocopying and recording, or by any information storage and retrieval system, without permission in writing from the publisher.

The publisher is not responsible for third-party websites or their content. URL links were active at time of publication.

Library of Congress Cataloging-in-Publication Data

Names: Gibson, Cynthia M., editor. | Cardona, Chris, editor. | Johnson, Jasmine McGinnis, editor. | Suárez, David F., editor.
Title: Participatory grantmaking in philanthropy: how democratizing decision-making shifts power to communities / editors, Cynthia M. Gibson, Chris Cardona, Jasmine McGinnis Johnson, David Suárez.
Description: Washington, DC: Georgetown University Press, 2024. | Series: Georgetown studies in philanthropy, nonprofits, and nongovernmental organizations | Includes bibliographical references and index.
Identifiers: LCCN 2024008530 (print) | LCCN 2024008531 (ebook) | ISBN 9781647125165 (hardcover) | ISBN 9781647125172 (paperback) | ISBN 9781647125189 (ebook)
Subjects: LCSH: Grantmaking—United States. | Endowments—United States.
Classification: LCC HV16 .P37 2024 (print) | LCC HV16 (ebook) | DDC 658.15/224—dc23/eng/20240916

LC record available at https://lccn.loc.gov/2024008530
LC ebook record available at https://lccn.loc.gov/2024008531

♾ This paper meets the requirements of ANSI/NISO Z39.48-1992 (Permanence of Paper).

26 25   9 8 7 6 5 4 3 2   First printing

Printed in the United States of America

Cover design by Jeremy John Parker
Interior design by Westchester

CONTENTS

Introduction: Participatory Approaches to Philanthropy: The Distinct Role of Participatory Grantmaking   1
Cynthia M. Gibson, Chris Cardona, Jasmine McGinnis Johnson, and David Suárez

Part I: Mapping Participatory Grantmaking Practice   33

1 Institutional Change or Shooting Star? The Landscape of Stakeholder Participation among Large Foundations in the United States   35
Emily Finchum-Mason, Kelly Husted, and David Suárez

2 From Collaboration to Ceding Power: The Impact of Participation on Grant Decisions   62
Jasmine McGinnis Johnson

3 Participatory Grantmaking Practices among Women's Funds: What Has Been Learned?   80
Elizabeth Barajas-Román and Mirenda Meghelli

Part II: Case Studies of Participatory Grantmaking in Action   97

4 Grounding Practice in a Movement's Principles: Why the Disability Rights Fund and the Disability Rights Advocacy Fund Continue to Prioritize Participation   101
Melanie Kawano-Chiu and Jen Bokoff

5 The Haymarket People's Fund: Evaluating an Antiracist Grantmaking Model   127
Eva King, Jaime Smith, and Kathryn Destin

6 Revolutionizing Philanthropy: Inclusive Participatory Processes in the New England Grassroots Environment Fund   162
Bart Westdijk and Sarah Huang

7 Global Participatory Grantmaking: Through a Climate Justice Lens   187
Laura García and Teresa Odendahl

8 Participatory Grantmaking and Giving Traditions in Communities of Color: The CLLCTIVLY Case   217
Stephanie Clintonia Boddie and Tracy R. Rone

Part III: The Challenges for and Limits of Participatory Grantmaking   259

9 Community Representation, COVID-19, and the Challenges of Shifting Grantmaking Power: How a Public LGBTQ+ Foundation Weighed the Options   261
Elizabeth J. Dale and Katie Carter

10 Community Foundations and Community Leadership: An Approach to Participatory Philanthropy   285
Melody MacLean, Caroline Merenda, and Len Bartel

11 "Participatoriness" in Philanthropy: A Conservative Perspective   312
Michael E. Hartmann and William A. Schambra

12 What Will It Take to Change? Traditional Foundations and Megadonors Experiment with Participatory Grantmaking   328
Anne Katahira with Marissa Jackson

Conclusion: Future Directions for Participatory Grantmaking Research and Implementation   354
Chris Cardona, Cynthia M. Gibson, Jasmine McGinnis Johnson, and David Suárez

Editors' and Contributors' Affiliations   365

Index   367

INTRODUCTION

Participatory Approaches to Philanthropy
The Distinct Role of Participatory Grantmaking

Cynthia M. Gibson, Chris Cardona, Jasmine McGinnis Johnson, and David Suárez

Philanthropy, in its purest form, is "love of humanity."[1] Historically, this has taken the form of mutual aid, collective giving, tithing, and other forms of community-minded generosity not necessarily tied to formal institutions.[2] Even when those institutions began emerging, the community mind-set prevailed. Established in 1914 in Cleveland, the nation's first community foundation was to "pool donor resources and use them to directly benefit the community."[3]

This community mind-set—particularly in relation to stakeholder voice, empowerment, and self-determination—has waned with philanthropy's gradual professionalization.[4] Philanthropy is now an organizational field comprising hundreds of thousands of foundations, philanthropic advisors, donor-advised funds, academic programs, and research centers across the country that control trillions of charitable dollars.[5] Philanthropy has also been transformed in its practice—moving from what was largely a values-based tradition to one that has become more technocratic. This reached a peak in the early 2000s, when solving social problems—which had for decades been treated as the purview of the nonprofits to which foundations made grants—became the modus operandi of many foundations themselves. Hallmarks of the latter included top-down approaches to grantmaking that were focused on clear and limited goals, theories of change and logic models, and evidence-based processes.[6] Local, small-scale, community-based organizations, in contrast, were viewed as incapable of addressing complex social issues, leaving them "consigned to the periphery . . . with large-scale, national, expert-driven efforts taking center stage."[7]

The pendulum, however, appears to be swinging back. During this time of dramatic change, people are becoming distrustful of established institutions and are demanding more accountability and transparency.[8] Across sectors, elite-driven decision-making is increasingly viewed with suspicion, if not outright hostility. And the staggering amount of wealth held in a relatively small number of hands has fueled a ferocious debate about the disproportionate amount of power that comes with it—including philanthropic power. Joanne Barkan, Anand Giridharadas, Rob Reich, and Emma Saunders-Hastings are just a few of the ever-growing circle of critics publicly challenging the notion that "all giving is good" and that philanthropy, "far from being an antidote, could and does actually support the structures that perpetuate inequality and reinforce the social advantages . . . of the wealthy."[9]

One of the tensions these and other critics have surfaced is the relationship between institutions and communities. Can the spark of human generosity, cultivated in individual and collective settings, be preserved when carried into an institution with rules, procedures, and agendas? One of the ways this can happen is through participation, specifically, inviting people outside the walls of established organizations or systems to weigh in, cocreate, offer feedback, and especially, form partnerships in making decisions that affect their lives and communities.

Many organizations are starting to supplant traditional top-down, elite, and impenetrable systems with these kinds of participatory processes. They have not yet, however, permeated philanthropy to the degree one might expect, given its roots in an ethics of mutuality, fellowship, and comity. As Gates and Rourke note, "While the media, politics, government, nonprofits, and businesses have been trying to find ways to meet the new demands of these hyper-connected times, one part of society has until recently remained nearly immune from such pressure. That is organized philanthropy," [i.e., tax-exempt public and private foundations] institutions that "make decisions behind closed doors . . . out of the glare of public review."[10]

Organized or "institutional" philanthropy is a key qualifier when it comes to whether and to what extent the field has embraced participation. Some argue that philanthropy actually has moved toward more democratization through crowdfunding, giving circles, digital giving, and other platforms that make it easier for anyone to be a philanthropist.[11] A number of smaller foundations include community members, or what some call their "peers," in grantmaking processes that are deliberately inclusive of and accessible to the larger community.[12] These funders are moving away from unilaterally deciding what gets done to working with the community to set priorities and funding criteria, develop strategies, review proposals, govern, and evaluate. All these are components of a participatory approach to philanthropy, and all can be—and are being—used by these institutions at different points in their process.

Some, however, are taking it one step further and involving outsiders in making decisions about who receives financial support—what is more commonly referred to as "participatory grantmaking." Generally, *participatory grantmaking* is defined as a process that cedes decision-making power about funding to the communities a foundation or donor aims to serve. Although participatory grantmaking is gaining traction across the field, two groups, in particular, have been reluctant to embrace it: traditional foundations and megadonors.

The first group consists of grantmaking organizations, such as private foundations, family foundations, corporate foundations, and community foundations. Generally, these organizations are governed by a board of directors, have professional staffs, and enjoy financial endowments (or a relationship with a corporate entity) that allow them to exist in perpetuity and make grants to charitable, nonprofit organizations.

The second group that has been somewhat hesitant to embrace participatory grantmaking is mega donors. These are individuals with assets of more than $30 million who may not use the traditional foundation model for their giving but operate with administrative setups (staff, lawyers, consultants, and management firms) that make them functionally similar to foundations, and thus they are often considered alongside them.[13] What they have in common is a tendency to rely on top-down decision-making, usually by the donors and/or professional staff members who are far removed from the communities or constituencies they are supporting.

Why have these two groups lagged behind in adopting participatory grantmaking? The ability to make decisions about money is a form of power, which, once accumulated, is given up reluctantly. Also, grantmaking decisions are fraught with power imbalances, institutional and personal priorities, legal regulations, and potential conflicts of interest. As noted, the cult of expertise continues to reign supreme in many foundations and other forms of philanthropy, which provides justification for their role as philanthropic decision-makers. And, unlike other fields that have strict certification, credentialing, and continuing education requirements, philanthropy does not, leaving foundations and megadonors with little incentive to change.

Moreover, research and assessment about participation in philanthropy—not just in grantmaking but also across other parts of this process, including strategy development, priority setting, evaluation, and application creation—have been relatively scarce, leaving proponents to skew toward values-based arguments for its broader adoption (i.e., "it's the right thing to do"). Although this belief may resonate with some funders, it may be insufficient to persuade a larger swath that participatory grantmaking has merit. Some perhaps will be swayed by peer pressure or reminders of philanthropy's long history with—and roots in—participatory values and practice, yet many will want data showing that it produces desired outcomes.

Recognizing the need for research that can demonstrate the effects of participatory frameworks and practice in philanthropy—as well as lay a foundation for the development of shared language, typologies, and theoretical constructs that are necessary for field building, and from which other participatory fields might benefit—in 2019, the Ford Foundation (which has supported efforts to improve philanthropic practice by making it more equitable and inclusive) approved funding to fill this gap. It also used a participatory grantmaking approach to the entire process, which ended with nine research projects receiving funding.[14] The cohort spanned a mix of projects that covered a variety of methodologies, including mapping current participatory philanthropic practice across different subsectors; developing tool kits for individual donors and foundations experimenting with the practice; and documenting the experiences and lessons learned by longtime participatory grantmaking institutions.

This book captures the findings of several of these research projects, as well as a few additional contributions that illuminate distinctive opportunities and challenges associated with participatory grantmaking. Taken together, its chapters highlight the potential of participatory grantmaking to reflect philanthropy's communitarian roots while also recognizing the limitations and unresolved tensions associated with this philanthropic approach. Most important, they provide a springboard for further discussion and study.

Because the tensions that emerge in participatory grantmaking (and other participatory approaches in philanthropy) have been—and continue to be—endemic to the practice of participation across other sectors, the editors of this collection believe it is important to begin by providing an overview of the literature on participation, organizations, and democracy. The latter situates participatory grantmaking and other philanthropic power-sharing innovations in this broader context because the study of voluntary participation in organizations and democratic processes has been occurring for decades and has surfaced a considerable amount of research and insights to offer philanthropy, which is relatively new to these theories and approaches. It also helps to inform our and the chapter authors' research on participatory grantmaking, which we hope will expand on this literature in a way that has not yet been undertaken. After that, we present the historical roots and contemporary drivers of participatory grantmaking. We then discuss several challenges associated with establishing an evidentiary basis for participatory grantmaking. In the remainder of the introduction, we explain how this book advances the literature, and we also clarify how each chapter makes a distinctive contribution that grows the field.

PARTICIPATION, ORGANIZATIONS, AND DEMOCRACY

The academic literature on participation and its links to democracy is extensive, spanning social science disciplines like sociology, political science, and economics, as well as the fields of urban planning, public management, nonprofit studies, and others.[15] This literature also has a long historical legacy, dating back at least to Tocqueville's nineteenth-century publication of *Democracy in America* and his observation that the people of the nascent American Republic had a distinctive commitment to voluntarism.[16] This study spurred voluminous research about the role of community groups and associations as "laboratories of citizenship" that could serve as vehicles for teaching and implementing democratic practice at the local level.[17]

There is still a considerable debate regarding how much and under what conditions participation in an organization generates subsequent civic engagement, particularly after accounting for the predisposition for an individual to volunteer, but the extant research demonstrates that volunteering in organizations can have long-term effects on civic engagement.[18] Research on participation has explored many additional salient questions as well, such as: What types of organizations have the greatest success in developing activists? Are "citizen groups" as effective in achieving their policy goals as professionalized advocacy organizations and interest groups? Why does participation (in organizations, elections, etc.) increase or decrease over time in a society?[19]

More recently, two opposing perspectives have coalesced in reaction to the same ongoing trends: (1) the growing implementation of novel tools for direct democracy or forms of "empowered participatory governance"; and (2) expanding stakeholder participation in the regular activities of organizations in all sectors of society (for-profit, nonprofit, and public). The first line of research tends to have a positive, normative view of individual participation in political processes (e.g., voting) and in the work of government and public agencies more generally (e.g., deliberative democracy and public problem solving). As a result, many studies in this line of research are encouraged by the ongoing trends in participation and seek to bolster them by demonstrating "what works" or by revealing the conditions or contexts that mediate effective participation.[20]

The second line of research investigates participation with a more critical lens. An older literature on "bad civil society" reflects this approach somewhat, demonstrating for instance that associations can employ democratic processes for antidemocratic purposes.[21] Newer studies, under the label of "new public participation," point out that research must attend to the political context for participation; and to do so, they ask questions such as: How do new participatory forms help to produce and reinforce inequality? How does the new public participation produce new forms of authority and legitimacy for elites? What unintended consequences emerge from participatory projects in unequal contexts?[22]

Studies in this tradition are less interested in the effects of participation than in how rising participation masks and may even accelerate growing inequality: "What many see as today's participatory renaissance appears to be richer and deeper than the programmatic efforts of earlier generations. Yet it also coincides with a dramatic expansion in socioeconomic inequalities over the past forty years, which have entailed a growing polarization between institutional elites and everyone else. The new participatory revival also coincides with the neoliberal turn in policymaking."[23] This "revival" is also correlated with two other phenomena: the rise of social media and communications technologies that allow wider numbers of people to participate visibly in public life; and the fact that private foundations are beginning to experience a sudden and vast accumulation of wealth. With regard to the latter, we acknowledge that some foundations will launch participatory initiatives solely to burnish their reputations.

At the same time, the distinctive emphasis on stakeholder decision-making in philanthropy, especially about grantmaking decisions, contrasts markedly with the paternalistic and technocratic approaches that have characterized the recent history of foundation grantmaking—and, as we discuss in greater detail below, the decision-making element is critical because of its relevance for community strength, agency, and capacity.[24]

THE HISTORICAL ROOTS AND CONTEMPORARY DRIVERS OF PARTICIPATORY GRANTMAKING

The growth of participatory grantmaking is quite recent, yet precursors to the approach can be traced back to long-standing philanthropic traditions. This section explores why participatory grantmaking has emerged and gained momentum at this particular moment in time by illuminating its historical roots and contemporary drivers.

Historical Roots

Participation may seem a relatively new focus for philanthropy, but its history indicates otherwise.[25] Long before it became a professionalized organizational field, informal giving and various forms of community-minded generosity characterized philanthropy. Communities of color have particularly rich traditions of giving on which to draw, often forged out of necessity when the larger society actively sought to discourage their collective action.[26]

These and other traditions—some dating back centuries—are the bedrock on which participatory grantmaking has been built. One of the dominant historical lines of participatory grantmaking can be traced to the 1970s, with the appearance of philanthropic institutions using more inclusive approaches that aligned with their interest in advancing economic equality, racial equity, and civil and human rights.[27] The Funding Exchange, for example, was a national network of public foundations embracing social justice that was established in 1979 by young activists with inherited wealth. With a "change, not charity" vision, these founding members pioneered what they saw as a new approach to philanthropy, which would transform power dynamics by involving community activists in grantmaking decisions.[28] While the Funding Exchange itself ceased operations in 2018, many of the social justice public foundations it convened continue to operate and innovate in their use of participatory approaches.[29]

While community involvement in institutional philanthropy was still far outside the norm, the participatory values embedded in the era's social justice movements fueled new philanthropic organizations and networks dedicated to those values. Among these were the Ms. Foundation for Women, National Committee for Responsive Philanthropy, Funders for LGBTQ Issues, and the Tides Foundation. These innovative participatory initiatives, nevertheless, were limited to smaller, typically public foundations until the early 1990s, when the Charles Stewart Mott Foundation's Community

Foundations and Neighborhood Small Grants Program gave rise to Grassroots Grantmakers, a network of place-based funders in the United States and Canada that involves nongrantmakers in their activities, including grantmaking.[30] Then, in 1999, the Annie E. Casey Foundation's Making Connections antipoverty initiative emphasized resident voice in strategy development and included a resident-led grantmaking component.[31]

One of the first attempts by a private foundation to undertake a national participatory grantmaking initiative was made in 2007, when the Case Foundation created and launched Make It Your Own, a grants program that involved the public in every step of the grantmaking process.[32] Also in 2007, the Knight Foundation added a public participation component to its then-nascent News Challenge, which invited the public to submit innovative ideas for gathering local news and information, as well as to comment on them.[33]

While notable, these twenty-first-century efforts have been relatively rare as examples of national foundations experimenting with participatory approaches to philanthropy, including, although to a lesser extent, grantmaking. But this situation has begun to change, for a variety of reasons.

Contemporary Drivers

Today, four larger trends are prompting philanthropic institutions to move toward more participatory approaches. *First, traditional foundations and megadonors have become the focus of sustained critique from activists, nonprofit leaders, and academics, as part of a larger questioning of established institutions.* Trust in institutions generally has been on the decline for many years.[34] More recently, this has led to calls to divest power and money from traditional institutions such as the fossil fuel industry and the prison-industrial complex.[35] Traditional foundations that invest their financial endowments in these industries are no longer immune from such pressures. Their reliance on top-down, expert-driven decision-making is also increasingly seen as an example of "old power," in contrast to network-based and distributed forms of "new power."[36] This perspective emerged publicly in 2018 with the near-simultaneous publication of *Winners Take All*, *Decolonizing Wealth* and *Just Giving*—three books that launched a cycle of philanthropic critique with an intensity that had not been seen since the 1960s, when the Filer Commission was established to assess federal policy on foundations.[37] The upshot of these critiques is that traditional foundations are elitist, nontransparent, and plutocratic—and thus focused on their own, rather than society's, interests. Megadonors have been subjected to similar critiques, particularly as the lines between their personal giving and that of the foundations bearing their names become blurred. Examples include critiques of the Bill & Melinda Gates Foundation's investments in public education, and MacKenzie Scott, who made headlines for giving away billions by simply writing no-strings-attached checks for hundreds of nonprofits but who used a process to make those decisions that was overseen by a well-heeled consulting firm and not made public.[38]

Second, *"people power" is on the rise—an ethos that participatory grantmaking embodies.* Today, technologies are giving people access to systems and institutions once controlled by experts and other gatekeepers. Amid growing fears that democracy is under threat, there has been a surge in the number of civil society organizations internationally—a part of a global associational revolution—that emphasizes civic participation, empowerment, equality, and justice.[39] The latter are inherent in participatory practice, which has exploded as a result, including in the philanthropic sector, where a growing number of organizations are now dedicated to this ethos—among them, the Trust-Based Philanthropy Project, Fund for Shared Insight, Justice Funders, Feedback Labs, and a rapidly growing community of practice comprising five-hundred-plus participatory grantmakers around the world that meets regularly to share knowledge and best practices.

Third, *calls for greater racial and other equity, diversity, and inclusion necessarily involve greater participation in decision-making by marginalized communities, or "nothing about us without us."* The US civil sector is in the midst of a reckoning about its systemic failure to recognize and address the historic legacy of racial, gender, sexual orientation, disability, and class exclusion that have shaped national history and generated the social needs that nonprofits seek to remedy. This reckoning includes a reexamination of the role nonprofits themselves play in perpetuating inequality across multiple dimensions, which is often reflected in how they function, as well as how they are funded, governed, and staffed.[40] As more nonprofits and funders have sought to acknowledge and repair these structural issues, participation has emerged as one means to operationalize equity.

Fourth and finally, *though they were once viewed as "fringe," participatory approaches to philanthropy, including participatory grantmaking, have been validated by mainstream sources, fueling further interest by a wider range of funders.* In late 2018, *Inside Philanthropy* announced its annual philanthropy awards, calling participatory grantmaking one of the sector's "most promising reforms," and more recently it included the approach as the "trend we hope sticks around."[41] And in 2019, the World Economic Forum wrote, "New efforts are required to help philanthropy adapt to changing times ... and to find models and approaches that can [respond to growing] criticism. . . . Participatory grantmaking is one of them."[42] This kind of recognition has led to a growing demand for more information about participatory philanthropy as well as more attention to it.[43]

THE CHALLENGE OF ESTABLISHING AN EVIDENTIARY BASIS FOR PARTICIPATORY GRANTMAKING

Advocates of participatory grantmaking posit that it benefits the foundations that adopt the approach, the participants that contribute to such initiatives, and the communities those individuals represent. However, establishing credible evidence for these bold claims has been inhibited by ambiguity in how the approach is defined and by its conflation with several alternative power-sharing innovations in philanthropy.

Definitional Ambiguity

A formidable barrier to building evidence about the effects of participatory grantmaking is that the innovation is complex and means different things to different people. This has resulted in a lack of consensus about what participatory grantmaking is and what it looks like in practice. Generally, practitioners doing this work agree that it emphasizes "nothing about us without us" and shifts power in grantmaking decisions from foundation staff, board members, donors, or experts to the people most affected by the issues.[44] They also agree that the process itself gives agency to people who benefit from funding to determine the priorities of their own lives. And to varying degrees, they see participatory grantmaking as one element of a larger project of democratizing the philanthropic sector.

In 2018, the Foundation Center (now Candid) published the "GrantCraft Guide"—part of a series of educational monographs aimed at foundation staff—on participatory grantmaking, which elicited the insights and experience of more than thirty practitioners around the world.[45] A key question was how it defined this approach. After much discussion with the project's steering committee, the publication defined participatory grantmaking as "ceding decision-making power about funding decisions—including the strategy and criteria behind those decisions—to the very communities that a foundation aims to serve."[46]

While this definition has gained some traction, it has yet to be embraced as a standard across the various parts of this nascent field. One reason is that proponents talk about both participatory *philanthropy* and participatory *grantmaking*, and it is not always clear whether they are meant to be one and the same. Though some practitioners use the terms interchangeably, others see participatory grantmaking as distinct because it moves decision-making about money—and, in turn, power—to the people most affected by the issues donors are trying to address. Still others see participation on a continuum or hierarchy based on the degree to which nongrantmakers are part of all grantmaking-related activities (e.g., strategy, proposal review). For example, engaging outsiders in making funding decisions would be seen as the "highest level" of participation, strategy decisions or issue foci would be in the middle, and listening to and getting input or feedback from communities would be at the other end. These three views are captured in figure I.1.

Suggesting that participation should be viewed as a hierarchy is a notion that has raised hackles among funders leading a movement calling on colleagues to adopt better listening and feedback processes with grantees or other constituencies.[47] These practitioners assert that this is a positive and long-overdue shift for a field in which there is a lot of talk about addressing the power dynamics rife in philanthropy, but there is comparatively less commitment to action, so it is equally as important as other participatory approaches to philanthropy. Others maintain that while providing feedback is necessary, it is not enough to break down power imbalances, especially if the people asking for that feedback are still making the ultimate decisions about the lives of the people providing it. The result is a loop back to the top-down, expert-driven system that is ingrained in traditional foundations.[48]

Participatory grantmakers agree that understanding and practicing the art of good listening are essential first steps toward authentic and meaningful participatory philanthropy, but if the goal is authentic participation, they are insufficient. They say that funders who do not commit to making changes based on what they hear from participants may lose credibility and participants' trust, because participants' actual feedback is not used in decision-making. Involving participants and then carrying on with business as usual does nothing to shift who has the power and disregards community knowledge, according to these practitioners.

Recognizing a need for more clarity but acknowledging the protean nature of participatory grantmaking, a publication produced in 2018 by the Ford Foundation included a draft framework for participatory grantmaking

VIEW ONE: It's one of several kinds of participatory philanthropy.

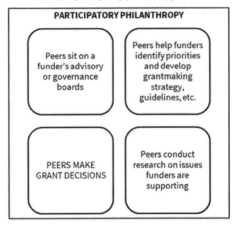

VIEW TWO: It's one kind of participatory philanthropy but the "highest level" in a hierarchy.

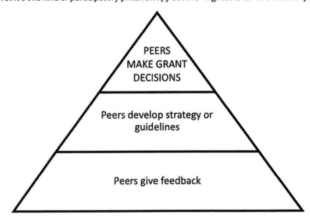

VIEW THREE: It's different from participatory philanthropy because it involves money, and money is power.

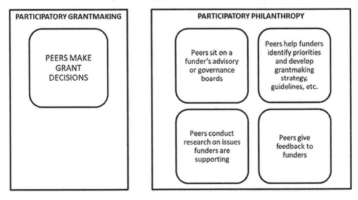

Figure I.1 Three Views of Participatory Grantmaking and the Role Peers Play in Each
Source: Cynthia M. Gibson, Cynthesis Consulting.

(see figure I.2) that laid out a set of stipulations that attempt to address the issues raised above. According to the monograph,[49] the draft framework (1) was a baseline—both grantmakers and nongrantmakers were encouraged to make modifications as they discussed and tested it in the field; (2) was not a hierarchy or continuum that assumed one level or tactic to be superior to another; (3) could be applied across different kinds of philanthropic institutions and networks; and (4) acknowledged that funding institutions may be at different points in their capacity or ability to incorporate participatory approaches, and that these efforts can be overlapping and fluid.

The framework also assumes that participatory grantmaking is a process rather than just one activity or tactic. That process occurs over three phases (pre-grant, grantmaking, postgrant), during which nongrantmakers can partner with grantmakers in several ways. In the pre-grant phase, stakeholders might identify funding priorities; conduct issue/environmental scans of issues, communities, and so on; design funding strategies; create funding criteria; review proposals; and make site visits. During the grantmaking phase, stakeholders might make grant decisions and support intermediaries that involve outsiders in making grant decisions. Finally, during the postgrant phase, stakeholders might decide on evaluation criteria and disseminate reports/results (figure I.3).

While this framework is largely focused on foundations, it can also be applied to megadonors, whose charitable giving, as noted above, tends to have some formal administrative structure. At the same time, the framework

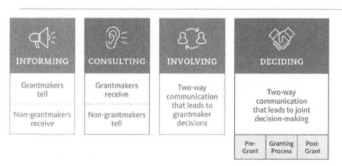

Figure I.2 Participatory Grantmaking Framework
Source: Cynthia M. Gibson, *Participatory Grantmaking: Has Its Time Come?* (New York: Ford Foundation, 2017).

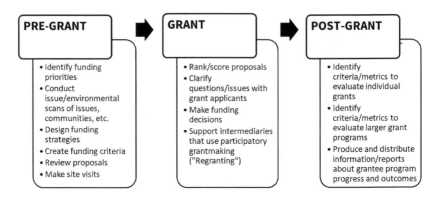

Figure I.3 An Expanded Definition of Participatory Grantmaking
Source: Cynthia M. Gibson, Cynthesis Consulting.

acknowledges that participatory grantmaking is embedded in the broader category of participatory approaches to philanthropy—and that not all participatory activity in foundations necessarily constitutes participatory grantmaking. For instance, a foundation might incorporate community representation into hiring and staffing decisions; restructure itself to be more collaborative and less hierarchical; increase transparency about its activities; or prioritize diversity, equity, and inclusion. We recognize that these efforts can engender a participatory organizational culture, which is an essential component of participatory grantmaking, but engaging in these activities does not always ensure that organizations will embody the ethos of participatory grantmaking.

Alternative Power-Sharing Innovations in Philanthropy

Another obstacle to establishing evidence about the effects of participatory grantmaking is its similarity to a set of giving/funding approaches that incorporate participatory elements or address power in philanthropy. Contrasting participatory grantmaking to its prominent alternatives can help sharpen its definition and identify its distinctive features:

- *Giving circles and giving projects:* Donors come together and pool their dollars, deciding together where to give the money and other resources such as volunteer time. Giving projects are a variation on

giving circles that incorporate a cross-class, cross-race membership and include political education.[50]
- *Crowdfunding:* The practice of collecting money from multiple individuals or sources in order to finance a new project. Often, crowdfunders use social media to share their platform or idea and inspire others to contribute to the funding campaign.
- *Trust-based philanthropy:* An initiative to address power imbalances between foundations and nonprofits that is rooted in a set of values to help advance equity, shift power, and build mutually accountable relationships. Grantmakers provide multiyear unrestricted funding; streamline their applications and reporting; and are committed to transparency, dialogue, relationship building, and mutual learning.[51]
- *#ShiftThePower community philanthropy:* Drawing on global experiences, this is an approach in which members of a geographic or identity community pool their resources to make decisions together about allocating those resources to benefit their own community. Community philanthropy is characterized in terms of "assets, capacities, and trust" by the Global Fund for Community Foundations, which launched the hashtag #ShiftThePower at its 2016 global summit.[52] Since then, the hashtag has become an online rallying point for efforts in the Global South to change the dynamics of power within traditional philanthropy and development aid.
- *Social justice philanthropy:* Though it has been supplanted in recent years by terms like "racial equity," "Just Transition," and "decolonizing wealth," social justice philanthropy remains a powerful intellectual current and tradition of practice, particularly among public foundations. It frames the *how* of grantmaking, including how decisions are made, as part of an overall transformation of how systems of power operate in society.[53]

As presented in figure I.4, one way to differentiate participatory grantmaking from many of these other approaches is to situate all of them in relation to two core dimensions of philanthropy: who is the decision-maker, and to what degree is power concentrated. The first dimension, the decision-maker, focuses on the philanthropic behavior of individuals and institutions. The second dimension, power, focuses on whether power over decisions is concentrated or distributed. Within this two-by-two matrix, we can situate participatory grantmaking and other forms of inclusion in philanthropy, and thereby clarify the focus of this book.

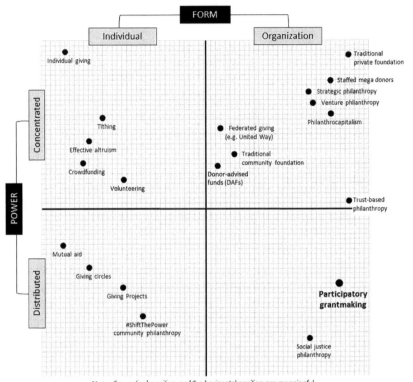

Figure I.4 The Matrix of Participation in Philanthropy by Decision-Maker Form and Power
Source: Author conceptualization.

The columns of this matrix distinguish two types of decision-makers in philanthropy: individual and institution. Individual philanthropy comprises conventional donations to public charities and mutual aid as well as newer approaches like effective altruism, giving circles, giving projects, and crowdfunding—forms of charitable giving used primarily by everyday individuals who tend to be self-organized rather than tied to larger institutions.[54] In contrast, institutional philanthropy attends to formal philanthropic organizations and their grantmaking, which includes private foundations, community foundations, and federated giving campaigns (like the United Way). Institutional philanthropy also applies to megadonors, who tend to make giving decisions with little public or "outsider" participation and have advisers, family offices, staff, or other kinds of institutional infrastructures that make them akin to foundations.

The rows of the matrix distinguish across the two types of decision-makers based on whether the power they hold is concentrated or distributed. For instance, while traditional giving to charities, crowdfunding, giving circles, and giving projects all are labeled as forms of individual giving shown in figure I.4, there are important differences regarding where decision-making power resides. Individual decision-makers can be distinguished as (1) everyday individual donors and contributors to crowdfunding campaigns (who act alone or in their household); and (2) mutual aid, giving circles, and giving projects, where multiple donors work together and develop relationships with each other in the course of their participation. With conventional donations, effective altruism, and crowdfunding, decision-making power is concentrated and typically has no relational element, as individuals give directly to the nonprofit they prefer. In contrast, power typically is distributed in mutual aid, giving circles, and giving projects, and these collective forms of participatory philanthropy entail social interaction. Participants concede some control over their donations when they contribute to a larger "pot" that gets disbursed according to rules established by the group.[55]

Organizational or institutional decision-makers can be distinguished as (1) traditional private foundations, community foundations, federated giving campaigns, and megadonors that exercise decision-making power in a concentrated manner; and (2) foundations (public and private) and megadonors that that make funding decisions in concert with nonprofit partners or members of the communities they seek to serve. In traditional private foundations, power is concentrated in the governing board, which usually consists either of the primary donor and members of their family or a body of elite leaders, such as bankers, lawyers, and corporate executives who rarely reflect the communities the foundation seeks to serve.. Power is concentrated in traditional community foundations and federated giving campaigns as well; their boards may include community members, but that does not mean those boards are very diverse or their grantmaking processes transparent.[56] Technocratic approaches to giving, like strategic philanthropy and venture philanthropy, are similar in that power is concentrated in program officers and the donors they serve retain decision-making power. While more inclusive and equitable than these other approaches, power is somewhat concentrated in trust-based philanthropy, too, because it preserves the prerogative of foundation staff members to make grant decisions. By contrast, power is distributed with participatory grantmaking and social justice philanthropy, as these approaches strive to integrate "locals" and individuals with relevant lived experience into the grantmaking processes of foundations.[57]

ADVANCING PARTICIPATORY GRANTMAKING RESEARCH AND PRACTICE

The preceding section did more than identify challenges associated with building evidence about the effects of participatory grantmaking; it highlighted core elements of the approach and distinguished it from alternative power-sharing approaches in philanthropy, both of which are essential for advancing participatory grantmaking research and practice. The overview of participatory grantmaking also provides multiple justifications for our focus on the bottom-right-hand corner of the matrix shown in figure I.4, where institutional decision-makers choose to distribute their power over grantmaking through participatory grantmaking. To begin with, we privilege this approach over other forms of participatory philanthropy presented in the matrix because it is uniquely attuned to current critiques of traditional foundations and megadonors, that is, those who tend to be more willing to engage in some participatory practices but not necessarily in ceding decisions involving financial resources.

Participatory grantmaking is neither the only way to infuse more participation into the practice of philanthropy nor the "best" way. But collective participatory approaches like mutual aid, giving projects, and donor circles are not directed at foundations (and in collective philanthropy, foundations are part of a broader ecosystem). Second, we privilege participatory grantmaking because, as figure I.3 suggests, the approach aligns with but can be distinguished from social justice philanthropy. To clarify, we consider participatory grantmaking to be more than a tactic; it is an ethos that can become marbled into all parts of the institution, its internal operations as well as external grantmaking. We nevertheless recognize the possibility that participatory grantmaking may contribute to democracy but not necessarily social justice.

Third, we focus on participatory grantmaking because it delegates decision-making power about all phases of the grantmaking process, including decisions about money, to stakeholders, which is critical for community voice, empowerment, and self-determination.[58] We take the position, then, that participatory grantmaking is a dimension of the broader phenomenon of participation in institutional philanthropy that bears special attention and study because it is centrally about who has decision-making power about grant funds, the primary currency of philanthropic action.

The decision-making role for stakeholders in the grantmaking processes clearly distinguishes participatory grantmaking from trust-based philanthropy, as well as the other approaches listed in the top-right quadrant of figure I.4.

The distinction we make between "deciding" and other forms of stakeholder participation draws very directly from the broader literature on the topic. Fields that have participation at their core—such as community organizing, community development, public problem-solving, and deliberative democracy—have grappled with how to engage ordinary people in public processes that goes beyond asking them for feedback and/or input (what deliberative democracy practitioners call thin participation) to how to involve them in planning, implementing, assessing, and developing efforts to strengthen communities (called thick participation).[59] We emphasize thick participation, or the top three rungs of Arnstein's ladder of participation—partnership, delegated power, and citizen control.[60]

We nevertheless support the effort to establish an inclusive definition of participatory grantmaking elaborated above. Instead of making the strong claim that other forms of participation in grantmaking processes (i.e., informing, consulting, involving) do not "count" as participatory grantmaking, we simply posit that the transformative, community-building potential of participatory grantmaking will depend on which elements are prioritized. Specifically, we expect the impact of participatory grantmaking to be significantly greater when it involves stakeholder decision-making than when it does not, which is just one of many assertions that research about participatory grantmaking can investigate.

Decision-making in participatory grantmaking, for instance, is not limited to the disbursement of charitable resources—who the recipients will be and how much they will receive. Crucially, setting the *strategy* that guides grantmaking, and defining the parameters of the *evaluation* that documents its impact, are also key decisions that in our definition, make up participatory grantmaking. Nonfunder (or stakeholder) participation in determining the criteria that will be used to make grant decisions, creating the overarching strategy that grantmaking seeks to achieve, and developing evaluative measures all constitute participatory grantmaking, in our view. And as a result, we expect the transformative, community-building potential of participatory grantmaking to be greater when it involves decision-making power over grant decisions than when it is limited to any of these other processes. Moreover, we expect the impact of participatory grantmaking to increase as stakeholder decision-making power over the number of components of the grantmaking process increases.

Finally, the "new public participation" literature has attuned us to the fact that foundation endowments, and societal inequality, have expanded more rapidly than all forms of participatory philanthropy. Much like the effects of volunteering in an organization on subsequent democratic participation, we expect the effects of participatory grantmaking on specific community outcomes (e.g., social capital, collective action, self-governance, and empowerment) will be contingent and conditional. Participatory grantmaking, furthermore, is not a silver bullet solution for democratizing philanthropy, strengthening community, and/or advocating for broader policy reform.

HOW THIS BOOK IS ORGANIZED

The authors of the studies that constitute this collection surfaced various findings regarding the theoretical underpinnings, practice, and outcomes of participatory grantmaking. These findings are described in the following chapters and organized into three parts: "Mapping Participatory Grantmaking Practice," "Participatory Grantmaking in Action: Case Studies," and "Challenges to and Limits of Participatory Grantmaking."

Mapping Participatory Grantmaking Practice

Part I of this book discusses three research projects focused on assessing the prevalence, types, and/or depth of participatory grantmaking across different philanthropic areas. The part begins, in chapter 1, with a study of participation approaches to philanthropy among America's largest private and community foundations, conducted by Emily Finchum-Mason, Kelly Husted, and David Suárez, of the Evans School of Public Policy and Governance at the University of Washington. Chapter 1 finds that, while 86 percent of large foundations report soliciting and utilizing feedback from their external stakeholders, few foundations indicate that they delegate decision-making authority to those stakeholders.

While there have been studies on deliberative participation involving technical or expert grantmakers and community members/residents making grant decisions jointly that used more analytical/traditional methods (e.g., scorecards), there has been little research examining the use of deliberative processes in which community members/residents were the primary decision-makers. In chapter 2, Jasmine Johnson, of George Washington University and the Urban Institute's Center on Nonprofits and Philanthropy, addresses this gap with her research that explores whether it matters *how* nongrantmakers are involved in these processes. Does the degree to which foundations cede power, consult, or collaborate with nongrantmakers affect the kinds of nonprofits that receive grants? If the participation of nonfunders in any or all of the components of the participatory grantmaking process leads to similar outcomes, it calls into question whether such participation is hierarchical. If not, it suggests that the variance may lie in how and to what degree participants are involved.

Although women's funds were one of the pioneers of participatory grantmaking, there has been little documentation of the current state of this practice and its evolution within the sector over the past decade. In chapter 3, Elizabeth Barajas-Román and Mirenda Meghelli of the Women's Funding Network—the largest alliance of women's funds and gender equity funders in the world—address this gap by creating a snapshot of this practice in community- and state-based women's funds. Their study finds that, while most of their network observes intentionally applied participatory funding principles, the practice has been identified differently depending on a variety of community-based factors. Further, some women's funds have evolved the practice to include other democratization strategies that help shift economic power to target communities.

Case Studies: Participatory Grantmaking in Action

One of the most commonly asked questions about participatory grantmaking is, "How do these processes work in real life?" Part II of the book attempts to provide some answers through five case studies (chapters 4–8) that delve into the nuts and bolts of the practice among different kinds of funds.

Many participatory grantmakers ground their approaches in the values of their field. The creation of the Disability Rights Fund and the Disability Rights Advocacy Fund (DRF/DRAF) was grounded in the disability rights community motto, "Nothing About Us Without Us," a principle that has been the guiding force for all DRF/DRAF international rights-based grantmaking practices, which include the active participation of persons with disabilities at all organizational levels. Chapter 4 outlines research on the fifteen-year history of DRF/DRAF's evolution as a participatory grantmaker, including its practices and how they distinguish DRF/DRAF's model of participatory grantmaking as a reflection of the larger disability rights movement. The authors also share how DRF/DRAF will continue to iterate on its participatory approaches and conclude by calling on the broader philanthropic field to adopt these approaches to better align with the social justice movements they support.

While participatory grantmaking has been gaining recognition among funders, Haymarket People's Fund has relied on community members to guide its grantmaking process for the past forty-eight years, a process it has simply called "grantmaking." In 2019—about thirteen years after Haymarket launched its transformational process to become an antiracist organization—it decided to take a step back and evaluate the effects of this organizational shift on its grantmaking model. In chapter 5, using a participatory action research process that involved academic researchers at Boston College, historical reviews, interviews, surveys, grantee reports, and data analysis, Haymarket presents key findings and recommendations for those interested in antiracist grantmaking models, a vital part of participatory decision-making.

Several years after its establishment in 1996, the New England Grassroots Environment Fund created a set of guiding values that included power shifting, transparency, and democracy. Since then, the fund has been deepening its comprehensive participatory decision-making process with frontline organizers, nonprofit colleagues, and funding partners. In chapter 6, Bart Westdijk, and Sarah Huang of the Grassroots Fund discuss how this approach—including participatory grantmaking—adds value or promotes diversity, equity, and inclusion. Working with a consultant, the fund has explored a set of key questions that inform its grantmaking practices and those of the broader philanthropic community.

Some of the most innovative approaches to participatory grantmaking are being undertaken by funders based in other parts of the world, which chapter 7 explores. In particular, participatory grantmaking across national borders requires additional cultural sensitivity and operational nuance. For decades, the Global Greengrants Fund has both facilitated such processes and advocated for their wider adoption within philanthropy. Based on this experience, and on related efforts like those of the Central American Women's Fund and FRIDA, the Young Feminist Fund, Terry Odendahl and Laura García unpack how participatory grantmaking can operate in global contexts and its implications for international philanthropy and development more broadly.

In chapter 8, Stephanie Clintonia Boddie of Baylor University and the University of South Africa and Tracy R. Rone of Morgan State University grapple with established philanthropic institutions' history of systematically ignoring or undervaluing giving traditions in communities of color as part of a broader disinvestment from those communities. These communal giving traditions share several features with participatory grantmaking, such as a collective approach to decision-making, an emphasis on relationships over transactions, and a connection with the act of giving to larger cultural practices. To highlight these common features, this chapter presents a case study of CLLCTIVLY, an evolving ecosystem and participatory grantmaking model for Black-led organizations and communities in Greater Baltimore. The study documents how the value and relevance of giving traditions in communities of color connect with the growing interest in participatory grantmaking.

Challenges to and Limits of Participatory Grantmaking

The chapters in part II of this book delve into specific contexts where participatory grantmaking has been applied successfully—that is, in ways that its practitioners believe enhance their pursuit of their missions. But this is not always the case. The four chapters (9–12) in part III present cases where practitioners decide that customary forms of participatory grantmaking do not fit their particular contexts, for an interesting variety of reasons.

In chapter 9, Elizabeth Dale of Seattle University discusses how the Pride Foundation, an LGBTQ+ public foundation working across five western US states, shifted its grantmaking practice to both align with the organization's racial equity core and include greater community participation in setting funding priorities and making grant decisions. The study documents the culture change efforts within the foundation through interviews with staff members, community groups, and grantee organizations, and it provides a road map for foundations wanting to adopt more participatory practices. Conducted during the height of the COVID-19 pandemic, the study raises important questions for foundations that want to align their grantmaking with an equity lens. One of these questions is under what circumstances should foundations explore and adopt alternative approaches to grantmaking. The chapter discusses how the Pride Foundation considered both participatory grantmaking and trust-based philanthropy and why it ultimately opted for the latter.

Chapter 9 further explores the manifestation of participatory grantmaking in community foundations, and whether it is a good fit. As charitable organizations that provide support for the needs of a geographic community or region, community foundations—compared with most philanthropic organizations—are particularly well positioned to employ a range of participatory approaches to philanthropy, including one that a group of community foundation leaders developed: community leadership. Through this approach, community foundations not only provide grants but also form partnerships with community stakeholders to identify important issues, commission research, convene decision-makers, engage in advocacy, and help marshal needed resources.

While the elements and goals of community leadership are similar to those of participatory grantmaking, in chapter 10, Melody MacLean, Caroline Merenda, and Len Bartels of CFLeads—a national network of community foundations committed to embedding this approach in their practices and cultures—show that there are important distinctions between the two. They suggest that while involving residents in grantmaking is one way to engage in participatory philanthropy and community leadership, it is not the only option. In particular, they recognize that most community foundations are reluctant to cede decision-making power on grants to community members, which some would view as the heart of participatory grantmaking. To expound on this assertion, the authors discuss how they have operationalized the community leadership approach, provide on-the-ground examples, and describe a research study they commissioned that included an assessment of community foundations' nongrantmaking roles, which served as a proxy measure of community leadership.

Chapter 11 tackles the ongoing question of why most participatory grantmaking seems to be occurring in progressive-leaning organizations and less so among more conservative foundations, especially given the latter's belief in community-based resolutions—rather than those that are government-funded or expert-driven/top-down—to poverty, food security, childcare, and other issues. This bottom-up perspective extends to philanthropy, which conservatives see as yet another system that favors elites and experts—but this time, in making funding decisions rather than involving the people most affected by those decisions in the process.

On the basis of this perspective, it is unsurprising that some conservatives have publicly voiced support for participatory grantmaking, including William Schambra of the Hudson Institute and Michael Hartmann of the Capital Research Center.[61] In chapter 11, they explain why this support—which confounds progressive funders, who see participatory grantmaking as inextricably linked to the social justice / liberal tradition—is aligned with their values and why more understanding of this perspective is critical for advancing the approach across a broader spectrum of philanthropic organizations.

At the same time, examples of efforts by conservative-leaning foundations and funders incorporating participatory approaches in their philanthropy—and a more formal argument for why they should—have been almost nonexistent. Schambra and Hartmann discuss the reasons for this seeming disconnect and also raise important questions/issues for conservative philanthropists to consider when more systematically moving toward practicing participatory grantmaking.

In chapter 12, Anne Katahira and Marissa Jackson—formerly of Philanthropy Northwest, a network for philanthropists in the Pacific Northwest—examine how both traditional foundations and megadonors are experimenting with participatory grantmaking, the motivation for which is a new or renewed commitment to racial equity. Through interviews with these grantmakers, Katahira and Jackson explore how organizational conditions—both internally (e.g., culture and power sharing/moving) and externally (e.g., trust, track record, and transparency)—shape whether and to what extent participatory grantmaking can take root and grow. Intriguingly, most of these donors have considered expanding their experiments but ultimately have opted not to do so. Katahira reflects, based on her decades of experience as a philanthropy practitioner, on what obstacles may impede traditional foundations and megadonors from continuing to adopt participatory grantmaking beyond an experimental phase. These reflections, which center on the donors' need for power and control, connect to fundamental questions about the future of philanthropy and the extent to which democratic participation can take root in a field that privileges the authority of the donor.

In the conclusion to this collection, the coeditors identify common threads across the twelve chapters, highlight ongoing issues and questions about participatory grantmaking, and identify areas for continued research. Ultimately, our aim with this collection is twofold: to build the evidence base on participatory grantmaking for those in the philanthropy sector, and to connect participatory grantmaking with the broader practice of democratic participation for those who study this phenomenon.

NOTES

1. Kevin Robbins, "The Nonprofit Sector in Historical Perspective: Traditions of Philanthropy in the West," in *The Nonprofit Sector: A Research Handbook*, ed. Walter Powell and Richard Steinberg (New Haven, CT: Yale University Press, 2006), 13–31; Robert Payton and Michael Moody, *Understanding Philanthropy: Its Meaning and Mission* (Bloomington: Indiana University Press, 2008).

2. Ariel Aberg-Riger, "'Solidarity, Not Charity': A Visual History of Mutual Aid," *Bloomberg CityLab*, December 22, 2020, www.bloomberg.com/news/features/2020-12-22/a-visual-history-of-mutual-aid.
3. David Hammack, "Community Foundations: The Delicate Question of Purpose," in *The Agile Servant*, ed. Richard Magat (New York: Foundation Center, 1989); Olivier Zunz, *Philanthropy in America: A History* (Princeton, NJ: Princeton University Press, 2014).
4. Kenneth Prewitt, Mattei Dogan, Steven Heydemann, and Stefan Toepler, eds., *The Legitimacy of Philanthropic Foundations: United States and European Perspectives* (New York: Russell Sage Foundation, 2006); Joel Fleishman, *The Foundation: A Great American Secret* (New York: PublicAffairs, 2007); Helmut Anheier and David Hammack, eds., *American Foundations: Roles and Contributions* (Washington, DC: Brookings Institution Press, 2010).
5. Paul DiMaggio, and Walter Powell, "The Iron Cage Revisited: Institutional Isomorphism and Collective Rationality in Organizational Fields," *American Sociological Review* 48, no. 2 (1983): 147–60; Emily Barman, "An Institutional Approach to Donor Control: From Dyadic Ties to a Field-Level Analysis," *American Journal of Sociology* 112, no. 5 (2007): 1416–57; Emily Barman, "The Social Bases of Philanthropy," *Annual Review of Sociology* 43 (2017): 271–90.
6. William Schambra, "Is Strategic Philanthropy Yesterday's News?" *Nonprofit Quarterly*, June 10, 2014; Michael Porter and Mark Kramer, "Philanthropy's New Agenda: Creating Value," *Harvard Business Review* 77 (1999): 121–31.
7. William Schambra, "MVPs of Civic Renewal," Giving Review blog, *Philanthropy Daily*, December 3, 2019.
8. Kaifeng Yang, "Trust and Citizen Involvement Decisions: Trust in Citizens, Trust in Institutions, and Propensity to Trust," *Administration & Society* 38, no. 5 (2006): 573–95.
9. Joanne Barkan, "Plutocrats at Work: How Big Philanthropy Undermines Democracy," *Dissent*, Fall 2013, 1–18; Anand Giridharadas, *Winner Take All: The Elite Charade of Changing the World* (New York: Knopf Vintage Books, 2018); Rob Reich, *Just Giving: Why Philanthropy Is Failing Democracy and How It Can Do Better* (Princeton, NJ: Princeton University Press, 2018); Emma Saunders-Hastings, *Private Virtues, Public Vices: Philanthropy and Democratic Equality* (Chicago: University of Chicago Press, 2022).
10. Chris Gates and Brad Rourke, "Foundations Must Rethink Their Ideas of Strategic Giving and Accountability," *Chronicle of Philanthropy*, May 18, 2014.
11. Sheila Herrling, "Four Trends Democratizing Philanthropy," Case Foundation blog, July 10, 2017, https://casefoundation.org/blog/four-trends-democratizing-philanthropy/; Lucy Bernholz, Edward Skloot, and Barry Varela, *Disrupting Philanthropy: Technology and the Future of the Social Sector* (Scotts Valley, CA: CreateSpace, 2010); Lucy Bernholz, *How We Give Now: A Philanthropic Guide for the Rest of Us* (Cambridge, MA: MIT Press, 2021).
12. Gillian Gaynair, "Participatory Grantmaking Aims to Dismantle Power Imbalances Between Funders and the Communities They Serve," Urban Institute blog, May 12, 2021, www.urban.org/urban-wire/participatory-grantmaking-aims-dismantle-power-imbalances-between-funders-and-communities-they-serve.
13. Wealth-X, *Ultra High Net Worth Philanthropy*, https://go.wealthx.com/download-ultra-high-net-worth-philanthropy-report-2022.

14. More information about this process can be found at www.fordfoundation.org/work/learning/learning-reflections/participatory-grantmaking-matters-now-more-than-ever/.
15. Sherri Arnstein, "A Ladder of Citizen Participation," *Journal of the American Institute of Planners* 35, no. 4 (1969): 216–24; Kelly Leroux, "Nonprofits as Civic Intermediaries: The Role of Community-Based Organizations in Promoting Political Participation," *Urban Affairs Review* 42 (2007): David E. Campbell, *Why We Vote: How Schools and Communities Shape Our Civic Life* (Princeton, NJ: Princeton University Press, 2008); Kirk Emerson, Tina Nabatchi, and Stephen Balogh, "An Integrative Framework for Collaborative Governance," *Journal of Public Administration Research and Theory* 22, no. 1 (2012): 1–29; Anna Amirkhanyan and Kristina Lambright, *Citizen Participation in the Age of Contracting* (New York: Routledge, 2018); David Suárez, "Advocacy, Civic Engagement, and Social Change," in *The Nonprofit Sector: A Research Handbook*, 3rd edition, ed. Walter Powell and Patricia Bromley (Stanford, CA: Stanford University Press, 2020), 487–506.
16. Alexis de Tocqueville, *Democracy in America* (Garden City, NY: Doubleday, 1969; orig. pub. 1835–40).
17. Joshua Cohen and Joel Rogers, "Secondary Associations and Democratic Governance," *Politics & Society* 20, no. 4 (1992): 393–472; Elizabeth Clemens, "The Constitution of Citizens: Political Theories of Nonprofit Organizations," in *The Nonprofit Sector: A Research Handbook*, 2nd edition, ed. Walter Powell and Richard Steinberg (New Haven, CT: Yale University Press, 2006), 207–20; Jennifer Dodge and Sonia Ospina, "Nonprofits as 'Schools of Democracy': A Comparative Case Study of Two Environmental Organizations," *Nonprofit and Voluntary Sector Quarterly* 45, no. 3 (2016): 478–99.
18. Daniel McFarland and Reuben Thomas, "Bowling Young: How Youth Voluntary Associations Influence Adult Political Participation," *American Sociological Review* 71, no. 3 (2006): 401–25; Debra Minkoff, "The Payoffs of Organizational Membership for Political Activism in Established Democracies," *American Journal of Sociology* 122, no. 2 (2016): 425–68; Tom Van Der Meer and Erik Van Ingen, "Schools of Democracy? Disentangling the Relationship Between Civic Participation and Political Action in 17 European Countries," *European Journal of Political Research* 48 (2009): 281–308; Hahrie Han, "The Organizational Roots of Political Activism: Field Experiments on Creating a Relational Context," *American Political Science Review* 110, no. 2 (2016): 296–307; Carolina Johnson, H. Jacob Carlson, and Sonya Reynolds, "Testing the Participation Hypothesis: Evidence from Participatory Budgeting," *Political Behavior* 45 (2023): 3–32.
19. Robert Putnam, "Bowling Alone: America's Declining Social Capital," *Journal of Democracy* 6 (1995): 65–78; Theda Skocpol, *Diminished Democracy: From Membership to Management in American Civic Life* (Oklahoma City: University of Oklahoma Press, 2003); Cynthia Gibson, "In Whose Interest: Do National Nonprofit Advocacy Organizations Represent the Underrepresented?" *Nonprofit Quarterly* 13, no. 2 (Summer 2006), 14–17; Jeffrey Berry, *The New Liberalism: The Rising Power of Citizen Groups* (Washington, DC: Brookings Institution Press, 2010); Hahrie Han, *How Organizations Develop Activists* (Oxford: Oxford University Press, 2014).
20. Archon Fung and Erik Olin Wright, "Deepening Democracy: Innovations in Empowered Participatory Governance," *Politics & Society* 29, no. 1 (2001): 5–41; Archon Fung,

"Varieties of Participation in Complex Governance," *Public Administration Review* 66 (2006): 66–75; Tina Nabatchi, John Gastil, G. Michael Weiksner, and Matt Leighninger, eds., *Democracy in Motion: Evaluating the Practice and Impact of Deliberative Civic Engagement* (New York: Oxford University Press, 2012); John Bryson and Kathryn Quick, "Designing Public Participation Processes," *Public Administration Review* 73, no. 1 (2013): 23–34; Brian Christens and Paul Speer, "Community Organizing: Practice, Research, and Policy Implications," *Social Policy Issues and Policy Review* 9, no. 1 (2015): 193–222; Gianpaolo Baiocchi and Ernesto Ganuza, *Popular Democracy: The Paradox of Participation* (Stanford, CA: Stanford University Press, 2017); Nicole Curato, John Dryzek, Selen Ercan, Carolyn Hendriks, and Simon Niemeyer, "Twelve Key Findings in Deliberative Democracy Research," *Daedulus* 146, no. 3 (2017): 28–38.

21. Sarah White, "Depoliticising Development: The Uses and Abuses of Participation," *Development in Practice* 6, no. 1 (1996): 6–15; Simone Chambers and Jeffrey Kopstein, "Bad Civil Society," *Political Theory* 29, no. 6 (2001): 837–65; Elizabeth Theiss-Morse and John Hibbing, "Citizenship and Civic Engagement," *Annual Review of Political Science* 8 (2005): 227–49.

22. Edward Walker, "Privatizing Participation: Civic Change and the Organizational Dynamics of Grassroots Lobbying Firms," *American Sociological Review* 74 (2006): 83–105; Nina Eliasoph, *Making Volunteers: Civic Life after Welfare's End* (Princeton, NJ: Princeton University Press, 2011); Nina Eliasoph, "Measuring the Grassroots: Puzzles of Cultivating the Grassroots from the Top Down." *Sociological Quarterly* 55, no. 3 (2014): 467–92; Edward Walker, *Grassroots for Hire* (Cambridge. Cambridge University Press, 2014); Caroline Lee, *Do-It-Yourself Democracy: The Rise of the Public Engagement Industry* (Oxford: Oxford University Press, 2015); Caroline Lee, "Participatory Practices in Organizations." *Sociology Compass* 9 no. 4 (2015): 272–88; Caroline Lee, Michael McQuarrie, and Edward T. Walker, eds., *Democratizing Inequalities: Dilemmas of New Public Participation* (New York: New York University Press, 2015); Jeremy Levine, "The Paradox of Community Power: Cultural Processes and Elite Authority in Participatory Governance," *Social Forces* 95, no. 3 (2017): 1155–79.

23. Caroline Lee, Michael McQuarrie, and Edward T. Walker, eds., "Rising Participation and Declining Democracy," in *Democratizing Inequalities*, 13.

24. Elinor Ostrom, *Governing the Commons* (Cambridge: Cambridge University Press, 1990); Michael McGinnis, "An Introduction to IAD and the Language of the Ostrom Workshop: A Simple Guide to a Complex Framework," *Policy Studies Journal* 39, no. 1 (2011): 169–83.

25. Cynthia Gibson, "The Historical Case for Participatory Grantmaking," *HistPhil*, August 15, 2019, https://histphil.org/2019/08/15/the-historical-case-for-participatory-grantmaking/.

26. Edgar Villanueva, *Decolonizing Wealth: Indigenous Wisdom to Heal Divides and Restore Balance* (Oakland: Berrett-Koehler, 2018); Tyrone Freeman, "400 Years of Black Giving: From the Days of Slavery to the 2019 Morehouse Graduation," *Conversation*, August 22, 2019, https://theconversation.com/400-years-of-black-giving-from-the-days-of-slavery-to-the-2019-morehouse-graduation-121402; Abby Rolland, "Philanthropy in America: Diverse, Historic, Generous," Lilly Family School of Philanthropy blog, September 26, 2019, https://blog.philanthropy.iupui.edu/2019/09/26/philanthropy-in-america-diverse-historic-generous/.

27. Susan Ostrander, *Money For Change: Social Movement Philanthropy at the Haymarket People's Fund* (Philadelphia: Temple University Press, 1995).

INTRODUCTION   29

28. Funding Exchange, "Funding Exchange History," 2021, https://fex.org/.
29. Giving Project Network, "Giving Project Network," https://www.givingprojects.org. A network of public social justice foundations that were formerly members of the Funding Exchange has incubated and disseminated the Giving Project model, a cross-class, cross-race giving circle with an explicit political-education component.
30. Tom Burns, Laura Downs, and Janis Foster, *A Legacy of Leadership and Support for Grassroots Grantmaking: A Retrospective Assessment of the Charles Stewart Mott Foundation's Community Foundations and Neighborhoods Small Grants Program* (Hallettsville, TX: Grassroots Grantmakers, 2007).
31. Annie E. Casey Foundation, "Making Connections," www.aecf.org/work/past-work/making-connections.
32. Peter Deitz, Cynthia Gibson, and Peter Levine, *Citizen-Centered Solutions: Lessons in Leveraging Public Participation from the Make It Your Own Awards*, September 2010, https://search.issuelab.org/resource/citizen-centered-solutions-lessons-in-leveraging-public-participation-from-the-make-it-your-own-awards.html; Stephanie Strom, "Foundation Lets Public Help Award Money," *New York Times*, June 26, 2007.
33. Knight Foundation, "The Knight News Challenge is 10; Here's What We've Learned," https://knightfoundation.org/knc10/.
34. Jasmine Aguilera, "'An Epidemic of Misinformation': New Report Finds Trust in Social Institutions Diminished further in 2020," *Time*, January 13, 2021; Edelman, "2022 Edelman Trust Barometer," www.edelman.com/trust/trust-barometer.
35. Incite!, ed., *The Revolution Will Not Be Funded: Beyond the Non-Profit Industrial Complex* (Durham, NC: Duke University Press, 2017).
36. Jeremy Heimans and Henry Timms, *New Power: How Power Works in Our Hyperconnected World—And How to Make It Work for You* (Toronto: Random House, 2018).
37. David Callahan, *The Givers: Wealth, Power, and Philanthropy in a New Gilded Age* (New York: Alfred A. Knopf, 2017).
38. Maria DiMento, "MacKenzie Scott Is Criticized for Not Providing Details in Latest Round of Grants," *Chronicle of Philanthropy*, December 9, 2021.
39. Lester Salamon, "The Rise of the Nonprofit Sector," *Foreign Affairs* 73 (1994): 109–22.
40. Incite!, *The Revolution Will Not Be Funded*; Claire Dunning, "No Strings Attached: Philanthropy, Race, and Donor Control from Black Power to Black Lives Matter," *Nonprofit and Voluntary Sector Quarterly* 52, no. 1 (2022), https://doi.org/10.1177/08997640211 0573.
41. "Philanthropy Awards," *Inside Philanthropy*, December 31, 2018, www.insidephilanthropy.com/home/2018/12/31/philanthropy-awards-2018; "2021 Philanthropy Awards," *Inside Philanthropy*, December 28, 2021, www.insidephilanthropy.com/home/2021/12/28/philanthropy-awards-2021.
42. Rhodri Davis, "Philanthropy Is at a Turning Point. Here Are 6 Ways It Could Go," World Economic Forum, April 29, 2019, www.weforum.org/agenda/2019/04/philanthropy-turning-point-6-ways-it-could-go/.
43. Candid, "Funders Beginning to Embrace Participatory Grantmaking, Report Finds," *Philanthropy News Digest*, October 3, 2018, https://philanthropynewsdigest.org/news/funders-beginning-to-embrace-participatory-grantmaking-report-finds; Tate Williams, "Power in Letting Go: How Participatory Grantmakers Are Democratizing Philanthropy," *Inside Philanthropy*, November 8, 2018; Chris Cardona, "Participatory Grantmaking Matters More Than Ever," Ford Foundation blog, 2020, www

.fordfoundation.org/work/learning/learning-reflections/participatory-grantmaking-matters-now-more-than-ever/; Ariel Madeline LoBosco Platt, Lance Bitner-Laird, Jaré Akchin, and Evan Bartlett, *Participatory Grantmaking in the Jewish Community and Beyond* (New York: Jewish Funders Network, 2021); Ben Wrobel and Meg Massey, *Letting Go: How Philanthropists and Impact Investors Can Do More Good by Giving Up Control* (independently published, 2021).

44. Marc Gunther, "Participatory Grantmaking: Power to the People," *NonProfit Chronicles*, December 12, 2017.
45. Cynthia Gibson, *Deciding Together: Shifting Power and Resource through Participatory Grantmaking* (New York: Foundation Center, 2018).
46. Gibson.
47. Fay Twersky and Hilary Pennington, "Listening to Beneficiaries Helps Nonprofits Learn What Doesn't Work," editorial, *Chronicle of Philanthropy*, December 20, 2016.
48. Cynthia Gibson, "Moving Beyond Feedback: The Promise of Participatory Grantmaking," *Nonprofit Quarterly*, August 28, 2019; and Participatory Grantmaking Collective, "Empowering Communities: Participatory Grantmakers Say We Must Go Beyond Feedback," *Nonprofit Quarterly*, August 28, 2019.
49. Cynthia Gibson, *Participatory Grantmaking: Has Its Time Come?* (New York: Ford Foundation, 2017), www.fordfoundation.org/media/3599/participatory_grantmaking-lmv7.pdf.
50. See www.givingprojects.org for a network of progressive, place-based community foundations that are using Giving Projects as a form of donor engagement.
51. Stanford Center on Philanthropy and Civil Society, "Trust-Based Philanthropy and Participatory Philanthropy," in *The Stanford PACS Guide to Effective Philanthropy* (Stanford, CA: Stanford University, 2020): 223–43; Trust-Based Philanthropy Project, "A Trust-Based Approach," www.trustbasedphilanthropy.org/overview.
52. Jenny Hodgson and Barry Knight, "#ShiftThePower: The Rise of Community Philanthropy," *Alliance*, November 29, 2019, www.alliancemagazine.org/feature/shiftthepower-rise-community-philanthropy/.
53. G. Albert Ruesga and Deborah Puntenney, *Social Justice Philanthropy: An Initial Framework for Positioning This Work* (New York: Ford Foundation, 2010). Social justice philanthropy includes a wide variety of approaches, eight of which are anatomized in this work.
54. Thomasina Borkman, *Understanding Self-Help / Mutual Aid: Experiential Learning in the Commons* (New Brunswick, NJ: Rutgers University Press, 1999); Global Fund for Community Foundations, *The Case for Community Philanthropy: How the Practice Builds Local Assets, Capacity, and Trust—and Why It Matters* (Flint, MI: Charles Stuart Mott Foundation, 2013).
55. Angela Eikenberry, "Giving Circles: Growing Grassroots Philanthropy." *Nonprofit and Voluntary Sector Quarterly* 35, no. 3 (2007): 517–32; Angela Eikenberry, *Giving Circles: Philanthropy, Voluntary Association, and Democracy* (Bloomington: Indiana University Press, 2009).
56. Kristen Grønbjerg, "Foundation Legitimacy at the Community Level in the United States," in *The Legitimacy of Philanthropic Foundations*, ed. Kenneth Prewitt et al. (New York: Russell Sage Foundation, 2006), 150–76; Chao Guo and William Brown, "Community Foundation Performance: Bridging Community Resources and Needs," *Nonprofit and Voluntary Sector Quarterly* 35, no. 2 (2006): 267–87; Elizabeth Graddy and

Lili Wang, "Community Foundation Development and Social Capital," *Nonprofit and Voluntary Sector Quarterly* 38, no. 3 (2008): 392–412.

57. Nwamaka Agbo, *Powershift Philanthropy: Strategies for Impactful Participatory Grantmaking* (Los Angeles: California Endowment, 2021). It is important to note that social justice philanthropy is more comprehensive in its aims and systemic approach, not just to philanthropy but to a larger economic system in which charitable giving is seen as a proxy for—rather than an addition to—resources that should be available to everyone. This "justice" approach is one that has recently surfaced more publicly and that some see as the next incarnation of participatory philanthropy.

58. Ostrom, *Governing*; Robert Putnam, "Bowling Alone"; McGinnis, "Introduction to IAD"; Gianpaolo Baiocchi and Ernesto Ganuza, *Popular Democracy: The Paradox of Participation* (Stanford, CA: Stanford University Press, 2017); Nicole Curato, John Dryzek, Selen Ercan, Carolyn Hendriks, and Simon Niemeyer, "Twelve Key Findings in Deliberative Democracy Research," *Daedulus* 146, no. 3 (2017): 28–38.

59. Tina Nabatchi and Matt Leighninger, *Public Participation for Twenty-First-Century Democracy* (Hoboken, NJ: Jossey-Bass, 2015).

60. Arnstein, "Ladder"; Gibson, *Deciding Together*.

61. William Schambra, "Philanthropy's Call to Action," Giving Review blog, *Philanthropy Daily*, March 24, 2020; Michael Hartmann, "William F. Buckley's Phone Book vs. the Ford Foundation's Participatory Grantmaking," editorial, *Philanthropy Daily*, December 8, 2017.

PART I

Mapping Participatory Grantmaking Practice

This part of the book comprises three chapters that empirically explore the practice of participatory grantmaking (PGM) among different constituencies in the foundation world. Because participatory grantmaking research is still relatively nascent, these chapters answer questions that are foundational, such as (1) What kind of participatory approaches are philanthropic organizations engaging in? (2) Why are some philanthropic organizations adopting participatory approaches when others are not? And (3), What factors mediate the outcomes of participation in organizations? Answering these questions requires a better understanding of the participatory approaches that are actually being pursued by philanthropic organizations, particularly participatory grantmaking as defined in the book's introduction. Once there is more understanding of this, future research can address additional questions, such as why organizations only engage in certain forms of participation, what the goals of certain participatory approaches are, and why organizations do not further engage in participatory approaches that give stakeholders more voice. In the meantime, by being among some of the first to document the prevalence, types, and effects of participatory grantmaking, these studies provide important contributions to this relatively new field.

In chapter 1, Finchum-Mason, Husted, and Suárez report on the findings of a survey of large foundations regarding their practices of participation and inclusion across a variety of dimensions. They find that while the practice of seeking input on foundation practices is fairly widespread, precious few foundations extend decision-making power about grants to communities.

In chapter 2, McGinnis Johnson documents how different forms of structuring a participatory grantmaking process can lead to different outcomes in the kinds of organizations that receive grants, compared with a traditional program-officer-led process. This question is an important one for traditional foundations and megadonors, which often ask whether the additional time and resources that participatory grantmaking requires on the front end can lead to a sufficient payoff in substantively different outcomes on the back end. McGinnis Johnson finds that there are, in fact, differences and that they are shaped by the way the process is structured, particularly whether staff from traditional foundations engage in it.

In chapter 3, Barajas-Román and Meghelli share the results of a survey of participatory grantmaking among women's funds—philanthropic entities set up to channel funding specifically to women-led and -serving organizations. The authors describe the nuanced ways in which the practice of participation actually manifests in women's funds, whose history and values make them "most likely cases" for the adoption of participatory grantmaking.

CHAPTER 1

Institutional Change or Shooting Star?
The Landscape of Stakeholder Participation among Large Foundations in the United States

Emily Finchum-Mason, Kelly Husted, and David Suárez

Philanthropic foundations in the United States wield a great deal of power—and nearly $1 trillion in assets—to define not only the nature of societal challenges but also the manner in which these problems will be solved. Although foundations can choose to share this power with stakeholders, they have no obligation to do so, and initiatives to generate meaningful participation are quite recent to institutional philanthropy.[1] The historical development of the field likely has exacerbated the lack of power sharing, and it also reveals some of the barriers to change. For instance, at the inception of institutional philanthropy in the United States, during the Gilded Age, wealthy individuals like John D. Rockefeller set out to organize the process and delivery of their charitable funds by creating foundations—many of which endeavored to understand and treat the "root causes" of social problems.[2] This development has been described as a shift from charity to philanthropy, or away from almsgiving and toward social innovation.[3] These novel foundations were unlikely to share power with stakeholders, however; Andrew Carnegie expressed the prevailing view that a philanthropist should manage their giving "in the manner which, *in his judgment*, is best calculated to provide the most beneficial results for the community" (emphasis added).[4]

The early obstacles to power sharing presented by philanthropic paternalism were exacerbated by the systematic and "scientific" approach to problem-solving embraced by many general-purpose foundations like the

Rockefeller Foundation.[5] Moreover, foundations' reliance on technocrats, "experts who identify the general interest from rational speculation," has only grown over time.[6] The Tax Reform Act of 1969, especially, which for the first time imposed meaningful new restrictions on foundations, led foundations to expand the hiring of credentialed staff, formalize internal decision-making structures, and approach philanthropy more as an arms-length service than as a collaboration with stakeholders.[7] Since then, several philanthropic approaches or movements have contributed to additional professionalization and rationalization of the field. Models like strategic philanthropy, effective altruism, venture philanthropy, and philanthrocapitalism emphasize unemotional cost-benefit calculations and the pursuit of outcomes defined by a foundation's theory of change.[8]

Importantly, the foundation is the locus of the strategy in these models, not the grantees that implement it or the stakeholders that will be affected. Philanthrocapitalism—a movement that espouses the importance of identifying social change agents that stand to increase social return on investment to advance social change—is a particularly potent example of this type of philanthropic logic. Large foundations holding billions of dollars in assets, like the Bill & Melinda Gates Foundation and the Chan Zuckerberg Initiative, also are strong proponents of this approach and have channeled billions into their strategic initiatives. Two tenets are at the core of these models: (1) a logic that the "right" people, the "right" resources, and the "right" types of knowledge can solve the most intractable societal challenges; and (2) a focus on the outcomes of giving, rather than the process of giving. In these approaches, foundations demonstrate commitment to their missions through the efficient and strategic use of resources.[9] Many of these methods also utilize market-oriented strategies (e.g., scaling and revenue generation) that made philanthropists successful in business, despite the role of markets in generating or perpetuating many of the social inequities that foundations seek to solve.[10]

Foundations nevertheless face persistent legitimacy concerns that create an opportunity for novel power-sharing models.[11] Private foundations, in particular, are not held accountable to the same extent as other nonprofits or public organizations, as they do not have a broad range of citizens or elected officials to which they are obligated to respond. Critics of large philanthropy have drawn attention to this lack of accountability since private foundations are not only seeded with money from the wealthy, but those who establish them also receive generous tax subsidies from the federal government to do so. Critics further argue that the lack of accountability and transparency in foundation decision-making reinforces the power of the wealthy.[12]

Others highlight that this is particularly problematic, given that foundations' assets are often generated through the exploitation of communities of color, serve to maintain extractive capitalist systems, and are rarely used to address systemic inequities.[13] Legitimacy concerns extend more broadly to the awkward role of plutocratic, tax-sheltered institutions in a democracy, which foundations have fueled with paternalistic, technocratic, and market-oriented activity.[14]

At the same time, stakeholder participation has become more common in other societal sectors.[15] In the for-profit sector, for instance, corporate social responsibility implies that businesses have some responsibility for stakeholders, as does the growing attention to environmental, social, and governance activity.[16] And in government—in contrast to the hierarchical, command-and-control approach of the 1940s and 1950s and to the "running government like a business" market-oriented approach of the 1980s and 1990s—public agencies in recent decades have become more receptive to deliberative approaches that emphasize coproduction with stakeholders.[17] Moreover, in what has been labeled as collaborative public management and collaborative governance, the public sector has sought to increase stakeholder participation and democratize decision-making by promoting collaborative networks of public service delivery.[18] In short, legitimacy concerns create pressure for foundations to consider power-sharing models, and relevant developments in other sectors have made this pressure difficult to ignore. Perhaps not surprisingly, then, several forms of "participatory philanthropy" have started to gain traction.

Participatory philanthropy is an umbrella term that refers to initiatives aimed at involving donors and other external stakeholders, but some attributes differentiate this phenomenon from other forms of participation in philanthropy. For instance, crowdfunding has the potential to democratize philanthropy by utilizing technology to increase participation in philanthropy; but participatory philanthropy implies more than making a charitable donation.[19] Better approximating the ethos of participatory philanthropy are giving circles, an approach in which individual contributors collectively determine where and sometimes how to allocate their shared charitable resources.[20] Like other donor-centered initiatives, however, giving circles differ from stakeholder forms of participatory philanthropy because they are "rooted in empowering the donors participating in the giving circle to decide where the funds are directed, rather than the community or organizational leaders who are benefiting from the resources."[21] Participatory grantmaking is an example of the latter approach, as external stakeholders are given an opportunity to steer donors by engaging in matters of foundation priorities and grantmaking.[22] Boston's

Haymarket People's Fund and the Disability Rights Fund are key examples of public foundations that pioneered the approach. Closely related, social justice philanthropy challenges systems and advocates for social change, and participatory grantmaking is a core strategy.[23]

Is the emergence of stakeholder-oriented approaches to participatory philanthropy in foundations a harbinger of institutional change in the field? Or is it just a fad, a shooting star that shines brightly for a moment and then burns out? These questions matter because participatory approaches to foundation governance and grantmaking hold promise for democratizing existing practices and for increasing equity by improving accountability pathways between elite foundations and the communities they aim to benefit. The questions also are important because increased stakeholder participation could play an important role in shifting power to marginalized communities. Indeed, calls for increased power sharing in philanthropy have become especially urgent considering the COVID-19 pandemic's disproportionate impact on communities of color and the protests after the murder of George Floyd, which have focused global attention on systemic racial inequities.[24] Answering our ambitious and speculative questions is a core goal of our research agenda, but a dearth of empirical research currently exists regarding the participatory repertoires of foundations and the extent to which participatory approaches have been adopted, leaving a significant gap in knowledge about these powerful institutions.

In this chapter, we take an important first step toward understanding change over time in the participatory repertoires of large foundations. We explore these two research questions about the extent to which large philanthropic foundations engage external stakeholders, such as their grantees and marginalized communities, in governance and grantmaking:

1. What is the scope of direct engagement in participatory practices and grantmaking among large philanthropic foundations in the United States?
2. What is the scope of indirect engagement—through funding—in participatory practices and grantmaking among large philanthropic foundations in the United States?

To address each question, we assess the extent to which large private and community foundations are both adopting participatory practices and funding their grantees' participatory practices and grantmaking along these three dimensions: Who participates? In what processes do stakeholders participate? To what degree do participants influence decision-making?

Our first research question aims to understand how foundations utilize participatory practices internally. For instance, a foundation could invite stakeholders to influence its own programs or grantmaking. But because we focus on the largest foundations in the United States, the second research question is intended to acknowledge that some of these foundations might be more likely to provide grants for other organizations to engage stakeholders in participatory initiatives than to implement such initiatives directly. As a hypothetical example, a foundation might choose to support the infrastructure for, and the growth of, participatory philanthropy by providing a community organization with $1 million—and local stakeholders then would decide how and where to disburse those resources. In the next section, we begin by elaborating the theoretical framework used to define stakeholder participation in the context of philanthropic governance. We then outline the survey distribution and weighting methodologies and describe the analytic sample. Findings based on our central research questions are then provided and discussed. Finally, we conclude by discussing the implications of these findings for our understanding of institutional change in organized philanthropy and outline areas for future research on stakeholder participation in philanthropy.

CONCEPTUAL FRAMEWORK

Stakeholder participation has been practiced and theorized in several fields, ranging from public administration to political science to international development. Across these fields, there is an understanding among practitioners and researchers that the people affected by a government's or organization's actions should have a voice in those decisions. Seminal work by Arnstein posits a ladder of participation from manipulation to citizen control.[25] Arnstein acknowledges the power differential inherent in the provider-beneficiary relationships and theorizes participation in governance on a continuum from least to greatest authority sharing. In this framework, forums where citizens or residents are allowed to express their opinions—but where the government is not accountable to act on those opinions—occupy the lowest rung, while more deliberative and co-determined enterprises occupy higher rungs.

Several scholars and practitioners have since built upon this work and suggested that ideal participation exists when individuals with diverse experiences are both provided a forum to voice their preferences and an accountability framework that ensures those preferences will be acted upon. Fung's "democracy cube" highlights the varying degrees of power-sharing between a governing entity and the governed, but it also brings in dimensions regarding participant identities and the mode of communication and decision-making.[26] Emerson and Nabatchi further offer a comprehensive framework for understanding how citizens and residents can inform and contribute to complex systems of governance through principled engagement, shared motivation, and a capacity for joint action.[27]

With respect to the nonprofit sector, Amirkhanyan and Lambright note that while many scholars have ventured frameworks on the forms and degrees of intensity of citizen participation, there has been little empirical exploration that attempts to parse out how the participatory spaces created by modern nonprofits rank on these frameworks.[28] On the practitioner side, the International Association for Public Participation puts forth a spectrum of participation characterizing the degree of power sharing—from informing and consulting to involving, collaborating, and empowering—between organizations and the communities they serve. The sum of these frameworks and related research points to the importance of the identities of participants, the activities in which they participate, and the extent to which a government or organization distributes power among stakeholders in their participatory practices.

What participation looks like in practice varies widely across contexts, and the landscape of potential participatory approaches in institutional philanthropy is unique and underexplored. Gibson highlights a growing recognition within the field of institutional philanthropy of the need to share power and democratize decision-making.[29] As noted earlier in the chapter, several public foundations and social justice funders have long prioritized participatory practices in both governance and grantmaking. Recent evidence shows that some private and community foundations also are starting to implement participatory practices, such as using community advisory boards to influence organizational priorities and grantmaking decisions.[30]

Our conceptual framework of participation and participatory grantmaking among foundations builds on the extensive prior work by researchers and practitioners. Synthesizing the participation and philanthropy literatures, we conceptualize stakeholder participation in philanthropic foundation governance and grantmaking along four major dimensions, which are shown in figure 1.1:

- *Who participates?* One of the key questions about participation in any sectoral context is who actually comes to the table to contribute ideas and make decisions. Participants could include internal stakeholders, such as foundation staff, or external stakeholders, such as nonprofit leaders, community leaders, or individual beneficiaries. The unique constellation of participants will likely determine whose concerns are given voice. Therefore, it is critical to understand how foundations enact participation by virtue of those they call upon to participate. Participant identity—whether the stakeholder is directly affected by the foundation's giving—is also a critical consideration in differentiating participation as a democratizing tool versus participation as a means of increasing equity, as the former does not necessarily involve those individuals most affected by the social challenges that the foundation aims to ameliorate.

- *In what processes do stakeholders participate?* Existing evidence shows the potential for stakeholder involvement in the processes of both foundation governance and grantmaking. One of the major sources of variation is the point at which stakeholders are called to participate: in guiding foundation priorities, in the design or review of requests for proposals, or in the process of making grant decisions and conducting evaluations.
- *To what degree do participants influence decision-making?* This dimension draws on the pervasive theme across literatures regarding the extent to which organizations share power with stakeholders. Building on the work of Gibson and the International Association for Public Participation spectrum of participation, we define the degree of participant influence according to three levels: consulting, involving, and deciding.[31] Consulting (e.g., surveys, focus groups) includes efforts by the foundation to solicit stakeholder input, without the assumption that this input will necessarily be incorporated into the foundation's processes. Involving (e.g., advisory committees) implies both the solicitation of feedback from stakeholders and the incorporation of that feedback to influence the foundation's processes. Deciding indicates that the foundation has placed decisions on governance or grantmaking in stakeholders' hands.
- *How does the foundation execute stakeholder participation?* Foundations can support stakeholder participation in their own internal governance and grantmaking processes—a process that we call *direct* stakeholder participation. In direct stakeholder participation, foundation staff might work with community members to develop a participatory grantmaking process. Foundations can also fund their grantees' stakeholder participation efforts, which we call *indirect* stakeholder participation.[32] In indirect stakeholder participation, the

foundation may fund its grantees to implement their own participatory grantmaking process. Whereas direct stakeholder participation presumes that the foundation has the internal capacity to implement a participatory initiative, indirect stakeholder participation relies on grantees' capacity and their stakeholder relationships. Hypothetically, foundations can engage stakeholders directly, indirectly, or both.

This framework focuses primarily on the people, processes, and influence of stakeholders in relation to institutional philanthropy. These are certainly not the only important dimensions for understanding participation and participatory grantmaking within the sector. Understanding *why*

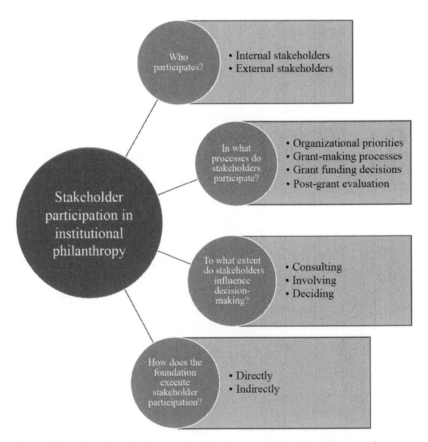

Figure 1.1 Stakeholder Participation in the Institutional Philanthropy Framework
Source: Author conceptualization.

foundations engage in participatory practices and the desired goals and outcomes of such practices are also critical. Furthermore, the extent and quality of these interactions matter greatly, as does the extent to which these practices become engrained in the organizational ethos (especially if foundations hope for these changes to last). However, we view these four dimensions as key building blocks of participation within institutional philanthropy and as necessary for understanding the extent to which foundations are engaging stakeholders.

An important challenge to note is that the line between participation and participatory grantmaking is blurred, as differing definitions of participatory grantmaking currently exist within the sector. Following the framework established in the introduction to this edited volume, we view participatory grantmaking as a process and not just as one activity or tactic—a process that involves some form of stakeholder participation in grantmaking. Nevertheless, varying ideas about what constitutes participatory grantmaking make it particularly difficult to measure. With this in mind, we aim to capture the full realm of participatory practices that foundations utilize to engage external stakeholders in their governance and grantmaking and to provide conceptual clarity as to what participatory grantmaking can look like in practice.

METHODOLOGY

Data for this descriptive study come from a nationwide survey of large philanthropic foundations. We sampled the five hundred largest private and community foundations (by total assets) in the United States, as determined from the Foundation Directory Online (FDO) database, a national repository of foundation and grant information administered by Candid.[33] The FDO data were obtained in 2018 and, as a result, some organizations have since spent down their funds, merged with others, transitioned to an alternative organizational designation, or had operations subsumed by a related foundation, leaving an effective sample size of 489 foundations.

To inform the development of the survey, interviews were conducted with foundation and nonprofit practitioners from January to March 2020, and the survey was piloted in late March 2020 with practitioners. (See this chapter's appendix 1.1 for information on the survey instrument.) The survey link was first emailed to foundations in late May of 2020—targeting the chief executive officer or other high-level executives in our survey distribution when possible. At survey closing in January 2021, 148 foundations had completed the survey, yielding a response rate of 30.3 percent. We apply inverse probability of response weighting to all results in our findings section to address nonresponse bias. (Again, see appendix 1.1 for a more comprehensive description of this weighting strategy.) Applying this weighting system provided more representative estimates, but it did not substantially change the findings from the unweighted analysis.

The survey asked a series of questions about whether the foundation had engaged in a range of participatory practices within the last two years. We chose this time frame to clearly delimit the questions and reduce ambiguity. In line with our conceptual framework, we asked large foundations about their engagement of different external stakeholder groups along two dimensions: (1) organizational and grantmaking processes (i.e., organizational priorities, grantmaking processes, funding decisions, and postgrant evaluation) and (2) stakeholder influence on decision-making (i.e., consulting, involving, and deciding). External stakeholders considered in these questions include the foundation's grantees, nongrantee nonprofits or community-based organizations, community members directly affected by the foundation's funding, and members of the public.

We further asked foundations about whether they funded grantees to engage stakeholders, realizing that this may be an important pathway that private and community foundations take to support participation. Here, too, we asked about whether the foundation funded grantees to engage stakeholders along the dimensions of (1) organizational priorities and grantmaking and (2) stakeholder influence on decision-making. The external stakeholder groups considered were peer nonprofits / community-based organizations, affected community members, and members of the public.

With questions about indirect forms of participatory grantmaking, there are concerns about foundation intentionality regarding specific purposes (i.e., stakeholder participation in determining organizational priorities) as well as the fidelity of grantees in using the foundation funding for those purposes. In our survey, we structured the questions to mitigate these concerns, requiring foundations to stipulate whether they granted funds for the purposes of supporting specific grantee stakeholder participation efforts. Appendix 1.2 illustrates one of the decision matrixes used to assess indirect stakeholder participation. Each respondent received three such matrixes, one regarding the stakeholder consultation, one regarding stakeholder involvement, and the last regarding the conferral of decision-making authority upon stakeholders. There is a risk that respondents misattributed the specific intention of their funding, but we believe that the responses shed some light on how foundations develop the legitimacy of—and capacity for—participatory grantmaking.

Table 1.1 provides an overview of foundation respondent characteristics. These data were obtained through the survey and the FDO database. The mean total assets of respondents are approximately $1,043,000,000, with median total assets of $417,214,000, which approximates that of our overall sample ($472,942,717). Community foundations are slightly overrepresented; where our sample features 23 percent (*N* = 34), roughly 15 percent of the largest foundations are community foundations. Finally, this sample underrepresents foundations located in the Northeast and slightly overrepresents foundations from each other region, relative to the overall sample. Education was the primary giving area of many foundations in this sample.

FINDINGS

We begin by presenting aggregate findings across all levels of participation, activities, and stakeholders. Then we discuss results specific to direct participation, in which foundations conduct efforts to engage stakeholders through their own internal capacity. Finally, we attend to indirect participation, where foundations fund their grantees to conduct stakeholder engagement efforts.

In the aggregate, the survey responses indicate that the vast majority of large foundations (82.7 percent) engaged stakeholders directly through participatory practices employed by the foundation itself, and 35.8 percent of foundations funded grantees to engage in some form of stakeholder participation (see table 1.2). Overall, 84.3 percent of foundations engaged external stakeholders either directly *or* indirectly, and 34.1 percent of foundations engaged external stakeholders *both* directly and indirectly.

Direct Stakeholder Participation

Next, we analyze direct participation—as conducted through the foundation itself—by the degree of stakeholder influence, the stakeholder group, and the stage in the organizational and grantmaking process. The effective sample size is 148 foundations for the results shown in figure 1.2.

We first measured whether large foundations consulted different stakeholder groups at varying points in their organizational and grantmaking processes. "Consulting" refers to the solicitation of feedback through activities such as surveys and focus groups. As figure 1.2 indicates, about 30 percent of foundations reported soliciting feedback on organizational priorities from

Table 1.1: Survey Respondent Characteristics

Characteristics of respondent	N	Percentage of respondents
Foundation type		
Community foundation	34	23.0
Private foundation	114	77.0
Geographic region		
Midwest	42	28.4
Northeast	37	25.0
Southeast	14	9.5
Southwest	15	10.1
West (Mountain and Pacific)	40	27.0
Staff size (full-time-equivalent hours)		
No staff	4	2.7
1–5	14	9.5
6–10	22	14.9
11–20	30	20.3
21–30	20	13.5
31–40	17	11.5
41 or more	41	27.7
Primary giving area		
Education	66	44.6
Environment	4	2.7
Health	14	9.5
Human services	26	17.6
Other	38	25.7
Total assets (in 2018 dollars)		
Mean		1,033,895,422
Standard deviation		1,875,941,031
Median		452,382,124
Minimum		243,819,481
Maximum		13,584,110,000

Sources: Author survey data; Candid, Foundation Directory Online database, 2023, https://fconline.foundationcenter.org/.

INSTITUTIONAL CHANGE OR SHOOTING STAR? 47

Table 1.2: Overall Foundation Engagement in Stakeholder Participation

Aspect of engagement	Percent (N = 148)
Foundation directly engages external stakeholders in some form of participation	82.7
Foundation funds grantees to engage external stakeholders in some form of participation (indirectly engaging stakeholders)	35.8
Foundation engages external stakeholders in any form of participation directly *or* indirectly	84.3
Foundation engages external stakeholders in some form of participation directly *and* indirectly	34.1

Source: Author survey data.

grantee nonprofits, affected community members, or nongrantee nonprofits. Just over half of large foundations (55.4 percent) consulted grantees regarding the foundation's grantmaking processes, but far fewer foundations consulted affected community members, nongrantee nonprofits, or members of the public. Less than a quarter of foundations consulted grantee nonprofits, affected community members, or nongrantee nonprofits with respect to grant funding decisions, and less than 10 percent consulted members of the public. A substantial proportion reported soliciting grantee feedback

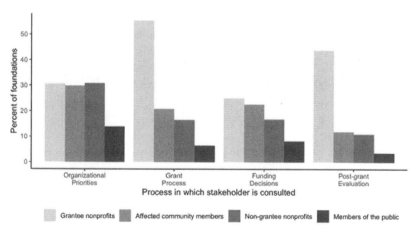

Figure 1.2 Foundations That Solicited Feedback from External Stakeholders Regarding Governance and Grantmaking

Source: Author survey data.

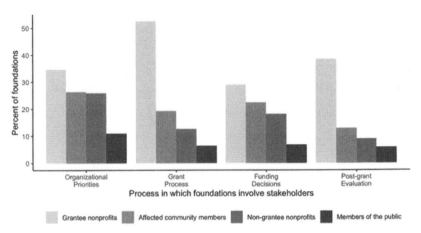

Figure 1.3 Foundations That Incorporated Feedback from External Stakeholders to Influence Governance and Grantmaking
Source: Author survey data.

on postgrant evaluation (43.8 percent), but much less so from other stakeholder groups.

Second, we assessed whether large foundations involved different stakeholder groups at multiple points in their organizational and grantmaking processes. "Involving" refers to the incorporation of stakeholder feedback—through activities such as advisory committees—to influence the organization's priorities and grantmaking. We see similar trends overall for involvement as we do for consultation, but the rates tend to be slightly lower. As figure 1.3 shows, about one-third of foundations involved grantee nonprofits in setting their organizational priorities, and about a quarter involved affected community members or nongrantee nonprofits in setting their organizational priorities. Most foundations (52.5 percent) involved grantees in the foundation's grantmaking processes; far fewer involved community members, nongrantee nonprofits, and members of the public in those processes. Furthermore, about a quarter of foundations involved grantees in their grant funding decisions, but fewer foundations involved other stakeholder groups. Not surprisingly, there was a significant percentage of foundations that incorporated grantee feedback to influence postgrant evaluation (38.5 percent), while other groups were involved far less with respect to evaluation.

Third, we assessed whether large foundations conferred decision-making authority to stakeholder groups at various points in their organizational and grantmaking processes. Rates of conferring decision-making authority to external stakeholders were low across the board (see figure 1.4). Fewer than 10 percent of foundations conferred decision-making power over organizational priorities to grantee nonprofits, affected community members, nongrantee nonprofits, or members of the public. Similarly, fewer than 10 percent of foundations reported conferring decision-making authority to any external stakeholder group in their grantmaking processes. Regarding grant funding decisions, 10.5 percent of foundations conferred decision-making authority on grantee nonprofits with respect to their grant funding decisions, and 9.9 percent conferred decision-making authority on community members directly affected by the foundation's funding. Fewer than 10 percent of foundations reported conferring decision-making power on any external stakeholder groups in relation to postgrant evaluation.

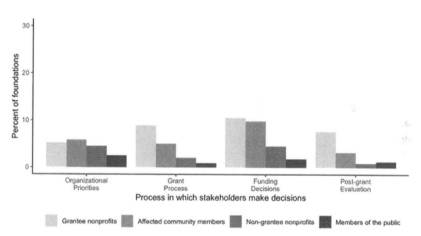

Figure 1.4 Foundations That Conferred Decision-Making Authority on External Stakeholders to Influence Governance and Grantmaking
Source: Author survey data.

Indirect Stakeholder Participation

Foundations can also implement stakeholder participation indirectly through funding their grantees' stakeholder engagement practices. Consistent with the conceptual framework for stakeholder participation in institutional philanthropy, we theorized that foundations could support a grantee's stakeholder participation efforts in determining their own (the grantee's) organizational priorities (n_g = 145). Foundations that fund grantees that then make grants to other organizations (n_r = 97) could also support stakeholder participation in any processes within the grantee's funding cycle. In figures 1.5 through 1.7, the denominator reflects all 145 grantmaking respondents. The proportion of foundations that engage stakeholders in matters pertaining to the grant cycle uses a denominator of 97, considering only foundations that reported regranting. With the goal of minimizing survey attrition, this question set was designed such that foundations were not exposed to questions that did not apply to them.

Overall, rates of funding grantees to engage external stakeholders in the grantee's governance and grantmaking are lower than through direct engagement, with only 36 percent of grantmaking foundations indicating some form of indirect stakeholder participation. We do, however, see similar trends as with direct participation, where reported funding for grantees' stakeholder engagement processes decreases as the level of power-sharing increases.

As figure 1.5 indicates, large grantmaking foundations most commonly fund grantees to consult community members directly affected by the foundation's funding in processes of determining organizational priorities. Fewer than 10 percent of foundations reported funding grantees to consult with their peer nonprofits, community-based organizations, or members of the public at large. Foundations most commonly funded a grantee's stakeholder decision-making for funding decisions. Nearly a quarter of foundations (24.1 percent) funded grantees to consult affected community members about the grantee's funding decisions. Across the board, foundations funded grantees to consult community members affected by their funding more often than to consult peer nonprofits / community-based organizations or members of the public.

As with stakeholder consultation, figure 1.6 highlights that grantmaking foundations most commonly funded a grantee's community member involvement efforts, although reported rates of funding a grantee's involvement of peer nonprofits and community-based organizations were statistically indistinguishable. Large foundations were especially likely to provide support for grantees to involve stakeholders in grant funding decisions. Across all processes, foundations provided resources to involve affected community members more so than other stakeholder groups. However, the rates of funding grantees to involve stakeholders in determining who gets funded and postgrant evaluation processes are slightly less than consultation in those processes. The results in figure 1.6 also show that foundations

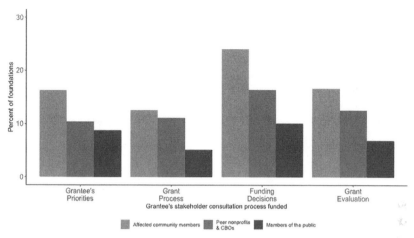

Figure 1.5 Foundations That Funded Grantees to Solicit Feedback from Stakeholders
Source: Author survey data.

funded their grantees' involvement of peer nonprofits / community-based organizations, community members, and members of the public to influence organizational priorities and grantmaking processes slightly more often than they reported funding analogous consultation efforts.

Funding grantees to confer decision-making authority upon stakeholders in determining organizational priorities is extremely rare among grantmaking foundations, as indicated by figure 1.7. Just 6.2 percent of foundations report funding their grantees to share decision-making power with affected community members. This is merely a third of the reported rates of funding for grantee's community member consultation and involvement. Figure 1.7 shows that foundation funding for grantee's stakeholder decision-making is far less common than funding for stakeholder consultation and involvement. Notably, large foundations funded grantees to confer decision-making power on external stakeholders over funding decisions at higher rates than other stages of their governance and grantmaking processes. For example, 10 percent of foundations reported funding grantees to confer decision-making power on affected community members regarding who the grantee funds. Overall, rates of funding grantees to confer decision-making authority on external stakeholders are markedly lower than rates of funding stakeholder consultation and involvement; this follows the same trend observed in direct stakeholder engagement by foundations.

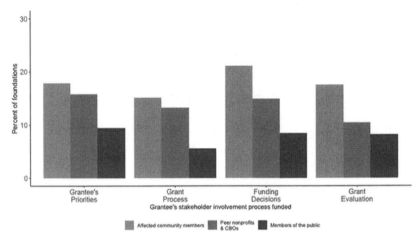

Figure 1.6 Foundations That Funded Grantees to Incorporate Feedback from Stakeholders
Source: Author survey data.

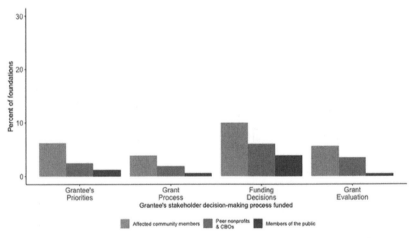

Figure 1.7 Foundations That Funded Grantees to Confer Decision-Making Authority on Their External Stakeholders
Source: Author survey data.

DISCUSSION

Foundations in the United States have made many important contributions to society, from strengthening tertiary (i.e., university-level) education to bolstering or pioneering innovations like the 911 emergency telephone call system and the Green Revolution.[34] Foundations nevertheless have faced persistent scrutiny, and their legitimacy remains contested.[35] Institutional philanthropy may be more controversial now than at any other point in time, as perceptions of undemocratic and excessive foundation influence have increased alongside the growth in foundation size (with respect to total number and total assets) and policy assertiveness.[36] It is in this context that we ask why foundations have become receptive to participatory grantmaking and question what influence this novel practice is having on the field. Viewed cynically, interest in participatory grantmaking among foundations could be nothing more than a public relations maneuver, a strategy to placate critics by offering rhetorical and performative support for the practice. However, the emergence and ongoing development of participatory grantmaking may reflect genuine institutional change in the field—much more than a "shooting star" that leaves no lasting impact on philanthropic practice.

Our cross-sectional landscape of stakeholder participation among large foundations in the United States cannot answer what direction institutional philanthropy is taking, but it does establish several relevant benchmarks for assessing change over time in the breadth and depth of participatory grantmaking. At the most general level, our findings indicate that many foundations have embraced at least some degree of stakeholder participation in their governance and grantmaking. Our conceptual framework also addresses four narrower issues, beginning with the "who" of participatory grantmaking. The majority (83 percent) of large philanthropic foundations in the United States have engaged their stakeholders directly—grantee nonprofits, nongrantee nonprofits and community-based organizations, community members affected by the foundation's funding, or members of the public—to some degree in their governance or grantmaking.

This summative percentage, however, masks considerable variation in who participates. For instance, we found that foundations consulted, involved, and conferred decision-making authority on grantee nonprofits and affected community members in governance and grantmaking more often than they did members of the public, supporting the suggestion that foundations may be more motivated to utilize these methods to work toward social equity rather than as a tool to democratize philanthropy more broadly. But it is interesting to note that foundations often frame this work as a matter of effectiveness, rather than as a means of breaking down power silos. To illustrate, more foundations reported utilizing stakeholder participation to increase grantmaking effectiveness (80 percent) and to generate innovative solutions to social challenges (66 percent) than to shift power (39 percent) or to work toward social equity (46 percent). Importantly, our stakeholder categories only capture participant identity groups at a high level. Further research is needed to unpack more specific aspects of participant identity—such as race, gender, and socioeconomic class—to determine whether foundations are actually engaging historically marginalized stakeholders in an effort to increase equity.

The second issue our conceptual framework explored was stakeholder participation in several key aspects of foundation governance and grantmaking (i.e., priorities, grant processes, grant decisions, and postgrant evaluation). Overall, we found that 66 percent of foundations reported engaging stakeholders (either directly or indirectly) in determining aspects of the grant process, and that this engagement largely takes the form of soliciting feedback from or involving grantee nonprofits in decisions regarding the grant cycle. We also found that 58 percent of foundations reported involving stakeholders in postgrant evaluation processes, which is, again, mainly driven by soliciting feedback from and involving grantee nonprofits. Taken together, these findings may reflect the fact that grantees are simply closer to the foundation and may require a "lighter lift" for the foundation to implement. However, these findings may also signal a shift in the grantee–funder relationship to a more collaborative dynamic, which previous literature has suggested could be tumultuous.[37] Further longitudinal research is needed to assess this trend.

We also explored a third issue—the degree to which participants influence foundation decision-making (i.e., consulting, involving, and deciding). Stakeholder participation among large foundations drops off precipitously as we move from consulting and involving stakeholders to allocating authority to stakeholders to make decisions regarding foundation governance and grantmaking. Our evidence suggests that foundations largely retain control over much of the decision-making, including decisions about which organizations are ultimately awarded grant funds. Just 10 percent of foundations reported allowing grantees or community members most affected by the foundation's funding to decide how to allocate grant funds. Further, only a handful of foundations reported engaging nongrantee nonprofits and members of the public to make governance and grantmaking decisions. These two findings provide further support for the notion that stakeholder participation efforts aim to increase social equity rather than to democratize institutional philanthropy.

The fourth and final issue we considered is how the foundation executes stakeholder participation (i.e., direct or indirect). Apart from implementing stakeholder engagement practices directly, foundations can also fund their grantees' stakeholder participation efforts. Our findings indicate that funding stakeholder engagement through grantmaking is an emerging strategy. Overall, about 35 percent of foundations reported providing grants for stakeholder participation. Like the observed trend in direct stakeholder engagement, the percentage of foundations that reported funding the various stakeholder participation efforts of their grantees was roughly constant at the levels of consulting and involving, but the percentage of foundations that funded grantees to confer decision-making authority on stakeholders was significantly lower. Interestingly, the proportion of foundations that supported indirect stakeholder participation was the same as supported direct stakeholder participation. Funding participation may not be so much a substitute for doing the work directly as a complement to it. This finding suggests that internal infrastructure, external relationships, and degree of comfort with participatory processes may support both direct and indirect stakeholder participation.

Taken together, our results suggest that participatory grantmaking is more than a passing phase in the field—more than a philanthropic shooting star—but instead is making a clear footprint in institutional philanthropy. Though most initiatives in large foundations so far have been narrow and shallow rather than broad and deep, participatory grantmaking is a recent innovation in foundation practice. Further longitudinal research is needed to ascertain how foundations' stakeholder engagement practices will change over time, especially with respect to growing movements calling for transparent and accountable institutions. An immediate next step in this research agenda is to develop theoretical expectations as to the change in nature of stakeholder participation as these practices become institutionalized.

CONCLUSION

Despite the pervasiveness of technocratic and impact-oriented practices among large philanthropic foundations, the findings of this study indicate that many of these same foundations value stakeholder participation. We highlight the many ways foundations are engaging external stakeholders, yet we also find that few foundations are sharing decision-making power with those stakeholders. These results raise questions regarding what drives participatory philanthropy. Some participatory practitioners have posited certain motivations for adopting participatory process, but specific drivers remain unknown.[38] Are there specific organizational attributes that make foundations more or less likely to engage stakeholders, such as a social justice ethos, a diverse staff and leadership, or an expansive peer network? Our findings also raise practical questions regarding what these approaches look like in practice, how foundations upend existing practices to incorporate stakeholder participation into their repertoire, and what types of support foundations need to continue to do this work.

Finally, while participatory grantmaking research typically focuses on stakeholder participation in relation to the processes and practices within a foundation, our conceptual framework challenges boundaries by proposing that participatory grantmaking can be direct or indirect. Even if a foundation does not bring participatory grantmaking within its own organizational boundaries, we suggest that it can strengthen the legitimacy and prevalence of innovative reform by providing grants for others to implement participatory grantmaking initiatives. Questions remain, however, about where to draw these boundaries—whether indirect stakeholder participation as we have defined it constitutes *funding* participatory grantmaking or *practicing* participatory grantmaking, and what this distinction means for philanthropic practice. Future stages of our research will contribute to the growing base of knowledge on participatory approaches within institutional philanthropy, not only by subjecting all dimensions of our conceptual framework to scholarly and practitioner critiques but also by addressing many of the empirical questions we have raised here.

APPENDIX 1.1: SURVEY WEIGHTING METHODOLOGY

We use a propensity score weighting technique to account for nonresponse bias. Using logistic regression, we modeled the likelihood of survey responses as a function of various measures of professionalization, geographic location, and subject matter focus (specifically, a human service orientation). These covariates were chosen by method of stepwise deletion based on model fit (measured by Akaike's and Bayesian Information Criteria) from a broader array of foundation covariates. These data were obtained from archival research of foundation websites as well as data aggregated from the Foundation Database Online. Foundation responses are then weighted by the inverse of the probability of a response. We find that the weighted results presented here do not deviate significantly from the unweighted results nor have an impact on the substantive interpretation of any of the results presented in this work.

APPENDIX 1.2: DECISION MATRIX FOR INDIRECT STAKEHOLDER PARTICIPATION

Indicate all the activities for which your foundation funded grantees to solicit feedback from stakeholders. Please select all that apply.

	Grantee's organizational priorities	Grantee's grantmaking processes	What the grantee funds	Grantee's evaluation of programs	Not applicable
Our foundation funded grantees to solicit *feedback from peer nonprofits/ CBOs*					
Our foundation funded grantees to solicit feedback from *community members directly affected by the foundation's funding*					
Our foundation funded grantees to solicit feedback from *members of the public*					

Source: Author survey data.

NOTES

1. Susan Ostrander, *Money for Change: Social Movement Philanthropy at Haymarket People's Fund* (Philadelphia: Temple University Press, 1995); Cynthia Gibson, *Participatory Grantmaking: Has Its Time Come?* (New York: Ford Foundation, 2017), www.fordfoundation.org/media/3599/participatory_grantmaking-lmv7.pdf; Cynthia Gibson, *Deciding Together: Shifting Power and Resources through Participatory Grantmaking* (New York: Foundation Center, 2018), https://learningforfunders.candid.org/content/guides/deciding-together/.

2. Olivier Zunz, *Philanthropy in America* (Princeton, NJ: Princeton University Press, 2014); Barbara Shubinski, "Evolution of a Foundation: An Institutional History of the Rockefeller Foundation," Rockefeller Archive Center, 2022, https://resource.rockarch.org/story/rockefeller-foundation-history-origins-to-2013/.
3. Barry Karl and Stanley Katz, "The American Private Philanthropic Foundation and the Public Sphere 1890–1930," *Minerva* 19, no. 2 (1981): 236–70; Anne-Emanuelle Birn and Elizabeth Fee, "The Rockefeller Foundation and the International Health Agenda," *The Lancet* 381 (2013): 1618–19, https://doi:10.1016/S0140-6736(13)61013-2.
4. Andrew Carnegie, *The Gospel of Wealth* (New York: Carnegie Corporation of New York, 2017; orig. pub. 1899), 12.
5. Donald Fisher, "The Role of Philanthropic Foundations in the Reproduction and Production of Hegemony: Rockefeller Foundations and the Social Sciences," *Sociology* 17, no. 2 (1983): 206–33; Emma Saunders-Hastings, "Benevolent Giving and the Problem of Paternalism," in *Effective Altruism: Philosophical Issues*, ed. Hilary Greaves and Theron Pummer (Oxford: Oxford University Press, 2019), 115–36; Emma Saunders-Hastings, *Private Virtues, Public Vices: Philanthropy and Democratic Equality* (Chicago: University of Chicago Press, 2022).
6. Daniele Caramani, "Will vs. Reason: The Populist and Technocratic Forms of Political Representation and Their Critique to Party Government," *American Political Science Review* 111, no. 1 (2017): 54.
7. Peter Frumkin, "The Long Recoil from Regulation: Private Philanthropic Foundations and the Tax Reform Act of 1969," *American Review of Public Administration* 28, no. 3 (1998): 266–86; Hokyu Hwang and Walter Powell, "The Rationalization of Charity: The Influences of Professionalism in the Nonprofit Sector," *Administrative Science Quarterly* 54, no. 2 (2009): 268–98; Theda Skocpol, *Diminished Democracy: From Membership to Management in American Civic Life* (Norman: University of Oklahoma Press, 2003).
8. For information on strategic philanthropy, see Paul Brest, "Strategic Philanthropy and Its Discontents," *Stanford Social Innovation Review* (2015), https://ssir.org/articles/entry/strategic_philanthropy_and_its_discontents#; Paul Brest and Hal Harvey, *Money Well Spent: A Strategic Plan for Smart Philanthropy* (Stanford, CA: Stanford Business Books, 2008); and Peter Frumkin, *Strategic Giving: The Art and Science of Philanthropy* (Chicago: University of Chicago Press, 2006). For information on effective altruism, see William MacAskill, "The Definition of Effective Altruism," in *Effective Altruism: Philosophical Issues*, ed. Hilary Greaves and Theron Pummer (Oxford University Press, 2019). For information on venture philanthropy, see Tamaki Onishi, "Venture Philanthropy and Practice Variations: The Interplay of Institutional Logics and Organizational Identities," *Nonprofit and Voluntary Sector Quarterly* 48, no. 2 (2019): 241–65, https://doi:10.1177/0899764018819875; and Michael Moody, "'Building a Culture': The Construction and Evolution of Venture Philanthropy as a New Organizational Field," *Nonprofit and Voluntary Sector Quarterly* 37, no. 2 (2008): 324–52. For information on philanthrocapitalism, see Kristin A. Goss, "Policy Plutocrats: How America's Wealthy Seek to Influence Governance," *PS: Political Science & Politics* 49, no. 3 (2016): 442–48; Sarah Reckhow, "More Than Patrons: How Foundations Fuel Policy Change and Backlash," *PS: Political Science & Politics* 49, no. 3 (2016): 449–54; Rob Reich, "Repugnant to the Whole Idea of Democracy? On the Role of Foundations in Democratic Societies," *PS: Political Science & Politics* 49, no. 3

(2016): 466–72; and Matthew Bishop and Michael Green, *Philanthrocapitalism: How the Rich Can Save the World* (New York: Bloomsbury Press, 2008).
9. Angela Eikenberry and Roseanne Mirabella, "Extreme Philanthropy: Philanthrocapitalism, Effective Altruism, and the Discourse of Neoliberalism," *PS: Political Science & Politics* 51, no. 1 (2018), 43–7.
10. Linsey McGoey, *No Such Thing as a Free Gift: The Gates Foundation and the Price of Philanthropy* (Brooklyn: Verso Books, 2015); Kavita Ramdas, "Philanthrocapitalism Is Not Social Change Philanthropy," *Stanford Social Innovation Review*, 2011, https://doi.org/10.48558/H52X-6T07; Christine Ahn, "Democratizing American Philanthropy," in *The Revolution Will Not Be Funded*, ed. Incite! (Cambridge, MA: South End Press: 2007), 63–76; Patricia Nickel and Angela Eikenberry, "A Critique of the Discourse of Marketized Philanthropy," *American Behavioral Scientist* 52, no. 7 (2009): 974–89.
11. Kenneth Mattei Dogan Prewitt, Steven Heydemann, and Stefan Toepler, eds., *The Legitimacy of Philanthropic Foundations: US and European Perspectives* (New York: Russell Sage Foundation, 2006); David Callahan, *The Givers: Wealth, Power, and Philanthropy in a New Gilded Age* (New York: Alfred A. Knopf, 2017); and Jenny Harrow, Gemma Donnelly-Cox, John Healy, and Filip Wijkström, "The Management and Organization of Philanthropy: New Directions and Contested Undercurrents," *International Journal of Management Reviews* 23, no. 3 (2021): 303–11.
12. Joanne Barkan, "Plutocrats at Work: How Big Philanthropy Undermines Democracy," *Dissent* (Fall 2013): 1–18; Anand Giridharadas, *Winners Take All: The Elite Charade of Changing the World* (New York: Alfred A. Knopf, 2018); Harrow et al., "Management."
13. Ahn, "Democratizing American Philanthropy"; Joan Roelofs, *Foundations and Public Policy: The Mask of Pluralism* (New York: State University of New York Press, 2003); Erica Kohl-Arenas, *The Self-Help Myth* (Berkeley: University of California Press, 2015); Edgar Villanueva, *Decolonizing Wealth: Indigenous Wisdom to Heal Divides and Restore Balance* (Oakland: Berrett-Koehler, 2018).
14. Stanley Katz, "What Does It Mean to Say That Philanthropy Is 'Effective'? The Philanthropists' New Clothes," *Proceedings of the American Philosophical Society* 149, no. 2 (2005): 123–30; Reich, "Repugnant"; Rob Reich, *Just Giving: Why Philanthropy Is Failing Democracy and How It Can Do Better* (Princeton, NJ: Princeton University Press, 2018); Emma Saunders-Hastings, "Plutocratic Philanthropy," *Journal of Politics* 80, no. 1 (2018): 149–61; Saunders-Hastings, *Private Virtues*.
15. Jeremy Levine, "The Paradox of Community Power: Cultural Processes and Elite Authority in Participatory Governance," *Social Forces* 95, no. 3 (2017): 1155–79; Amanda Barrett Cox, "Powered Down: The Microfoundations of Organizational Attempts to Redistribute Power," *American Journal of Sociology* 127, no. 2 (2021): 285–336.
16. Emily Barman, *Caring Capitalism: The Meaning and Measure of Social Value* (New York: Cambridge University Press, 2016).
17. Christopher Hood, "A Public Management for All Seasons?" *Public Administration* 69, no. 1 (1991): 3–19; David Osborne and Ted Gaebler, *Reinventing Government* (New York: Penguin Press, 1993); Elke Loeffler and Tony Bovaird, eds., *The Palgrave Handbook of Co-Production of Services and Outcomes* (London: Palgrave, 2021).
18. Carmen Sirianni, *Investing in Democracy: Engaging Citizens in Collaborative Governance* (Washington, DC: Brookings Institution Press, 2009); Kirk Emerson, Tina Nabatchi,

and Stephen Balogh, "An Integrative Framework for Collaborative Governance," *Journal of Public Administration Research and Theory* 22, no. 1 (2012): 1–29; Kirk Emerson and Tina Nabatchi, *Collaborative Governance Regimes* (Washington, DC: Georgetown University Press, 2015).
19. Lucy Bernholz, *How We Give Now: A Philanthropic Guide for the Rest of Us* (Cambridge, MA: MIT Press, 2021).
20. Angela Eikenberry, *Giving Circles: Philanthropy, Voluntary Association, and Democracy* (Bloomington: Indiana University Press, 2009).
21. Ariel Madeline LoBosco Platt, Lance Bitner-Laird, Jaré Akchin, and Evan Bartlett, *Participatory Grantmaking in the Jewish Community and Beyond* (New York: Jewish Funders Network, 2022), 68.
22. Gibson, *Participatory Grantmaking*, 2017; Nwamaka Agbo, *Powershift Philanthropy: Strategies for Impactful Participatory Grantmaking* (Los Angeles: California Endowment, 2021).
23. David Suárez, "Grant Making as Advocacy: The Emergence of Social Justice Philanthropy," *Nonprofit Management and Leadership* 22, no. 3 (2012): 259–80; Sean Dobson, *Freedom Funders: Philanthropy and the Civil Rights Movement 1955–1965* (Washington, DC: National Committee for Responsive Philanthropy, 2014).
24. Chris Cardona, "Participatory Grantmaking Matters Now More than Ever," Ford Foundation, 2020, www.fordfoundation.org/work/learning/learning-reflections/participatory-grantmaking-matters-now-more-than-ever/; Donna Daniels and Kelley Buhles, "Truly Shifting Philanthropy's Power Dynamics Requires New Structure for Giving," *Inside Philanthropy*, 2020, www.insidephilanthropy.com/home/2020/11/6/truly-shifting-philanthropys-power-dynamics-requires-new-structures-for-giving; Emily Finchum-Mason, Kelly Husted, and David Suárez, "Philanthropic Foundation Responses to the COVID-19 Crisis," *Nonprofit and Voluntary Sector Quarterly* 49, no. 6 (2020): 1129–41; Bill Pitkin, "Moving the Rooms of Power: Participatory Philanthropy Is Gaining More Traction," *Inside Philanthropy*, 2020, https://www.insidephilanthropy.com/home/2020/6/24/moving-the-rooms-of-power-participatory-philanthropy-is-gaining-more-traction.
25. Sherry Arnstein, "A Ladder of Citizen Participation," *Journal of the American Institute of Planners* 35, no. 4 (1969): 216–24.
26. Archon Fung, "Varieties of Participation in Complex Governance," *Public Administration Review* 66 (2006): 66–75.
27. Emerson and Nabatchi, *Collaborative Governance Regimes*.
28. Anna Amirkhanyan and Kristina Lambright, *Citizen Participation in the Age of Contracting* (New York: Routledge: 2018).
29. Gibson, *Participatory Grantmaking*, 2017.
30. Jasmine McGinnis Johnson, "Necessary but Not Sufficient: The Impact of Community Input on Grantee Selection," *Administration & Society* 48, no. 1 (2016): 73–103.
31. Gibson, *Deciding Together*, 2018; International Association for Public Participation, "IAP2 USA Resources," 2022, https://iap2usa.org/P2_Resources.
32. Chris Cardona, "Who's Getting Paid to Advance Grantee Inclusion?" *Stanford Social Innovation Review*, 2016, https://doi.org/10.48558/GX12-3375.
33. Candid, "Foundation Directory Online (FDO) Database," 2023, https://fconline.foundationcenter.org/.

34. Joel Fleishman, *The Foundation: A Great American Secret* (New York: PublicAffairs, 2007); Zunz, *Philanthropy in America*, 2014.
35. Prewitt, Heydemann, and Toepler, *The Legitimacy of Philanthropic Foundations*, 2006; Helmut Anheier and David Hammack, eds., *American Foundations: Roles and Contributions* (Washington, DC: Brookings Institution Press, 2010).
36. Peter Dobkin Hall, "Philanthropy, the Nonprofit Sector and the Democratic Dilemma," *Daedalus*, Spring 2013, 139–58; Callahan, *Givers*, 2017; Reich, *Just Giving*, 2018; Benjamin Soskis and Stanley Katz, *Looking Back at 50 Years of US Philanthropy* (Palo Alto, CA: William and Flora Hewlett Foundation, 2016); Saunders-Hastings, *Private Virtues*.
37. Ann Goggins Gregory and Don Howard, "The Nonprofit Starvation Cycle," *Stanford Social Innovation Review* 7, no. 4 (Fall 2009): 49–53.
38. Gibson, *Participatory Grantmaking*, 2017; Hannah Paterson, "Drivers of Participatory Grant Making," *Medium*, 2020, https://hannah-paterson.medium.com/drivers-of-participatory-grant-making-e286c3276f69.

CHAPTER 2

From Collaboration to Ceding Power
The Impact of Participation on Grant Decisions

Jasmine McGinnis Johnson

Participatory grantmakers use panels with nonfunders as members to help make grantmaking decisions. However, participatory grantmakers choose different ways of involving grantmaking panel members in the final grant decisions—from collaborating to consulting to ceding full decision-making power. Practitioners and deliberative governance scholars debate whether ceding power is more authentic participation than collaborating or consulting with grantmaking panels. They also argue that outcomes are affected by how much power is shared. This chapter uses summary data to compare ceding full decision-making power with collaborating or consulting with grantmaking panel members and the nonprofits that receive grants.

INTRODUCTION

In recent years, a small but growing group of funders have begun to use participatory approaches in their grantmaking, upending how resources are allocated, by whom, and to what end. They are inviting nongrantmakers to help set priorities, develop strategies, sit on foundation boards or advisory committees, and conduct research. These are essential components of the participatory approach to philanthropy, and these institutions are using them all at different points in their process.

What has not been as prevalent is participatory grantmaking, which draws on broader participatory philanthropy approaches but zeroes in on how funding decisions get made. While some see participatory grantmaking as one of many types of participatory philanthropy, others see it as a distinct category because it moves decision-making about money to the people most affected by the issues donors are trying to address.[1]

This chapter defines participatory grantmaking as a process that can comprise one or several of the components above, but that also involves nonfunders in making grant decisions. However, this practice is still relatively rare; even among those who engage in participatory grantmaking, there is still considerable variance in how much power (and for what) they cede to nonfunders. Grantmakers for Effective Organizations, for example, found in 2010 that while 48 percent of grantmakers sought information from grantees or community representatives, and 36 percent sought advice from grantee advisory committees, only 14 percent delegated funding decisions to grantees or community representatives when making grant decisions.[2]

This raises a question: Does it matter how nongrantmakers are involved in these practices? In other words, does the degree to which foundations cede power to nongrantmakers affect the kinds of nonprofits that receive grants?

These questions are essential because there is a debate between those who see that involving nonfunders in any part(s) of the grantmaking process is equally valuable in shifting power and others who believe that participation is on a continuum based on the degree to which non-grantmakers are part of decision-making.[3] This debate has been part of other participatory fields, including deliberative democracy, which characterizes participation as "thin" or "thick," and others that use frameworks that begin with "informing" and end with "empowering" stakeholders.[4] In an initial participatory framework originally put forward in a 2018 Ford Foundation monograph, the process begins with "informing" and ends with "joint decision-making."[5] Recently, another column was added by Justice Funders that cedes all decision-making power to nongrantmakers.

If the participation of nonfunders in any or all of the components of a participatory grantmaking process leads to similar outcomes, it calls into question whether such participation is hierarchical. If not, it suggests that the variance may lie in how and the degree to which participants are involved.

POWER IN PARTICIPATORY GRANTMAKING: LITERATURE REVIEW

Power is a central tenet of participatory grantmaking since it influences who makes decisions and controls how resources are distributed. Power also affects whose voices are included and whose voices are not.

Practitioner insights and formal theories attempt to understand the relationship between the amount of voice a person has in the significant decisions of a government or organization and how much a person's voice affects final decisions. Arnstein's ladder of participation, for example, outlines several levels of power—ranging from nonparticipation to citizen power—which people potentially have in influencing the decisions of government agencies.[6] Another model, which the deliberative democracy field uses to assess how much residents are involved in local priority setting and decision-making, is the International Association for Public Participation's Spectrum of Participation. This model starts with "informing the public," then moves to consulting, involving, collaborating, and, ultimately, "empowering" it. Ebdon and Franklin's participatory budgeting model has five components—environmental, process design, mechanisms, goals, and outcomes—that can be analyzed by which are least or most supportive of public participation.[7] While each may have different foci, they all focus on how much power participants have to make/change decisions, how these decisions shape decision-making, and their influence on the end decision.

Although many participatory grantmakers involve stakeholders in grant decisions, not all funders cede complete power in making those decisions. The Liberty Hill Foundation, for example, involves stakeholders in site visits and asks them to provide their lived expertise to staff; but, ultimately, the staff makes final grant decisions. The Headwaters Foundation for Justice asks community members to decide which organizations will receive a grant and for what amount, but the board still has veto power. Finally, the Disability Rights and Global Greengrants funds cede total power to community members to decide which organizations will receive grants and for what amount.[8]

While there have been attempts to codify these practices into a more formal framework, there has yet to be one that the larger field sees as its standard. In 2017, Gibson laid out an initial baseline framework with four components: informing, consulting, involving, and decision-making.[9] This framework is nonhierarchical and indicates how participatory grantmakers can and do involve nonfunders. The framework was introduced, in fact, with an invitation to the field to iterate on it—an invitation that Justice Funders responded to by adding a fifth component: ceding power.

For this study, this author created a new participatory grantmaking framework that consolidates the above-noted frameworks based on the depth and level of nonfunders' participation in the grantmaking process, especially in funding decisions. This framework has three levels (see table 2.1).

The first level of the framework—what this author calls "consultation"—occurs at the pre-grant and grant stages. At this level, participatory grantmakers' staff will often select a group of potential grantees for consideration and invite grantmaking panels that include nongrantmakers to make site visits to those groups. However, the board of directors (or another governance body) makes the final grant decisions. Also, grantmaking panels are made passive in their relationship with funders since they do not have much control over final grant decisions.

Table 2.1: A Power-Sharing Framework

Stage	Level of power sharing		
	Consultation	Collaboration	Ceding power
Pre-grant	Staff or board develop the application and/or decision-making guidelines	Staff or board develop the application and/or decision-making guidelines	Grantmaking panels develop the application and/or decision-making guidelines
Grant	Staff and/or grantmaking panels review applicants, conduct site visits, and tell grantmaking panels about their decision; the board or staff makes final grant decisions, including amounts	Grantmaking panels review all applications and conduct site visits; staff often intervene when grantmaking panels make decisions about grant awards	Grantmaking panels review all applications and do site visits; grantmaking panels make final grant decisions or determine grant amounts
Postgrant	Staff reviews evaluations of grantees and communicates this information to stakeholders	Staff review evaluations of grantees and communicates this information to stakeholders	Grantmaking panels review evaluations of grantees and communicate this information to stakeholders

Source: Author-generated data.

At the second level—what this author calls "collaborating"—grantmaking panels share their ideas about which grantees should receive grant awards at the pre-grant stage, but often these ideas are not implemented at the final grant stage. For example, staff and grantmaking panels may share responsibilities in all facets of the grantmaking process, but grantmakers often make the final funding decisions themselves.

At the third level, "ceding power," grantmaking panels are given complete power over the entire process, including selecting potential grantees, conducting site visits, awarding final grants, and making decisions about amounts.

As noted, there is some debate in the philanthropy and public participation fields that consultation and collaboration are lower forms of—or less "authentic" than—participation than ceding power through joint or independent decision-making.[10] However, there has been little analysis to determine whether one type of participatory grantmaking is better than another. Grantmakers may have reasons for choosing a particular power-sharing approach over another. For example, some staff may not want grantmaking panels to spend volunteer hours reading many applications. Alternatively, grantmakers may have policies that require the board to approve final grant decisions and amounts.

Because it is unknown whether ceding power is better than consultation in affecting grantee decisions, the framework proposed in this chapter does not assign any value to them. Instead, it aims to provide an initial quantitative analysis to determine whether there is a difference in grant decisions, depending on whether participants are involved in the consultation, collaboration, or ceding power levels.

LEVELS OF POWER IN PARTICIPATORY GRANTMAKING AND GRANTEES AWARDED FUNDING

The intentional recruitment of a heterogeneous group of community members to engage in a participatory grantmaking process automatically introduces a broader array of interests, perspectives, and networks into the grant selection process.[11] Grant decisions involving nonfunders will be immediately affected because the latter brings information that foundation boards and staff do not have.[12] This information and lived experience are an essential resource for foundation boards and staff, who tend to make grant decisions in environments with high degrees of information asymmetry.[13] The latter occurs when one decision-maker has more information than another;

in grantmaking, for example, nonprofits often have more information on their performance than grantmakers.

Several foundations create metrics or indicators for grantees to use in assessing their performance and outcomes. While seemingly objective, these indicators are difficult to use, let alone attain, due to the complexity of most nonprofits' goals and services, which do not usually lend themselves to narrowly proscribed outputs. Additionally, these measures are not necessarily those the nonprofit might choose to use in assessing its efforts because they have a better understanding of and more direct experience in identifying what matters to funders, their own organizations, and end users.[14]

Participatory grantmaking helps to lessen a foundation's reliance on these kinds of performance proxies by involving those community members who are closest to the problems in evaluating which organizations are performing well or have the potential to do so.[15] Bourns notes that participatory grantmakers describe this approach as an opportunity that "extends our reach and knowledge of who is doing what in the community."[16] According to initial studies, it can also enhance decision-making, improve organizational effectiveness, increase trust, and reduce cynicism.[17]

However, other studies conclude that community involvement in participatory grantmaking is sufficient but does not automatically yield grantmaking panels that make different grant decisions.[18] Only when citizens have opportunities for deep participation, defined as those in which community members are given the power and authority to influence or alter organizational decisions, can the idealized benefits of participatory governance transpire.[19]

One understudied aspect of participatory grantmaking (and participatory processes in general) is whether the decisions made by stakeholders (of any kind) differ from those made exclusively by traditional power brokers and influential board members. McGinnis finds that grant decisions that emerge from a participatory grantmaking process differ from those made by traditional foundation boards.[20] Grant decisions are different because community members, who live and work in the same areas as potential nonprofit grantees, are involved in those decisions—a contrast to traditional funders, whose boards and staff often do not live or work where they make grants.[21]

Additionally, participatory grantmaking panels tend to be heterogeneous, with members usually having weak ties to one another (i.e., they are acquaintances rather than close friends or family). These acquaintances have access to a breadth of knowledge about their communities, the issues at stake, and some of the existing nonprofits that are working well and those that are not. Alternatively, traditional funders typically recruit from existing board members' personal and professional networks.[22] These closed networks may limit board members' heterogeneous perspectives and influence and insert biases into decisions about which nonprofits receive grant awards.

McGinnis, for example, compared six foundations with both a participatory grantmaking program and a traditional foundation and looked at the characteristics of the nonprofits that received funds.[23] Participatory grantmakers selected smaller, less professionalized grantees and nonprofits that had not been awarded a grant in the previous year compared with traditional funders' grantees. However, older nonprofits—those that more traditional foundations would usually favor—were more likely to be chosen by participatory grantmakers.

Another study that corroborated this finding stemmed from a joint initiative between the Centers for Disease Control and Prevention (CDC), the CDC Foundation, and the Robert Wood Johnson Foundation, which created a competition through which researchers and practitioners submitted their ideas for creating cross-sector collaborations able to address complex issues.[24] The study compared reviewers who used a rubric to score applications versus a popular voting platform. Small applicants were more likely to move forward when reviewers used a rubric to score proposals; the popular voting platform led to the selection of more prominent, traditional applicants. These studies demonstrate that participatory grantmaking does not automatically alter grant decisions.

HYPOTHESES

To explore these issues, this author conducted a study that examined the various ways foundations engaging in participatory grantmaking gave decision-making power to "outsiders," and then whether and how these variations influenced which nonprofits received funding. Three specific hypotheses guided the study:

> Hypothesis 1: Funders that cede power at every stage of the grantmaking process (versus those that collaborate or consult) are more likely to select grantees that are new applicants.

There is evidence that participatory grantmakers are more likely than more traditional grantmakers to select new applicants for funding.[25] According to Grønbjerg, Martell, and Paarlberg, when nonprofits have received a grant in the previous year from a traditional grantmaker, they are more likely to receive renewed funding.[26] Faulk, McGinnis Johnson, and Lecy discovered that it is challenging for nonprofits that have never received a grant from a foundation before to start receiving grants.[27] This evidence suggests that when participatory grantmaking panels have the power to make final grant decisions, they will be more comfortable selecting first-time grantees because members are more likely to have personal insight into nonprofits' work in their communities:

> Hypothesis 2: Funders that cede power at every stage of the grantmaking process (versus those that collaborate or consult) are more likely to select fewer "professional nonprofit" grantees, defined as those organizations that file tax returns using Internal Revenue Service Form 990-N or 990-EZ.[28]

Previous research indicates that traditional grantmakers are more likely than participatory grantmakers to select "professional nonprofits" for grants than participatory grantmaking panels.[29] This suggests that when grantmaking panels have the power to make final grant decisions, they are more likely to select less-professional grantees because members are more likely to have personal knowledge about local nonprofits:

> Hypothesis 3: Funders who cede decision-making power (versus those that collaborate or consult) are more likely to select small nonprofits, defined as nonprofits with smaller total revenues.

Traditional funders tend to give more significant grants to larger nonprofits.[30] This suggests that when grantmaking panels have the power to make final grant decisions, they will be more comfortable supporting smaller nonprofits because they are more likely to have personal knowledge about or experience with these groups.

Data Collection and Sample

This author interviewed eight social justice participatory funders (defined in this chapter as funders who support environmental, social, and economic issues) from December 2020 to March 2021.[31] Primarily, these funders made grants to youth funds, community organizers, race-conscious causes, and environmental organizations. To compile a list of these funders, the author conducted Google searches for "social justice participatory grantmakers" (and similar phrases/words) and pulled names from both the Funding

Exchange member list (network of social justice funders) and those that were mentioned in previous publications about participatory grantmaking.[32] After the initial list was created, the author conducted qualitative interviews with participatory grantmakers who said yes to the interviews. At the end of each interview, the author asked each interviewee if they could provide the names of additional participatory grantmakers doing similar work. Interviewees answered questions about nonprofit grantee decisions, who makes them, and how. (For a complete list of these questions, see the appendix to this chapter.) This author also collected data about each participatory grantmaker's organization, which are summarized in table 2.2.

Out of the eight funders, one's total assets are unknown, and six have total assets of over $5 million.[33] Nationally, 71.5 percent of foundations have assets under $5 million.[34] Additionally, three grantmakers in the sample are between twenty and thirty years of age, and four are between forty and fifty years. The median age of foundations nationally is eleven years.[35] The foundations in this sample are older and larger than national foundations' average total assets and age and are medium-sized. (Due to institutional review board rules at the Urban Institute, interviewees must be anonymous.) As we see in table 2.2, the eight funders in the sample are in three categories based on the typology the author has created (foundations that consult, collaborate, or cede power).

Of the eight grantmakers in this sample, four cede full power to participatory grantmaking panels in making grant decisions, one is collaborating with nonfunders at some point in the grantmaking process (e.g., reviewing

Table 2.2: Descriptive Statistics and Power-Sharing Categories of Foundations (Full Sample)

Foundation ID	Total assets, in millions of dollars	Age (years)	Level of participation
A	5–10	20–30	Collaboration
B	10–15	40–50	Consultation
C	10–15	40–50	Ceding power
D	15–20	40–50	Consultation
E	5–10	40–50	Ceding power
F	1–5	20–30	Ceding power
G	Unknown	10–20	Ceding power
H	50–100	20–30	Consultation

Source: Author-generated data.

grant applications and making site visits and recommendations for funding alongside staff; but staff or the board make final decisions), and three are consulting (i.e., inviting participation for one component of grantmaking decision, such as conducting site visits) but are not involved anywhere else in the process.

Sample and Variables

During 2021 and 2022, 451 nonprofit organizations received grants from the 8 grantmakers in the sample.[36] Grant amounts and information about whether that foundation supported the grantee during the past year were also collected when available. Each foundation's organizational and financial characteristics were collected manually from its Internal Revenue Service Form 990.[37]

Variables

Using each grantmaker's website and reports, this author began by collecting information about whether nonprofits that received grants from that foundation in 2021 or 2022 had received a grant the previous year. The author then identified what type of Form 990 series returns the nonprofit uses: Form 990-N (also called an e-Postcard), Form 990-EZ, or Form 990. Nonprofits with gross receipts of $50,000 or less complete a Form 990-N; those below $200,000 can complete a Form 990-EZ, and those with gross receipts over $200,000 can complete a Form 990. However, previous research indicates that regardless of gross receipts, nonprofits often fill out a 990, even when they do not need to as a signal or proxy to funders of their professionalism.[38]

The size of grantees was determined using proxy variables, such as total revenues and total assets.[39] Other financial characteristics that research has shown to influence whether nonprofits receive donations or grants were also collected and included: total contributions (donations, gifts, and contracts), total expenses, and program revenue (the sale of goods and services).[40] Total liabilities and net assets represent nonprofits' financial savings and health.[41]

Methodology and Descriptive Statistics

Because of the small sample size, this study uses descriptive statistics such as means, medians, percentages, and correlations. Stata, a statistical software program, was used to analyze descriptive statistics.

Of the 451 grants, 211 were found in various 990 databases and website searches when looking for organizations that file a 990-EZ or 990 for which there are financial characteristics (table 2.3). Over half the grants funded by participatory grantmakers in this sample were made to organizations that do not file a 990, 990-EZ, or a 990-N, which indicates that participatory grantmakers are funding small, local, community-based organizations—which is one of many participatory grantmakers' primary goals.

Of the nonprofits that received grants, 67 percent filed a 990; 17 percent completed a 990-EZ; and 16 percent completed a 990-N. For those nonprofits that filled out a 990 or 990-EZ, the average grant award was $31,711 and the median grant was $16,000. Fifty-six percent of nonprofits received a grant in the previous year. The average nonprofit grantee had annual revenues of $6.2 million and total assets of $23.4 million.

Table 2.3: Descriptive Statistics for Nonprofit Grantees (Full Sample)

IRS Form type	Grantees filing (%)
990-N	16
990-EZ	17
990	67
Grants	**Amount received ($)**
Average	31,711
Median	16,000
Received grant previous year?	**Grantees (%)**
Yes	55.68
No	44.32
Overall financial data	**Average ($)**
Total revenue	6,229,782
Total expenses	5,196,873
Total contributions	5,529,263
Program service revenue	410,651
Total assets	23,400,000
Total liabilities	3,224,505
Net assets	20,300,000

Source: Author-generated data.

Analysis

Using this information, this author then compared the foundations' level of power-sharing, the characteristics of the nonprofits that received grants, and whether/how their organizational and financial characteristics differ. Table 2.4 shows that a majority (53 percent) of new grantees were awarded grants from grantmakers that ceded control of grant decision-making to community members/panels. Grantmakers that ceded control or collaborated with grantmaking panels awarded, respectively, 46.6 percent and 47.4 percent of their grant budgets to new grantees. This finding supports hypothesis 1. Specifically, foundations that invite more participation to take more risks in supporting new organizations. Foundations with less participatory practices are more likely to fund the tried and true.

Funders that cede power award 54.8 percent of their grants to organizations that file Form 990 (defined in this study as professional nonprofits). Funders that collaborate with grantmaking panels award grants to

Table 2.4: Descriptive Statistics Comparing Levels of Power Sharing by Nonprofits That Receive Grant Awards

IRS form filed by grantees	Funders and level of power sharing (%)		
	Cede power	Collaborate	Consult
990-N	28	33	7
990-EZ	17	8	18
990	55	59	75
Received grant previous year			
Yes	53	53	37
No	47	47	63
Grants received			
Average			
Median	$27,648	$23,874	$45,000
Average total revenue	$3,110,906	$399,653	$8,109,237
Average total expenses	$2,658,134	$501,992	$6,723,745
Average program service revenue	$784,787	$59,000	$248,215

Source: Author-generated data.

58.3 percent of organizations with 990s,[42] and funders that consult with panels award grants to 74.5 percent of nonprofits with 990s. Since 990 status is a proxy for professionalism, this finding supports hypothesis 2 (funders that cede grantmaking power to grantmaking panels are more likely to award grants to fewer professionalized nonprofits). Funders ceding power also made more grants to those with 990-EZ and 990-N than funders collaborating or consulting. Again, funders that cede power are more likely to award grants to more risky, less professional nonprofits. Funders that consult or collaborate are more likely to make decisions with more traditional nonprofits.

Funders that collaborate with grantmaking panels are more likely to award grants to nonprofits with smaller total revenues (defined as donations and contributions) when compared with funders that cede power or consult with grantmaking panels. The average revenue of grants awarded to nonprofits from funders that collaborate is nearly $400,000, compared with more than $3 million in revenue from grantmakers that cede power and more than $8 million with funders that consult. These findings do not support hypothesis 3 (funders that cede decision-making power to grantmaking panels are more likely to award grants to smaller grantees).

Another variable collected was nonprofit grantees' program service revenue (defined as money raised by charging fees for programs and services). The average program service revenue for grantees of funders collaborating with participatory grantmaking panels is $59,000 and $248,215 from grantmakers that consult with grantmaking panels (table 2.5).

Table 2.5: Overall Findings Comparing Funders That Consult, Collaborate, and Cede Power to Grantees (Percentage)

Funder action	Work with new grantees	Nonprofit grantees' level of professionalism	Nonprofit grantees' size
Consult	Low	High	Medium
Collaborate	Medium	Medium	Smallest
Cede power	Highest	Lowest	Biggest

Source: Author-generated data.

DISCUSSION

This study's descriptive statistics and findings identify mixed support for its three hypotheses. Funders that cede decision-making power to grantmaking panels are more likely to select new and less professionalized grantees. The opposite pattern is true for funders collaborating and consulting on grantmaking decisions with grantmaking panels. Funders that collaborate and consult with grantmaking panels when making grant decisions are more likely to select tried-and-true organizations that were previously funded by the foundation.

However, another pattern emerges when looking at the financial characteristics of nonprofits awarded grants in this sample. Funders collaborating with grantmaking panels select organizations with lower total revenues, assets, and program service revenues.

One new insight from the financial characteristics of nonprofits is that foundation staff members who collaborate and consult with grantmaking panels are doing a good job selecting smaller grantees. Interviews indicated that many participatory grantmaking staff members are racially diverse, are former community organizers, and have lived in the local area for a long time. One staff member in particular, who wished to remain anonymous, indicated in an interview that they are a fifteenth-generation resident of their neighborhood and a former youth activist.

One limitation of this study is that it is cross-sectional and has a small sample size, which precludes more rigorous statistical analysis. Another limitation is that the interviews did not generate complete information about the postgrant stage since many participatory funders do not involve grantmaking panels in evaluations or other postgrant assessments. This understanding could lead to different groupings of the funder's levels of participation.

Future research could investigate other organizational and financial characteristics of nonprofits that are not available in tax data, such as the diversity of nonprofit leadership, the nonprofit ecosystem, and community reputation. As a representative from Foundation C noted, "We are intentional about diversity—asking nominators about the experience, level of organizers, age and experience on the ground, race, and geography—various other forms of diversity. We also have a rich conversation about what is needed [in a local area] right now—and people feel a sense of community and understand the ecosystem." Future research could also explore the relationship between staff and grantmaking panels in participatory grantmaking, and the role of board approval as a process that hinders or catalyzes funders' goals.

APPENDIX: INTERVIEW PROTOCOL QUESTIONS

1. Introduction / background information
   - What is your role in this process?
     - How many staff members are dedicated to this process?
     - Describe the entire process of community involvement from start to finish, or from recruitment of community members to awarding grant monies.
   - What are the goals/strategy of having this board?
     - Probe the different strategies. If they answer one strategy, probe the next few.
   - What type of representation are you trying to achieve with this community board?
     - Is demographic representation important to your organization? Why or why not?

2. Who makes the decisions?
   - To what extent does the community board take the lead during the grantmaking process?
     - Why is it important that this is community led?
     - Do you have any staff involvement in the application reviews or during site visits?
   - Are grant decisions made by community boards reflective of final grant awards?
     - If yes, why don't you have another board approve these decisions?
     - If no, why do you allow community members this discretion?
     - Why is this important to your organization?
   - Does your organization have opportunities during the grantmaking process for members of the community board to record their individual evaluations?
     - Can you describe the scoring system you use?
     - Why do you use this scoring system?
     - Why is this important to you?

NOTES

1. Cynthia Gibson, *Deciding Together: Shifting Power and Resources through Participatory Grantmaking* (New York: Foundation Center, 2018), https://learningforfunders.candid.org/content/guides/deciding-together/.

2. Courtney Bourns, "Do Nothing About Me Without Me: An Action Guide for Engaging Stakeholders," Grantmakers for Effective Organizations, www.geofunders.org/resources/do-nothing-about-me-without-me-an-action-guide-for engaging-stakeholders-688.
3. Cynthia Gibson, "Moving Beyond Feedback: The Promise of Participatory Grantmaking," *Nonprofit Quarterly*, Summer 2019, https://nonprofitquarterly.org/moving-beyond-feedback-the-promise-of-participatory-grantmaking/.
4. Tina Nabatchi and Matt Leighninger, *Public Participation for 21st-Century Democracy* (Hoboken, NJ: Jossey-Bass, 2015); Organizing Engagement, "Types of Engagement: Thick, Thin, and Conventional," blog, https://organizingengagement.org/models/types-of-engagement-thick-thin-and-conventional/; International Association for Public Participation, "IAP2 Spectrum of Public Participation," 2007, http://iap2.affiniscape.com/associations/4748/files/IAP2%20Spectrum_vertical.pdf.
5. Cynthia Gibson, *Participatory Grantmaking: Has Its Time Come?* (New York: Ford Foundation, 2017), www.fordfoundation.org/media/3599/participatory_grantmaking-lmv7.pdf.
6. Sherri Arnstein, "A Ladder of Citizen Participation," *Journal of the American Institute of Planners* 35, no. 4 (1969): 216–24.
7. Carol Ebdon and Aimee Franklin, "Citizen Participation in Budgeting Theory," *Public Administration Review* 66, no. 3 (2006): 437–47.
8. Gibson, *Deciding Together*, 2018.
9. Gibson, *Participatory Grantmaking*, 2017.
10. Arnstein, "Ladder"; Sarah C. White, "Depoliticising Development: The Uses and Abuses of Participation," *Development in Practice* 6, no. 1 (1996): 6–15.
11. Bourns, "Do Nothing"; Kathleen Enright and Courtney Bourns, "The Case for Stakeholder Engagement," *Stanford Social Innovation Review* 8, no. 2 (Spring 2010): 40–45, https://ssir.org/articles/entry/the_case_for_stakeholder_engagement; Jasmine McGinnis, "Necessary but Not Sufficient: The Impact of Community Input on Grantee Selection," *Administration & Society* 48, no. 1 (2016): 73–103.
12. Enright and Bourns, "Case."
13. McGinnis, "Necessary."
14. Dale E. Thomson, "Exploring the Role of Funders' Performance Reporting Mandates in Nonprofit Performance Measurement," *Nonprofit and Voluntary Sector Quarterly* 39, no. 4 (2010): 611–29; Joanne G. Carman, "Nonprofits, Funders, and Evaluation: Accountability in Action," *American Review of Public Administration* 39, no. 4 (2009): 374–90.
15. McGinnis, "Necessary"; Mayer Zald, "Urban Differentiation, Characteristics of Boards of Directors, and Organizational Effectiveness," *American Journal of Sociology* 73, no. 3 (1967): 261–72; Enright and Bourns, "Case"; Rebecca Kissane and Jeff Gingerich, "Do You See What I See? Nonprofit and Resident Perceptions of Urban Neighborhood Problems," *Nonprofit and Voluntary Sector Quarterly* 33, no. 2 (2004): 311–33. Research has found that nonprofit board members and staff members tend to live far away from the communities they serve. This distance is hypothesized as one of the reasons why surveys of nonprofit executives and community members reveal distinct differences between community members' description of problems, solutions, and high-performing nonprofits, and the perspectives of nonprofit executives on these same issues.
16. Bourns, "Do Nothing," 28.

17. Thomas Bryer and Ismail Sahin, "Administrators as Deliberative Representatives: A Revised Public Service Role," *International Journal of Public Administration* 35, no. 14 (2012): 925–33; Carol Ebdon and Aimee Franklin, "Searching for a Role for Citizens in the Budget Process," *Public Budgeting and Finance* 24, no. 1 (2004): 32–49; Ebdon and Franklin, "Citizen Participation"; Aimee L. Franklin and Carol Ebdon, "Are We All Touching the Same Camel? Exploring a Model of Participation in Budgeting," *American Review of Public Administration* 35, no. 2 (2005): 168–85.
18. Laurence Bherer, "Successful and Unsuccessful Participatory Arrangements: Why Is There a Participatory Movement at the Local Level?" *Journal of Urban Affairs* 32, no. 3 (2010): 287–303; Bryer and Sahin, "Administrators"; Ebdon and Franklin, "Citizen Participation."
19. Arnstein, "Ladder"; Thomas Bryer, "Toward a Relevant Agenda for a Responsive Public Administration," *Journal of Public Administration Research and Theory* 17, no. 3 (2007): 479–500; Ebdon and Franklin, "Citizen Participation."
20. McGinnis, "Necessary."
21. Kelin Gersick, *Generations of Giving: Leadership and Continuity in Family Foundations* (Lanham, MD: Lexington Books, 2004).
22. Gersick.
23. McGinnis, "Necessary."
24. Oktawia Wojcik, LesLeigh Ford, Keely Hanson, Claire Boyd, and Shena Ashley, "Participatory Grantmaking: A Test of Rubric Scoring Versus Popular Voting Selection in a Blinded Grantmaking Process," *Foundation Review* 12, no. 1 (2020).
25. McGinnis, "Necessary."
26. Kirsten Grønbjerg, Laura Martell, and Laurie Paarlberg, "Philanthropic Funding of Human Services: Solving Ambiguity Through the Two-Stage Competitive Process," *Nonprofit and Voluntary Sector Quarterly* 29, issue 1 supplement (2000): 9–40.
27. Lewis Faulk, Jasmine McGinnis Johnson, and Jesse Lecy, "Competitive Advantage in Nonprofit Grant Markets: Implications of Network Embeddedness and Status," *International Public Management Journal* 20, no. 2 (2017): 261–93.
28. Nonprofits that have gross annual receipts of $50,000 or less can file a Form 990-N. Nonprofits that have gross annual receipts between $50,000 and $200,000 can file a Form 990-EZ.
29. McGinnis, "Necessary."
30. Heather MacIndoe, "Understanding Foundation Philanthropy to Human Service Organizations: Funding Stratification in an Urban Grants Economy," *Human Service Organizations: Management, Leadership & Governance* 46, no. 3 (2021): 1–22; Faulk et al., "Competitive Advantage."
31. Ten qualitative interviews were conducted, but two funders did not make grant decisions to organizations, so they were eliminated from the sample.
32. Gibson, *Participatory Grantmaking*; Gibson, *Deciding Together*, 2018.
33. One funder is a program of a larger foundation, and the total assets of the program are unknown.
34. Foundation Source, "Report on Private Foundations—Grantmaking," 2021, https://20294318.fs1.hubspotusercontent-na1.net/hubfs/20294318/Resource-Hub/2021-Report-on-Private-Foundations-Grantmaking_FINAL.pdf.
35. Foundation Source.

36. Most funders did not want to share their grantee data, so to compile lists of grantees, the first step was to visit each funder's website and download its grantmaking reports (which are typically issued annually; it is important to note that some funders had grant data from 2022 but others had data from 2021). Next, grantees' employer identification numbers were collected through ProPublica's Nonprofit Explorer and through Charity Navigator.
37. The existing databases typically used to collect 990 data were not updated to 2020 or 2021.
38. Kristen Grønbjerg and Laurie Paarlberg, "Extent and Nature of Overlap Between Listings of IRS Tax-Exempt Registration and Nonprofit Incorporation: The Case of Indiana," *Nonprofit and Voluntary Sector Quarterly* 31, no. 4 (2002): 565–94.
39. John Trussel and Linda Parsons, "Financial Reporting Factors Affecting Donations to Charitable Organizations," *Advances in Accounting* 23 (2003): 263–85.
40. Cagla Okten and Burton Weisbrod, "Determinants of Donations in Private Nonprofit Markets," *Journal of Public Economics* 75, no. 2 (2000): 255–72.
41. Christopher Prentice, "Understanding Nonprofit Financial Health: Exploring the Effects of Organizational and Environmental Variables," *Nonprofit and Voluntary Sector Quarterly* 45, no. 5 (2016): 888–909.
42. Because we are only comparing grantee descriptive statistics and are not using higher-level statistical analysis, only one funder is power sharing.

CHAPTER 3

Participatory Grantmaking Practices among Women's Funds
What Has Been Learned?

Elizabeth Barajas-Román and Mirenda Meghelli

While women's funds were one of the pioneers of participatory grantmaking, there has been little documentation of the current state of this practice or its evolution within the sector over the past decade. To address this gap, Elizabeth Barajas-Román, Megan Murphy Wolf, and Mirenda Meghelli of the Women's Funding Network—the largest alliance of women's funds and gender equity funders in the world—created a snapshot of this practice in community- and state-based women's funds by surveying and conducting focus groups with representatives from sixty-five women's funds in the United States. The study found that although most of their network intentionally applied participatory funding principles, the practice was identified differently depending on a variety of community-based factors. Further, some women's funds had evolved the practice to include other democratization strategies that help shift economic power to the communities they serve.

INTRODUCTION

The Women's Funding Network (WFN) is a growing community of more than 130 women's funds, foundations, gender equity funders, allies, and individuals spanning fourteen countries. Together, they create a community of practice that applies intersectional feminist approaches to philanthropy across the United States and around the globe.[1] Its members create an interesting and complex landscape of philanthropy, with varied experiences and participatory practices, including grantmaking. As such, examination of these variations presents a unique opportunity to explore the benefits and challenges of participatory grantmaking principles and practices. This chapter offers insights and the expertise of WFN members, early pioneers, and enduring practitioners of participatory approaches (see box 3.1).

3.1 The Women's Funding Network's Ecosystem

- WFN has over 130 members representing over $1.4 billion in combined annual grantmaking.
- Fifty-five percent of the WFN consists of place-based women's funds: they are public organizations that build power in communities where they are located and range in geographic scope from municipal and statewide funds in the United States to national funds based outside the United States.
- Twenty-one percent of member organizations have a global reach, with a combined focus on fifty-five different countries in all habitable regions of the globe.
- US-based members represent thirty-three states; Washington, DC; and Puerto Rico.
- Thirteen percent of member organizations are based outside the United States.

From inception, WFN has included public and private foundations, women's foundations, and women's funds (generally housed within community foundations) engaging in strategic philanthropic efforts that invest in women and girls at the intersection of race, class, gender, demographics, and other identities through a cadre of approaches. Launched thirty-eight years ago as a response to the marginalization of women's leadership within philanthropy, along with the need for more philanthropic investment targeted specifically at women and girls, WFN continues to be a catalytic force in the social movement to ensure access, equity, opportunity, dignity, and security.

WFN brings its members together to support their leadership, to share best practices, and to replicate and scale methods, models, and programs that advance the lives of women and girls. A long-standing benefit of membership in WFN is the collaborative research that it regularly conducts and is made possible through its network of gender-based funders. This collaborative and participatory approach to learning provides context, thought leadership, and evidence to support funding practices that propel movements forward.

CONTEXT

In 1984, during a joint meeting of the National Black United Fund and National Committee for Responsive Philanthropy, leaders from several women's funds discussed creating what would later become WFN. A year later, twenty funds gathered for the first conference of women's funds in Washington. At that time, WFN and its members adopted principles of social justice philanthropy, placing racial and gender equity at the center and identifying these values as critical and defining the characteristics of a new wave of philanthropy designed to make lasting change. In 2018, WFN, which had grown to ninety-six members, recommitted to these principles, including intersectionality, and to continuing to engage in practices that give women, girls, and other marginalized genders a powerful voice and role in decision-making that affects their lives. To do so requires participatory approaches that are centered and grounded in the understanding that those most affected have the insight, information, and ability not only to define the problems but also to serve as an integral and necessary participant in the implementation of their interventions and solutions. WFN has learned alongside its members that commitment to these values requires deep engagement in communities, as well as in organizational governance, fundraising, advocacy, and in making grant decisions.

In 2017, WFN received funding from the Fund for Shared Insight, a national funding collaborative that invests in opportunities for foundations and nonprofits to listen and respond to the people and communities that have been most harmed by the systems and structures they are seeking to change. With this funding, WFN facilitated online focus groups and surveyed forty-four of its individual member organizations. WFN also conducted in-depth interviews with nine of these members to explore their openness practices. These practices were defined by the Fund for Shared Insight as foundations sharing their goals and strategies, making decisions and measuring progress, listening and engaging in dialogue with others, acting on what they hear, and sharing what they have learned with people and organizations outside their philanthropic institutions. As a part of this research, participatory grantmaking practices and approaches emerged as key to sharing goals, strategies, decision-making, incorporating feedback, and understanding progress. The information and contextual understanding gleaned from this scan provided important learning and insights to share with WFN members and the broader philanthropic community.

One learning was that the majority of WFN members were conducting participatory research to better understand the lived experiences of women, girls, and other marginalized genders in the community. This research process included listening tours, which took various forms, such as joining existing gatherings at community centers, churches, schools, and other centers of public life. These events provided an opportunity for WFN members to hear directly from the women, girls, and marginalized genders in the communities they seek to serve. WFN members also used listening tours to collect qualitative data as part of a place-based research methodology to ensure that findings, as well as proposed approaches to philanthropic intervention, accurately reflected the experiences of women, girls, and other marginalized genders.

With this research as leverage, WFN members were able to convene key stakeholders, such as other funders, nonprofits, government entities, and community leaders. Through discussions with these partners, WFN was able to develop more equitable targets and evaluation measures, which would help ensure that any proposed strategies and solutions would be focused on meeting the needs of the intended population.

It is worth noting that the overwhelming majority of WFN members surveyed said that participatory grantmaking and funding practices are important practices for philanthropic openness and transparency with the communities they support. These findings supported anecdotal evidence gathered from decades of grantee partner testimonials on how WFN member funds approach grantmaking strategy. They also helped shape a series of additional issues that WFN was eager to explore, including the factors preventing some foundations from deeper community engagement, and more details about the diverse participatory approaches women's funds were undertaking beyond their grantmaking. With its interest in learning more about participatory practices among foundations, the Ford Foundation provided WFN with the opportunity to dig deeper into how participatory practices support WFN members' missions, visions, and values; track and assess their progress; and advance their commitment to diversity, equity, and inclusion. The remainder of this chapter provides an overview of this process and an analysis of learning from the study.

STUDY DESCRIPTION AND PROCESS

The study, conducted across two member cohorts, was guided by and sought to understand six questions:

- What does a cultural ethos of participation look like?
- How has participatory grantmaking been successful?[2]
- How is success measured in terms of process and results on the ground?
- What are the effects of participatory grantmaking on the people who are participating?
- How does participatory grantmaking promote and advance diversity, equity, and inclusion?
- What are the practical considerations funders need to address when implementing participatory grantmaking?

The research process included a mixed-method approach for data collection and analysis that included virtual hour-long focus groups and an online survey. WFN has used this approach in previous studies because it provides richer insights and, in true participatory fashion, benefits both researchers and respondents. Focus groups allow members to hear colleagues' first-hand experiences; build relationships across and between members; and offer ideas for methods, tools, and resources that WFN might adopt or explore while providing it with the opportunity to collect qualitative and quantitative data.

Given the challenge of many time zones and schedules, which prevented some members from participating in the focus groups, WFN created and distributed an online survey with the same focus group questions to these members. The participants were all US-based members of WFN, and comprise the vast majority of community, regional, and state-based women's funds.

Data collection took place in the late fall of 2019 through the early spring of 2020. Analysis of the findings and dissemination of the results to WFN members happened in the late spring of 2020.

Participant Selection

The sample included sixty-five US-based community, regional, and state-wide women's funds engaged in participatory grantmaking practices; of these, forty-four participated in an online survey. Participants were recruited through WFN's weekly newsletter, which briefly described the research study and invited members to complete a survey to identify those engaged in participatory grantmaking practices. At the end of the survey, members who self-identified as using participatory grantmaking practices were invited to participate in the study.

Due to many leadership transitions occurring across the network, WFN provided members with a clear definition of participatory grantmaking: where decision-making power about funding—including the strategy and criteria behind those decisions—is ceded to the very communities that funders aim to serve.[3] Further, the grantmaking practices passed down from one leader to the next over the past thirty-five years—or that were adopted by new women's foundations mentored by existing foundations—were now being named and labeled by the broader philanthropic sector as participatory grantmaking (see box 3.2).

3.2 Women's Funding Network participatory grantmaking research participants:

85: Percentage of leaders of member organizations who participated (CEO, executive director, or program director)
65: Number of member participants
60: Percentage of participants who have an annual grantmaking budget of below $500,000
35: Number of states from all regions, representing state, regional, and local foundations

---

Data Collection

See the discussion questions in box 3.3.

3.3 Discussion Questions

- Why do you practice participatory grantmaking?
- Identify how participatory grantmaking has advanced your mission, vision, and values.
- How do you evaluate impact through participatory grantmaking?
- What participatory grantmaking evaluation practices do you engage in?
- What are the most compelling reasons you undertake participatory grantmaking?
- Identify how participatory grantmaking promotes/advances our commitment to diversity, equity, and inclusion.
- What are some of the challenges of participatory grantmaking?

WFN conducted three focus groups with a minimum of five people from at least four member organizations participating in each session. These focus groups, conducted virtually and lasting 1 hour, provided an opportunity to ask both qualitative and quantitative questions. The focus group protocol ensured the same set of questions were asked across sessions for qualitative responses and the polling feature was used to collect quantitative responses. Forty-four WFN members participated in an online survey. Five WFN members who were not engaged in participatory practices participated in one-to-one interviews, which provided WFN with an opportunity to surface the beliefs, practices, and/or challenges preventing them from doing so.

Data Analysis and Findings

While the different research approaches (focus groups, surveys, and one-to-one interviews) added texture to the findings, there were some distinct throughlines:

- Overall, 73 percent of total respondents from each research approach, indicated that they use some level of participatory grantmaking practices.
  ○ Among total respondents who indicated some level of participatory grantmaking practices, 10 percent indicated that they engaged potential grant recipients in the highest level of grantmaking integration including community members reviewing and scoring letters of intent and grant proposals, conducting site visits, and selecting grant recipients and funding amounts.
  ○ Among total respondents who indicated some level of participatory grantmaking practices, 86 percent expressed hesitancy over going as far as letting potential grantees decide on recipients and funding amounts, indicating that they felt this level of involvement to be a conflict of interest. Instead, these respondents integrated potential grantees up to recommending, but not finalizing, grant recipients and funding amounts. For these member organizations, grant decisions were presented to the board of directors or advisory committee (e.g., a women's fund within community foundations) for final approval.
  ○ Among total respondents who indicated some level of participatory grantmaking practices, 2 percent indicated that beyond engaging community reviewers for grant proposals, the only other level of integration they had was involving reviewers and grant recipients in stipulating shared evaluation outcomes.

- Twenty-seven percent of total respondents indicated they were not engaged in participatory grantmaking. However, after interviewing five individuals from these member organizations, it was clear they were confused or not aware that some of their practices were indeed participatory.
  ○ These member organizations indicated that they were applying participatory grantmaking principles to a smaller, more specific funding portfolio or program area and not their entire portfolio.
  ○ These respondents also believed that if their practices include a range up to, but not including, grant decision-making, they were not engaged in participatory grantmaking at all. It is worth noting, however, that nearly all these respondents indicated their practices included either community members involved in grant reviews but not decision-making.

- Two respondents indicated that they engaged in participatory grantmaking for a specific funding pool or issue area but not for all their grantmaking. "We were not sure if we could say we were doing participatory grantmaking, since all except for one grant program are traditionally decided," said one respondent.
- Three respondents representing family or corporate foundations indicated that while they were exploring participatory grantmaking practices, the principles conflicted with the current organizational structure and/or interests of the donor/founder. No additional detail was provided.

- The rationale for use of participatory approaches varied, with wide overlap among the following responses: It
  - aligned with social justice and equity values;
  - advances commitment to racial and gender equity, inclusion, and diversity;
  - provides an opportunity for donor education and engagement;
  - provides an opportunity for cultivation of new donors and leaders for the organization; and
  - a combination of both donor education, engagement, and securing new donors and leaders.

- Deeply held beliefs, rooted in trust and power dynamics, impede some members' desire to explore participatory grantmaking and other participatory practices. Some of the beliefs that emerged during interviews included doubt about the intelligence/sophistication of those living in poverty or need (which is also a stand-in for anti-Blackness beliefs), the question of whether people leading nonprofits can act without self-interest, and the position that it is a funder's job to shape strategy and make decisions. Until these beliefs are unpacked, questioned, and examined, the full range of opportunity to engage with participatory practices by many members will continue to be aspirational.

- Respondents cited three issues they wanted to learn more about and incorporate into their practice: (1) the evaluation of individual participants' experience, (2) whether the intentions and aims of participatory grantmaking practices are achieved, and (3) the impact of these practices on communities and constituents.

- Participatory practices beyond grantmaking have evolved across WFN to include other democratization strategies that help shift economic power to target communities.
  - Women's foundations/funds use participatory practices to build community and engagement in their gender equity movements to advance women's economic power and security.
  - WFN respondents are using participatory practices to select, train, and equip women to advance policy change via Women's Policy Institutes. These institutes, sponsored by women's funds and foundations in various jurisdictions, are designed to engage women to identify policy issues, develop policy solutions, and learn how to implement policy at the municipal, regional, state, and national levels.
  - Women most affected by economic disparities lead and form partnerships with women's funds to determine programmatic and policy strategies that address needs, priorities, accelerators, and barriers to advancing systemic change.
  - Participatory learning, research, and relationship building, as well as listening tours to understand lived expertise and learn about community-driven solutions, are creating sustained relationships, building trust, and facilitating community-led transformational change.

DISCUSSION

In the broader philanthropic sector, participatory approaches continue to be the exception rather than the rule.[4] For WFN members, participatory approaches are more often the rule rather than the exception: more than 73 percent of WFN members who participated in this study reported engaging in participatory grantmaking practices. Many use participatory principles to democratize other strategies and initiatives to share power, invest and grow in community leadership, and innovate. These findings are key and are consistent with WFN's position that women's funds were early pioneers that regularly used participatory grantmaking practices to engage in openness and transparency necessary to build relationships and trust, and to sustain lasting change led by the communities they serve.

In addition to documenting the network's use of participatory grantmaking practices, this study also surfaced important questions and challenges that warrant further exploration—all of which were raised

What Does a Cultural Ethos of Participation Look Like?

The fundamental and underlying belief that guides WFN members' engagement in participatory grantmaking is the importance of agency and voice of women, girls, and nonbinary people. WFN members believe that when women, girls, and nonbinary people from diverse backgrounds come together, the power dynamic shifts from "power over" to "relational power within" the community. As such, WFN members believe that those most affected by the issues can articulate and drive what is most needed to sustain change efforts.

WFN members report that participatory grantmaking supports the mission, vision, and values of their organization in several ways, which together illustrate what a "culture ethos of participation" looks like. This culture

- allows for a more thoughtful and informed decision-making process when awarding grants;
- strengthens the trust and credibility of the foundation with constituents, grant partners, funders, and donors by inclusion in and exposure to the grantmaking process;
- assesses and strengthens organizational program and grantmaking process and outcomes focused on diversity, equity, and inclusion;
- identifies new initiatives, partners, leaders, and solutions for issues that affect the communities WFN members are seeking to serve; and
- builds community and collaboration to support the gender justice movement.

How Has Participatory Grantmaking Helped WFN Members Who Use These Practices Achieve Their Goals?

WFN members are committed to evolving their openness and transparency practices and to engaging in participatory approaches (including participatory grantmaking) as ways to ensure that they align with their organizational culture and values and are responsive to the needs of the community, donors, and funders.

WFN members note that participatory grantmaking advances their missions, visions, and values by building local, state, regional, municipal, and national movements toward gender equity. Participatory grantmaking offers creative solutions to complex, deeply entrenched barriers to gender equity. By sharing power and access with the community through participatory grantmaking practices, members report that they can invite others who are external to their organizations to dismantle inequitable institutional practices and move toward inclusion.

How Do WFN Members Engaging in Participatory Grantmaking Practices Assess Their Progress in Terms of Both the Process and Results on the Ground?

WFN respondents say they measure success primarily by assessing the level and quality of participants' experience in the grantmaking process. These assessments, however, are still largely anecdotal, though several WFN members use surveys and focus groups to collect data on the participation experience.

Participatory grantmaking practices tend to be more inclusive of communities most affected by issues; allow organizations to make more thoughtful and informed decisions; strengthen trust and credibility among organizations, their donors, and the community; and promote equity in both processes and outcomes. Given these advantages, it may behoove women's foundations/funds to engage in reflection and inquiry conversations with their grant partners and applicants to collectively define and then design strategies to determine whether these objectives are being achieved.

Many WFN members indicate that participation on the grant review committee is an opportunity to educate the community on gender justice and the work being done on the ground to advance equity. Others believe that participation in a grant review committee also offers nongrantmakers opportunities to engage with donors directly and to screen and assess possible committee and board members. That said, most do not collect or analyze data that might support these assumptions.

What Benefits Do Participants Obtain from WFN Members' Participatory Grantmaking Processes?

WFN members report that people who participate in their grantmaking process enjoy gathering with groups of like-minded people to discuss issues affecting women, girls, and other marginalized genders in their community and to learn more about the organizations working to advance gender and racial equity. All members, especially volunteers, report a high level of engagement and participation, although they also indicate the process is time-consuming and sometimes arduous.

Despite the time and energy these processes often require, most participants return year after year because they value and enjoy the experience. As a result, some WFN members have had to place term limits for participation. Others, however, have expanded their committee size to incorporate more participation from the community and to allow continued participation from long-standing committee members. Anecdotally, WFN members report that many grantmaking committee participants become long-term donors.

Further, they support other gender-equity-focused organizations, either financially or through volunteering, or by engaging in advocacy, joining other committees, and/or becoming board members. As noted earlier in the chapter, there may be readily available data that could support these claims and strengthen their case for participatory grantmaking practices.

How Does Participatory Grantmaking Promote and Advance Diversity, Equity, and Inclusion in the WFN?

Overwhelmingly, all WFN members engaging in participatory grantmaking believe this supports their commitment to diversity, equity, and inclusion—or whichever terms they prefer for equity and justice. Without exception, WFN members have explicit values on equity and justice and employ participatory grantmaking practices to support their intention to bring a gender equity lens to create positive social change for all. WFN members also bring together grant reviewers that reflect their communities through a variety of criteria—age, race, ethnicity, sexual orientation, education, zip code, profession, and, increasingly, gender. WFN members shared specific ways in which participatory grantmaking promotes and advances their commitment to equity and justice. These include the ability to

- identify new initiatives and take risks;
- encourage collaboration and larger movement building by forging relationships among diverse group of individuals and institutions;
- promote openness and transparency practices;
- offer deeper transparency by revealing the inherent power dynamics that come with making decisions about money and how those decisions are made;

- diversify decisions about resource allocation and by whom;
- enable them to walk the talk of social change by affirming that a foundation's funding process is as important as what gets supported;
- empower communities by putting resources (power, money, visibility, access) in the hands of women, girls, and other individuals with marginalized genders who are leading and problem-solving a broad array of issues;
- shift from the foundation being the expert to learning from and alongside those most affected by a problem; and
- advance diversity, equity, and inclusion by building the leadership capacity of community participants typically overlooked for leadership.

What Do WFN Members See as Challenges for Participatory Grantmaking?

The vast majority (90 percent) of total respondents engaged in participatory grantmaking practices indicated that the approach is resource intensive, with significant staff time needed to recruit, train, support, and facilitate community review processes. This can take months of training before the review process begins, and then take anywhere from three to six months to score and discuss applications, conduct site visits, and make decisions. Resources are also needed to support participants' meals and travel, as well as meeting spaces.

Members who are not currently engaged in the practice of participatory grantmaking cite the challenges noted above, along with having to deal with their philanthropic institutions' hesitancy to cede decision-making power to people outside those institutions. Traditionally, foundations have seen program staff and their leadership—rather than community residents or other external stakeholders—as having the expertise to guide, inform, and make grant decisions.

Some respondents said they are reluctant to pursue participatory grantmaking given that it can invite and even exacerbate bias because, in many cases, the foundation decides who will be invited to participate in the process or limits the participant pool in ways that are not fully representative of the larger community. Members also expressed concern about exploring participatory grantmaking because of the potential for conflicts of interest when there are current or potential grantees at the decision-making table. However, this study suggests that there is a wide range of definitions of participatory grantmaking—and that a majority of self-identified participatory grantmakers in this study do not integrate grantees into final decision-making.

Some of these beliefs are rooted in power inequities and a lack of trust and, if left unaddressed, will hamper efforts to advance participatory practices to the full democratization and potential of grantmaking. Addressing these barriers will require acknowledging and examining the sources of foundation assets (e.g., the predominance of white donors and other sources of assets, such as toxic capitalism, slavery, or stolen land) and philanthropy's white-dominant culture and privilege, which reinforces beliefs, practices, and processes that misalign with the missions, visions, and values that advance intersectional gender equity. Participatory grantmaking, while a step in the right direction, needs to be centered in intersectional equity, challenging white-dominant organizational culture and decentering whiteness; anything less perpetuates, rather than advances, participatory approaches.

CONCLUSION

This study's exploration of WFN's participatory grantmaking practices has provided an opportunity to deepen the conversation and better understand how WFN members are engaging in participatory approaches. It has also confirmed members' experiences with participatory approaches as being critical for building relationships, trust, and credibility in the community; providing transformative experiences for the women, girls, and nonbinary people who participate; shifting power and decision-making back to the community; and increasing WFN members' ability to make progress on key economic indicators of progress for women, girls, and nonbinary people. The ability to compare experiences across and within the WFN membership also encourages wider consideration and adoption of participatory approaches throughout the network by providing empirical evidence of their value, benefits, outcomes, and effects—as well as insights and assistance—from peers.

From the onset of the research, WFN understood that participatory grantmaking has many entry points and opportunities for engagement and that members may find themselves at various places along the spectrum. This openness has encouraged and supported member engagement and thus, their eagerness to share practices and processes, willingness to be forthcoming about some of the challenges and frustrations, and excitement about the opportunity to hear and learn from their peers.

Although the vast majority of WFN members are engaged in participatory grantmaking practices, a few questions warrant further exploration. These include whether some practices on community member recruitment designed to support organizational needs (donors, board members, et al.) may impede intentions of centering those most affected by the issues, and their ability to advance social justice and democratizing principles from where the approach developed as bias may shape who is recruited. There are some promising approaches—such as engaging grantees and/or former grantees on the community review team, engaging community in grantmaking strategy to inform portfolios and funding, and using participatory evaluation practices to set shared expectations and outcomes—that have the potential to engage communities most directly affected by the issues, honor community members' expertise to solve and make decisions for themselves, and develop relationships based on a shared understanding of progress, outcomes, and impact. Further, evaluation of the processes, aims, and intentions of participatory grantmaking by the funder and its grant review committee are in fact being achieved not only for the women's foundations/funds but also for the communities they serve.

Additionally, it is important to note that this study was completed on the eve of the global COVID-19 pandemic and the historic social justice reckoning in the United States. This research and the new world context created a rare opportunity for the WFN community to examine deeply held beliefs around power and mutual trust that impeded their organizations from the full ceding of decision-making and evaluation to communities. In the years that followed, WFN has been able to help more of its member organizations unpack and address concerns and barriers about participatory grantmaking through new communities of practice, executive peer coaching, and new programs that support member organizations' full integration of grantees into decision-making. The result has been an expansion and iteration of practices already in place and an invitation to those not currently in the practice into a deeper examination of their organization's culture and feminist ethos.

Given WFN members' long history and commitment to equity, their expertise in participatory grantmaking practices can be leveraged to support others in the philanthropic ecosystem that are encountering participatory grantmaking. There are many examples of how a variety of participatory practices, including grantmaking decisions, are being explored and iterated to encompass other democratization approaches. There is much to offer. Participatory grantmaking practices are not new. These practices are deeply rooted in feminist, social justice philanthropy, which is designed to redistribute money as one mechanism for redistributing power.

NOTES

1. "Intersectional feminism [centers] the voices of those experiencing overlapping, concurrent forms of oppression in order to understand the depths of the inequalities and the relationships among them in any given context." UN Women, "International Feminism: What It Means and Why It Matters Right Now," blog, July 1, 2020, www.unwomen.org/en/news/stories/2020/6/explainer-intersectional-feminism-what-it-means-and-why-it-matters.
2. Success in this study was primarily measured by the participation level and quality of the experience of participants in the grantmaking process.
3. Cynthia Gibson, *Deciding Together: Shifting Power and Resources through Participatory Grantmaking* (New York: Foundation Center, 2018), https://learningforfunders.candid.org/content/guides/deciding-together/.
4. Gibson.

PART II

Case Studies of Participatory Grantmaking in Action

This part of the book comprises five chapters that explore participatory grantmaking (PGM) from the perspective of practitioners. Each organization profiled in this part has been engaged in participatory grantmaking for many years, and four of the five chapters are written by the practitioners themselves. As such, they constitute an exercise in self-reflection, evaluation, and process improvement. Taken together, they provide a broad overview of the variety of contexts in which participatory grantmaking can be applied in "real life"—information that is often requested by an ever-growing practitioner community wanting to learn more about "what works" across a variety of contexts, topic areas, geographies, and participants' cultural backgrounds. What is also notable is that each of these five cases connects to a different social justice topic area or movement—including disability rights, antiracism, environmental justice, climate justice, and Black self-determination—and in so doing, illustrates how PGM interacts with broader social justice efforts. These cases also identify and discuss nuances that often affect how organizations will employ PGM, especially in social justice work.

In chapter 4, Kawano-Chiu and Bokoff document how the Disability Rights Fund and the Disability Rights Action Fund—twin organizations that mobilize philanthropic resources to advance disability rights globally—have implemented PGM throughout their fifteen-year history. They describe how DRF/DRAF's participatory grantmaking model has evolved during this time as the organizations have sought to more closely align their grantmaking practices with the values of the disability rights movement.

In chapter 5, Smith, King, and Destin share the results of an external evaluation of the Haymarket People's Fund, which has looked to community members to guide its grantmaking process for almost half a century. It is also an example of an organization for which participatory grantmaking is not an end in itself but an expression of one of its core values: antiracism. The authors describe the organizational transformation process it began in 2006 to become an antiracist organization, which involved developing a shared analysis of racism across the organization, consulting outside organizations, rebuilding a base of support, prioritizing people of color for leadership, and establishing antiracist principles in its mission, policies and practices, and culture.

In chapter 6, Westdijk and Huang describe how the New England Grassroots Environment Fund used an external evaluation of its PGM model to reconsider how best to live its values and its connection with the environmental justice movement through its grantmaking. An external consultant created a detailed process map that led the fund to revisit its practices, such as what kinds of community members to invite to the decision-making table, placing a greater emphasis on demonstrating connections with the broader environmental justice movement.

In chapter 7, García and Odendahl examine participatory grantmaking in the global context, considering both the Global Greengrants Fund, of which they are the current and prior executive director, respectively, and two related cases: the Central American Women's Fund and FRIDA, the Young Feminist Fund. They find that practicing PGM in the context of the climate justice movement requires a rigorous commitment to interrogating power structures within the grantmaking process, as well as creating accountability systems between actors in the Global North and Global South that seek to collaborate through PGM. This represents an additional layer of complexity that, though present in domestic PGM processes, is particularly salient when PGM is practiced across borders.

The first four chapters in this part are written by the practitioners themselves, often in dialogue with external evaluators. For the fifth and final entry in this part, chapter 8, two academics, Boddie and Rone, provide a case study of CLLCTIVLY, a philanthropic entity in Baltimore that embodies a deep tradition of African American giving and cultural resistance. The authors offer a more expansive view of philanthropy, which they connect to an existing framework for understanding individual giving, while also tracing the multiple strands of African American culture over the last few hundred years that inform CLLCTIVLY's approach. They situate the organization's work in the context of Baltimore's racial history, and they offer a call to institutional philanthropy to place greater attention and investment in philanthropic traditions in communities of color.

CHAPTER 4

Grounding Practice in a Movement's Principles
Why the Disability Rights Fund and the Disability Rights Advocacy Fund Continue to Prioritize Participation

Melanie Kawano-Chiu and Jen Bokoff

When the Disability Rights Fund (DRF) and the Disability Rights Advocacy Fund (DRAF) were established in 2007, participatory grantmaking was not a formally defined philanthropic practice, nor was including persons with disabilities in decision-making, despite the disability movement's call for "Nothing About Us Without Us." The latter principle has been the guiding force for all of DRF/DRAF's rights-based grantmaking practices, which include the active participation of persons with disabilities at all organizational levels. This chapter outlines research on the history of DRF/DRAF's evolution as a participatory grantmaker, including its practices and how they distinguish DRF/DRAF's model of participatory grantmaking as a reflection of the larger disability rights movement. The authors also share how DRF/DRAF will continue to iterate and adjust its participatory approaches and they conclude by calling on the broader philanthropic field to adopt these approaches to better align with the social justice movements they support.

INTRODUCTION: FROM A GLOBAL MOVEMENT TO A GLOBAL FUNDER

Since their joint founding, the Disability Rights Fund (DRF) and the Disability Rights Advocacy Fund (DRAF), twin organizations with complementary missions, have been grounded in a rights-based approach that personifies "Nothing About Us Without Us," a powerful slogan that originated in the disability rights movement and underscores the necessity of participation by persons with disabilities in everything that affects them. This principle has guided the manifestation of DRF/DRAF's rights-based approach, which necessitates the active participation of persons with disabilities at all organizational levels (e.g., grantee, staff, grantmaking committee, and board) as well as in strategy design and collaborations.

From 2019 to 2021, DRF/DRAF undertook a research study to document the evolution of its participatory grantmaking model, understand perceptions about how that model is experienced by its stakeholders, and provide recommendations for other funders striving to use a similar approach. As the first and largest grantmaker focused solely on supporting disability rights globally using a participatory grantmaking framework, this documentation and reflection were important parts of DRF/DRAF's executive leadership transition and opportunities to codify its deep experience in ways that can inform foundations interested in this approach.

To understand this research and the context in which DRF/DRAF operate, the remainder of this section situates these organizations in the context of the broader global disability rights movement and the United Nations Convention on the Rights of Persons with Disabilities(CRPD)—both of which made the formation of DRF/DRAF possible and necessary. The section then concludes with a brief discussion of the creation of DRF/DRAF and presents evidence of the impact these organizations have had since that time.

The Prevalence of Disability and the Leadership of Activists with Disabilities

The driving force behind the CRPD and the need for DRF/DRAF is a broad and diverse disability rights movement that has spanned the globe for more than sixty years. While accurate global data collection is still needed, the World Health Organization and World Bank estimate more than 1 billion people, or 16 percent of the global population, have a disability.[1] Additionally, the disability community is quite diverse, ranging from disability identity to other aspects of identity (e.g., race, gender, age, geography, religion) to perspectives and experiences.

Organizations of persons with disabilities (OPDs), which are also referred to as disabled persons' organizations (known as DPOs), are representative groups of persons with disabilities who constitute a majority of the overall staff, board, and volunteers at all levels of the organization.[2] OPDs also operate with a social model of disability, which sees barriers as caused by society rather than by a person's disability. While the global rights movement does not have a single nexus, the International Disability Alliance brings together over 1,100 OPDs and their families from across eight global and six regional networks, which promote the inclusion of persons with disabilities in advancing human rights and sustainable development around the world.[3]

Disability activism globally has been significant over time, starting in the 1960s and 1970s, as activists started to collectively mobilize and demand rights. South African disability activists coined "Nothing About Us Without Us," which became the disability community's slogan. In 1975, the United Nations passed the Declaration on the Rights of Disabled Persons, the first rights-based international statement on disability. Disability activists, academics, and legal experts continued to mobilize—efforts that led to the UN's establishment of the World Program of Action Concerning Disabled Persons and the Decade of Disabled Persons (1983–92). The early 1990s brought the adoption of the Standard Rules on the Equalization of Opportunities for Persons with Disabilities by the UN General Assembly and the UN Committee on Economic, Social, and Cultural Rights General Comment on persons with disabilities.[4]

In 2008, the UN Convention on the Rights of Persons with Disabilities entered into force and became a legally binding international manifesto articulating the rights held by persons with disabilities. This issuance was transformative in that it codified the view of persons with disabilities not as "objects" of charity, medical treatment, and social protection but as "subjects" with fundamental human rights who are capable of making decisions for their lives based on their free and informed consent. A major strength of the CRPD was that it was created using a global participatory process in which persons with disabilities took the lead in ensuring that the resulting documentation represented their needs and priorities and that it used the language and frameworks of the disability rights movement. Since its adoption, the CRPD has had the fastest rate of ratification of any UN treaty, with 164 signatories and 185 states parties that have ratified the treaty to date.[5]

Although disability activism has had remarkable traction in the larger world, the same level of participation and influence is not yet true in philanthropy. Persons with disabilities receive only 2 percent of foundations' human rights funding and 3 percent of bilateral and multilateral human rights funding. Further, only 1 percent of gender-focused rights funding supports women with disabilities.[6] Within the philanthropic field, persons with disabilities are underrepresented and marginalized, with less than 1 percent of more than seven hundred foundations in the United States employing full-time staff members with disabilities.[7] Moreover, philanthropic giving to disability often goes to services, health, and rehabilitation (following a charity or medical model), rather than to helping persons with disabilities fully participate in society and move toward independent living (a rights-based model).

DRF/DRAF AND PARTICIPATORY GRANTMAKING FROM 2007 TO 2019

As the disability movement and its partners celebrated the success of the CRPD, they recognized the need for funding to support its implementation. In 2007, DRF and DRAF were formed to meet that need. DRF's mission is to support persons with disabilities around the world to build diverse movements, ensure inclusive development agendas, and achieve equal rights and opportunity for all. DRAF's mission is to support persons with disabilities in the developing world to advance legal frameworks to realize their rights. The funds work in tandem and use intersecting grantmaking, advocacy, and technical assistance strategies to support OPDs across low- and middle-income countries (primarily in Africa, Asia, the Pacific Islands, and Caribbean), so they can participate in the CRPD's ratification and implementation, and in ongoing efforts to ensure the inclusion of persons with disabilities in the UN's Sustainable Development Goals.

Since they began operations in 2008, the funds have practiced participatory philanthropy, including participatory grantmaking.[8] The latter is a process through which a grantmaking committee of disability activists and a small number of donor representatives—some of whom self-identify as persons with disabilities—make the majority of final funding decisions.[9] The funds' participatory practice is not limited to grantmaking decisions, however. Persons with disabilities participate at all levels of operations and constitute the majority of the funds' boards and staff. In recent years, DRF/DRAF has hired activists with disabilities from its focus countries to manage grantmaking portfolios in these areas, a community-centered approach that reflects the CRPD's participatory mandate.

When the funds launched, participatory grantmaking was not a formally defined or discussed philanthropic practice. Moreover, the mainstream philanthropic field had yet to fully understand the deep history and wisdom of centuries-old community practices—such as African American mutual aid benefit societies, Chinese benevolence societies, and Indigenous community care—as participatory grantmaking approaches or precursors.[10] In these instances and in others where a form of participatory grantmaking was practiced, community-focused philanthropy tended to focus on critical community needs such as education, social justice, and economic development.[11] The mainstream philanthropic field, meanwhile, operated with a very top-down decision-making approach and traditionally employed those with relative privilege compared with the communities those donors were serving. The concept of including persons with disabilities in decision-making at the global level to advance the rights of persons with disabilities had not been applied before the establishment of DRF/DRAF, making these funds and their founding executive director, Diana Samarasan, significant trailblazers in modeling participatory approaches across the larger philanthropic arena.

In early 2008, as the CRPD was about to become legally binding, DRF and DRAF were launched under the fiscal sponsorship of the Tides Foundation, a philanthropic intermediary, to channel resources to the disability movement in the Global South and thus to advance the CRPD's ratification and implementation. The participatory grantmaking process that would accompany DRF/DRAF's advocacy and technical assistance approaches to disburse these resources was developed through a consultative process that envisioned the engagement of persons with disabilities at all levels of decision-making (governance, advisory, and staffing). This approach not only incorporated "Nothing About Us Without Us" but also the CRPD's mandate for the full participation of persons with disabilities and OPDs in the achievement of rights.

It was also an opportunity to model a set of inclusive participatory decision-making practices that had yet to be recognized and implemented in mainstream philanthropy—or by other participatory grantmakers as it related to disability inclusion. It is often asserted that decision-making by focus communities adheres to a human rights-based approach and may result in more effective and relevant philanthropic outcomes.[12] Modeling this approach and sharing it within the philanthropy sector contributed to its ever-growing credibility and gave traction to participatory approaches.[13] Further, including persons with disabilities in decision-making roles within the organization became an essential value and a significant enabling factor in supporting persons with disabilities to make progress toward the achievement of rights.

To assess the value of this approach more rigorously, DRF/DRAF commissioned four external independent evaluations from 2012 to 2019, all of which concluded that its participatory model was effective, efficient, a good value for the money, responsive, and sustainable.[14] Specific achievements from DRF/DRAF's inception in 2008 through 2021 include:[15]

- allocating $40 million to 408 OPDs in thirty-nine countries and disbursing more than 54 percent of these funds to OPDs of persons with disabilities who are further marginalized by their intersectional identities (e.g., women, LGBTQI+, persons with intellectual disabilities, persons with psychosocial disabilities, persons with albinism, persons with Deafblindness, and little people);
- grantmaking, technical assistance, and global advocacy that led to changes in 346 national and local legal frameworks in the funds' focus countries that reflected disability inclusion;
- helping to ensure that persons with disabilities are included in pressing social and policy conversations, such as the UN Sustainable Development Goals and in inclusive health communications and services in the COVID-19 context;[16]
- supporting persons with disabilities to participate in global forums, such as the UN Conference of State Parties to the CRPD and the UN Commission on the Status of Women, through the submission of sixty-eight state and alternative monitoring reports; and
- establishing representative spaces, such as the Indigenous Persons with Disabilities Global Network, and building relationships with new donors from adjacent movements to support the disability intersection (e.g., the funds' work with Purposeful's Global Resilience Fund changed their participatory grantmaking process to be more inclusive[17]).

With these achievements documented as a baseline, the organizations decided to undertake a systematic analysis of their participatory grantmaking model to identify and understand potential connections between its grantmaking model and its contributions to the disability movement.

EXAMINING DRF/DRAF'S PARTICIPATORY GRANTMAKING FROM 2019 TO 2021

The remainder of this chapter shares insights from research conducted from 2019 to 2021, which describes both DRF/DRAF's participatory grantmaking evolution and perceptions about its relevance and effectiveness. Additional reflections from DRF/DRAF staff, a founding former board member, and participatory grantmaking peers shared in 2022 are also included.[18]

Methodology

The research methodology focused on assessing the relationship between the DRF/DRAF participatory grantmaking model and the funds' organizational, advocacy, and programmatic achievements. Conducted by a research team and guided by a research board (see the acknowledgments for a list of members), the research had four components:

1. Literature review: The research team reviewed nineteen published blogs, articles, and peer-reviewed research on how participatory grantmaking is practiced in a variety of contexts.
2. Evaluation reviews: The research team reviewed three of the four previously completed independent evaluations that addressed the DRF/DRAF participatory practices and its effectiveness and relevance to grantees. Synthesized findings from these evaluations informed the primary data collection approaches to the 2019–21 research.
3. Interviews: The research team conducted twenty-one interviews with key stakeholders, 85 percent of whom were persons with disabilities, persons with a chronic illness, or family members of persons with disabilities. Interviewees included past and current grantees, past and present staff members, and people from nine different countries who had been involved in DRF/DRAF's participatory grantmaking process at different points in the funds' history.
4. Sensemaking workshop: The research team held a virtual sensemaking workshop with the research board to review the findings from the literature review, evaluation review, and interviews, and to reflect on questions that emerged from them. The workshop enabled the research team to share and validate early findings while collecting additional information.

This research documented DRF/DRAF's participatory grantmaking model as it currently exists and how it evolved over the funds' history. It also gathered stakeholder perceptions about how DRF/DRAF's participatory grantmaking model affects the funds' relevance and effectiveness. To ensure that the research was voluntary, inclusive, and respectful of the participants in the project, the research used a utilization-focused approach, which prioritizes making the evaluation useful for intended users, as well as a human rights-based approach, which centers on the dignity of the research subjects.[19]

In conducting this research, DRF/DRAF sought to understand contribution, rather than attribution, as it better aligns with the rights- and justice-based principles of participatory grantmaking and those in which DRF/DRAF are grounded. Attribution connects specific interventions with outcomes and outputs; contribution takes a systemic approach and acknowledges multiple stakeholders' efforts in a complex system. Attribution methodology also tends to prioritize holding constant as many factors as possible in order to draw the conclusion that one factor was one of the main forces of change. Because DRF/DRAF prioritizes accessibility, participation, and utilization in its learning and evaluation practices, it eschews evaluation and research methods that seek to determine attribution.

DRF/DRAF's decision to ask a representative sample of key stakeholders for their feedback on the research's findings reflects this preference. These stakeholders include current staff, current/former board members, peer participatory grantmakers, and disability movement actors.

FINDINGS: INTENTIONAL EFFORTS TO CENTER PERSONS WITH DISABILITIES MATTER

The key research finding is that DRF/DRAF deepened the participation (especially an increase in the decision-making power) of persons with disabilities at all levels of operations—including the board, grantmaking committee, and staff. This was its original intent. One interviewee commented on the significance of establishing and valuing a participatory model from the beginning of DRF/DRAF: "For far too long persons with disabilities were separated from their communities and the medical and charity approach were prevalent. In light of [the] CRPD, we needed to shift to a social model to disability in which the principle of participation was paramount.... Persons with disabilities have the right and capacity to be involved. They are making good choices about what they need because they are experts in their situations and countries."

In addition to this key finding, the research project generated six core insights. *Steady growth and listening necessitate ongoing iteration.* The model DRF/DRAF uses now is not the one with which it started, reflecting its commitment to iteration—as is fundamental for any rights-based, participatory approach. This practice emphasizes listening to stakeholders and integrating their insights and feedback in ways that change the work and the organization's grantmaking structures.

In the DRF/DRAF framework developed at the start of the funds, the original model consisted of a global advisory panel and a steering committee.[20] The twelve-member global advisory panel comprised nine disability activists with diverse backgrounds (diversity of impairments, gender, age, geography) and three people from other human rights movements (women's rights, Indigenous Peoples' rights, and economic/social/cultural rights) to encourage cross-movement learning and disability inclusion within other movements. The global advisory panel provided DRF/DRAF with important advice about all aspects of the funds' grantmaking, including country selection, funding priorities, grant sizes, and creating an accessible application process.

Given the low level of familiarity and few existing opportunities for engagement between donors and activists with disabilities, the funds initially designed the steering committee (now called the grantmaking committee, in its updated iteration) to comprise equal numbers of donors and disability activists. The eight-member steering committee consisted of the four founding donor representatives and four global advisory panel disability activist members selected by other disability activists. According to one interviewee, "When we first started out, very few donors knew anything about the disability rights movement in the Global South. It seemed really important to have a learning mechanism so that donors could learn from activists. The fact that most OPDs had never received donor funding told us that there was much learning required on the activist side as well. Building that relationship was key. It still is."

Interviewees noted that this donor–activist model resulted in greater understanding within the group, including the necessity of including persons with disabilities in grant decision-making and on the steering committee. As one interviewee shared, "While I have always seen donor representatives being passionate about disability rights, [at the beginning] it did look like it was still an 'us and them' matter. It seemed donor representatives sat on one side, talked with fellow donor representatives, while the activists with disabilities would often talk with each other such as during breaks/lunch. Now, donor reps are very engaged and eager to talk to activists with disabilities to tap into their knowledge wealth. I also see donor reps more happy to defer to the activists with disabilities to have the higher hand in making the final decision."

From the initial global advisory panel to the present-day grantmaking committee to the input grantees provide on country-level advocacy priorities, disability activists weigh in substantially on strategy and funding decisions. The main areas where these decisions take place are in the grantmaking process and in the development of global strategy, country-level strategies, and annual grantmaking guidelines. This model of participatory grantmaking "involves bringing in practitioners, sector experts or individuals with lived experience to add depth and knowledge to discussions and decisions."[21]

Inclusion and accessibility are critical for authentic participation. Within all social movements, hierarchies exist, and intersectional identities can exacerbate marginalization. This is also true within the disability movement. A person with a disability can be further marginalized by their type(s) of impairment, age, gender, sexual orientation, sexual characteristics, race, ethnicity, or Indigeneity. To address this reality and ensure authentic inclusion, DRF/DRAF established diversity criteria early on to ensure that different identities were represented throughout its participatory mechanisms—including the grantmaking committee and its board.

Participation was woven into not only the funds' governance structures but also its hiring practices, and into its staff roles and responsibilities, particularly for program officers. One interviewee noted the "absolute importance" of having program officers who self-identify as persons with disabilities from the countries in which DRF/DRAF was actively grantmaking, stating, "One of the reasons is to show donors—most of whom were not persons with disabilities at the time—that people with disabilities have the capacity to do things just like everyone else."

As DRF/DRAF grew, the program officer role evolved from persons with disabilities who worked (primarily) in the Global North and were responsible for oversight of several countries or regions where the funds worked, to persons with disabilities hired in and responsible for grantmaking in the country where they are based. This was important because program officers have a direct relationship with disability movements, applicants, and grantees. They are responsible for gathering information from OPDs on DRF/DRAF's country-level grantmaking strategies and the objectives DRF/DRAF develops for its grantmaking. It facilitates deeper inclusion practices because the local contexts—from language to intimate knowledge of local environmental and political factors—are more actively centered.

When DRF and DRAF were established as independent nonprofits in 2011, the funds began deepening their participatory grantmaking by creating their own boards of directors and by instituting bylaws stipulating that half of board membership would consist of persons with disabilities, including one cochair who would always be a person with a disability.[22] In 2018, DRF/DRAF further evolved the participatory grantmaking model by giving the grantmaking committee—whose role was to discuss and advise on grant proposals—full decision-making power to approve grants.[23]

Part of this deepening participation means promoting accessibility and supporting activists as much as possible. DRF/DRAF intentionally include a diversity of disability activists in the grantmaking committee—and carefully plan materials, processes, and interactions to optimize participation from everyone. The funds provide an honorarium to members of their participatory bodies and cover costs related to travel, accessibility, and reasonable accommodations (e.g., accessible hotels and meeting venues, braille documents, sign language interpreters, professional captioners, and personal assistants). Ensuring such accommodations is a basic right and a principle of inclusion.

For in-person grantmaking committee meetings, activists arrive the day before the official starting time, which allows them to prepare. This is especially important for activists with intellectual disabilities who may need additional support to understand various documents and prepare contributions. All these practices illustrate the difference between accessibility and inclusion, which was described this way by one interviewee:

> You can have accessibility, but that is not inclusion. You can have a sign language interpreter for a person who is Deaf, which is accessibility, but that does not create inclusion if people do not sit next to the person and engage in conversation. You could have provided braille or a PowerPoint ahead of time for someone who is visually impaired—that is accessibility. But if you do not describe what's happening in the room, or what's up on the PowerPoint while it is being shown, that's a lack of inclusion... Inclusion needs to be a team effort and not simply the responsibility of one person.

Structurally, the funds have worked to ensure a broad range of diversity and inclusion over the years through staggered term limits that ensure a variety of voices over time while preserving the larger structure that values and benefits from the entire group's lived experience. The funds also receive activist nominations from the International Disability Alliance, which sets out diversity criteria for activist nominations with input from DRF/DRAF based on the geographies and diverse identities missing on the grantmaking committee, and a requirement that the committee's activist members represent the interests of the broader disability community, rather than themselves, their organizations, or their networks.

DRF/DRAF's participatory grantmaking approach builds an invaluable foundation of trust. As in all relationships and values-driven work, trust is essential currency. Meaningful participation requires it. Through the research, DRF/DRAF learned that its participatory grantmaking approach lays the groundwork for trust with grantees and persons with disabilities more broadly. According to grantees, DRF/DRAF grantmaking committee and board members who are persons with disabilities "know our reality" and "represent us well." The fact that persons with disabilities provide input and make decisions on grants gives disability community members confidence in DRF/DRAF's funding decisions. As described by one grantee, "Without the grantmaking committee, it would not be the same. . . . It is important to include persons with disabilities in grantmaking decisions. Their voices are our voices. When someone with disabilities is part of the decision-making process, they express what we feel."

Based on interviews with DRF/DRAF's board and committee members as well as grantees, its participatory grantmaking model matters to persons with disabilities for three reasons: (1) it gives them an authentic and meaningful voice in grant decision-making, (2) it aligns with the CRPD and the "Nothing About Us Without Us" framework, and (3) it is rooted in rights-based approaches and inclusion principles. Interviewees also shared that having persons with disabilities at the grantmaking table is critical because their perspectives are grounded in the realities of the disability community.

While it was not an explicit topic of inquiry, this research affirmed that the funds' practice of hiring program officers from the disability rights movement and from the countries or regions where they will work is a strong tool for building trust. DRF/DRAF's program officers conduct outreach in disability communities, work closely with grantees to support their proposal development, and summarize proposals for grant recommendations that are then submitted to the grantmaking committee for review and, most often, approval. Through this process, as well as with grants oversight, program officers build essential knowledge of and trust with grantees. Because of this, the grantees interviewed for this research note that some of the greatest value they currently gain from DRF/DRAF's participatory approach comes from their interaction with the funds' program officers.

Through participation in funder networks and affinity groups, DRF/DRAF is also increasingly being approached by other donors, both individual and institutional, which are intrigued by its deep experience with participatory grantmaking, inclusion, and rights-based strategies and want to learn more. As one donor representative, Daryl Lloyd—who is the statistics and results adviser for disability inclusion at the Foreign, Commonwealth, and Development Office of the United Kingdom—notes: "We are now using the DRF model as a model for designing other Foreign, Commonwealth, and Development Office grantmaking programs. It has very strong links to the grassroots disability movement."

Participatory grantmaking is a powerful way to live rights-based values. The funds' commitment to a participatory grantmaking model, as well as to a broader participatory approach, is core for its adherence to the culture of human rights—one in which entities (e.g., governments, the private sector, and the health care industry) or people (e.g., government officials and those in the health care professions) must understand their duties to respect, protect, and promote human rights, and where rights holders must know their rights and how to exercise them.

The research found that by living its values through this structure, DRF/DRAF gains more credibility with OPDs, disability rights activists, donors, and others in the global disability movement. According to many interviewees, the model demonstrates that DRF/DRAF takes "Nothing About Us Without Us" seriously. When persons with disabilities are involved in deciding which OPDs should receive DRF/DRAF grants, this increases confidence in the relevance and appropriateness of DRF/DRAF's funding decisions.

Taking this rights-based approach also recognizes persons with disabilities as having full agency over their lives—something the research showed is built through the funds' participatory grantmaking. Specifically, activists who are part of the grantmaking committee said that this participation helps increase their visibility, build relationships with other activists and donors, and have more opportunities to share their experiences in regional and global venues, such as the Conference of State Parties to the CRPD.

Board and grantmaking committee members also say that DRF/DRAF's participatory grantmaking structure increases knowledge and understanding between activists and donors, and that they value learning from each other. Donors say they better understand the experiences and perspectives of persons with disabilities, while activists say they have more insight into how donors think and operate. Both groups report increasing their knowledge of what is happening with the disability community in more countries.

Learning does not only take place in meetings; it also emerges from the networking between activists and donors that occurs as a result of the participatory grantmaking process. In some cases, these connections have led to increased donor funding for activists' work within the movement and greater advocacy collaboration at a global or national level. For instance, one donor recalled meeting the newly appointed UN special rapporteur on the rights of persons with disabilities at a grantmaking committee meeting and decided to provide needed funds to support the special rapporteur's work.

The research also indicated another benefit to living the rights-based approach: it is diversifying the funds' grant portfolios by increasing the number of grants to organizations representing people with impairments who have historically been underresourced. Multiple funding streams (small grants, national coalition grants, etc.) were developed because activists on the grantmaking committee pointed out the need for grants of different sizes with different purposes to go to OPDs with varying experience.[24] According to one interviewee, "By having diverse representation of activists with disabilities on the grantmaking committee and board, their recommendations and expertise have helped us do more, such as defining what is considered to be marginalized. In creating a specific definition of marginalization, we are seeing more grant applications from these populations, as well as more collaborations between different OPDs of different disability types and also more collaborations with civil society."

There will be challenges, and these challenges can enable growth. The interviews revealed that participatory grantmaking is not without challenges, many of which other participatory grantmakers have experienced.[25] Rather than see these challenges as barriers, DRF/DRAF actively acknowledges and grapples with them in ways that can help inform and strengthen its ongoing participatory practices.

One challenge, for example, is balancing the diversity and size of the grantmaking committee to maximize representation of impairment groups, geographies, and other demographic characteristics but keeping it small enough to give members a strong sense of belonging, ownership, mutual trust, and responsibility. To address this challenge, DRF/DRAF has developed a clearer nomination and selection process, as well as role and term clarity through revisions to its terms of reference. Similarly, interviewees noted the time and resources required to make participatory grantmaking worthwhile outweigh the costs because, ultimately, involving people with relevant lived experience in grants decision-making processes can help lead to more effective grantmaking with a greater impact (although more research is required to test this hypothesis).[26]

Simple planning ahead allows DRF/DRAF extra time for participatory processes. For example, as of this writing, the funds are revising their technical assistance strategy through a process that so far has involved over seventy grantee representatives and all staff members. Although the strategy will take longer to finalize, we believe the time and resources to make this a participatory process will result in a strategy that is more reflective of the movement's priorities and has greater relevance for grantees.

Another way DRF/DRAF has addressed time and resource issues is by shifting more grants decision-making authority back to program officers. This process might seem completely at odds with DRF/DRAF's participatory grantmaking focus,. However, because program officers are hired based on their experience with and knowledge of the disability rights movement, the grantmaking committee increasingly became more comfortable with ceding most proposal review responsibilities to program officers, thereby freeing up the committee's time to focus on larger strategic issues, although it still has the final say on grant decisions. "I think that's a good thing," one interviewee said, "because national staff, largely from the disability movement, make the recommendations based on their knowledge of the context and the budget."

DRF/DRAF's program officer for Nigeria, Theophilus Odaudu, added: "As a program officer, I think about the grantmaking committee when doing my job of reviewing the grant applications. At the back of my mind I wonder if the grantmaking committee can approve of the grant or not. That also has a way of making me put the best work of the grantees forward so that the grantmaking committee has no reason to say no to this proposal at the end of the day."

DRF/DRAF's evolving approach has been both a challenge for and a strength of its work. At the core of the iterative process is inviting and responding to feedback, but that is also a challenge because it requires that the funds constantly interrogate how to strengthen the work with their staffs, boards, grantmaking committees, grantees, and donors. For example, we are thinking about how to shift some more of our grantmaking to multi-year grants, based on feedback from grantees over the years through external evaluations and annual grantee surveys who requested longer grant periods. This sounds good on paper, and is in line with the trust-based philanthropy practices to which DRF/DRAF aspires—which emphasize sharing more power with grant partners—but there are challenging implications for DRF/DRAF's sustainability and own resources to think through, from operational, risk, grants management, and donor reporting perspectives.[27] Sitting in the tension of iteration is an important part of doing the work. Other participatory grantmakers agree, including Katy Love, a peer in the

Global Community of Participatory Grantmakers, who says "participatory grantmaking is a commitment to learn, iterate and improve, acknowledging that the world is constantly changing, and we all make mistakes, so we need to learn from them and do better tomorrow."

Designing processes to address inherent power dynamics is needed. The funds' grantmaking committee was purposefully designed so that activists could educate donors about disability rights and learn from donor perspectives and practices. However, this pairing inevitably comes with an unequal power dynamic. To address this, DRF/DRAF shifted the grants decision-making process from an open and real-time discussion of all grants to a pre-meeting, confidential survey that each member completes to formalize their comments and decisions on each grant. This allows grantmaking committee members to share their thoughts on grants without others knowing what they decided. Members then use the results of this meeting to discuss overarching strategic issues, as well as any grant recommendations that any committee member did not approve.

While this shift has mitigated some of the power dynamics, grantmaking committee members stated that some remain. Interviewees described the power dynamic as resulting from a number of factors, some of which are related to position (donor representative vs. activist), gender, and race. Interviewees also noted that some dynamics may be related to culture, with some donors coming from cultures where people are more likely to speak up in a public setting, and some activists coming from cultures where people are expected to be quiet and defer to others. A few DRF/DRAF staff members and grantmaking committee members noted the importance of skilled and trained meeting facilitation to help address these dynamics, which is valuable feedback that is helping us to strengthen the decision-making meetings.

Another factor that has influenced unequal power dynamics is the level of familiarity of grantmaking committee members: those who are more familiar with its dynamics and processes are more willing to speak up, while those less familiar might prefer to listen. One grantmaking committee member suggested that greater continuity of membership could help address this challenge, but this dovetails with another challenge mentioned above: balancing longer membership terms with the need for diversity and new voices over time.

Finally, many interviewees pointed to a power dynamic created by the time required to prepare for grant decisions and meetings. Many members mentioned the large amount of reading, which includes country contextual documents and recommendations for each grant under review. Interviewees noted that while donor representatives have larger teams available to help them digest the documents, activists do not. As a result, donor representatives may arrive at grantmaking committee meetings better prepared to participate and are therefore more likely to comment and raise questions. To address this problem, activists and some donor representatives have suggested giving more time to review the documents, and activists have also welcomed more support from DRF/DRAF, including the provision of more simplified information. We are also using this insight to inform process revisions that would reduce paperwork even further and build greater dialogue and connection among grantmaking committee members in the process.

DISCUSSION: A CALL TO ACTION—FOR DRF/DRAF AND FOR OTHERS

The recommendations from the original research conducted in 2019–21 prompted DRF/DRAF to reflect further with current staff, peer participatory grantmakers, and disability movement actors on the implications for its work and the broader philanthropy field. The first subsection shares these reflections. The subsequent subsection puts forward a call to action to the broader philanthropic field, based on the recommendations from the 2019–21 research, that DRF/DRAF will also apply to its own work and operations.

Upon Further Reflection: Cycles of Trust and Even More Participation

As DRF/DRAF completed this research and documented it through various publications, including this book chapter, we asked two program officers, a founding board member, a current board member, and participatory grantmaking peers to reflect on the research findings. Two themes arose: the importance of building trust, and the need for more participation. Theophilus Odaudu has outlined how building trust with grantees starts with listening: "Program officers, for the most part, are from the disability movement and persons with disabilities themselves, but at the same time program officers cannot unilaterally design what the objectives and priorities should be at the end of the day. Participation also means trying to get different groups represented as much as possible." Dwi Ariyani, a former program officer and the first DRF/DRAF regional head of programs for Asia, has shared how this listening needs to result in changes: "Program officers are the front line of our organization [working with each] grantee to understand how this different approach will be reflected in their project implementation. Listening to our grantees means we need to ensure that we provide space where they can speak to us and inform us what they need to support their advocacy. On the other hand, when program officers share what happens at the country level, then DRF/DRAF develops a new policy or changes our approach, we are living our participatory approach to our grantees."

However, on further reflection, there is an awareness that DRF/DRAF is still in limited company with its participatory approach because it is still not the way most donors ground their grantmaking. As Ola Abu Al Ghaib—the manager of the UN Partnership on Persons with Disabilities Fund at the United Nations Development Program, a past DRF/DRAF board member, and a current OPD leader—notes: "Whenever/whoever is serving marginalized communities, looking at equality, engaging with persons with disabilities, they want to abide by the participation principle. The implication is that persons with disabilities would be [making decisions that affect them]. But unfortunately, that is not happening. . . . Decisions on funding are still be done behind closed doors. We are not there yet." Sikelelwa Alexandrina Msitshana, the CEO of the Deaf Empowerment Firm and a current DRF/DRAF board member, agrees: "In most instances you find donors wanting to impose their will on OPDs and wanting to channel OPDs' activities in a particular direction. Often times, this limits what OPDs would like to achieve and, in most cases, why they exist in the first place." While we are grateful that there is more research taking shape on participatory grantmaking, it still remains a fringe practice, which affects our grantees' and DRF/DRAF's ability to obtain critical resources to do this work.

Recommendations for Funders Considering Participatory Grantmaking and Broader Participatory Approaches

As an early and evolving practitioner of participatory grantmaking, DRF/DRAF and the many people interviewed for the 2019–21 research are advocating for its use, particularly when supporting human rights work. This model of grantmaking is guided by the principles and values of the disability movement and the broader human rights movement. For funders considering adopting a representative participatory grantmaking approach and/or a broader participatory approach, here are recommendations based on this research:

- *Recognize that the members of each community are most knowledgeable about how funding can benefit their community and that they have the right to weigh in on matters that affect their lives.* While outsiders might have important technical knowledge to contribute, the members of a focus community best understand the community's culture, needs, priorities, and the kinds of interventions that are best designed to respond to them. This ethos is critical for understanding and striving to design a representative model of participatory grantmaking that centers community members, their perspectives, and their priorities in grantmaking decisions.[28]
- *Make the goals of the participatory grantmaking model explicit to better illustrate the benefits of the participatory process.* DRF/DRAF's grantmaking committee, consisting of both donors and activists, was designed for mutual learning and networking, in addition to grantmaking. This mix has helped raise the profile of some of the activist members involved, potentially contributing to leadership development. These kinds of goals are important to articulate so as to better share the results of the participatory grantmaking approach.
- *Establish clear criteria for the identification, selection, scope, and terms of people responsible for grantmaking decisions to ensure diversity of experiences, transparency in who is involved, and clarity about roles.* This transparency will ensure that committee members represent their communities well and simultaneously strengthen their trust in the process. Members should represent the diversity within their community and/or be known through the groups in which they are active. They are meant to represent the community as a whole, not just their interest group. If possible, grantmakers should form partnerships with a broadly representative body, as DRF/DRAF does with the International Disability Alliance, to receive nominations for grant review committee membership. This may contribute to the maturation of a movement and its internal dynamics. Setting term limits on committee membership also enables the critical rotation of members and, over time, representation by different subgroups within the community.
- *Value the time that community members spend on the grant review and decision-making process to ensure a commitment to participation.* This might include covering travel costs, offering a stipend to cover members' time spent engaged in committee activities (including for reviewing materials in preparation for their participation), providing

preparatory materials that are simple to digest, ensuring they are familiar with the committee's expectations and procedures, and/or briefing them ahead of a committee meeting.

- *Offer additional information to help all grant review committee members fully understand information related to the collective decisions that will be made.* This might include in-person visits or webinars with current grantees, discussions with staff members, providing relevant—but not too lengthy—reading materials, and educating community members about grantmaking and donors' priorities and perspectives.
- *Build in a variety of review and feedback processes to mitigate the power dynamics within the grant review committee.* These processes should be reflective of members' different backgrounds, communication styles, languages, impairments, and the like, which will facilitate equal participation. Any facilitator should also take these power dynamics and differences into account.
- *Offer grant review committee members opportunities for networking and increasing their visibility to strengthen the leadership of the focus community in new contexts.* Facilitating introductions with other community members, donors, and those working to advance human rights in other capacities, as well as offering opportunities to speak in relevant forums, can all help committee members strengthen their own work and influence. While some committee members will be established leaders, for others, this can serve as an opportunity to strengthen their leadership skills and networks. Even for established leaders, being affiliated with the grantmaking process may strengthen their existing connections and positioning within the focus community.
- *Hire staff members from focus communities to enhance the relevance and effectiveness of funding decisions.* Staff members drawn from focus communities are well positioned to understand the community's culture, priorities, strengths, and challenges, which in turn may increase donor confidence to shift decision-making power to persons with lived experiences. Donors also need to be aware of community dynamics so as to be able to select staff members who will represent the community as a whole and avoid favoring any subgroup. Additional research needs to be done to examine the benefits of hiring taff from the communities with whom donors seek to form partnerships.

Kaberi Banerjee Murthy, the chief impact officer at Meyer Memorial Trust, makes this call to collective action: "DRF is a leader in what it means to center community in every aspect of the work. Most foundations didn't create operations with a participatory approach so there can be many obstacles to moving in that direction because we have to essentially change the way we do everything—from how we structure our calls for proposals to how we engage the community and how we talk with our board and staff about power. But that doesn't mean we shouldn't do it; participation is the best way for us to fully live our values."

Responding to Our Own Call: DRF/DRAF's Continued Participatory Evolution

The DRF/DRAF staff members are not objective authors. This research and discussion will continue for each of us personally—in our work, and in our lives:

> I'm a person with chronic illnesses and lived experience with disability—at times apparent but mostly invisible. For me, our participatory model is a powerful reminder to always center lived experiences—and particularly those lived experiences marginalized within the disability community—in meaningful, intentional ways. In my role as a fundraiser for our work, this informs how I craft proposals, call in philanthropy for disability inclusion, and otherwise engage with donors. This includes thinking deeply about language, voice, and ethical storytelling. Not only do I work for DRF/DRAF, but I also participate on movement-building nonprofit boards, in the global participatory grantmaking community, and as a member of Disability Lead. This research also motivated me to raise deeper, more intentional conversations about how power dynamics show up and push for more nuanced and ongoing reflections about what shifting power means and looks like beyond the #ShiftThePower hashtag. My identity and lived experience give me opportunities to be an advocate and ally in important ways—and both of these roles must happen in community.
>
> —Jen

> As a mother of a joyful and brave child who self-identifies as neurodivergent, life over the past decade has become a path of shifting power and releasing my ideas of who gets to be involved in decision-making.

I've been privileged to have the frame of letting go evolve through motherhood. I began living this shift in power when I shared my body with my daughter, who needed it as her gestational home and then helped her navigate how to sleep more than twenty minutes at a time once she was born. More recent years have included walking with her through assessments, therapies, and growing to find self-discovered solutions on everything from how to comfortably wear socks to how to find peace and calm in a stimulus-rich world. I get to continue on this path both personally and professionally. Because of my experience at home, at work I know that centering the voice of the person who is most directly affected or who knows their experience the best only leads to better outcomes: relationships, trust, people, and systems. Remembering that each voice—no matter how small, soft, or sidelined—is powerful and needs to be heard. We need to place our grand solutions aside and listen deeply.

—Melanie

This research has been a powerful tool for informing and shaping DRF/DRAF's work at DRF/DRAF. By the time this book is published, we will be embarking on our next organizational strategic planning process. It will be a time, too, for grantees, staff, grantmaking committees, boards, and other stakeholders to reflect upon what is working, to iterate and improve on challenges, and to reimagine. Thankfully, this research lends excellent guidance to our team as we forge ahead. It has validated the strengths of our participatory model, such as the role of DRF/DRAF program officers and the value of the dialogue with the grantmaking committee. It has also helped us to understand ways we can continue to evolve and strengthen our work.

There are at least two key area of improvement that we will focus on: (1) reconsidering grantmaking committee members' roles and grant review, given the growth of the DRF/DRAF grantmaking portfolio; and (2) building in a variety of review and feedback processes to mitigate power dynamics within the grantmaking committee created by day-job roles, disability identities, and geographies.

This call for further reflection and iteration comes from a place of growth in an evolved context. As the research has shown, shifts in contexts and growth in organizations necessitate change. Each of these areas includes elements of our model that have evolved in the past and will continue to evolve in the future—iteration that is important for us to be fully participatory. We want to follow the lead of the movement in every aspect of how we work. As persons with disabilities strive for and call for the fulfillment of their rights, we will continue ceding our power as grantmakers to practice the principles that drive the community and bind us together. As the disability movement needs evolves, so too will DRF/DRAF.

ACKNOWLEDGMENTS

One of DRF/DRAF's core organizational values is celebration, which is grounded in the value of appreciation for the humans who power the work. While we coauthored this chapter, we could not have done so without the generous time and perspectives shared by interviewees (grantees, past and present staff members, donor representatives, and activist advisers), Research Board members, and colleagues who reflected with us on the published research. The Research Board provided guidance and leadership on the research's validity and coherence and included persons with disabilities, former and current DRF/DRAF grantees, former DRF/DRAF staff members and Global Advisory Panel members, and a participatory grantmaking researcher. The Research Board's members include Lisa Adams, a consultant focused on disability and gender justice and a former DRF/DRAF program director; Bhargavi Davar, founding DRF/DRAF Global Advisory Panel member and founder of TCI Asia and Pacific (a regional network of persons with psychosocial disabilities); Hannah Paterson, the 2019 Winston Churchill Fellow on participatory grantmaking; Diana Samarasan, DRF/DRAF's founding executive director; and Alberto Vasquez, the research coordinator of the Office of the UN Special Rapporteur on the Rights of Persons with Disabilities, the president of SODIS (an OPD in Peru and former DRF/DRAF grantee), a former member of the DRF/DRAF Global Advisory Panel and grantmaking committee, and a DRF/DRAF board member. For their additional reflections on the research findings, we would also like to thank Dr. Ola Abu Al Ghaib, manager of the UN Partnership on Persons with Disabilities Fund at the United Nations Development Program; Dwi Ariyani, the DRF/DRAF regional head of programs for Asia; Kaberi Banerjee Murthy, the chief impact officer at the Meyer Memorial Trust; Katy Love, a peer in the Global Community of Participatory Grantmakers; and Theophilus Odaudu, the DRF/DRAF program officer for Nigeria.

We would like to gratefully acknowledge the contributions of Carlisle Levine, PhD, president and CEO of BLE Solutions, who was a member of the research team. We also deeply thank our founding executive director, Diana Samarasan, not only for her inputs into the research but also for her trailblazing leadership, which has made all the work and learning shared here possible. The research and this book chapter were funded by a generous grant from the Ford Foundation.

NOTES

1. World Health Organization, *World Report on Disability* (Geneva: World Health Organization, 2011).
2. United Nations (UN), *Report of the Committee on the Rights of Persons with Disabilities on Its Eleventh Session (31 March–11 April 2014)*, UN Convention on the Rights of Persons with Disabilities, Annex II, paragraph 3.
3. For more information, visit the International Disability Alliance website, www.internationaldisabilityalliance.org/.
4. UN, *Report of the Committee on the Rights of Persons with Disabilities*, 14–15.
5. Read more at the UN Department of Economic and Social Affairs website, "Convention on the Rights of Persons with Disabilities," www.un.org/development/desa/disabilities/convention-on-the-rights-of-persons-with-disabilities.html.
6. Candid and Human Rights Funders Network, *Advancing Human Rights: Annual Review of Global Foundation Grantmaking; 2017 Key Findings* (New York: Candid, 2020), 9.
7. Council on Foundations, "2020 Grantmaker Salary and Benefits Report," https://cof.org/content/2020-grantmaker-salary-and-benefits-report.
8. As Lani Evans defined it in *Participatory Philanthropy: An Overview* (Wellington: Philanthropy New Zealand, 2015), a representative participation model involves bringing individuals with lived experience to add depth and knowledge to discussions and decisions.
9. The term *donor representative* indicates an individual employed by an institutional donor that supports DRF/DRAF.
10. Examples of scholarship on philanthropy and community giving include publications by Tyrone McKinley Freeman, or the essay by Him Mark Lai, "Historical Development of the Chinese Consolidated Benevolent Association / *Huiguan* System," in *Chinese America: History and Perspectives*, ed. Chinese Historical Society of America and San Francisco State University (San Francisco: San Francisco State University, 1987).
11. For more on the roots of participatory practice in community organizing and deliberative democracy, see Cynthia Gibson, "The Historical Case for Participatory Grantmaking," *HistPhil*, August 15, 2019, https://histphil.org/2019/08/15/the-historical-case-for-participatory-grantmaking/.
12. This was a stated by the UK Department for International Development representative at the 2019 Buenos Aires Global Disability Summit, June 6–8, 2019.
13. For more descriptions of the DRF/DRAF participatory grantmaking model, which has added to the philanthropic field's based of knowledge on modern participatory grantmaking, see Gemma Bull and Tom Steinberg, *Modern Grantmaking: A Guide for Funders Who Believe Better Is Possible* (London: Modern Grantmaking, 2021); and Ben

Wrobel and Meg Massey, *Letting Go: How Philanthropists and Impact Investors Can Do More Good by Giving Up Control* (published independently, 2021).

14. These are part of the Organization for Economic Cooperation and Development's evaluation criteria. For more information, see www.oecd.org/dac/evaluation/daccriteriafor evaluatingdevelopmentassistance.htm. For more on external independent evaluations, see the Disability Rights Fund's evaluation page, https://disabilityrightsfund.org/our-impact/evaluation/.
15. These studies are documented in DRF/DRAF's annual reports, which may be found online at https://disabilityrightsfund.org/about/annual-reports/.
16. For examples of how OPDs responded to the COVID-19 pandemic, see https://disabilityrightsfund.org/covid19/.
17. Ruby Johnson and Rosa Bransky, "Building Resilience through Participation with a New Global Fund," Candid Learning for Funders, blog, October 28, 2020, https://learningforfunders.candid.org/content/blog/building-resilience-through-participation-with-a-new-global-fund/.
18. For additional details on the findings of the 2019–21 research, see the Disability Rights Fund and Disability Rights Advocacy Fund's full report: *Reflecting a Movement's Principles in Grantmaking Structure: Evidence of the Benefits of Participation from the Disability Rights Fund and Disability Rights Advocacy Fund*, November 2021, https://disabilityrightsfund.org/wp-content/uploads/ReflectingMovementsPrinciples_Nov2021_noQ.pdf.
19. Many helpful resources from Michael Quinn Patton and the utilization-focused evaluation team may be found at www.utilization-focusedevaluation.org/books. Another resource is *A Human Rights-Based Approach to Data: Leaving No One Behind in the 2030 Agenda for Sustainable Development*, UN High Commissioner for Human Rights, 2016, https://www.ohchr.org/sites/default/files/Documents/Issues/HRIndicators/GuidanceNoteonApproachtoData.pdf.
20. For more on the DRF/DRAF original framework, visit Disability Rights Fund, "Our Story," https://disabilityrightsfund.org/about/more-drf-info/our-story/. Since DRF/DRAF began under the fiscal sponsorship of the Tides Foundation, the governance mechanism was a steering committee in lieu of a board of directors.
21. Evans, *Participatory Philanthropy*.
22. The Tides Foundation was the fiscal sponsor of DRF/DRAF from 2007 to 2011. Fiscal sponsorship is a practice of nonprofit organizations offering their legal and tax-exempt status to groups engaged in activities related to the sponsoring organization's mission. For more information about this practice, see "What Is a Fiscal Sponsor?" Foundation Group, CEO's Blog, August 2, 2021, www.501c3.org/what-is-a-fiscal-sponsor/.
23. For the most recent information on DRF/DRAF's leadership composition, visit its GuideStar profile at www.guidestar.org/profile/27-5026293.
24. For another example of how participatory grantmaking and more open and discursive processes helped overcome bias against small organizations, see Oktawia Wojcik, LesLeigh Ford, Keely Hanson, Claire Boyd, and Shena Ashley, "Participatory Grantmaking: A Test of Rubric Scoring Versus Popular Voting Selection in a Blinded Grantmaking Process," *Foundation Review* 12, no. 1 (2020). This research provides interesting insights; however, its use of the term *blinded* to describe anonymous grantmaking is problematic given its perpetuation of using ableist language.

25. In addition to other works previously cited, see also Ceri Hutton, *Monitoring and Evaluating Participatory Grantmaking: Discussion Paper for the Baring Foundation* (London: Baring Foundation, 2016); Cynthia Gibson, *Deciding Together: Shifting Power and Resources Through Participatory Grantmaking* (New York: Foundation Center, 2018); Hannah Paterson, *Grassroots Grantmaking: Embedding Participatory Approaches in Funding* (London: Winston Churchill Memorial Trust, 2018); and Tierney Smith and Katy Love, "Exploring Participatory Grantmaking with Grants Managers," Grantbook blog, February 11, 2020, www.grantbook.org/blog/participatory-grantmaking-grants-managers.

26. While more research is still needed on the benefits of participatory grantmaking, a growing body of research has started to explore this area of work. See, e.g., Matthew Hart, *Who Decides: How Participatory Grantmaking Benefits Donors, Communities, and Movements* (Paris: Lafayette Practice, 2014); and Hutton, *Monitoring and Evaluating Participatory Grantmaking*, which includes a brief discussion of participatory grantmaking and increased value for money.

27. For more information on trust-based philanthropy practices, visit Trust-Based Philanthropy, "Practices," https://www.trustbasedphilanthropy.org/practices.

28. A staff member noted that when a donor chooses not to include members of a focus community among grants decision-makers, they can support regranting through organizations that are more participatory. For an example of one foundation's journey into greater proximity and participatory grantmaking, see Nicholas Randell and Megan MacDavey, "Human-Centered Design and Foundation Staff: A Case Study in Engaging Grant Beneficiaries," *Foundation Review* 12, no. 1 (2020).

CHAPTER 5

The Haymarket People's Fund
Evaluating an Antiracist Grantmaking Model

Eva King, Jaime Smith, and Kathryn Destin

While participatory grantmaking has been gaining recognition among funders, Haymarket People's Fund has relied on community members to guide its grantmaking process for the past forty-eight years, a process it has simply called "grantmaking." In 2006, Haymarket underwent an organizational transformation process to become an antiracist organization, which involved developing a shared analysis of racism across the organization, consulting outside organizations, rebuilding a base of support, prioritizing people of color for leadership, and establishing antiracist principles in its mission, policies and practices, and culture. In 2019—approximately thirteen years after Haymarket launched its transformational process—it decided to take a step back and evaluate its progress in becoming an antiracist organization by examining the effects of this organizational shift on its grantmaking model. Using findings culled from a historical review, interviews, surveys, grantee reports, and data analysis, Haymarket here presents key findings and recommendations for those interested in antiracist grantmaking models, a vital part of participatory decision-making.

INTRODUCTION

Founded in 1974, the Haymarket People's Fund is an antiracist, multicultural foundation committed to strengthening the movement for social justice in New England. Haymarket uses grantmaking, fundraising, training, and capacity building to support grassroots organizations that are addressing the root causes of injustice, increasing sustainable community philanthropy across the region, and backing social change movements.

As participatory grantmaking begins to gain traction among other funding organizations, it is important to note that the Haymarket People's Fund has looked to community members to guide its grantmaking process for almost half a century. In 1998, Haymarket embarked on a deliberate process to address the internal racism that, despite the fund's commitment to ceding decision-making power to those most affected by the issues it was trying to resolve, was still permeating every aspect of the organization. This necessitated a deep assessment of Haymarket's internal structure with the goal of creating an organization that would live, breathe, and remain dedicated to antiracism principles. From 1998 to 2003, Haymarket engaged in this process, which led to numerous internal and external struggles and shifts, including tokenism that "filled the multicultural basket." At times, it was unclear if Haymarket was going to be able to weather the storm that came from engaging in an antiracist reorganization.

At the height of these struggles, in 2003 Haymarket formed a partnership with the People's Institute for Survival and Beyond (commonly known as the People's Institute), "a national, multiracial, antiracist collective of organizers and educators dedicated to building a movement for social transformation," and ChangeWorks, to assist with this organizational change process.[1] This partnership led to Haymarket making several changes that reflected its long-standing commitment to sharing and ceding power to community activists in grantmaking decisions, including:

- rewriting funding guidelines and criteria to reflect and incorporate antiracism principles in evaluating grant applications;
- replacing individual state funding boards with regional funding panels to create consistency across decision-making processes;
- requiring all funding panel members to participate in the People's Institute's Undoing Racism workshop, which provides members with a shared language and understanding of Haymarket's antiracism analysis; and
- prioritizing people of color for leadership in Haymarket's funding panels and board membership.

In 2019, Haymarket took a step back to evaluate these and other efforts that resulted from its antiracism organizational transformation to determine to what degree these principles and values had been seamlessly integrated into its internal and external policies and activities in its antiracist grantmaking processes. What follows is an overview of this research and key findings, the most important of which is that Haymarket's efforts to deepen its antiracism structure is not done—and it never will be. This journey is life-long work, individually and collectively. While the lessons and findings shared in this chapter may not resonate with every funder or advocate in the social justice movement, the authors believe that the information gleaned from this research is generalizable to any organization hoping to learn more about antiracist grantmaking.

WHAT IS HAYMARKET?

Based in Boston, Haymarket is a public 501(c)(3) foundation named after the 1886 Haymarket affair, a worker-led demonstration that paved the way for the eight-hour workday and one of the most important landmarks in the history of the labor movement. Haymarket sees social change philanthropy as a form of community organizing. In 1979, Haymarket was one of the founders of the Funding Exchange, a national membership organization of regionally based community foundations. The organization was a unique partnership of activists and donors dedicated to building a permanent institutional and financial base to support progressive social change through fundraising for local, national, and international grantmaking programs. Its motto, "Change, Not Charity," continues to influence all the work that Haymarket does.

Each year, Haymarket awards grants to local organizations across New England (Connecticut, Maine, Massachusetts, New Hampshire, Rhode Island, and Vermont). This money is strategically allocated by a funding panel composed of volunteer community organizers from the region who are actively involved in social change in their communities and know where resources are needed most.

Over the course of forty-eight years, Haymarket has provided over $33 million to organizations in New England. One hundred percent of those funds have supported grassroots organizations that are challenging the status quo by addressing the root causes of injustice.

Haymarket currently offers two kinds of grants for social justice organizing in New England. Sustaining grants provide up to $20,000 for grassroots social change organizations that meet funding criteria. Urgent response grants provide up to $5,000 to help these kinds of organizations respond quickly to unforeseen crises, events, and/or opportunities they and their constituencies may be facing.

To receive funds, groups can apply for general operating support or specific project-based work. Grantees are not required to have 501(c)(3) tax status or a fiscal sponsor, which can be a huge barrier for small or emerging groups working to fully organize toward systemic change. Funds are not provided for direct services responding to individuals' basic needs, self-help programs, or advocacy work unless they are part of an organizing strategy.

A critical part of Haymarket's grantmaking is upending systemic racism, which requires a shared analysis and language among those working toward this goal. That is why, in addition to providing grants, Haymarket supports social change movements through training and capacity building. One of Haymarket's cornerstone training programs, Undoing Racism, is a workshop provided by the People's Institute. This training—which is required for all staff, board, and funding panel members and is offered (but is not required) to all grantees—has been essential for developing and guiding Haymarket's shared analysis and strategy.

Haymarket also holds annual grantee gatherings that are hosted by multiple funders and led by grantees, giving them the chance to network, collaborate, and learn from one another. In addition, Haymarket provides grant-writing training, leadership development workshops, and other capacity-building opportunities for grantees.

HAYMARKET'S GRANTMAKING DEVELOPMENT

Haymarket is one of the pioneers in the field of social change philanthropy. It was founded in the 1970s when young radicals with revolutionary intentions to create societal change wanted to invest in movements (e.g., Black liberation, women's, anti-apartheid, and welfare rights) and other collective actions. These movements also generated new models of philanthropic engagement with a social change bent, including funding grassroots groups committed to radical activism with grant decisions made by the activists themselves—an intentional model that trusted people from a community to make decisions about where resources should go in their community.

Since its inception, Haymarket has used this model to support urban and rural organizing across the region—including start-up and emerging organizations as well as those with a long history of grassroots/community organizing—a strategy Haymarket believes is the most effective for achieving its vision of an equitable, peaceful, and humane world. Haymarket defines organizing as efforts that are led by those most affected by injustice, that focus on the root causes of the problems, and that aim to change the institutions and structures of power that stymie justice.

Haymarket also believes that for real change to occur, organizing must address the intersection of racism and other forms of oppression. This is based on Haymarket's recognition of racism's many pernicious effects, which have divided and obstructed US-based social change movements and community-based organizing for decades.

To that end, Haymarket focuses on groups that have strong constituency leadership and accountability, antiracist and anti-oppression values and practices, and a commitment to movement building. An important part of this focus is supporting cultural work and resources to support antiracist organizing in communities and in larger social change movements.

While the values, approach, and practices outlined above have been at Haymarket's core since its inception, in the early 2000s, Haymarket realized that it had a higher comfort level in addressing class and economic inequality issues than in directly confronting racism. In 2003, Haymarket launched an in-depth transformation process that forced it to grapple with the history of racism and white superiority—as well as its present-day manifestations—a reckoning that led to it centering an antiracism grantmaking approach. This process, which the People's Institute helped to facilitate, was long, intensive, and required a complete organizational restructuring. The organization's new structure would be led by people of color.

HAYMARKET'S ANTIRACIST ORGANIZATIONAL CHANGES

The transformational process that Haymarket undertook led to several organizational changes, including significantly revised grantee criteria, board restructuring, and others. These are detailed in this section.

Revised Grantee Criteria

In 2004, Haymarket began the process of revising its grantee criteria in partnership with the People's Institute, which worked intensively with Haymarket's diverse staff, community leaders, and a voluntary working group to help create, write, and implement new antiracist principles for the foundation.

These principles, described on its website and which Haymarket believes are essential to effective broad-based social transformation movements, are:

- Be inclusive.
- Let people speak for themselves.
- Work together in solidarity and mutuality.
- Honesty.
- Commitment to self-transformation.
- Sharing culture.
- Internal dynamics of leadership development (grassroots leadership needs to be developed intentionally and systematically within all Haymarket's structures).
- Networking.
- Openness and commitment to the process (encouraging Haymarket members to participate in open dialogue—which often involves dissent—with the intention of making the organization stronger).
- Taking responsibility.
- Sharing information.
- Support.
- Humor.

Haymarket then began operationalizing these principles across the organization, which included rewriting its funding guidelines and criteria; creating a development plan with new fundraising tactics; writing new bylaws, job descriptions, and union contracts; and establishing equitable salary structures.

Haymarket also incorporated antiracism grantmaking criteria into its funding evaluation process to assess grantee / grant applicants' commitments to antiracism across all aspects of their work. Specifically, the funding panel could determine if prospective grantees clearly identified their constituencies and the root causes of the oppression they organized against, as well as whether they were developing genuine leadership by people of color in their organizations. The funding panel also began to encourage grantees to use an antiracist lens in taking a deeper look at their organizational structure and operations as part of the application process.

Since the new criteria were implemented, the funding panel has agreed to review and update them annually to determine whether any changes need to be made. Members are also asked to share any reflections or thoughts for consideration at the end of semiannual grant cycles. Often, working groups of members and grantees are formed to explore ways of improving the process:

Haymarket's Anti-Racism Grantee Funding Criteria

1. **Self-determination and accountability:** Is the organization or project led by and accountable to its constituency or community? Do constituents have real leadership and voice in all aspects of the organization?
2. **Leadership development:** Is the grantee strengthening the skills and experience of its constituency in all aspects of their organization's work? How is leadership development built into its process?
3. **Anti-racism and anti-oppression values and practice:** Does the organization understand racism, and is it working to develop and incorporate anti-racist visions, values and practices, both internally and externally in the community? Is it helping its members and leadership develop a clear understanding of racism and White privilege? Does the grantee understand how racism and White privilege impact its community and the issues it is facing? Is its organization changing as a result of this work? Does it understand other areas of oppression and their intersection with racism?
4. **Organizing for systemic change:** Does the grantee understand the underlying causes of the problems it is addressing, and does it have plans and strategies to address these root causes? Is the group working to create systemic change—i.e., is it working to change the culture, institutions and/or structures of power in its community? Does the organization have a power analysis?
5. **Movement building:** Is the organization building relationships and unity with other groups working on similar or related issues? Is the group able to see its work as part of a larger struggle for change?
6. **Diversified funding base:** Is the group working to build a strong, diverse, and sustainable funding and resource base in its community? Does it have a good mix of funding sources (i.e., grants, grassroots, etc.)?
7. **Limited access to traditional funding:** Haymarket is committed to funding groups that, because of their analysis and vision, have limited access to traditional funding sources such as government and corporate funding. It has a history of funding start-ups and smaller, grassroots organizations.

From Six State Funding Boards to One Regional Funding Panel

During its early years, Haymarket used funding boards in six states to collectively determine grant awards according to its mission, vision, and principles. Each of these boards had a diverse group of activists and community leaders, who, through their work, played important roles in advancing Haymarket's regional justice and equity efforts for three decades.

In 2006, under the guidance of the People's Institute, Haymarket decided to merge these six state funding boards into one regional funding panel that included representation from each state. This change was made to ensure that there was more consistency in the decision-making processes across all the funding boards and that each was grounded in and able to apply the organization's new antiracism principles and values in those processes. The regional panel would work with Haymarket's staff to carry out grantmaking duties and be accountable to Haymarket's board of directors. Panel members would also be required to participate in the People's Institute's Undoing Racism workshop to provide members with a shared language and an understanding of Haymarket's antiracism analysis.

Today, this New England funding panel consists of up to eighteen community organizers from across the six New England states. Terms last for three years with the option of a fourth-year extension. Ideally, there are three members from each state representing a range of issues and geographic regions. The panel's membership must be majority people of color and committed to Haymarket's values of inclusion around age, gender, sexuality, ability, and class. The process to become a funding panel member is a collective decision made by current panel members, staff, and the board.

All Haymarket's funding decisions are made collectively by the funding panel using a consensus-based decision-making model through which group members develop and agree to support a decision they determine to be in the best interest of the whole community. Consensus may be defined as an acceptable resolution (i.e., one that can be supported even if it is not everyone's favorite). This approach is different from more traditional group decision-making processes, which tend to focus on debate and the passage of proposals approved through majority vote or full agreement.

Haymarket has found that panel membership is helpful to local activists because it provides them with an opportunity to collaborate with diverse groups of organizers working in other communities and with other constituencies across New England. It also gives members the chance to develop and employ their leadership skills in new ways, collaborate on campaigns and other initiatives that leverage individual groups' impact, deepen their political analysis and creative and critical thinking, and connect with national antiracist and progressive funding networks.

The Group Interview Process

Haymarket's grant interview process is unique in that multiple organizations with either an interest area or geography in common are interviewed together. Since its inception, Haymarket has used this practice, and it continues to be a core component of its grantmaking within its antiracist framework.

This process does more than elicit information for the grantmaking process. Because all organizations are eligible for funding—and not competing with each other—these interviews provided (and continue to provide) activists with rare opportunities to engage in authentic relationship building and networking that can (and do) lead to collaborations and potential movement building.

Currently, each of the organizations participating in the interview are encouraged to include up to three people in the process: ideally, a person familiar with the application as well as one or two constituents. At least one of the participants should be a member of their organization's constituency (people who are most affected by their work) who is not a paid staff person.

Each organization is given 10 to 15 minutes to respond to two general questions about how their work aligns with Haymarket's values and their vision for change. Afterward, time is given for funding panel members and the other grantee organizations to ask questions and network.

HAYMARKET'S ANTIRACIST GRANTMAKING PROCESS

An important part of Haymarket's process is continually revising and updating its grantmaking process each year through working groups, community meetings, grantee gatherings, and panel recommendations. As noted, since 2006, many of the major changes made through this process have occurred as part of Haymarket's transition to an antiracist organization. The flowchart given in figure 5.1 illustrates how these changes are now integrated into Haymarket's grantmaking process.

HAYMARKET'S ANTIRACIST GRANTMAKING FIVE-YEAR EVALUATION

The authors categorized the feedback we received into three groups: grantees, the funding panel and board members, and peer funders. These are detailed in this section.

What Did the Research Project Entail?

In 2019, about thirteen years after Haymarket launched its transformational process, it decided to take a step back and evaluate its progress in becoming an antiracist organization to examine the effects of this organizational shift on its grantmaking model.

The goals of the research project were to:

- develop tools and processes for participatory evaluation of Haymarket's grantmaking;
- deepen an understanding of Haymarket's grantmaking process; and
- assess the ways that Haymarket's antiracist grantmaking influences grantee organizations and their communities.

Research Questions

1. How do various stakeholders perceive the strengths and challenges of Haymarket's antiracist grantmaking model?
2. How did Haymarket funding and support affect grantee organizations' internal and external antiracist community organizing?

Methodology

In partnership with Haymarket stakeholders (which included grantees from 2017 to 2021, funding panel and board members, staff, and peer funders), the study used a participatory evaluation research approach that was aligned with Haymarket's overall participatory model (in contrast to more traditional or technocratic processes that employ linear logic models or industrial/additive metrics). Researchers collaborated with people closest to the issues, striving to center their historically marginalized knowledge and

HAYMARKET PEOPLE'S FUND   137

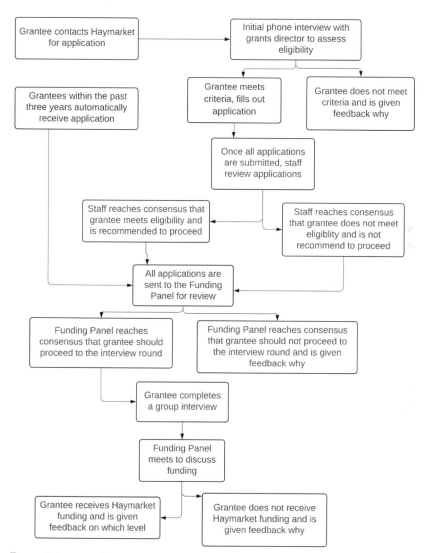

Figure 5.1 Haymarket Antiracist Grantmaking Flowchart
Source: Haymarket People's Fund.

voices while also closely attending to power and privilege dynamics. Working with outside researchers and consultants, Haymarket engaged a diverse group of community and regional stakeholders in conducting document reviews, coding follow-up reports, making observations, doing interviews, and administering surveys. While Haymarket staff helped to initiate the assessment and oversee the general process, independent researchers from Boston College, Harvard University, and Boston University created, administered, and summarized the findings. Researchers included four principal investigators—Eva King, Kathryn Destin, Courtnye Lloyd, and Nadia Brashier—and six research assistants—T'Ajmal Hogue, Brian Rudolph, Larissa Truchan, Baris Tezel, Gia Mitcham, and Mawerisa Mekonen.

Researchers used email to recruit grantee organizations for one-to-one interviews through randomized stratified sampling. Table 5.1 summarizes the data collection tools used in the research. The three strata were organizations that had received high, medium, and low funding over the past five

Table 5.1: Data Collection Tools

Collection tool	Participation	Description
Grantee follow-up reports analysis	57 grantee follow-up reports from 2018–19	One year after receiving a sustaining grant, organizations are required to submit a follow-up report. Over two years of these reports were analyzed and coded using Dedoose software to qualitatively and quantitatively evaluate grantees' level of commitment and implementation of Haymarket's antiracism and anti-oppression values during grant periods.
Grantee interviews	11 interviews	One-hour interviews were conducted with 11 grantee organizations to evaluate how they perceived the strengths and challenges of Haymarket's antiracist grantmaking model. Interviewees were a representative, diverse sample of organizations representing different funding amounts, locations, and issues.
Grantee surveys	41 out of 100 grantees responded	Surveys, including the two research study questions, were sent to every grantee organization that received a grant from Haymarket during the past 5 years.
Funding panel and board member interviews	10 interviews	One-hour interviews were held with 10 funding panel and board members to gauge their analysis, understanding, opinions, and feedback on Haymarket's antiracist grantmaking process.
Peer funder interviews	4 interviews	Researchers conducted interviews with four peer foundations familiar with Haymarket's work to elicit their perceptions of the fund's efforts to incorporate an antiracism lens into its grantmaking process.

Source: Author survey data.

years. Equal numbers of grantees from each of those categories—as well as by state/location and issue focus—were contacted. Each grantee was scheduled for a 1-hour video interview, received $100 in compensation for their time, and was asked the same questions.

Given the power dynamic between grantmaker and grantees, only researchers were able to access transcripts and recordings. To complement the depth of interviews, a survey was distributed to every grantee within the past five years to collect data from a larger, more diverse sample of grantee organizations. The survey was anonymous. Funding panel and board members were also recruited by email for 1-hour video interviews. Responses were kept anonymous, and compensation of $100 was given. Members were chosen based on their engagement during the past five years on either the funding panel or board. Peer funders were recruited for 1-hour video interviews, and permission was received to share their feedback in this report.

To assess how various stakeholders perceive the strengths and challenges of Haymarket's antiracist grantmaking model, researchers conducted eleven grantee interviews and forty-one grantee surveys (anonymously), ten interviews with funding panel and board members, and four interviews with peer funders. All participants had either received a grant or worked with Haymarket within the past five years to ensure they were knowledgeable about and/or had employed Haymarket's current antiracist grantmaking model. The findings of common themes, statistics, and observations broken down by stakeholder categories are given in the next subsections.

Research Question 1: How Do Various Stakeholders Perceive the Strengths and Challenges of Haymarket's Antiracist Grantmaking?

Grantees' Feedback

Based on interviews and anonymous surveys from grantees who received a grant from Haymarket at least once between 2016 and 2021:

- 97 percent said that funding from Haymarket positively affected their organization;
- 73 percent said that since receiving funding from Haymarket, their organization has deepened their antiracist values and practices; and
- 78 percent said that the participatory grantmaking decision process led by the funding panel was fair and accessible.

These are specific findings from grantees on Haymarket's application process, funding, peer networking, Undoing Racism training, and antiracism focus. *First is the application process:* The first-time application process for potential grantees includes an initial phone consultation to assess eligibility, a five-page written application with supporting documents, a group interview (which, as noted, includes three other grantee or applicant organizations working in a similar area) with the funding panel, and written feedback provided by the funding panel to help make an application stronger or to help explain why a group does not receive funding.

According to the survey results, 80 percent of grantees said that Haymarket's application process was clear in its explanation of grant requirements and expectations. The main challenges that grantees mentioned were the length of the process and reduced accessibility for groups where English is a second language. While Haymarket provides interpreters for group interviews, grantees pointed out that important detail and nuances can still be lost, especially when working with immigrant and refugee organizations. Grantees also expressed appreciation for Haymarket's policy of giving applicants written feedback to improve their application and the opportunity to submit missing information or clarify their answers to application questions after the application deadline. This flexibility helps smaller organizations that may not have professional grant writers on staff with the application process.

Haymarket's written application asks groups to describe their constituency, funding/sustainability plans, systemic organizing, and budgets. Fifty percent of grantees found that filling out the written application helped their organizations think more deeply about their antiracist approaches. Some grantees attributed this to Haymarket's requirement that grantees annually reassess their internal and external antiracism work. Some grantees, however (BIPOC-led organizations in particular), said the question about their antiracist approach was difficult to answer because it "was what we live and breathe"—that is, it was hard to separate their antiracism approach from the entirety of the work they do.

A challenge that grantees mentioned was the length of the application process. One grantee said, "It was a relatively involved process for a small amount of money. There was leadership development involved but it is a lot of writing for a maybe grant. I do think they are valuable questions but in a small organization there is an additional burden." While most said they appreciated the intentionality of the Haymarket grantmaking process, many noted the length and requirements to be above average.

Second is funding: Many grantees appreciated Haymarket's provision of general operating support, which organizations can use in whatever way they see as having the most benefit for their communities and to advance their missions. One grantee explained why this flexibility was beneficial: "One of the things that is very different when working with immigrants and other marginalized groups is that there is no such thing as planning or following a plan. We are at the mercy of the national or international climate." When grants are more restrictive on how funds must be spent, it can be hard for small organizations to respond effectively in the face of unanticipated events or crises.

While 78 percent of grantees said that the grantmaking decision process led by the funding panel was fair and accessible, some expressed a need for more clarity about why those funding decisions were made. One grantee stated, "There are a set of principles and values that affect the ways funding is distributed or grantees are considered but I think they have to be more transparent."

Third is peer networking: Surveys and interviews indicated that Haymarket's annual grantee gathering and group interview process were viewed as the most positive aspects of Haymarket's influence on grantees' antiracism work. Grantees also saw Haymarket's understanding of peer networking and community building as positive and necessary aspects of community organizing—and their support and facilitation of these efforts—as important: "Haymarket is creating spaces for grantees to be in dialogue together. *That* is where it is happening—where you can talk about reverse racism, race equity, and antiracism. While we have been talking about racial justice for a long time, we really started to dig into that with our engagement with Haymarket."

Fourth is Undoing Racism training: Of the eleven grantees interviewed for this study, ten had participated in Haymarket's required Undoing Racism training, which is run by the People's Institute. Of those, seven said that the workshop significantly influenced their work by deepening their analysis of structural racism and highlighting the importance of leadership by people of color. Three grantees felt that the workshop could have "gone deeper" or provided more of an intersectional component—a gap that additional antiracism training focused on these issues could address.

Fifth is an antiracism focus: Grantees agreed that since receiving funding from Haymarket, their organizations "positively benefited." Figure 5.2 shows that at least 70 percent said that Haymarket's antiracist approach had affected its organization positively across six different categories.

Some respondents provided more specific comments. Seventy-eight percent of grantees, for example, saw Haymarket's antiracism focus as unique among funders. While some grantees would like to see Haymarket continue its antiracism focus, others pointed out that by asking these kinds of

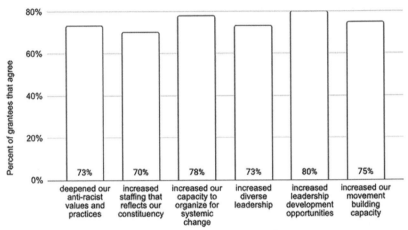

Figure 5.2 Grantees' Survey Responses
Source: Author survey data.

questions in its applications, Haymarket may be assuming grantees or applicants do not already have an antiracism approach or foundation. In so doing, Haymarket could be inadvertently positioning itself as an "educator" about these issues, rather than ceding that responsibility to community organizers or others doing the work on the ground. As one grantee noted, "I always feel bad about the question as to whether Haymarket influenced how we engage in anti-issue work—not because we aren't doing the work [to undo racism] or encouraging it, but as a founder-director/co-director, we are very clear what antiracism is and what system change should look like so if anything it has felt like Haymarket has helped us continue the work instead of influencing how we do it."

Funding Panel and Board Members' Feedback

All funding panel and board member interviewees felt Haymarket's grantmaking model demonstrated antiracist values and principles. This subsection presents specific findings from funding panel and board members on Haymarket's Undoing Racism training, group interviews, consensus-based decision-making, leadership development, and expectations and guidelines.

Undoing Racism training: The feedback on the training, which all funding and board members are required to attend, was split. Some members found it particularly helpful and an important initial step in understanding

Haymarket's antiracist grantee criteria. As one panel member said, "I took the Undoing Racism workshop and thought it was a good foundation of where Haymarket was at. If I know that other people have gone through that same training, then I know at least we are using a shared understanding of what antiracism means." Other funding and board members felt that the training was insufficient, and that Haymarket should consider offering workshops and educational components focused on intersectionality.

Group interviews: Funding panel and board members viewed the group interview process as a crucial aspect to building stronger regional advocacy and organizing systems. They also noted that the interview process strengthens Haymarket's commitment to peer networking and systems building. A quarter of the funding panel respondents who had conducted an interview process said it was "one of the most essential parts of Haymarket's grantmaking."

Consensus-based decision-making: The funding panel makes consensus-based decisions when distributing grant funds, which requires considerable time, discussion, and patience even in the best of circumstances. It is even more challenging for Haymarket because its grantmaking panel annually cycles in new members with diverse backgrounds, experiences, and locations. This ever-changing heterogeneity makes consensus building more time-intensive, given the need to continually learn from and teach others, especially newer members. Even when there is a consensus among panel members, disagreements can emerge, which require energy and patience to resolve. One funding panel member explained, "I think it is a work in process to be antiracist. Haymarket is always pulling people in from the ground to bring them into the process. There is a lot of internalized oppression. At times, I didn't have the willpower to have the larger conversation with the group. I'm too burnt out."

Despite these challenges, none of the funding panel interviewees suggested that the consensus-based, community-driven process be changed, stating that it "was worth the work." Some members, in fact, mentioned that on many occasions, disagreements that may have thwarted other organizations were resolved because of members' strong commitment to Haymarket's mission and vision, the participatory grantmaking process itself, and support from Haymarket's staff.

Leadership development: All funding panel members said that their engagement with Haymarket led to changes in their own community-organizing work. Some said their participation on this panel deepened their views of organizing and how it can be done; others said it expanded their political analysis of and faith in organizing work occurring across New England.

Expectations and guidelines: All funding panel members felt that the expectations and guidelines for their participation were clear when joining. One interviewee, however, said Haymarket should be more up front about the time demand, and another noted that it took completing one full cycle of grantmaking to fully understand the process. Half the panel members said the workload was "manageable," and the other half said, "sort of manageable." Those that expressed more of a mixed opinion thought that membership should be seen as a part-time job and that the demands of that job were especially high during the grantmaking season.

Current and past board member interviewees felt that being in a governance role at Haymarket comes with overwhelming workload pressure. A few said that serving as a Haymarket board member was different from other board service they had done because the work was more complicated. One prior board member said, "The work on the board was different [than my other work,] so I had to think about policies, governance, and had to figure it out. It was harder. With the budget, it was a different language and took more time to understand. It's why I wouldn't be prepared. I didn't have the time to figure it all out."

Peer Funders' Feedback

Four peer funders familiar with Haymarket's work and participatory approach were interviewed for this study: the Social Justice Funders Network, Resist, Resource Generation, and the Hyams Foundation. Each funder knew about Haymarket's work before the interview and had either worked with Haymarket or adopted parts of its grantmaking model. This subsection presents findings from peer funders regarding Haymarket's niche, social justice focus, Haymarket as a role model, and the funding panel model.

Haymarket's niche: All the peer funders pointed to Haymarket's grantmaking model and its long history of supporting community-driven organizing as its two greatest strengths. According to David Moy of the Hyams Foundation, Haymarket has carved out a unique niche in the philanthropic ecosystem because of its track record on identifying and funding smaller, emerging community-organizing groups that have been instrumental in advancing important issues. That is important for those funders, such as the Hyams Foundation, that focus on grantees that are typically larger with a more established foundation and budget.

Social justice focus: Haymarket's commitment to social justice and empowering communities for nearly fifty years was another strength that funder interviewees identified. That commitment never wavered, but in fact was strengthened because of the antiracism efforts Haymarket undertook. Sheryl Seller, a member of Social Justice Funders Network, explained how "everything we focus on is social justice aligned. I think Haymarket is a model for that work and that is one of their biggest strengths. They have really stuck to this participatory community-based work."

Haymarket as a role model: All the funders expressed how their own organizations had been inspired by various parts of Haymarket's participatory grantmaking approach, principles, and grantee funding criteria—so much so that they adopted one or more aspects of these for their own organizations.

The funding panel model: Peer funders said that the main challenge in implementing Haymarket's participatory grantmaking approach was working with a funding panel whose membership is constantly changing, which makes it difficult to achieve a consensus and be consistent in using similar criteria for funding decisions. As one funder said, "Having a community panel of decision-makers is awesome but you have to make sure that people on that panel have the right training and resources to make informed decisions. That is a lot of work and in some ways is more challenging than having the staff make those decisions."

Summary of Findings on Research Question 1

Overall, grantees spoke positively of Haymarket's grantmaking process. They felt its grant process requirements and expectations were clear and aligned with its antiracist values. The three processes respondents identified as especially helpful to their organizations in refining their antiracist approach were the group interviews (70 percent), the act of writing the grant application (50 percent), and the funding panel's written feedback (25 percent). The annual grantee gatherings were also seen as helpful for peer networking and systemic organizing among grantees. Grantees were generally aware of Haymarket's grantmaking model but felt there should be more transparency in how the funding panel made its decisions. Grantees liked the interview process but noted the length of the written application and time needed to prepare for and participate in interviews as a large ask for the grant amount.

Funding panel and board members felt that Haymarket upholds its antiracist values and practices when it comes to the grantmaking process. All interviewees from both groups said that serving in these positions deepened their own work as community leaders and that the expectations and guidelines regarding their roles and responsibilities were clear. The biggest challenge the funding panel noted was working with a diverse group of community organizers to reach a consensus about grant decisions because they come from different backgrounds and varying levels of understanding race analysis. While the Undoing Racism training was seen as a helpful starting point in this process, there was still a considerable amount of time and work needed throughout the grantmaking process to reach a consensus. They also expressed that this training needs to be more intersectional and that offering additional training programs would be helpful.

Peer funders saw Haymarket as a strong guide on social justice issues with clear principles and values, and they deeply appreciated its long history working in the field of philanthropy and community organizing. Multiple funders mentioned that Haymarket would be playing an important leadership role in sharing what it has learned because of the antiracist grantmaking model it has adopted—something it could accomplish more effectively by enhancing its online presence.

Research Question 2: What Impact Does Haymarket's Grantmaking Have on Its Grantees' Antiracist Infrastructure and External Antiracist Community Organizing?

After conducting preliminary readings[2] and team discussions, researchers defined and distinguished between grantees' internal and external organizing efforts by utilizing their knowledge of antiracist organizing theory; participatory grantmaking (defined as the cession of grantmaking power to the communities and constituencies the grants support[3]); Weber's three-component theory of stratification, a sociological theory that asserts that political power is determined by and accessed through class, status, and collective power; and Haymarket's *Courage to Change*, a retelling of Haymarket's transformation journey to becoming an antiracist organization and recommendations to other philanthropic organizations of how to become antiracist.[4]

Antiracist infrastructure was defined as the activities, policies, and processes aimed at affecting change that occur in grantees' internal structure, mission/values, and staffing. Examples included placing people of color, particularly grantees' constituents of color, into positions of decision-making power in their organizations (e.g., executive director, board member, or senior leadership), dismantling hierarchical staffing structures in favor of more democratic approaches to grassroots management, and revising mission statements and values to be explicit about antiracism as part of their grassroots community-organizing approach.

External antiracist efforts were defined as actions that the grantees made in—and in partnership with—actual communities. Examples included grantees hosting town halls for their constituents to meet with local politicians, police officers, and school district officials to discuss the resources and support they need in their community; creating petitions advocating antiracist and/or anti-oppressive community policies; and collaborating with other antiracist, grassroots organizations to host protests and strengthen a deeper sense of community among neighborhoods.

Once these terms were defined, researchers began their investigation into Haymarket's impact on their grantees' internal and external organizing. Two years of data, culled from follow-up reports prepared and submitted by grantees that received sustaining grant funding during 2018–19, were analyzed. Sustaining grants varied from anywhere between $3,000 and $9,000 and were awarded to both emerging and more established movement-building organizations to support general operations or projects. Haymarket staff selected the grantees they deemed were aligned with the fund's Anti-Racism Grantee Funding Criteria and that displayed a commitment to strengthening an antiracist movement in New England. At the end of the grant year, grantees were required to submit a brief two- to three-page follow-up report detailing how Haymarket support had affected their organization.

These reports included descriptions of how grantees used the funds; summaries of their achievements, challenges, and lessons learned; assessments of if and how this funding contributed to their ability to engage in different or new kinds of work; and evaluations of any shifts that might have occurred in their organizational practices/infrastructure due to their relationship with Haymarket.

To interpret these data, Haymarket's research coordinator and five student researchers used Dedoose software, a cross-platform app optimized for mixed methods research and data analysis. This software allowed the researchers to synchronize the information from the follow-up reports, keep track of grantees' ratings, and create charts to find data trends.

Coding

To assess grantees' progress and accomplishments during the grant year, researchers created a coding system based on Haymarket's antiracist grant-making criteria (see figure 5.3). When analyzing the follow-up reports, researchers specifically looked for grantees' use of antiracist theory language

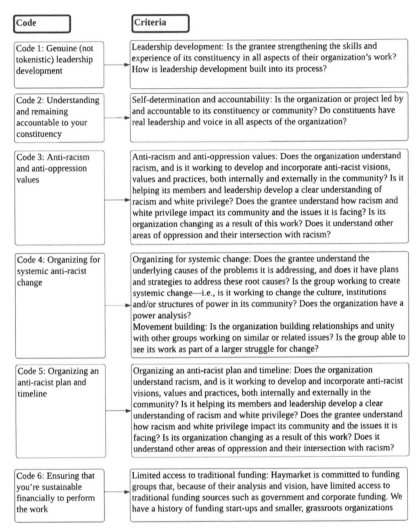

Figure 5.3 Follow-Up Report Coding System
Source: Author survey data.

in descriptions of their community-organizing approach, recollection of recent shifts in their organizations' structure (e.g., putting people of color into positions of power), and attendance at Haymarket-recommended trainings. Finally, researchers also noted any reference to grantee-hosted community events and the level of their constituents' involvement in these events.

Rating

After coding, researchers established a rating system on a scale from 0 to 5, as described in table 5.2. The researchers established this rating system to go beyond merely identifying what grantees did in the grant year to assessing how well they implemented Haymarket's understanding of antiracism in their community work (e.g., hosting their own antiracist training for constituents to attend and displaying an understanding of how crucial antiracism theory is in their grassroots organizing approach). Considering the goal of this research question was to investigate Haymarket's impact on grantees' becoming more antiracist, researchers returned to Haymarket's *Courage*

Table 5.2: Ratings and Numerical Scores in Research Code

Rating/ score	Description	Explanation
0	No mention of the Haymarket criteria	The follow-up report does not mention the grantee working toward implementing the criteria into their structure.
1	Acknowledgment of the existence of the Haymarket criteria	The follow-up report mentions the criteria and expresses an awareness of its importance to their organizational structure and values.
2	Planning and participation in the practice of the Haymarket criteria	The follow-up report details the actions the grantee took to begin implementing the criteria in their internal and external antiracist and anti-oppressionist efforts.
3	Active performance of the Haymarket criteria	The follow-up report explains how the grantee actively incorporated the criteria into their internal and external antiracist and anti-oppressionist efforts.
4	Engagement (internally) with the Haymarket criteria	The follow-up report reveals that the grantee internally questioned how deep their commitment is to the criteria to go beyond their present performance of the criteria in their internal and external antiracist and anti-oppression efforts.
5	Engagement and evaluation (internally and externally) of the Haymarket criteria	The follow-up report states that the grantee worked with their constituents, community leaders, staff, and/or external partners to evaluate how deep their commitment is to the criteria as an organization to go beyond the performance of the criteria in their internal and external efforts to be antiracist and anti-oppression.

Source: Author survey data.

to Change booklet, which outlined these steps to becoming an antiracist organization:[5]

- Planning stage: hiring antiracism, community-organizing experts to guide the process.
- Participate in an antiracism training to obtain a racial analysis and develop a common language to discuss antiracism.
- Perform an organizational assessment.
- Create an internal planning team.
- Work to obtain leadership and organization buy-in and support.
- Engage in a strategic planning process.
- Evaluate impact, document learnings, and capture accomplishments along the journey.

Researchers then used the same language (i.e., planning, performance, and evaluation) that Haymarket used in its stated steps to inform its construction of the rating system. Each follow-up report received six individual ratings for each code based on Haymarket's grantmaking criteria. Recognizing that there would be diversity in grantees' execution of the criteria—likely performing well in some areas and needing to improve in others—researchers decided against giving grantees a singular overall score across all the codes and, instead, averaged all six individual codes. Figure 5.4 shows the average score across all of Haymarket's grantees in each of the six codes developed by researchers.

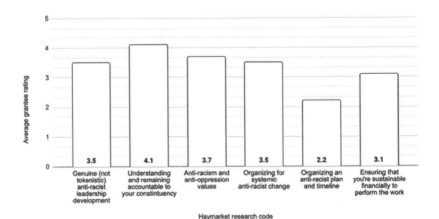

Figure 5.4 Average Grantee Rating among Haymarket Codes
Source: Author survey data.

CODE 1: GENUINE (NOT TOKENISTIC) ANTIRACIST LEADERSHIP DEVELOPMENT
The average rating is 3.5, between "Performing" and "Engaging." On average, the follow-up reports grantees submitted between 2018–19 had people of color in leadership with genuine access to power. Eighty-one percent of grantees scored at least a 3 in this code as they had hosted antiracist trainings for their leadership and had begun or were continuing to institute an antiracist culture in their organization. After participating in antiracism training, leaders and staff who attended would return to their organizations ready to share what they had learned with other members and grantee constituents, which included the common language and analysis used to examine racism in the United States, the racist assumptions that interfere with organizations' ability to do their work, and the power of multiracial coalitions in community organizing. Several dozen respondents referred to the People's Institute's training and indicated their attendance had led to a deeper and more genuine antiracist leadership development in their organizations and were confident it would be sustained. Many grantees also showed signs of making efforts to include those who were directly affected by the issues that their organizations were addressing in the organization's power structure or created pipelines to facilitate the gradual movement of community members into leadership positions that would eventually lead to their running the organization itself.

The 19 percent of grantees who fell short in receiving a score of 3 or higher in this code struggled to perform, engage, and evaluate this aspect of becoming an antiracist organization. In order to improve, these grantees should consider working on taking more input from people of color when it comes to decision-making, attending more antiracist leadership training sessions, and restructuring leadership.

In 2018, a representative from Students for Educational Justice (SEJ) shared in their follow-up report, "SEJ is a Black-led organization that, through youth-led organizing, spearheads efforts for racial and educational justice in Connecticut. . . . We know that organizing efforts are best led by those most directly affected by the issue, and with the guidance and insight of our program coordinator, Briyana Mondesir—who at the time was a high school senior—we have developed an organization consistent with that ideal."[6]

CODE 2: UNDERSTANDING AND REMAINING ACCOUNTABLE TO YOUR CONSTITUENCY
The average rating is 4.1, between "Engaging" and "Engaging and Evaluating." On average, grantees are extremely committed to understanding the makeup and needs of their constituencies (e.g., cultural competency education for

Indigenous youth, legal assistance for asylum seekers, and transition services for formerly incarcerated constituents). Ninety percent of grantees scored a 3 or higher in this research code, indicating that they are holding themselves accountable to their constituencies, as opposed to being primarily responsible to their local government or organizational board and trustees. Grantees involved their constituents in their community-organizing planning processes and asked for their constituents' opinions on their organization's overall efforts. This high average score is most likely because Haymarket's grantee organizations stay true to their grassroots mission and are most often spearheaded by the very members of the communities in which they operate.

The remaining 10 percent of grantees that received a lower score in this code struggled to express in their follow-up report an understanding of or a commitment to their constituency. Some shared they were in the process of planning community initiatives but had not yet enacted them. These grantees also received a lower score if they did not detail how their constituents were affected by their community organizing or did not express an interest in internally evaluating how intertwined antiracism is in the core of their mission.

A representative from the Beantown Society noted in the organization's 2018 follow-up report that "during our relationship with Haymarket People's Fund, Beantown has recommitted to the leadership of people of color at all levels of the organization—specifically the leadership of Black and Latinx people. All of Beantown's adult and youth staff are Latinx or Black and from Boston, representing the communities that Beantown organizes in. Beantown's board has also made a shift to more representation of people of color; out of the thirteen current members, only three are White, and the co-chairs are both Black."

CODE 3: ANTIRACISM AND ANTI-OPPRESSION VALUES
The average rating is 3.7, between "Performing" and "Engaging." On average, grantees had a good understanding of antiracism and anti-oppression values. Eighty-five percent of grantees received a score of 3 or higher because they expressed an awareness that racism is not only an issue of racial prejudice but also a result of an unbalanced power dynamic that marginalizes people of color. Additionally, grantees were beginning to take steps toward transitioning from understanding these values to actually enacting them. Steps included creating their own antiracist trainings for staff, using anti-oppressive language (e.g., referring to concepts such as the "model minority," "myth," "systemic heterosexism," and "land is wealth"), and making their meetings more accessible to their constituents to encourage community participation

(e.g., using online resources to translate board meeting communications into their constituents' native languages).

Researchers found that there is room for improvement in terms of the depth to which grantees are operationalizing antiracism and anti-oppression values to be part of their infrastructure. For the remaining 15 percent of grantees that scored a 2 or lower in this code, this gap could be addressed by leadership and staff conducting internal processing and examination to ensure equal access to power for all those serving and/or benefiting from the grantee organization.

One grantee, Maquam Bay in Missisquoi, indicated in 2018 that "our relationship with [Haymarket] has made us more aware of our work as [it] relates to putting antiracism in the forefront. It has helped leadership develop a more clear understanding and a connection to the work of educating Vermonters about racism in our state and connect with antiracism activists and leadership from other tribes and people of color."

CODE 4: ORGANIZING FOR SYSTEMIC ANTIRACIST CHANGE

The average rating is 3.5, between "Performing" and "Engaging." This code showed the most variation in responses. Eighty-four percent of grantees scored a 3 or higher, revealing that a majority understand that racism is an institution that must be dismantled and that there are systemic inequities such as higher poverty rates, lower educational attainment, and housing shortages that disproportionately affect people of color. However, even among these higher-scored grantees, community organizing still tends to be centered on reactive advocacy (e.g., hosting protests against incidents of police brutality or organizing to support immigrant communities at risk due to a rise in deportation) rather than proactive advocacy that attempts to introduce alternative, more progressive legislation and systems benefiting their constituents in the long run (e.g., policies to require mental health first responders be dispatched first to address mental health crises rather than untrained police officers). The need to shift to more proactive efforts is even more so the case for the remaining 12 percent of grantees that scored a 2 or lower in this code.

All in all, Haymarket grantees can continue to work on going beyond just responding to acts of racism when they occur as their primary approach to dismantling systems of oppression. During their analysis of the follow-up reports, researchers noticed a recurring barrier of government hesitation, on all levels, to enact policies that would better the conditions and quality of life for grantee organizations' constituents. Considering Haymarket's criteria of "self-determination and accountability" and antiracist theories, researchers determined that those grantees that heavily relied on reactive change (e.g., provocation of political leaders and legislators through protests) would not see the long-term change both they and Haymarket aspire to see and not challenge oppressive powers. Grantees that displayed an understanding of the necessity to shift to using collective power and enact proactive advocacy tactics (e.g., mutual aid, legislative petitioning, and the provision of antiracist education in curricula) received a higher score in this code.

A representative of Pioneer Valley Workers Center (PVWC) stated in 2018 that "PVWC is also combating racism on a more public level. First, when groups across the country mobilized to hold demonstrations about family separation at the border, PVWC worked with a local activist group to redirect their proposal event from ally-led in the majority-White city of Northampton to being a coalition-led event in Springfield that also addressed broad issues of systemic racism and mass incarceration. Together we welcomed over 600 people to hear from more than twenty community leaders about state-sanctioned violence separating Brown and Black families."

CODE 5: ORGANIZING AN ANTIRACIST PLAN AND TIMELINE

The average rating is 2.2, between "Planning and Participating" and "Performing." This code had the lowest average score, with many grantees falling short in expressing how they implemented an antiracist plan and a timeline during the grant year. While grantee organizations were required to submit a plan and timeline in their grant application to be considered for Haymarket funding, few were able to indicate in their follow-up reports the concrete progress they had made. Fifty-one percent of grantees scored a 3 or higher, but often still focused their community efforts and resources toward responding to policies, practices, and social norms that were racist and/or oppressive rather than on developing and enacting strategies aimed at establishing new systems that would be inherently antiracist and anti-oppressive. For a higher average in this code, grantees needed to display that their efforts would have been more focused on dismantling the roots of persistent problems rather than responding to them with temporary solutions. Doing so will require organizations to dedicate time, staff, and resources to actually progress in implementing their plan and clear timeline to stay the course and monitor progress along the way. Currently, grantees were either working on creating a plan of attack to implement their timeline or operating with a plan that is somewhat proactive but was not yet being executed fully. For example, while many of Haymarket's grantee organizations are made up of the community members where they are operating and have antiracism embedded in their organizing work, many struggle to execute and evaluate a longer-term plan to enact antiracism structurally within their organization and in external institutions.

In 2019, a staff member from Essex County Community Organization noted that "responding to this analysis, we set forth three major goals last year: (1) expand beyond legislative tactics to mass protest and movement building strategy; (2) increase participation by communities of color and public conversation around race; [and] (3) continue to focus our work on dismantling the root causes of racism and classism."

CODE 6: ENSURING THAT YOU ARE SUSTAINABLE FINANCIALLY TO PERFORM THE WORK
The average rating is 3.1, between "Performing" and "Engaging." Grantees provided surface-to-mid-level details of their financial abilities. Seventy-three percent of grantees scored at least a 3 on this code because they were usually able to cover their basic costs and necessities such as transportation to events, campaigns, protests, and leadership training throughout the grant year. Funds were also used to cover general operational expenses such as staff pay, office space, and office utility bills. Those grantees that scored higher in this code also consistently met all their expenses with income from a diverse set of funding sources and even began to pursue or secure additional funding to serve as a buffer for unforeseeable costs.

Haymarket recognizes the challenges raised by this funding criteria as the organization itself is committed to helping grantees become self-sufficient instead of relying solely on philanthropic support. At the same time, Haymarket is aware that many of the groups doing antiracism work are those that often find it most difficult to secure this—or any kind—of financial support. Researchers took this into account while analyzing the data and recommended that Haymarket, in the short term, not only continue to support these organizations but also encourage and help them secure financial support from other funders that share Haymarket's commitment to this work. Researchers also advised that Haymarket reevaluate how it can deepen its impact on grantees so that they eventually are able to obtain the sustained funding they need to thrive.

In 2019, grantee Alliance Mobilize Our Resistance described these organizational practices that have changed because of Haymarket: "Increasing capacity for training and ensuring that we have food at all of our events for our constituents, increasing our capacity to organize trainings and activities to provide culturally competent mental health services and healing space for the community by the community, [and] increasing capacity for outreach, specifically to young people."

Summary of Findings on Research Question 2

Based on the 2018–19 follow-up reports, it appears that Haymarket is helping its grantees move toward becoming stronger antiracist and anti-oppressive organizations, both internally and externally. The majority of grantees had people of color with genuine access to positions of decision-making power, held antiracist training sessions for their leadership, and were instituting antiracism into the cultural fabric of their organizations. With Haymarket's support, grantees also held themselves accountable to their constituents through activities such as hosting feedback forums, hiring community members for staff positions, and bringing together political leaders with community members to cocreate social change campaigns and platforms. The follow-up reports expressed a solid understanding of antiracism and anti-oppression values as well as a stronger shared antiracist language and framework across all grantee organizations that emerged from the People's Institute training and Haymarket's grantmaking process (which encourages applicants to demonstrate how they are applying—or will apply—its antiracist criteria in their work).

There is still work to be done, however, by both Haymarket and its grantees. Research revealed that while grantees are using an antiracist lens to make tangible change in their communities, they are not evaluating those efforts consistently and in ways that are essential to continual learning and improvement. And while they are taking immediate action in becoming antiracist organizations, they still need to deepen their commitment to creating and adhering to a longer-term, proactive plan that lays out how they will continue to advance toward a fully antiracist structure within their organizations and their communities, how they will assess progress, and in what time frame. An important part of that plan is channeling a large amount of organizational resources toward building institutions, public policies, and other systems that are inherently antiracist instead of reacting to the symptoms of the systems that are structurally racist and oppressive. Researchers and Haymarket staff hypothesize that this is not likely the case for most grantees because many of Haymarket's grantees already have antiracism as part of their organizing work on the ground but are still determining how to make antiracism part of their infrastructure. Furthermore, many of the racist and oppressive conditions grantees' constituents are subjected to are extreme and often violent, and therefore require immediate support to ensure their safety and well-being. Many grantee organizational members are also subjected to these volatile conditions and can be overwhelmed in trying to support both themselves and their fellow community members.

During 2018 and 2019, Haymarket's grant staff selected smaller grassroots organizations to support with a sustaining grant. Some of these organizations would be unable to cover operating funds without Haymarket's support; therefore, researchers also acknowledge that these grantees might not always be able to meet expectations immediately during a time of growth. During this early time of foundation establishment, researchers understand why some grantees might have scored within the rating system lower in certain codes as they were actively learning what it means to be antiracist internally and externally. While the ideal goal for grantees' is their achieving self-sufficiency and allocating most of their resources to proactive antiracist and anti-oppressive change, that is not reality. Therefore, researchers realize more research can be done to determine what balance must be struck between grantees' reactively responding to the racism and oppression they encounter and grantees' instituting inherently antiracist and anti-oppressive systems that prevent these circumstances.

CONCLUSION

This research project began in 2019, but due to the COVID-19 pandemic and other various unforeseen challenges, it took more time than anticipated. This was actually a positive development because it gave Haymarket the opportunity and time to make some changes in its grantmaking process based on the findings described in this chapter as well as the feedback it has received from a grants working group, created after the research project, that was made up of grantees and members from the funding panel, board, and community.

While this research project sought to provide an accurate evaluation of how Haymarket's organizational shift to an antiracist organization affected its grantmaking model, there were several limitations to this study. There is always the question of how honest interview participants are, especially in a power-dynamic relationship such as grantor and grantee. To address this, Haymarket hired an independent researcher to conduct interviews and keep all responses anonymous. Further, the cultural and personal bias of the researchers is an ever-present challenge, affecting how they wrote, conducted, and synthesized their findings. Since the actual interview transcripts are kept anonymous in this report, making independent confirmation of sources impossible, the bias of the researchers can affect the legitimacy of the study. To address this, Haymarket had multiple researchers write and oversee the structure of the research report to limit the bias that may arise from one perspective.

Additionally, the follow-up reports from which data were derived were only two or three pages (a parameter set by Haymarket); thus, grantees did not have much room to provide expansive details of their progress over the grant year. Because many Haymarket grantees have staff who are multicultural and speak other languages, researchers suspect that a language barrier also might have affected grantees' ability to clearly describe what they accomplished or struggled with over the grant year in these reports. Finally, the data elicited for this study came from self-reports, which can be subjective—especially when being submitted as a condition of receiving additional funding.

Despite these limitations, several important lessons emerged from the study. One of the most important is that part of becoming an antiracist organization is knowing that the work is never complete and being open to change and adaptations, especially when centering folks most affected (grantees) by the fund's actions (grantmaking). Since this research project, Haymarket has responded to grantees' request for more sustained support by creating a multiyear grant of up to $20,000 a year for three years. This request addresses grantees' criticism of the length of the application process for the amount of funds given and the large burden that it can place on a small organization. To expand accessibility—another request from grantees—it is also allowing for applications to be submitted in Spanish and planning for additional languages in future cycles. Finally, Haymarket has updated its grant materials to clarify the meaning of organizing and other terms that may have different connotations to different people and organizations.

However, Haymarket has gleaned additional, and perhaps even more significant, lessons from this project, as well as from its own antiracism work thus far:

- Before Haymarket was able to prioritize antiracism grantmaking, it had to look internally first and go through a major organizational transformation and decide whether it was ready and willing to make the commitment necessary for becoming a truly antiracist organization.
- One person cannot be the sole voice for addressing racism; it requires a group, including at least some people of color in leadership positions. Having a diverse critical mass of advocates is important because without it, it is easier for leadership to ignore the demand for change and for those demanding that change to become marginalized.

- Recognizing that part of building a strong antiracist organizational foundation requires creating new principles, expectations, and guidelines that are laser-focused on undoing racism, Haymarket hired an outside organization in 2003 to assist in creating and implementing these new processes.
- Funding panel members need considerable support in using a consensus decision-making model. Creating shared training that builds trust within the group is a crucial step to facilitating a mutually beneficial, productive, and thoughtful process. Additionally, it is important for funders that are using or supporting these approaches to be clear in their expectations for the work, as well as the role it will play.
- Peer networking is one of the most powerful tools for undoing racism because this work cannot be done alone. Networking allows for greater advocacy and community-organizing opportunities. Examples of this kind of peer networking are Haymarket's unique shared interview process, which gives grantees the opportunity to strengthen and build relationships, and its annual grantee gathering.
- It is important for philanthropic organizations to support grantees' work and trust them to carry out that work without dictating how it should be done. Haymarket created its general operating support category for grantees based on the assumption that they know best how to spend the funding. On-the-ground organizing is constantly changing, and grantees should be able to adapt and respond to this changing environment.
- Create processes that continually update funders' grantmaking processes, protocols, and assessment systems. The process should not be stagnant and can always be improved. Be open to creative new ideas while holding true to guiding principles.

A LETTER TO FUNDERS INTERESTED IN ANTIRACISM

Despite nearly fifty years of experience in social justice organizing and funding, Haymarket continues to be reminded that for systems of power and leadership to change, organizations and individuals holding that power must be willing to share it across race and culture. This will only come when everyone in the organization understands and faces the history of racism and white superiority (as well as its present-day manifestations) and adopts an organizational culture that dismantles behaviors and dynamics that undermine people of color's leadership, voice, and advancement.

We have learned this ourselves—and it has not been easy. We realized that it is not enough for funders—including those with a social justice mission—to simply talk about diversity, equity, and inclusion or to create funding streams for people of color; they have to prioritize looking inwardly, honestly and critically, at their organizations to determine whether and to what extent they acknowledge and understand racism in its many forms, including those that can and do manifest in organizational cultures and activities. Moreover, the good intentions embedded in philanthropic organizations are not enough; funders must also be committed to changing their organizations in ways that help dismantle racism in all its forms and across all parts of the institution. These include rising above defensiveness and denial because this work is "too painful" or "irrelevant" or to the claim that there is not enough time or resources.

Before Haymarket was able to instill its antiracist grantmaking model, a full internal restructuring had to occur; only then could it begin to address racism in every aspect of its organization. But the work did not stop there. It needed to then implement its antiracist grantmaking framework, which began by making sure this process was led by those most affected by the problems it was trying to resolve. This process will look different for every organization and require new learning curves and lessons.

This transformation did not happen overnight. When Haymarket first began its own organizational transformation and shifted its grantmaking to an antiracist model, everything felt as if it was going to fall apart. To weather the storm, Haymarket needed help and support from outside organizations, a strong team of leadership of color, a new outlook on its mission, revised criteria and a vision that reflected antiracist values and principles, and a process that was continually open to evolving, listening, and learning.

This process also required acknowledging that one way to continue to dismantle racism's foundations is to increase access to all resources—including but not limited to money—and acknowledge the role of foundations as gatekeepers in the nonprofit industrial complex. That is not easy for most funders, including even those with a social justice focus like Haymarket. It is a goal, however, that is worth pursuing, and one of the ways to move toward it is to drop the barriers surrounding grant funding. By placing power and trust in community members, funders that are dedicated to social and racial justice issues will not only be strengthening grantees' ability to achieve their organizational goals but also providing them with opportunities to share and wield the power needed to make lasting change.

NOTES

1. "About Us: Mission," People's Institute for Survival and Beyond, accessed December 27, 2022, https://pisab.org/about-us/. For a more in-depth analysis of Haymarket's antiracism transformation, see Haymarket People's Fund, *The Courage to Change: The Journey towards Transformation and Anti-Racism in Philanthropy at Haymarket People's Fund*, https://www.levellerspress.com/product/the-courage-to-change/.
2. Readings included Daniel Martinez HoSang, "The Structural Racism Concept and Its Impact on Philanthropy," Philanthropic Initiative for Racial Equity: Critical Issues Forum, vol. 5, *Moving Forward on Racial Justice Philanthropy*, June 2014; Keith Lawrence, "Reconsidering Community Building: Philanthropy Through a Structural Racism Lens," *Souls* 4, no. 1 (2002): 45–53; and John A. Powell, "Proposal for a Transformative, Racially Just Philanthropy," *Souls* 4, no. 1 (2002): 41–44.
3. John Kabia, "Fund 101: Intro to Participatory Grant-Making," Commentary blog, Fund for Global Human Rights, February 25, 2021, https://globalhumanrights.org/commentary/fund-101-intro-to-participatory-grant-making/.
4. "8.1D: Class," LibreTexts Social Sciences, February 20, 2021, https://socialsci.libretexts.org/Bookshelves/Sociology/Introduction_to_Sociology/Book%3A_Sociology_(Boundless)/08%3A_Global_Stratification_and_Inequality/8.01%3A_Systems_of_Stratification/8.1D%3A_Class; Max Weber, "Class, Status, and Party," no date, https://sites.middlebury.edu/individualandthesociety/files/2010/09/Weber-Class-Status-Party.pdf.
5. Haymarket People's Fund, *Courage to Change*, 12.
6. Quotations from representatives of specific organizations were derived from 2018–19 follow-up reports.

CHAPTER 6

Revolutionizing Philanthropy
Inclusive Participatory Processes in the New England Grassroots Environment Fund

Bart Westdijk and Sarah Huang

The New England Grassroots Environment Fund uses participatory grantmaking to support community-based, volunteer-run environmental justice organizations in six New England states. To examine how the use of participatory grantmaking approaches has influenced the fund's evolution during the past twenty-six years, staff members worked with a consultant on a nine-month process evaluation that sought to understand the fund's work, organizational structure, theory, approach, and implementation strategies. This chapter describes the fund's evaluation process, provides an overview of the findings and how it has incorporated them, and discusses the issues with which it is still grappling.

INTRODUCTION

The New England Grassroots Environment Fund, Inc., uses participatory grantmaking to support a wide range of volunteer-run, community-based (and often unincorporated) environmental justice groups and organizations across New England. Through this approach, the Grassroots Fund convenes and engages community members in all aspects of the grantmaking process: setting program guidelines, designing grant applications, reading and reviewing applications, and making grant decisions.

With support from the Ford Foundation, the Grassroots Fund worked with a consultant, Christine Robinson, on a nine-month process evaluation to understand the fund's work, organizational structure, theory, approach, and implementation strategies. This chapter describes this process and provides background on the development of the Grassroots Fund, including the history and evolution of its participatory grant programs. The chapter also provides an overview of the evaluation report and discusses how the Grassroots Fund has adapted some of Robinson's findings—and how it is still grappling with others, and why.

HOW AND WHY THE GRASSROOTS FUND WAS FOUNDED

In 1995, four New England foundations held a listening exercise with members of the environmental community to elicit their perspectives about the state of the regional environmental organizing movement. During this convening, members identified a need for greater attention to community-based environmental actions—especially dominant philanthropy's reluctance to support unincorporated volunteer efforts and/or those that did not have a fiscal sponsor but were developing locally rooted solutions to environmental problems in the region. This meeting led to the creation of the New England Grassroots Environment Fund in 1996. Its primary focus was to support these kinds of efforts as part of a larger mission: "Fostering an environmental ethic based on stewardship, to support and maintain a vibrant and diverse grassroots network and enhance community participation in local and regional environmental issues."[1]

With support from the four convening foundations, the Grassroots Fund was initially housed as a donor-advised fund at the New Hampshire Charitable Foundation. The fund's governance and policies were managed by an advisory committee consisting of representatives from the four foundations and grassroots community members based in Maine, Massachusetts, New Hampshire, and Vermont.

In 2000, this committee decided to spin off the Grassroots Fund as an independent, private nonprofit organization that would provide programming in all six New England states. As a nonendowed fund, the Grassroots Fund would also fundraise and regrant to smaller grassroots organizations. Most important, the committee recommended that the fund commit to a participatory governance structure, in which a majority of its grantmaking committee and board of directors would be environmental activists.

THE FIRST STEP TOWARD EVOLVING THE GRASSROOTS FUND: GUIDING VALUES

Since then, the Grassroots Fund has implemented participatory processes in myriad aspects of its work. In 2016, this ethos and value system was embedded more formally in the fund's work when a leadership change prompted the establishment of Guiding Values for the organization's overall planning and programming. Co-created with grantees and community partners, the final published Guiding Values document challenged the organization to declare and commit to equity as a core value and to working with grassroots groups in facilitating and evaluating decision-making processes. At the center of these discussions and decisions was a recognition of the importance in having a broad range of voices and lived experiences participating in all facets of the grantmaking process.

A key aspect of the Guiding Values document was its use of "Just Transition," a framework from the labor and environmental justice movements that advocates moving from an extractive economy to one that is regenerative, just, and supports bottom-up organizing. This framework encourages attention to the process as much as the end result, a perspective that deeply informs the fund's Guiding Values.

The fund viewed that document as an opportunity for working more closely with environmental organizers to explore who should be involved in co-creating local solutions; how a volunteer-run, ad hoc group's work could contribute to advocating for the Just Transition across Northeast communities; and how the fund could support these kinds of on-the-ground efforts. The fund categorized its Guiding Values into seven sections (see table 6.1), nearly all of which align with values that are frequently associated with participatory grantmaking.

LEANING INTO ITERATION: GUIDING VALUES THAT BECAME GUIDING PRACTICES

By codifying a giving approach that connected Grassroots Fund to larger local, regional, and national processes, Guiding Values (see table 6.2) was essential to laying a foundation for the fund's Guiding Practices, which was developed in 2018 and emerged from the iterative and reflective nature of the fund's equity work. This process underscored the need for the fund to move beyond the broad and more static statements outlined in Guiding Values and toward operationalizing these concepts in and across all organizational functions,

Table 6.1: Guiding Values of the New England Grassroots Environment Fund, 2016

Guiding value	Definition	How we do this
Just Transition and strategic considerations	Strategies and programs are focused on efforts to move from an extractive, fossil-fuel-driven economy toward a local, living economy grounded in ecological and social well-being, cooperation, and regeneration.	• Leveraging resources and tools to support community activists • Identifying innovative and effective strategies that bridge issues and move toward social change
Shifting power: transparency, accountability, democracy	Grant decisions are made collectively by those who donate money and those who receive grants.	• Ensuring grantmaking committees consist of representatives of the grassroots community and funding community • Leveraging an online grant review system to allow a large pool of partners to share grant applications • Defining clear values and funding criteria
Lowering barriers to funding	Applicants are viewed as colleagues catalyzing innovative change or addressing systemic challenges.	• Funding applicants without tax-exempt status • Cultivating relationships across a broad range of focus areas • Accepting verbal applications and reports
Flexibility and risk-taking	Grant guidelines can be flexible at times and recipients trusted to use funds effectively. Grassroots Fund assumes the risks in our grantmaking to learn with grantees to understand what works and what does not.	• Contacting and facilitating conversations with each applicant to better understand project initiatives
Change versus charity	Commitment to provide grantees with a range of services that focus on the root causes of problems rather than their symptoms.	• Offering tiered grant programs that allow grassroots groups to match their work with project-development-based support • Providing technical resources to grantees
Community-based fundraising	Equity is at the center and Grassroots Fund recognizes the inherent inequities in philanthropy.	• Engaging a broad network of donors
Process is the product	Risks in the fund's structures, processes, and funding decisions are learning opportunities.	• Assessing and evaluating the fund's practices and seeing the Guiding Values as a living document

Source: Author survey data.

activities, and processes. This decision emerged from tough conversations and analysis of *how* the fund was living its Guiding Values, including making funding decisions through a participatory grantmaking process.

An important part of the Grassroots Fund's continued evolution has been centering the concept of environmental justice. The US Environmental Protection Agency defines this as the "fair treatment and meaningful involvement of all people regardless of race, color, national origin, or income, with respect to the development, implementation, and enforcement of environmental laws, regulations, and policies."[2]

The key elements of environmental justice—bottom-up organizing, centering the voices of those most affected, and shared community leadership—converge at the grassroots level. For this reason, the fund believes that moving toward environmental justice requires investing in and increasing the power of grassroots organizers who are directly experiencing the effects of environmental injustice.

Guiding Practices is essential to the fund's thinking about how to create a just and equitable space within the environmental justice movement. Its elements also serve as filters through which the fund's staff, board, frontline organizers, participants, and funding partners can reflect on their work by asking questions that are often prevalent across the larger movement. These include:

- Who has power, and how do they have it?
- Who is able to access resources?
- Who is participating and who is not? Why are they not?
- How are we moving toward a less extractive society?
- How are our solutions rooted in the history, cultures, and lived experiences of our community?

It is important to note that the Guiding Practices are not static; they evolve from grassroots organizers' work in their communities, which, in turn, shapes the fund's support for strategy building across its grantee network. This includes participatory decision-making not only on funding but also on other protocols and practices, such as alternative governance structures that emerge from mutual aid and solidarity processes.

This type of reciprocal learning is, in itself, a powerful example of how organizations can center participatory practice. For example, the participatory grantmaking process often creates an iterative interaction between the funding process itself and the work that is being funded to create a collectively developed set of values-aligned practices.

Table 6.2: Guiding Practices of the New England Grassroots Environment Fund, 2018

Guiding practice	Key focus	Reflection questions
Rooted innovation	Understanding how a project is grounded in a community—not only what the community's needs are but also how you understand these needs and create pathways for feedback	1. What are the needs of the folks who live in our community? 2. What existing partnerships and collaborations do we have? Are there any new connections that can be made to make sure that we are working in solidarity with our community? 3. How can we make sure that our community can provide active feedback on this work?
Shifting power in decision-making	How decisions are made, how those with diverse lived experiences can meaningfully weigh in, and what protocols are in place to navigate tension and conflict	1. Are the folks who are intended to benefit from this project also a core part of priority setting and decision-making? 2. Is the group's composition representative across race, ability, gender, class, and other self-identifiers or demographics? 3. Do our decision-making processes ensure that all voices are heard? 4. How are we navigating tension and conflict?
Equity in participation	Understanding the tangible and intangible barriers to participating and creating opportunities to collectively overcome them. An example of a tangible barrier is lacking access to transportation to attend a meeting. An intangible barrier to participation might be a lack of attention to equity and care.	1. How do group members voice their concerns about participation? Is this an explicit process that all members are aware of and able to engage with? 2. Do you understand the complexity of your community's identity? How do intersectional identities influence how members show up to each meeting? 3. How do you assess barriers to participation? Who was included in those assessments? When was the last time you asked these questions?

(continued)

Table 6.2: *(continued)*

Guiding practice	Key focus	Reflection questions
Centering a Just Transition	We reference Climate Justice Alliance's understanding of Just Transition, which has roots within labor organizing and environmental justice.[a] To move toward a Just Transition, the solutions and ideas of what is needed for community well-being must come from the bottom-up, which requires understanding of two of the fund's Guiding Practices: "rooted innovation" and "shifting power in decision-making." It also requires a problem-solving culture that trusts community members' lived experiences and that they know best the complexity and the diversity of their needs. It requires asking questions like, How are we working toward relationship building and connecting? This includes between people, between organizations, and between food, health, and housing issues.	1. What intersections exist within our work? For example, is hunger a result of lack of food access or are there other societal issues at play? 2. How is our work leading toward greater systems change? 3. How have we assessed our community's needs? What are the gaps and opportunities in our resources (including, but not limited to lived experiences, knowledge, skills)? 4. How are we centering regenerative or relationship-based practices? 5. Who are the non-traditional partners needed in our work? How can we move toward living well, but not at the expense of others living poorly?

[a]"Just Transition: A Framework for Change," Climate Justice Alliance, 2023, https://climatejusticealliance.org/just-transition/.
Source: New England Grassroots Environment Fund, 2018.

THE BASELINE FOR THE FUND'S PROCESS EVALUATION: HOW ITS GRANTMAKING WORKS TODAY

The evolution of the Grassroots Fund's values and practices has led to a particular approach to grantmaking, which became the baseline for a process evaluation the fund undertook in 2020. Three areas of the fund's work were studied: grantmaking, convening, and learning.

Grantmaking

The Grassroots Fund's theory of change supports bottom-up organizing and centering the voices of those most affected by the issues they see as most important. The fund implements this across its grant programs, which are structured using a framework developed by Bruce Tuckman, a psychological researcher focused on group dynamics.[3]

Tuckman outlines four phases of organizational development, which may be seen in the elements of the Grassroots Fund's Guiding Practices. (For complete descriptions of each practice, see table 8.2.) The first in Tuckman's model is the "forming phase," when members come together with a high level of drive and energy (and sometimes urgency) to move a project or campaign forward. During this phase, groups tend to focus on "rooted innovation" and "shifting power in decision-making" in the Grassroot Fund's Guiding Practices. Tuckman's second phase, "storming," is when group members align their work styles and define a specific vision or focus for their collective work. This phase is often where the fund's Guiding Practices of "rooted innovation," "shifting power in decision-making," and "equity in participation" are evident. In Tuckman's model, during the third or "(re-)norming phase," the group settles on a specific direction and approach, which is followed by the final "performing phase," when a project is implemented. These last two stages are when groups are better able to articulate how they are employing the fund's Guiding Practice of "centering a Just Transition." It is important to note that these phases are not necessarily linear; they can sometimes be cyclical as projects deepen their focus and broaden who is involved in their work and leadership.

The grant programs provide funding for organizers to launch and sustain projects that, in turn, become the context for implementing the Guiding Practices and strengthening environmental justice capacity at the local level. Since 1996, the Grassroots Fund has been able to fund 4,000-plus groups through this program, totaling more than $8.5 million.

The fund's participatory grantmaking process operates differently across all four grant programs but generally follows a cycle that begins with submitting applications to an online platform. Community grant readers—often, between 80 and 120 per round—respond to an open call asking them to review the applications and to provide comments and a score based on the Guiding Practices (see table 8.2). A staff member then reviews the application and conducts a phone call with the applicant, and a selected group of grassroots organizers are invited to make final decisions as a part of the grantmaking committee. Members of this committee are often previous high-scoring grantees with experience in implementing projects that are closely aligned with the Guiding Practices. After the review is conducted, staff members reach out to the applicant and provide feedback on their applications—based on input from all participants—for all applicants, regardless of funding level.

The fund provides four kinds of grants: seed, grow, young leaders, and shared gifting circle. Seed grants support grassroots leaders as their projects "form and storm."[4] The application questions focus on how the project is rooted in community needs (e.g., does the group know the demographics of core decision-makers?) and inquire about conversations that have taken place on governance, priority setting, and decision-making. At this level, answers can often be aspirational, and there is a higher level of flexibility, given that organizers are testing new practices. A diverse group of community grantmakers provides feedback and suggestions focused on these aspects of the work. Reviewers come to the Grassroots Fund through an invitation-only process that asks them to self-identify across a range of demographic characteristics and provide more detail about their lived experiences. Each community grantmaker cohort is approved by the board. Seed grant review processes are facilitated by seed community grantmakers and use a consensus-based decision model to make final decisions on grant applications. The fund receives 80 to 100 seed requests annually.

Grow and young leaders grants focus on the cycle of "(re-)norming and performing."[5] Application questions go deeper into power and decision-making (e.g., how conflict/tension is managed within the group). The application also focuses on how barriers to participation are lowered to ensure the voices of those most affected by environmental injustices are centered. With these key capacity components in place, the grow and young leader grant programs start seeing applicants centering intersectional solutions. The latter are defined as solutions that come from community members, involve them at the decision-making table, and focus on the root causes of the issues they see as priorities. At this level, applicants tend to have active projects already and can speak to or share direct experiences as examples of what the work looks like on the ground. The process for grow grants is described in figure 6.1.

The two-phase review process for these grants often offers spaces for rich conversations on both the process side of an application, as well as the specific issue area content and intersectionality of environmental justice work. Phase one brings in application readers through an open call. Community grant readers review up to fifteen applications online and provide a numeric score (1–4) based on a rubric that reflects the Guiding Practices. In phase two, final decisions are made by a grantmaking committee that is selected by staff and approved by the board. Committee members are active organizers who have direct experience implementing projects aligned with the Guiding Practices (often, representatives of high-scoring groups from previous grant rounds). The final decision-making process is facilitated by a grantmaking committee member, and the process for how decisions are made is decided upon by the grantmaking committee members themselves.

Finally, the fund has begun piloting a new grantmaking program focusing on a shared gifting circle / learning cohort model. Shared gifting is a democratic and collaborative exchange of funds that allows grantee participants to also be grantors. Rather than rely on a set application process, this participatory grantmaking approach creates space for Shared Gifting Circle cohort members to engage in conversation and relationship building, decide collaboratively how they want to learn together, build trust, and create a process for making funding decisions.

This program is currently by invitation only and is based on alignment with all Guiding Practices as determined through the fund's participatory process. Groups able to show strong examples of how they are implementing the Guiding Practices (as determined by seed and grow application readers and the grow grantmaking committee) take part in cocreating a shared gifting model through which the cohort sets parameters and makes all decisions on resource distribution. In 2022, the Grassroots

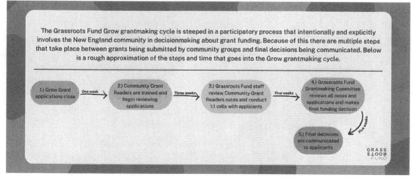

Figure 6.1 Grow Grant Cycle, 2022
Source: New England Grassroots Environment Fund.

Fund facilitated regional gifting circles focused on food system resilience and climate resilience.

Convenings

The Grassroots Fund's virtual and in-person convenings are designed to deepen and strengthen grassroots movements by facilitating connections across a broad spectrum of individuals, groups, and organizations, all working toward common goals. As described in table 6.3, the fund has four types of convenings.[6]

Table 6.3: Types of Convenings

Pop-up offices	Community-based pop-up offices that give activists/residents the opportunity to connect directly with Grassroots Fund staff who provide personalized assistance in everything from starting a grant application to exploring project ideas to discussing challenges and opportunities in those communities.
Catalyst convenings	Discussion-based events that bring community members together to strengthen cross-issue area collaboration, create space for new and creative ideas, and connect with Grassroots Fund's community from a shared region (which could be defined by shared water systems or food systems). Convenings typically focus on a specific framing topic based on the fund's Guiding Practices and are grounded in a specific community context (city, town, or bioregion). A planning committee of local representatives helps design the agenda and does outreach ahead of the convening.
Root Skills Trainings Series	One- or two-day in-person gatherings that strengthen relationships and offer skill-building opportunities focused both on issue content and organizing processes. The fund issues an open request for proposals to its contact list for potential workshops, which are peer-led interactive sessions focused on both process-based and issue area topics. Each event is designed with planning committee members from the hosting community who help with choices on venue and catering, lowering barriers to access, and selecting workshop proposals.
Community of Practice Series	Communities of practice help participants workshop and implement a Guiding Practice within their organizing group or their organizing work via a virtual space where organizers have a chance to get to know each other, connect, listen to and share challenges and ideas, as well as cocreate values-driven interventions for their groups or communities.

Source: Author survey data.

METHODS AND GOALS FOR PROCESS EVALUATION

In March 2020, the Grassroots Fund commissioned a consultant, Christine Robinson—a seasoned leader and strategist for philanthropic foundations, government agencies, and initiatives—to conduct a nine-month process evaluation. The goal of the evaluation was to assess whether the fund's program activities had been implemented as intended and aligned with anticipated outputs.

During the first three months, Robinson worked closely with the Grassroots Fund's leadership team to review the organization's founding documents and how its grant programs and convenings operate.[7] She also conducted interviews with eight staff and ten board members, and selected stakeholders (around thirty grantmaking committee members), reviewed previous survey responses collected by the fund following review rounds, and participated in virtual grantmaking committee retreats in the spring and fall of 2020.

After this initial learning, Robinson produced a report outlining whether and how the fund's work aligns with its Guiding Practices; the report also provided guidance and support for this work. Using these findings, she developed a process map identifying the key streams and approaches that the Grassroots Fund uses. The process map also shows what inclusivity looks like across the fund's internal operations and how the Guiding Practices of equity, power shifting, and rootedness are embedded (or not) in its programming. Figure 6.2, which is an excerpt from this process map, shows the different stages of the Grassroots Fund's programming and internal functions as it moves from its current state toward its desired outcome.

Overview of the Report's Findings and Recommendations

The general findings and recommendations of Robinson's report are organized into two categories: (1) who and what drives the organization's work (mission, values), and (2) how the organization does this work (programs, internal functions).

Who and What Drives the Work (Mission and Values of the Organization)

First, the Grassroots Fund continues to be committed to amplifying grantee partners' voices and strengthening and supporting their efforts as part of a generative social justice movement. However, the fund's primary focus continues to

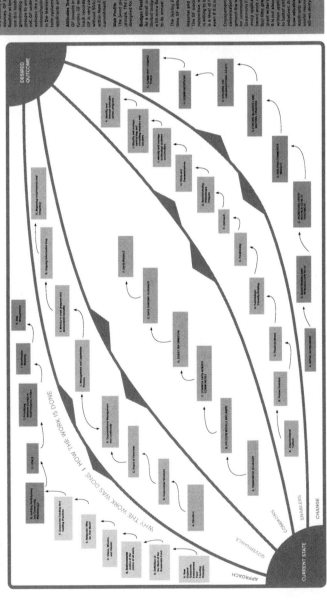

Figure 6.2 Excerpt from Process Map

Source: New England Grassroots Environment Fund, 2020.

be its grantmaking processes, with less of a focus on environmental justice issues themselves. While the focus on how decisions are made is a real contribution to leadership development, there is a need for the fund to balance this with a deeper focus on the "what" of the projects and building out a deeper understanding of successful and effective projects that lead to environmental justice.

Second, the Grassroots Fund is seen by peer funding partners and grassroots leaders as a grantmaker / grant seeker hybrid. In addition to helping more traditional funders explore participatory and equity-driven grantmaking practices, the fund also keeps its ear to the ground to ensure an ongoing understanding of mutual aid groups' needs, grassroots organizing strategies, and innovation. Because of these multiple perspectives, the fund has an opportunity to take the lead in grounding an integrated approach that weaves grassroots organizing and building pathways to equity and justice across both on-the-ground work and philanthropy.

How the Work Is Done (Internal Operations)

First, the Grassroots Fund seeks to convene grassroots partners to stimulate dialogues and collaboration on complex issues and to educate funders and traditional ecological movement leaders about the power of grassroots innovation and strategic approaches. There is a potential to significantly amplify grantees' voice and deepen the understanding of their interconnected endeavors. Where convenings and gatherings are currently disconnected from other program elements, there is an opportunity to integrate learning from the participatory process across convening spaces. The focus on Guiding Practices can be core components of efforts to connect program areas.

Second, the Grassroots Fund is starting to address issues of racism by undergoing self-examination and deepening insights on equity. Those working from historically marginalized communities must be placed front and center in the fund's work.

Third, the Grassroots Fund needs to continue to move toward more understanding and empathy about the role of oppression and "othering" in environmental justice work. It needs to build its own internal capacities to be more aligned with this goal.

Fourth, the fund can facilitate cross-disciplinary, geographic, and cultural coordination. Both the application and participatory processes provide the fund with rich data on participants, how they self-identify, what issues they are working on (and where), and other information. The participatory process offers insights into how groups or projects develop (and the degree to which they align with the Guiding Values in doing so), which creates an opportunity to connect organizers and groups with each other across a range of demographic identities.

Fifth, the Grassroots Fund can give more attention to leveraging collaboration and cohort building that will empower grassroots groups to tackle issues beyond the local level. And sixth, the fund can organize grassroots grantee partners into cohorts to catalyze deeper understandings, creativity, and a shared purpose.

FINDINGS FROM THE PROCESS EVALUATION AND HOW WE HAVE APPLIED THEM

The Grassroots Fund has applied several of these findings to its grantmaking and operations. This section examines how it did so under two headings, "Leveraging Collaboration and Cohort Building" and "Leveraging the Participatory Process at Different Scales." Each subsection outlines what was learned from the report, how it is being applied, and what the fund is still considering.

Leveraging Collaboration and Cohort Building: What We Learned from the Report

Findings indicate an opportunity for deeper cohort building and leveraging collaboration that empowers grassroots groups to tackle issues at different levels. Participatory grantmaking is one way this can happen, because it gives grassroots organizations and traditional funders an opportunity to meet and communicate directly with one another. The Grassroots Fund could become more intentional about how this happens and what it could look like by beginning to examine its stakeholder engagement processes and power-mapping analyses more closely to understand how grassroots organizations are coming to the fund, the resources and work the fund's grants are supporting, and the key levers for systemic change. Through these deeper connections between grassroots organizers, traditional funders, and new donors, there is great potential to build a stronger and more diverse environmental justice movement.

What Has Been Done Since the Report

Based on Robinson's findings, the fund has identified two ways to increase the level of collaboration and engagement that results from its grants process: (1) changing how it uses the surveys given to grant readers for evaluation purposes, and (2) taking a more active approach to convening the individuals who participate in that grantmaking process.

To deepen connections with the fund's own communities, it must dig further into what accountability and learning sharing looks like and become more intentional about creating spaces for community members to engage more authentically and see themselves within the participatory process. This requires setting up interactional spaces that allow for a flow of knowledge and experience in both directions, specifically drawing from grant reader experiences, organizing experiences, expertise, and resources.

In past grant rounds, community grant readers would finish the review of their applications and then receive an evaluation survey to gather their feedback about the review process and what could have been done differently. But the fund did not necessarily close the loop with readers by letting them know what it took away from their feedback and what it did differently as a result.

According to Robinson, this is a missed opportunity. Being more intentional about closing the loop with readers on how the fund uses evaluation surveys to improve its process would not only be enhancing transparency but also strengthening what Robinson calls bridge-building skills. In her view, these are an essential contribution the Grassroots Fund can make in thinking about—and developing strategies for—ways in which "environmental justice connects people, place, disparity, and overarching connections of community."[8]

Based on these reflections, the fund has redesigned how it surveys community members who participate as grant proposal readers. Originally, these evaluation surveys were designed to ask for feedback about how the fund carried out the volunteer grant reader experience. Now, evaluation surveys ask for detailed information about what readers are learning from the review process and how they are implementing that learning in their everyday lives. New surveys are also able to show whether and for what reasons activists continue to participate in the fund's grantmaking, which include the sense of community the fund has worked hard to embed in this process and that they are part of a larger movement. Readers' feedback has also revealed that there could be more intentionality in connecting the community and movement-level work, reinforcing a point made in the report.

Recognizing the need for more transparency, accountability, and bridge building that the findings given above indicate, the Grassroots Fund has created a new strategic communications and network-weaving position. This person will, for example, facilitate stronger connections between participants in the grantmaking process and applicant and grantee groups. They will also communicate more directly with community readers and grant applicants about final funding decisions. For example, the fund recently began publishing a snapshot of the grant cycle, which includes the names of grantee groups and demographic information about where and to whom funds were allocated, to demonstrate its commitment to transparency and accountability.

An example of this reporting is depicted in figure 6.3, which shows where grow grants were distributed in the spring of 2022. In that cycle, 49 percent of these funds went to groups with majority white leaders, whereas 25 percent went to groups with majority Black or African American leaders. The fund is continuing to use this type of tracking to get a better sense of where grant dollars are going.

The grassroots environmental justice community that the Grassroots Fund has fostered over the past twenty-six years already has a strong bridge-building capacity. And much of the infrastructure for supporting this work is also established, including the process for convening individuals, the participatory grant review, and a large community. However, questions of scale and movement building still need more focus. While the fund provides spaces for conversations in which these questions can be raised—such as through its grantmaking review processes and convenings—it is also well positioned to convene organizers and others working on environmental justice issues at a much broader scale to discuss these issues as well as their alignment with the Guiding Practices.

With the assistance of the new network weaver, the fund has also been strengthening its bridge-building skills by becoming more proactive in how it convenes community members who participate in the grant process. In the

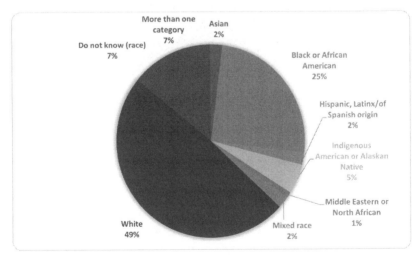

Figure 6.3 The Race and Ethnicity of Leaders of Organizations That Received Grow Grants, Spring 2022

Source: Author survey data.

spring of 2022, the fund hosted its first reader gathering—a 90-minute virtual gathering, during which fifteen readers had the opportunity to introduce themselves to the group, share why they participated, and to discuss challenges and opportunities from the experience. Readers' lived experiences ranged broadly, from serving as frontline organizers and/or nonprofit staff to those with grant writing or grantmaking experience. Readers who have participated for many years shared their insights and experiences with new participants about important issues (e.g., understanding the content of some applications, and community-based power shifting and what that looks like).

Updating the reader evaluation survey and beginning to convene readers have allowed the fund to understand more about how readers are joining the participatory process. This, in turn, has enabled it to be more intentional in identifying opportunities for making deeper connections among frontline organizers, current grassroots grant applicants, and grantees. While feedback from the survey and convening reveals that readers have a broad range of learning experiences, the fund hopes that, at a minimum, participants can experience what it looks like to shift power in decision-making processes, and to see examples of grassroots groups leading innovative changes in their communities. One reader shared that they came to learn more about the grant process but continued to engage as a reader because of the ability to learn more about the New England environmental justice field. This is the type of bridge building the fund hopes to see more of through its grants process.

What the Fund Is Still Considering

There is still work to be done with regard to how the fund is leveraging collaboration and cohort building. Aside from creating more cohort-aligned spaces through its shared gifting cohort pilot programs, the fund continues to engage with how these larger strategies of convening and supporting collaborations fit within its organizational strategic plan.

Leveraging the Participatory Process at Different Scales: What We Learned from the Report

The fund believes that placing equity at the heart and core of this kind of work is not easy. It is usually messy and requires a willingness to dig into hard conversations, such as who gets to make decisions and why. That can make folks feel uncomfortable—especially those who have never had their power or privileges challenged. And yet these issues show up across all areas of the Grassroots Fund's work: internal staff operations, collaboration with community members, and larger grassroots organizing movement building. These challenges to power occur at all points of the participatory process and across the organization, both internally and externally.

Robinson points out in her findings that there are two ways in which the Grassroots Fund can leverage the benefits of its participatory grants process at a larger scale. One is to pay attention not just to *how* grant recipients pursue their aims but also to *what ends*. The other is to connect the local work the fund supports more explicitly with regional and national trends.

The Grassroots Fund has traditionally focused more on the participatory grantmaking process and how the grassroots organizing work that is being considered for support (or supported) is done, rather than what elements of environmental justice that work addresses. In its grant applications, for example, the fund asks how groups are shifting power in their decision-making and centering equity in their projects. While the specific environmental justice issues that applicants are focusing on are seen as important, funding decisions are made primarily based on how those groups are organizing to address them. Robinson suggests that bringing so much attention to the process and not enough to the "what" of environmental justice work is a missed opportunity to broaden the focus of the fund's work.

There are also opportunities to think differently about the scale of the fund's work. Historically, it has focused on supporting local grassroots organizing on issues communities have identified as priorities (e.g., banning potentially harmful new development projects in urban neighborhoods and creating healing gardens for veterans). In thinking about future collaboration and cohort building, Robinson recommends that the fund create space for grassroots groups to develop and work collectively toward a shared purpose at all levels of the environmental justice movement: local, regional, and national.

While the participatory process is inherently a power-sharing approach and also provides many learning opportunities for participants, the evaluation indicated that there are additional ways in which the fund could move toward deeper power-shifting engagement. For example, much of the fund's participatory process, including the reader experience, occurs in isolation and often with static engagement rather than in spaces that allow for the more iterative and participatory processes that are necessary to achieve environmental justice. As Robinson notes, "The grant may be the entry point, but the work developed through the grant period, often through subsequent grant periods, is a power story, particularly in outcome-driven fields such as environmental justice."[9] Participatory grantmaking, as a process, can create new dynamic relationships between the funder and the grantee and between applicants and participants. It moves transactional relationships toward mutuality, power sharing, and capacity building, and it can create a shared movement toward desired outcomes. There is more that the Grassroots Fund can do to capture this potential in its current grants process.

What Has Been Done Since the Report

FURTHER OPERATIONALIZING THE GUIDING PRACTICES

Currently, the fund uses the grant application as an opportunity for grassroots organizations to test the alignment of their ideas with the environmental justice principles outlined in its Guiding Practices. The grant application provides questions that are connected to each practice and seeks to learn more about how the group is doing its work or what it is proposing to do.

To be able to answer these questions, the fund has observed that sometimes a group needs to carry out an actual test project or action experiment. For example, because one of the Guiding Practices is "rooted innovation," the grant application asks groups how they know whether the work they are proposing is rooted in the community they hope to serve. During staff review calls with grant applicants, some say they have used the process of filling out their application to talk to their board members or other organizers about engaging more deeply in their own equity practice. The application itself, therefore, serves as a reflection point for organizations not only on their proposed projects but also on how they intend to work with each other and the larger community to ensure they are addressing often-invisible problems like power, barriers, and inclusion.

Since beginning work with Christine Robinson, the Grassroots Fund has started bolstering its data collection and internal evaluation of the Guiding Practices. This has begun through the assumption that grassroots organizations come with a wealth of knowledge, strategies, tactics, culture, and ways of working that have been proven to work in their own communities and that are essential for the larger movement. Internally, the fund has started to dial into what each of the Guiding Practices actually means in practice (e.g., the proposed ways groups are shifting decision-making power, the methods or frameworks they are using to make decisions, and what is and is not working). Specifically, the fund has collected an inventory of practices that align with its own Guiding Practices (e.g., using a consensus decision-making model as an example of "shifting power in decision-making"). This inventory helps its staff gain a deeper understanding of practices and provides a resource that allows the fund to engage with grant applicants, grant readers, and the larger environmental justice community.

STRENGTHENING THE GRANTMAKING COMMITTEE'S LEARNING
Before Robinson's report, the fund's fifteen-member grantmaking committee was formed by selecting volunteer readers from a participant pool and inviting them to take part in a three-day virtual grantmaking committee retreat. Because of the fund's commitment to ensuring that committee members reflect the lived experiences and voices of those most affected, it has worked hard to include a broad cross section of identities (e.g., geographic, socioeconomic, gender, race, and education) as well as intersecting experiences from the LGBTQ+ movement, the disability rights movement, and economic justice organizing.

During the first day of the retreat, members participate in implicit-bias training to understand how bias shows up in decision-making. This includes naming various ways of decision-making (single individual, advisory, majority vote, consensus, consent) and how these sometimes align with certain values or group needs. Participants talk about blank spots and facades (e.g., what we know about ourselves but cannot always talk about and what others know about us that we may not directly be aware of). This is both an opportunity for folks to get to know each other (and themselves) and to start thinking intentionally around how they will proceed in decision-making processes.

The next day, participants engage in deeper discussions about grant applications, which builds relationships and provides more context and information about the application process and environmental justice work. These conversations also ensure that members have the space to challenge existing program guidelines, because the process is not just about making grant decisions but also about identifying barriers to funding and other issues for staff learning. Examples of theme discussions include defining community, distinguishing between constructive conflict and harm, making decisions about partial funding, and Guiding Practice examples that are necessary for a project to be considered under a particular grantmaking category.

Discussions like these lay the groundwork for the third day of the retreat, which focuses on grant application decision-making. Committee members are given a group of applications that have been reviewed by volunteer readers and staff (who often also do a phone call with applicants). Using the notes and scores from all these reviews—as well as the Guiding Practices framework—members discuss each of the applications and make a decision about whether the group will receive full, partial, or no funding. Often, committee members provide additional feedback to the applicant about how their application could score higher next time.

In response to Robinson's report, the fund has incorporated more emphasis on field building into its participatory process, which includes being more intentionally selective about who gets to participate as grantmaking committee members. While anyone can still be a community grant reader, the grantmaking committee is an opportunity for the fund to engage individuals with the ability to build connections across organizations and movements. For example, it has begun to invite past grantees representing organizations that have scored high on all the Guiding Practices to serve on this committee because they have demonstrated a deep understanding of what it looks like to center equity in their work and the importance of advancing the Just Transition framework across the larger movement.

The fund also now asks the organizations it invites to join the grantmaking committee to propose one of their individual members to participate as a grantmaking committee member in the retreat. This strengthens the fund's bridge-building work in two ways: (1) it includes folks with a wider range of experiences in movement organizing to support other grantees who are trying to engage in this work in their own communities, and (2) it forges cross-disciplinary, cross-regional, and diverse connections that are essential to larger movement building. Ultimately, the fund hopes that through these efforts, more movement leaders across the region will be able to support each other through culturally relevant strategies and tactics.

What We Are Still Considering

Thus far, the fund is finding that as a consequence of the more curated approach to composing the grantmaking committee, it needs to retool the retreat structure. New committee members are coming to the retreat with much of the lived experience and organizing experience that previous members might not have had. This means that the training that usually occurs on the first two days can look a little different.

The fund is also experimenting with what it looks like to shift accountability and power in the grantmaking committee's process beyond the retreat. For example, it is launching a grant round in which committee members who have participated in the past (as grantees or as previous grantmaking committee members) are invited to take on different roles (e.g., facilitator and evaluator) with different power to shape the agenda and outcomes of the process.

In these two new roles, the fund is hoping to have grantmaking committee members who are past grantees to design and facilitate conversations and evaluate the goals and process. This shifts power from staff members facilitating discussions or deciding what the evaluation process will entail and instead centers the voices of grantees across the entire grants process. By further embedding grantee leadership in the decision-making process, the fund hopes to identify different and more effective opportunities for collaboration and cohort building based on what grantee leaders prioritize.

Another way the fund is expanding this type of connecting and learning is by sharing anonymized reviews for each application. Previously, readers only saw the rating scores they gave. Now, they can compare the scores they give with those from other participants who bring different lived experiences. In doing so, they can reflect on blank-spot biases they may have and see where others raise questions or observe nuances they may have otherwise missed. Since participants also have connections with the larger environmental justice movement and field, they can bring this reflection and learning to other organizations.

CONCLUSION: TRACING THE RIPPLE EFFECTS OF PARTICIPATORY GRANTMAKING

Despite the Grassroots Fund's efforts to incorporate the recommendations of the evaluative study it undertook to improve its participatory grantmaking process in ways that reflect a stronger commitment to power sharing, racial equity, and field building, it still faces the challenge of working in a philanthropic industry whose values are somewhat antithetical to the environmental justice movement the fund exists to support. Fortunately, the study's findings are helping the fund grapple with that tension; here is an example.

In 2020, the Grassroots Fund received funding to sponsor a Food System Resilience Fund cohort. This funding came from a funder to regrant to grassroots organizations. The goal of the fund was to provide financial support to majority community-of-color organizers working in New England's food system. Grassroots Fund staff worked with food system organizers to design the fund, which would provide one-year grants to fifteen organizations that themselves are grassroots organizers across the region. The design team kept the definition of "food system organizer" intentionally broad because many folks are deeply engaged in food system organizing work but are often left out of traditional food system funding avenues because they are deemed as not being connected to food work or are excluded because of their tax status or lack of connections.

The fund was also structured as a shared gifting circle, giving full process and decision-making authority over the grant funds to community leaders.[10]

A big focus of this cohort was trust and relationship building because many of the organizers, who worked across the six-state region, did not know each other or had not worked together. Thus, the fund needed to ensure that these groups were comfortable discussing funding questions and issues with one another while acknowledging their diverse class status and relationships with money. This brought home a notable tension in participatory grantmaking: the need for participants to balance their own relationships with money, their organizing work, and others' relationships and work. The fund wanted to ensure that people felt comfortable doing this and that they had the power to make decisions about this funding from a mind-set of solidarity and abundance rather than competition and scarcity. To face this dynamic head on, the fund knew that the cohort needed to engage in a conversation about how they would talk about money.

This took much longer than anticipated. As a result, the fund quickly found itself five meetings into the yearlong cohort with many members identifying that they were not sure what they were doing in the group or feeling like they were not getting a sense of who was in the room. They were frustrated and asked the fund and the facilitator for more structure.

We reflect upon this as a moment when the fund realized that money was just getting in the way. The impending shared gifting circle, which was scheduled for the sixth cohort meeting, felt as if it was coming too soon, with the group not having spent enough time getting to know each other. They needed different conversations, more centered on how they were going to make decisions about what was needed to distribute the funding, and less focused on the everyday challenges of grassroots organizing. It felt as if the barriers were about planning, logistics, and outcomes of the process rather than relationality, trust, and support among the participants.

As a result, the Grassroots Fund's staff, along with the facilitator hired to work with it, drafted a proposal whereby instead of the funding being allocated at the end of the yearlong process, it could be allocated at the six-month mark so that groups could spend more time building relationships with each other. The cohort eventually decided to distribute some of the funding immediately to leave time for more meaningful conversations without money getting in the way of relationships. Robinson's point, mentioned earlier in the chapter, that grants are the inroads to something more, resonated with Grassroots Fund staff in this moment as participants verbalized the huge potential they saw in increased connections and peer sharing. It highlighted that perhaps the participatory process, the convening of change makers, and the holding of space are benefits that go far beyond what grants themselves can provide. Perhaps it is in those broader ripple effects, more so than in the distribution of funds, that the true power of participatory grantmaking lies.

This recent experience, which applies the lessons from the process evaluation, left the fund hungry for more. It introduced a different way of working and opened up a new set of questions. In particular, it left the fund with a yearning for more understanding of how the participatory process in itself is a form of field building. And if this is indeed true, then what does this field look like that other participatory grantmakers are supporting? What common ties could be strengthened? The Grassroots Fund is hopeful that the chapters of this edited collection can point the way to a larger discussion in the sector along these lines.

NOTES

1. New England Grassroots Environment Fund, "Founders' Document," 2000.
2. US Environmental Protection Agency, "Environmental Justice," https://www.epa.gov/environmentaljustice.
3. Bruce Tuckman, "Developmental Sequence in Small Groups," *Psychological Bulletin* 63, no. 6 (1965): 384–99.
4. Tuckman.
5. Tuckman.
6. These convenings were on pause after the beginning of the 2020 COVID-19 pandemic until the writing of this book chapter in 2022. The Grassroots Fund used this time to reassess how convenings can best play a role in our grantmaking work across the region.
7. In 2020, the leadership team included Julia Dundorf, executive director, and Bart Westdijk, director of operations. The Grassroots Fund underwent a leadership transition at the start of 2022.
8. Christine Robinson, *New England Grassroots Environment Fund: A Model of Participatory Grantmaking, a Participatory Organization, and the Essential Nature of Belonging* (Newmarket, NH: New England Grassroots Environment Fund, 2021), 27.
9. Robinson, 38.
10. A shared gifting circle is when a group of people come together to collectively distribute an already-fundraised pool of money.

CHAPTER 7

Global Participatory Grantmaking
Through a Climate Justice Lens

Laura García and Teresa Odendahl

As the adverse effects of climate change increase, philanthropy is beginning to pay more attention to climate justice as an orientation that addresses the root causes of the crisis, along with the inequalities experienced by those communities most affected by it. This orientation, however, requires philanthropy to radically shift the way that it has addressed climate and environmental issues to reach those whom it has most underresourced and undervalued. Participatory grantmaking is arguably the best practice to achieve this transformation and find the solutions that the climate crisis requires.

In support of this claim, the authors offer three case studies of global funders that have been making grants to climate justice groups and movements around the world using participatory models: Global Greengrants Fund; FRIDA, the Young Feminist Fund; and Fondo Centroamericano de Mujeres / Central America Women's Fund. Through conversations with representatives of these organizations, the authors provide an overview of their history and participatory approaches and a comparative analysis of their models, which fall on an evolving spectrum of participation. Ultimately, the authors show that by centering support on Indigenous Peoples, people with disabilities, women, and youth, these funders have been able to develop more integrated and interconnected approaches to resource allocation.

Finally, the authors explore potential issues that participatory grantmakers will need to address as the model continues to evolve in the face of the urgent global climate crisis. This includes challenging philanthropy to acknowledge, grapple with, and upend the patriarchal, racist, capitalist, and colonialist systems and structures that have been part of its own history. The authors suggest that shifting the structures of inequality and power will not only allow participatory grantmakers to strengthen their practices but also generate more impact in addressing the climate and other crises.

GLOBAL PARTICIPATORY GRANTMAKING AND MOVEMENT BUILDING

> "Participatory grantmaking decolonizes philanthropy and puts beneficiaries in the center. All grantmaking should be participatory so that philanthropy isn't about handouts, but rather, about both sides (funder and grantee) solving common problems and common issues. Grantmaking should not be unidirectional. It should be a relationship between the grantmaker and beneficiary".[1]
> —Samuel Nnah Ndobe, Central Africa Advisory Board, Global Greengrants Fund

Reflecting other forms of imperialism, Europe and the United States have exported their forms of charity and philanthropy around the world, which leaves decision-making power primarily in the hands of individuals and families with wealth or "experts" whom they employ.[2] Whatever the instruments or mechanisms used for funding, which often mirror the charitable values of the upper classes, this kind of elite philanthropy is more beneficial for the privileged and "their" institutions than for the disadvantaged, marginalized, overlooked, and poor.[3]

Outside this imported grantmaking style, global philanthropy has taken many different participatory forms. According to Titilope Ajayi, philanthropy in non-Western countries is not always giving for its own sake; it also fulfills economic and emotional needs. Communities and extended families care for each other. Mutual aid societies, which were formed over centuries, meet various, interconnected community needs. The Igbo people of wealth in eastern Nigeria, for example, train selected apprentices in trades and other crafts and set them up in business once they attain the required level of proficiency. In addition to providing economic empowerment, this kind of philanthropy enhances awareness of people's interconnectedness and upholds values of community, sharing, and reciprocity by encouraging beneficiaries to pay forward the kindness they have received. Through this practice, hundreds of young men and women have become self-reliant members of society who might not ordinarily qualify for strategic assistance from philanthropic foundations.[4]

This chapter focuses on the participatory grantmaking practices that some global grantmakers have developed that stem from the values that inspired them to develop these kinds of approaches. It is important to note that the term "global" participatory grantmaking is a misnomer because participatory grantmaking takes many forms in different parts of the world. A range of participatory practices are undertaken in majority countries (often referred to as the Global North or Western countries).[5] And there are funders such as FRIDA and Global Greengrants that make grants globally using participatory practices. We believe some of the most effective and innovative forms of grantmaking have originated outside the United States and Europe; however, to date, there has been no comprehensive research on this topic internationally.

While there is considerable variance in participatory philanthropic approaches across countries and regions, a common thread is a belief that resisting elite, class-based forms of philanthropy can help "decolonize philanthropy."[6] This belief is also at the core of climate justice philanthropy, which aims to decolonize the resources, information, decisions, and power of those engaged in climate-related action so that these resources can be redistributed back to the communities harmed by climate change. In participatory systems, grassroots and traditional knowledge—such as how communities are adapting to climate change through regenerative practices in agriculture, the preservation of land and livelihoods, and other localized initiatives—is acknowledged and elevated. This kind of knowledge is largely ignored or devalued by the larger climate narrative—to which many foundations still adhere—but is highlighted and supported by participatory practices that put communities' priorities front and center.

Perhaps one of the most important reasons why participatory approaches are useful and needed in climate change work is their focus on and support for movement building. This is in direct contrast to more mainstream US foundations, which tend to support specific projects, outcomes, or issues. Participatory grantmakers support an array of interconnected issues, populations, and efforts that make up and build grassroots climate justice movements because they believe that it is through movements that power is built and ideas proliferate. At the same time, the nonlinear, spontaneous progress and aims of movements make their growth and achievements difficult to quantify and meet preset objectives. For example, movements often have considerably diverse efforts, players, and issues because of the different needs that communities identify. This necessitates a more comprehensive approach where all these pieces are understood to be part of a larger, interconnected ecosystem, which is quite different from the one-size-fits-all strategy many traditional funders employ.

Participatory grantmakers around the world are comfortable with these challenges and nuances and see them as integral components of all participatory processes, including funding. What follows is a description of how this approach strengthens the climate justice movement and why those in mainstream philanthropy who are committed to climate justice need to take it seriously.

SUPPORTING THE CLIMATE JUSTICE MOVEMENT WITH PARTICIPATORY GRANTMAKING

> If we want to talk about climate justice, first of all, the most powerful must take responsibility for what they have done and what they are doing and what they have done to the planet. Secondly, we can also talk about our place as women within those spaces, and begin to say that if we want a comprehensive environmental justice that resolves all the violence that we experience as peasant women, Indigenous women in contexts of environmental pollution, mining, extractivism, agro-industry, half dams, etc., we need to talk about a feminist justice, especially because it is important to think about all these areas of violence.[7]
>
> —Carmen Aliaga, from Bolivia, and Colectivo Casa

The climate crisis requires us to reflect on alternative, collective futures. Capitalism, patriarchy, and racism have captured the modern imagination to the point that we have not yet been able to reshape our systems. Significant resources are invested in the discovery of technologies to mitigate climate change (e.g., hypothetical devices to pull carbon out of the atmosphere), while grassroots solutions are undervalued—even though larger-scale solutions at best ignore, and at worst perpetuate, the deep structural inequities that are at the root of the climate crisis and other environmental disasters.

For this reason, climate justice—perhaps more urgently than any other problem—demands grassroots responses that can be supported through participatory grantmaking, a core element of which is the participation of local people who are directly connected to the issue and who bring important diversity, knowledge, experience, and observational evidence to the table. Because mainstream philanthropy tends to operate from afar and limits its reach to grassroots organizations, it will be structurally difficult for them to play this kind of role. More than simply alternative models of philanthropy, participatory approaches (1) understand and value intersectionality and apply this perspective in decision-making, and (2) seek to dismantle power inequities and imbalances.[8]

Participatory Approaches Understand and Value Intersectionality

Developed by the legal scholar Kimberlé Crenshaw in 1989, "intersectionality" is at the heart of what has come to be known as modern critical theory. Systematic oppression—whether due to racism, sexism, classism, ableism, homophobia, transphobia, xenophobia, or other -isms and -phobias—are so interconnected that they cannot be understood without reference to each other. For example, an Indigenous woman—living in Sub-Saharan Africa, South or Southeast Asia, or Latin America—who may walk miles every day to collect water for her family, is not exacerbating the climate crisis but is at a much greater risk than a middle-class white American man or woman who drives a car with a combustion engine.

Part of what is understood and critiqued by those in climate justice movements are the ways in which the climate crisis and its solutions have different effects on different members of society, especially marginalized peoples living in majority countries who face many intersecting forms of oppression that exacerbate their climate-related obstacles. Extreme climate change coexists with anthropocentric, colonialist, racist, and xenophobic ideologies about which humans and/or species merit saving and which do not. These forms of crisis response are already shaping decisions and policy. Governments, for example, are paying poorer countries to lock up climate migrants to keep them from arriving to their shores. Billionaires are planning to colonize other planets to save themselves. And geoengineering techniques are injecting harmful aerosols into the stratosphere to reflect the sun away from the Earth.

In short, false climate solutions are not grounded in rebuilding a just world for everyone because they fail to consider the source of the problem, lack accountability to the most affected people, and usually exclude communities from participating in these decisions. Without their full participation—as well as societies outside the Global North elite, BIPOC and LGBTQIA2S+ communities, Indigenous Peoples, women, people with disabilities, and youth who are at the forefront and most affected in climate decision-making—the perspectives we need to fully challenge this complex global problem will be painfully absent.[9]

Grassroots activists understand that a sustainable future does not hinge on a single large-scale solution or a novel technology put forward by a few individuals in power, but rather on culturally specific, contextualized solutions led by people collaborating in organized groups. Climate justice grassroots movements, therefore, use diverse, intersectional approaches in their work.[10] The youth climate movement, for example, is helping people fight for democratic spaces to protect their own lives and future. Women's leadership in grassroots climate action is bringing attention to the interconnectedness between health and climate as well as the economy of care and local food production. Feminist climate justice is clarifying how violence against the land is another face of the same system that uses violence against women's bodies. Indigenous People are prioritizing the significance of local livelihoods, well-being, and traditional systems of governance to address climate change at the local level. With their knowledge, Indigenous Peoples are advancing efforts in agroforestry, biodiversity conservation, traditional medicine, and resource management—as well as to strengthen climate resilience mechanisms, from their observation to their natural environments.

These movements demonstrate that more diverse leadership leads to more diverse knowledge, approaches, and options that generate more resilient and workable solutions. In fact, local environmental work and grassroots climate efforts are already contributing to sustaining life in communities, protecting resources, and demonstrating alternative futures, despite receiving little or no philanthropic support.[11] For example, while 80 percent of the world's biodiversity is being stewarded by Indigenous Peoples, philanthropy allocates less than 1 percent of its resources to Indigenous Peoples' organizations to reduce deforestation, despite it being an effective strategy, as evidenced by the well-conserved natural habitats in which they live. To Indigenous Peoples, land is inseparable from existence, and we are human only in connection with our reciprocal relationship with Mother Earth—a stark contrast from the technocratic and individualistic perspectives that dominate current climate change policy development.[12] Philanthropy also falls short in supporting women-led climate action. Despite women being at the forefront of grassroots environmental work, only 0.2 percent of all foundation funding focuses explicitly on women and the environment.[13]

Both examples underscore the need for a paradigm shift in how governments, societies, and philanthropy respond to the climate crisis. Specifically, if philanthropy wants to resolve the climate crisis, it must find ways to democratize climate funding so that an equitable share of resources reaches grassroots groups and organizations. Given the structural inequities that exclude grassroots movements from philanthropy, the most effective path to reverse this trend is through participatory grantmaking.

Participatory Approaches Seek to Dismantle Power Inequities and Imbalances

We are here to ask ourselves how to continuously hold ourselves accountable to the movements we support and to acknowledge the power dynamics as we do that. We are very clear that having a space, a mechanism that was for and by young feminists would lead us on our path to being able to transform power.[14]
—Maria Alejandra Rodriguez Acha, from Peru,
co-executive director of FRIDA

When activists take control of where funding goes, they are challenging the power structures in philanthropy that reinforce inequality and colonial systems. Moreover, as the demands for intersectional and grassroots approaches permeate philanthropy, participatory grantmaking becomes the natural and most effective path to guarantee these shifts. Without participatory grantmaking, philanthropy will find it extremely difficult to guarantee that the money reaches grassroots movements and their agendas. This is because participatory grantmaking models are an effective way to identify what is typically outside funders' radar.

Furthermore, climate movements are calling for justice through radical and urgent systems shifting—an important part of the participatory process. Climate justice demands not only a perspective of just urgency but also a sense of urgent justice. Short- and long-term needs should be addressed simultaneously because "equity is not secondary to survival, as some suggest, it is survival."[15] For funders, participatory grantmaking is one of the most valuable tools for meeting this call and bringing grassroots stakeholders into climate spaces, conversations, and solutions.

One of the challenges for this process, however, is the perception that participatory grantmaking values fairness over wisdom—that is, equitable participation may conflict with traditional decision-making processes in which credentialed experts have more voice in making certain decisions because their perspectives are seen as more valuable.[16] When it comes to climate justice, the authors believe that "expert" versus "equitable participation" is a false dichotomy because the most informed experts on climate effects are those who have experienced them. The best solutions to the climate crisis will involve extensive changes that can only be brought about through a conversation that involves the full spectrum of global perspectives and experiences. The climate crisis urgently requires a more representative, inclusive public conversation where decisions about money and power are critically evaluated.

Learning from the experience of past decades, international efforts to address the climate crisis are (albeit slowly) shifting their attention to more integral, participatory approaches. Recommendations from panels of credentialed experts and scientists, in fact, include ensuring that climate solutions incorporate equitable representation as well as more participation of groups that are most vulnerable to climate change and that lack access to resources.[17] Some foundations and climate philanthropists are also turning their attention to grassroots action. At the United Nations Climate Change Conference in Glasgow in November 2021, governments and private funders announced a historic $1.7 billion pledge to "prioritise the inclusion of Indigenous Peoples and local communities in decision-making and in the design and implementation of relevant programmes and finance instruments, recognising the interests of vulnerable and marginalised groups including women and girls, people with disabilities, and youth."[18]

Commitments such as this one are significant steps forward to making philanthropy more accessible to and representative of grassroots climate solutions, yet many questions remain. If there is increased financing for grassroots movements, how is that funding going to be redistributed? What are the participatory and accountability mechanisms that will ensure the inclusion of Indigenous Peoples and local communities in the design and implementation phases? Given their current funding structures, how will foundations and governments frame their work to support grassroots climate action in a way that recognizes the interests of vulnerable and marginalized groups?

The CLIMA Fund—a collaborative of grassroots climate funders using participatory approaches that has leveraged $10 million and made 300+ grants during its first five years—highlighted these issues in *Soil to Sky: Climate Solutions That Work*, a report that uplifts grassroots climate solutions.[19] According to the report, "by tackling climate change through lenses such as health and gender equity, grassroots solutions more effectively tie climate action to broader development goals. Providing solutions to impacts of climate change, such as increased frequency of extreme climatic events and drought, also helps to support human rights, such as rights to food, water, health, and sustainable local livelihoods."

The publication adds that grassroots climate solutions "may have common characteristics globally but are unique to specific geographies, communities, landscapes, and ecosystems. Because the impacts of climate change are place-based, their solutions must also be customized to locales to maximize effectiveness and local buy-in, which help ensure success." Climate funding also needs to be especially intersectional, wide-encompassing and allow for thematic flexibility. Participatory grantmaking fits well into this approach because collective deliberation typically generates a wider frame in which more diverse, plural, and imaginative strategies are included.

Another strength of participatory grantmaking is that it can be a space for activists in the climate movement to practice deliberation, increase understanding of financing trends and their relationship to developing larger agendas, and advocate for climate justice priorities in other philanthropic spaces. In a study to assess the literature of participatory governance and its effectiveness in environmental planning to tackle climate change, Aylett argues that "participatory forums provide community-based organizations with an opportunity to institutionalize and scale up their concerns to the level of the city as a whole."[20] Participation, debate, and deliberation are transformative processes for climate activists who have the opportunity to learn the language of philanthropy and practice a political relationship with money that gives them the power to advance their agendas.

Potentially, participatory grantmaking also gives climate activists the chance to strengthen their ability to influence climate justice funding decisions, especially if that process is sufficiently open and not just concentrated on grantee selection. When it offers spaces for integral deliberation of ideas, participatory grantmaking is an instrument of movement building that not only ensures fairness but also strengthens activists' capacities to advocate for more and better funding for their diverse, intersectional agendas.

In summary, participatory grantmaking values and incorporates intersectionality, and it dismantles power inequities and imbalances—two core strengths of the approach. Nevertheless, achieving justice through participatory practices takes time. Participatory grantmaking for climate justice requires building trusted relationships, systems of accountability, and shared learning, among other processes that are slow but have a long-lasting impact. Calls to decolonize climate philanthropy demand moving beyond a "politics of urgency" to carefully examining the historical processes of patriarchy, racialization, colonialism, and imperialism. Given the urgency to respond to the climate crisis, funders are tempted to skip these meaningful but slow processes that shift power and create systemic change, and instead fund initiatives that prioritize scaling up and changing larger legal or political systems without the inclusion of the affected communities in the planning and the implementation of those initiatives.

THREE CASE STUDIES OF GLOBAL PARTICIPATORY GRANTMAKING

To demonstrate the need for philanthropy to shift from how it has traditionally addressed climate and environmental issues—specifically, by adopting a climate justice orientation—the authors offer three case studies of global funders that have been making grants to climate justice groups and movements around the world using participatory models. These organizations are the Global Greengrants Fund; FRIDA, the Young Feminist Fund; and Fondo Centroamericano de Mujeres / Central America Women's Fund.

Overview and Methodology

In 2022, the authors undertook three case studies that highlight the importance of participatory approaches in international climate justice funding. Fondo Centroamericano de Mujeres / Central America Women's Fund (FCAM) introduced and continues to use a highly participatory model, including applicants in decision-making about proposals. FRIDA, the Young Feminist Fund, inspired by and with the support from FCAM, expanded young women's grantmaking to majority countries. The Global Greengrants Fund (Greengrants, for short) was the earliest experimenter, with several deliberative participatory models on a worldwide scale. All three funds support grassroots climate justice and have been collaborating for years on different initiatives that support grassroots climate justice movements.

It is important to note that the authors used a case study approach to illustrate how participatory grantmaking is used to advance climate justice because there has not yet been a comprehensive mapping of participatory grantmakers, either based in majority countries or that support work in these regions, let alone those who work with climate justice. This complicates any attempt to analyze global tendencies or draw conclusions. Nevertheless, they hope these three cases can offer important insights about how climate justice grantmaking can incorporate grassroots participation in ways that reflect the interconnectedness of climate and other social justice issues.

Background

The people doing the work on the ground understand the context, the reality. They are the people who need to be informed about what philanthropy does, who it funds, and what it looks like. They are the people that need to be leading it.[21]
—Paige Andrew, from the Republic of Trinidad and Tobago, programs comanager for participatory grantmaking and operations at FRIDA

Three case studies—of FCAM, FRIDA, and Greengrants—illustrate how organizations are using participatory models to advance climate justice globally. Each was created to serve urgent needs that were being unmet by either governments or philanthropy. Each recognized a funding gap as well as a need to mobilize new resources, expand existing ones, and support crucial, groundbreaking work. All these funds see the voices, experiences, and knowledge of Indigenous Peoples, people with disabilities, women, and youth in decision-making as essential. And each understands the need for better and more funding for solutions to climate change.

These are also well-established funds that have been making participatory grants for a decade or more. For thirty years, Greengrants has used a participatory grantmaking model to support grassroots causes and groups advocating for environmental and human rights. With advisers from around the world recommending and accompanying grantees, Greengrants' goal has been to ensure that the power of decision-making is distributed widely and anchored in movements. For nearly twenty years, FCAM has been supporting the emotional, financial, physical, and political sustainability of women and feminist movements in Central America. Over a decade ago, FRIDA put decision-making directly in the hands of young feminists who decide where to distribute flexible funds globally to feminist youth.

It is important to note that FCAM, FRIDA, and Greengrants are all intermediary funders, which means that they raise money from foundations, individuals, and other sources to make grants to activist groups. While all participatory models involve the communities they serve in decision-making, each fund approaches these partnerships in its own way.

The Global Greengrants Fund

"There are a number of strengths in Greengrants' participatory grantmaking model. We are really connected with the issues on the ground and the grantmakers and activists in the country where we work. The most positive strength is that our network is global.... The decisions we take are informed by the people who are right at the center, the groups of communities that are seeing a problem firsthand and are looking into every angle to create a solution."[22]
—Hilma Angula, from Namibia, adviser on Greengrants' Next Generation Youth Climate Advisory Board reports

Greengrants was created by a small group of environmental activists and philanthropists who recognized the tremendous value of grassroots environmental and social justice action taking place outside of the United States and Europe, most of it with little or no access to funding. Greengrants' cofounders—three Americans and a Brazilian—saw that with ample support, the potential of these grassroots movements to bring about real change was enormous, but that the challenge was how to reach the multitude of small organizations at their heart.

[Greengrants] grew out of existing networks of environmental organizers who had, in many cases, learned to depend on each other for information, help, and even protection in some of these places. They're people with integrity who also know the lay of the land in their home countries and regions. They know who they can and can't trust, and they depend on each other for informal feedback and mutual support. So when we ask[ed] them to help us identify new and emerging groups and individuals as prospective grantees, they tend[ed] to suggest groups and individuals that they have faith in and that are in a position to strengthen and advance their specific causes as well as the civil society movement in general[23]
—Chet Tchozewski, Global Greengrants Fund's cofounder, who became its first executive director

Working from this original model since the early 2000s, Greengrants has built a network of more than 200 advisers, all respected activists and experts from around the world, who serve with their peers on regional or thematic advisory boards. Greengrants also works with international nongovernmental organizations to make funding decisions and is active in a number of collaborative funding efforts. All Greengrants advisers are trusted volunteers who are passionate about environmental justice and human rights. In addition to selecting grantees, many advisors accompany these groups, leaders, and members as their work evolves.

In about 2011, the new second executive director of Greengrants, Terry Odendahl, and other staff in the United States began raising funds earmarked for resourcing grassroots groups seeking solutions to climate change. Greengrants' advisory boards were offered an additional 10 percent to their budgets to identify local and regional efforts around climate change adaptation and mitigation. Advisory board coordinators responded positively but also noted they were already working on climate justice because they saw every environmental issue as interconnected; in fact, they felt that focusing so narrowly on climate would actually restrict advisers' autonomy and strategic responsibilities. Those insights led to Greengrants developing a method of tagging each grant in multiple ways, depending on the issue, constituency, and/or other activities it was undertaking. By doing so, the fund was explicitly acknowledging these interconnections and that climate grants rarely fall into a single category.

Greengrants' network has led to the funding of grassroots organizations across Africa, the Arctic, Asia, Latin America, the Pacific Islands, and most recently, the Middle East. This grantmaking has helped to grow and accelerate global movements for climate justice. Greengrants' model and infrastructure have enabled it to become one of the first funders capable of supporting grassroots movements at the most fundamental level: through grants to grassroots organizations that are just beginning or developing their work, and those that have traditionally had the least access to funding. Over nearly thirty years, Global Greengrants Fund has awarded more than 14,000 grants, totaling over $100 million to grassroots groups in 168 countries.

FCAM

> To achieve the structural changes we want, power relations must be transformed; power must be placed in the movements. And convinced of this, we decided to start from within our organization. The FCAM, since 2004, is one of the pioneering organizations at a global level in terms of participatory selection processes which has inspired other models, such as the FRIDA Fund, and adapted it to make it global.[24]
>
> —Carla López, FCAM's executive director

Based in Costa Rica, FCAM was formed in 2003 as the first feminist and participatory grantmaker in Central America. FCAM supports organizations led by women, trans, and nonbinary people who are part of women's and feminist movements in Central America.

FCAM currently has four major funding areas that support women's organizations in Central America that are working on the following issues:

- Justice and sustainability: organizations building resilience in the face of the environmental and climate crisis and oppressive economic and punitive justice systems (including the defense of territories and natural assets) and those influencing, leading, and building comprehensive alternatives that link gender justice with economic, environmental, climate, and restorative justice.
- Freedom and autonomy: organizations defending the right(s) of people to make decisions about their lives, bodies, identities, orientations, and gender expressions.
- Life in dignity: organizations advocating for a life free from violence (structural, physical, emotional, symbolic, and economic), the right to migrate in safe and dignified conditions, the rights of the *maquila* (factory workers) and domestic workers, and care work.
- Solidarity and resilience: organizations that are providing a variety of support and technical assistance aimed at strengthening climate justice groups' physical and emotional sustainability, as well as ensuring the well-being, care, and safety of those who defend human rights.

In its early years, the fund's work team were all adult women who recognized a need to include young women as central to the fund's mission. Eventually, this also led to FCAM's assistance in forming FRIDA.

FCAM also leads the Global Alliance for Green and Gender Action (GAGGA) in coordination with two other global grantmaking funds, Both ENDS and Mama Cash. With Dutch government funding, they have developed a grantmaking program focused on strengthening grassroots organizations' capacity to advocate at the intersection of women's and environmental rights. GAGGA is the result of a collaboration of many actors that have been key in the program's success: grassroots groups, nongovernmental organizations, women's funds, environmental justice funds, and other ally organizations. Together, they work collaboratively toward a common goal of creating a world in which women of all ages and conditions can exercise their right to water, food security, and a clean, safe, and healthy environment.

In the last eighteen years of work, FCAM has become a model of support for the diversity of women and feminists in Central American social movements, from the defense of water to the feminist movement for people with disabilities. FCAM continues to be the most important philanthropic institution in Central America providing support to feminist movements, particularly to organizations that are outside funders' radar and face obstacles in securing financing.

FRIDA

> I remember being in conversations at the very beginning and people asking why we needed a Young Feminist Fund if there were women's funds and they were already funding youth.... We wanted to shift power.... We were very clear that having a space, a mechanism that was for and by young feminists would lead us on our path to being able to transform power.[25]
> —Amina Doherty, a Nigerian/Antiguan feminist and FRIDA's first coordinator

The idea to create FRIDA, a fund to support young feminists, first emerged at a meeting supported by the Global Fund for Women, which was coordinated by the Association for Women's Rights. Continuing the conversations and ideations of the fund, the Association for Women's Rights joined efforts with FCAM to benefit from their experience in supporting youth-led activism through inclusive mechanisms. The young feminist activists leading the process invited other, multigenerational feminist networks and the women's funding community—with a special focus on majority countries—to participate. FRIDA is still the only global youth-led fund dedicated to supporting young feminist organizing.

FRIDA provides core flexible funding for emerging grassroots groups led by young feminists working on

- improving the lives of young women, girls, trans, and/or intersex youth at local, national, regional, and international levels;
- inclusive organizing; and
- collective action and feminist movement building.

In 2017, FRIDA established a special climate and environmental justice grantmaking funding program and welcomed the first cohort of grantee partners whose feminist work intersects with climate and environmental justice. They learned, however, that this grantmaking approach may have inadvertently separated groups that prioritized climate justice efforts from those whose work also addresses climate justice but have other priority issues. Working in this way boxed grantee partners into categories that did not fit the needs of organizing as it existed on the ground. As a result, climate was not specifically referenced in FRIDA's call for proposals in 2022.

Envisioning a world where young women, girls, and trans youth are recognized as experts of their own reality, enjoying their human rights and building a more just and sustainable world through collective power and transformative leadership, FRIDA provides funding and accompaniment to support and amplify the activism of girls, young women, trans, intersex, and nonbinary youth against all violence, oppression, and inequality. In the past eleven years, FRIDA has leveraged more than $7.5 million to support over 250 young feminist initiatives across 115 majority countries in the world.

Models of Participatory Grantmaking Processes

Global Greengrants Fund

The fund's participatory practices include activists, movement leaders, and other experts in finding and eventually deciding on potential grantees. Over the years, several more nuanced versions of this participatory model have been adopted and utilized by Greengrants.

The first model, developed in the early 2000s, was a partnership with existing progressive, international, environmental nongovernmental organizations whose staff recommended local groups for funding. This model continues today in an expanded version with these collaborations: 350.org, CLIMA, Earth Island Institute, Friends of the Earth International, GAGGA, International Rivers, Oilwatch International, Pesticide Action Network, and Rainforest Action Network.

The original model had limitations, however, because Greengrants was only reaching organizations connected to these networks, and the advisers recommending funding could be quite removed from the groups. A few years into Global Greengrants' operation, its cofounder and board member Wendy Emerick recommended expanding the pool of grant recommenders beyond the international partners by recruiting local activists in many different countries to serve as advisors. As Greengrants continued to expand its donor base and fund in several regions, there was a need to hire a second staff member, Chris Allen, and consultants who were instrumental in getting the earliest regional advisory boards started. Global Greengrants now has twenty-four regional advisory boards and organizational partners.

As this second participatory model was being created, regional advisers were identified and boards were formed around the world to provide grants that would meet grassroots actors where they were in terms of local needs, struggles, priorities, and aspirations. Compelling advantages included reliance on local knowledge, the ability to have trusted relationships with familiar local people representing Greengrants, more accessible grants, and the unanticipated discovery that most grantees were receiving their first outside funding.

Growing from the regional board model, Greengrants helped to establish and continues to provide substantial resources to local and regional environmental funds, some of which replaced advisory boards in certain regions. In 2003, the Samdhana Institute began allocating funds in Indonesia, the Philippines, and Southeast Asia. A couple of years later, CASA Socio Environmental Fund was founded in Brazil. In 2007, Fondo Acción Solidaria was founded in Mexico and, more recently, Fondo Tierra Viva in Central America and the He Yi Institute in China were established. To this day, Greengrants partners with and supports these regional organizations in their participatory grantmaking processes.

In 2002, a third model of participatory grantmaking emerged, which included thematic boards. The first focused on the International Financial Institutions Advisory Board, followed by the youth-led Next Generation Youth Climate Advisory Board. Diverse advisers operating at a global scale, rather than from a single organization or part of the world, were now able to work together as members of these boards on cross-regional learning and strategy, with the potential for more traction on specific issues.

FCAM

A core part of FCAM's participatory grantmaking process is including all applicant groups in each cycle of its final grantmaking decisions. A simple application process makes it easy for new and smaller groups to access resources. In addition to the opportunity to participate, current and potential grantee partners also meet potential allies and learn about new strategies for women's rights. The selection model is anonymous; groups have information only about the proposed initiatives. Because of this, participant organizations have the same opportunities to be selected in an inclusive, democratic, and transparent process. As Claudia Samcam, FCAM's development and alliances coordinator, notes, "The participatory selection process is an open process: we'll keep permanently learning, and we always can improve."

FRIDA

Modeled on FCAM, FRIDA has all the same participatory processes, but with some additional features. For instance, groups apply for a grant of $6,000 that is flexible and can be used over a period of twelve months for general support. It is open to renewal. As a language justice practice, FRIDA receives applications in Arabic, English, French, Portuguese, Russian, and Spanish.

Its grantmaking process includes these key steps:

- Call for application: Young feminist groups from any of the majority countries can submit an application.
- Screening process: FRIDA staff and regional advisers review proposals to consider the different contexts and confirm eligibility. Eligible applications are sent to the voting stage.
- Voting: Eligible groups are placed in subregional and/or thematic voting groups and applicants vote for the top applications in their region.
- Final decisions: A regional committee comprising FRIDA staff, advisers, and current grantee partners review the voting groups and the top-voted groups.
- Grants award: A final list of applicants is determined and emails are sent to successful applicants officially welcoming them to the FRIDA community as FRIDA grantee partners.

All FRIDA grantee partners have access to capacity-strengthening support as they begin to carry out activities. At the end of one year, FRIDA grantee partners are asked to submit an online report via FRIDA's grantmaking platform to share their achievements, challenges, and work throughout the year. Groups are also invited to apply for a renewal of their grants.

FRIDA's participatory practices go beyond selecting groups for funding to incorporating processes that include wide-ranging stakeholders in strategic thinking. For example, in 2020, FRIDA launched a strategic planning process that included advisers, staff, board, and grantee partners. FRIDA's new strategic plan acknowledges complexity and a process of learning that is agile, flexible, and adaptive.

Common Themes

Despite some differences in their approaches to participatory grantmaking, all three funds share several values and practices. One of the most important is that their agendas are set by grantees, not the grantmakers. Each fund is also consciously attempting to support change, rather than the status quo.

There is an element of political subversiveness to funding social movements that the funds recognize and endorse. The groups that FCAM, FRIDA, and Greengrants support are primarily activist organizations and, as such, are integral to local, regional, and/or international environmental, feminist, and human rights movements. While advisers and employees of the funds are often activists themselves, when they represent philanthropic organizations they are not "in" the movement but rather provide financial and capacity-building support for its infrastructure.

All three funds indicate that they "accompany" or provide "accompaniment" to their grantees and various movements—terms of art that can be both figurative and literal. At a basic level, the funds stand in solidarity with the movements and movement groups they support. At FCAM and FRIDA, the staff members consider themselves part of the movement as activists. At Greengrants, most of the advisers are activists. A specific duty or role of Greengrants advisers is accompaniment, and in some regions, mentorship. Even the notion of mentorship, however, points to the power of the funder in comparison with the grantee. Who is mentoring whom? The question of whether funders are part of movements is outside our scope here, although it has been debated at many Greengrants advisory board meetings.

For all three funds, issue interconnectedness is central to grassroots, environmental, and feminist movement building. Because there are no environmental issues that can be separated from climate or the people who live on Earth, the funds' participatory grantmaking processes understand these issues as inextricably linked. Rather than donors, foundations, or their employees making funding decisions, those most affected by interconnected issues are doing so—an approach that is changing the nature of philanthropy around the world.

WHAT CAN PHILANTHROPY LEARN FROM PARTICIPATORY GRANTMAKING?

Participatory grantmaking is not a magical tool that will allow philanthropy to adequately address all its shortcomings and save the world. It is a practice that, if in a constant state of revision and improvement, can significantly reshape philanthropy to become a better reflection of the world it wants to see. While participatory grantmaking is an evolutionary step in philanthropy and is constantly changing itself, it has much to offer traditional or mainstream funders that are committed to addressing climate change. Here are five takeaways.

Understanding and integrating intersectionality in funding strategies and allocations is important. Just as cultures and societies evolve, social movements are learning, shifting, and growing, but they still have gaps and oversights. A relevant example is the lack of connectivity between the disability rights movement and the climate justice movement. Yolanda Muñoz, a former program officer at the Disability Rights Fund and current Greengrants adviser, explains why the environmental justice movement has not had a disability lens:

> From my perspective, environmental justice is not the only field of social justice that has fallen behind the inclusion of disability in their agenda. It is actually very rare that environmental justice and climate action movements include people with disabilities in their strategies, because they have very low expectations about our potential to contribute to the community.... To promote a constructive dialogue, people with disabilities and environmental justice promoters need to learn from each other's agenda to determine the main common areas of interest.... Transitioning towards a more just and environmentally responsible culture requires avoiding working in silos: disability rights are also environmental rights. But ultimately, the narrative we have pushed regarding disabled people is one of transition from victims to leaders. This is extremely important to highlight for many reasons but mostly because it is an effective counter-narrative to disability stigma.[26]

When part of a movement is not seen or an issue that disproportionately affects certain groups is ignored, the whole movement suffers—including the climate justice movement. This issue also surfaces in philanthropy as well as in debates about who is missing and which rights and social justice issues need to be more connected. While issues and approaches can change over time, tending to become more inclusive and complex, this transformation tends to occur more quickly in social movements than in mainstream philanthropy, which still silos—rather than connects—diverse issues, perspectives, and organizations.

In contrast, participatory grantmaking encourages integration and collaboration by making learning one of its key goals. Participants' opportunity to incorporate an ecosystemic, integrated lens into the grantmaking process can potentially influence the interconnectedness of their own activist agendas. For example, Greengrants' advisory network's intentional outreach to disability rights organizations has helped that network identify and connect with more groups that had not originally been visible to them, reviewing existing challenges of accessibility and recognizing issues of ableism within different cultures.

Barriers that keep philanthropy from contributing to social change need to be dismantled. Dismantling barriers is another key recommendation, according to Sukuamis, to bring more intersectionality and representation in philanthropy:

> One of the challenges of a participatory model is ensuring that it is part of a broader process that represents social movements. Representing social movement means supporting their agenda rather than select groups that have the access and the connections to the spaces. For philanthropy to change profoundly, we must continue to push on this issue to ensure that we are not only creating a participatory process, but a truly community-centric space that is accessible (thinking about anti-ableist practices, language justice, as well as technology) by and for the community.[27]

In table 7.1, Sukuamis identifies different strategies and approaches that funders might implement in their participatory models. As shown, participatory grantmaking has various degrees of participation, access, representation, and reach. These nuances have different social and political implications for participatory grantmaking's impact.

As shown in table 7.1, the different strategies and approaches vary in how much control, access, representation, and decision-making are held by the communities and movements that philanthropy is serving. Clearly, power is at the center of the discussion in participatory grantmaking models. It determines who is included in the processes, to what extent and manner people participate, and which decisions are taken. While funders can finance and promote participatory spaces with activists, it is important to recognize

Table 7.1: Community-Centric Analysis of Participatory Grantmaking

Strategy	Approach
Internal representation	Staff is representative of the communities and social movements the organization is serving
	Board is representative of the communities and social movements the organization is serving
Access	Application process (types include open, invitation-only, and recommendations from grantee partners)
	Filtering of applicants (Who will be reviewing applicant information and how will they approach filtering them?)
Communities/movements as decision-makers	Communities/movements (applicants participate in the selection process)
	Community/movement representative (How will this person be nominated and selected, are there term limitations, will they be compensated for their time and labor?)
Resourcing movements	Terms of funding (< 1 year, 1–2 years, 2+ years)
	Type of funding (general/flexible, project)
	Emergency
Co-strategizing with the movements	Co-construction of strategic plans
	Co-construction of participatory grantmaking model
	Mutual accountability practices and collective impact analysis

Source: Author data.

that funders will always represent power. *Denying* the power that funders hold or attempting to fully erase power through participatory processes is a false and misleading path. Participatory grantmaking processes do not shift all of the power that funders have. Although funders shift decision-making to the hands of activists, it would be misleading to assume that they do not have any more decision-making power, let alone the power that is carried by having the money and giving it away, with all of the cultural and social implications therein.

Acknowledging and more systematically dismantling power imbalances and inequities are critical. A more genuine and ethical position for funders, especially funders from the Global North, is to continually acknowledge their power and be open to finding ways to deconstruct the colonial, patriarchal, and racist mind-sets embedded in culture. In doing so, funders can discover new resources or added value that they can bring into participatory models.

For example, many funders are part of larger networks with which they can connect grantees in need of financial resources, opportunities, and information. Participatory grantmakers could also facilitate connections among activists and invest in and coordinate spaces for them to exchange ideas that allow for power to be consciously questioned openly and contested. Shying away from the privileged position that funders have by not offering these resources and opportunities to movements they support is doing a disservice to those movements.

Community learning, deliberation, and knowledge-sharing are all important. If the purpose of participatory grantmaking is to cede power about the grantmaking process—of which learning is an important part—who decides what information is learned and through which channels? How can a participatory process support an exchange of ideas, discussion, and deliberation that sees both funders and activists as having valuable knowledge, experience, and insights to provide in pursuit of common goals?

If, however, a participatory grantmaking process is also a space for learning, deliberation, and exchange of ideas, is it valid that the funders offer information to the participants on opportunities to enhance more intersectionality and provide the tools to interconnect issues that are evident from the "global" lens that the funder has acquired through its work? In a participatory grantmaking round, could they promote the inclusion of other issues, groups, or movements that are not being considered by the participants if the reason for their exclusion is related to silos, biases, or lack of information?

Dialogue in participatory grantmaking enhances a constant practice of resistance and accountability to power. Attempting to avoid conflict and resistance reveals a superficial assumption of what power is. In contrast, participatory grantmaking encourages deliberation in open spaces where power is constantly checked and freedom is exercised, which often has much—if not more—value than making decisions of where the money actually goes. Through these conversations, funders have a huge opportunity to learn how inequalities are normalized and integrated into systems, as well as to identify the rationale of those systems of oppression that shape our institutions. In turn, participants have an opportunity to hold truth to power and reflect on the power of their own decisions.

Community ownership is critical for these efforts. According to Perla Vazquez and Laura Vergara from Sukuamis: "A reparative approach that prioritizes full community ownership is not an option, but a requirement. This means that the community is leading, envisioning, strategizing, represented, and deciding on all aspects of the grantmaking process. Participatory grantmaking potentially helps social movements gain more power because they get closer to controlling the money that goes to them. It is therefore a valuable movement-building tool."[28] However, there are different levels of participation and deliberation in grantmaking models, as evidenced throughout this book. A recommendation to participatory grantmakers who are interested in movement building is to critically evaluate whether their models allow for the two-way flow of ideas between movements and their participatory grantmaking spaces.

For global funds that finance climate justice, a key question for their learning and grantmaking practices is: What knowledge do they hold as funders that could help advance climate solutions? Funders have a considerable amount of information about grantees' work in different parts of the world. Can this knowledge strengthen understanding of the problem and possible solutions in ways that lead to better grantmaking priorities and choices? Funders can organize spaces where they share this information with their grantees to foster community learning. For example, FCAM and other feminist funds in majority countries have generated participatory processes for their learning, monitoring, and evaluation systems. Grantees share with one another their lessons learned, results, and challenges throughout their grant period. This is a fruitful exercise that promotes learning instead of merely reporting to the donor. Not surprisingly, this practice has also generated deeper collaboration among the grantees. Sustaining these structures and enabling the transformation from ideas into action is also a key role that funders can play.

Like all movements, climate justice is ever changing, and this affects funding. For climate justice participatory grantmakers, the context and history of the environmental movements are very important to consider. Youth climate activists, BIPOC, and women environmental defenders are at the frontlines of grassroots environmental movements and increasingly becoming the public face of a movement that has been historically dominated by Global North organizations. Moreover, there is an opportunity today to help larger movements—including feminist, labor rights, and racial justice ones—generate conversations that explore their overlapping goals and agendas, as well as potential opportunities for collaboration. The climate crisis urges the incorporation of climate-related implications to health care access, gender inequalities, racism, and economic inequalities, among other complex problems. This context represents an opportunity for climate justice participatory funders to continually evaluate their grantmaking models and align them with the evolutionary processes of the movements they support.

According to Peter Kostishack, Greengrants' former vice president and director of programs:

We still need to move towards better learning systems and finding ways to instrumentalize participatory decision-making processes. We recognize that the most valuable improvements of participatory grantmaking are much more centered around issues of power than techniques or technological systems, ranking systems, voting systems, [and the like. An] overreliance on procedural aspects might cause participants to be disingenuous in the process and feel distanced or unable to place their wisdom and reflections on those instruments. We cannot [idealize institutions and] ignore the role of debate. Power analysis allows us to improve who is included, what is discussed, and how decisions are made.[29]

In the context of intensifying polycrises (including the climate crisis), global grantmakers will be faced with increasing demands to address disasters and respond to emergencies. Contrary to what has been assumed, although participatory grantmaking processes require more time, it is not impossible to create participatory mechanisms that respond to emergencies. An example is the newly established Global Resilience Fund, launched in May 2020 to finance COVID-19 response efforts led by girls and young feminist activists.[30]

As seen in the history of FRIDA's conception, efforts such as the creation of the Global Resilience Fund are in themselves participatory processes where the learnings from other participatory funds shape the new systems. In this case, the Global Resilience Fund benefited from the insights of collaborating funds such as FCAM, FRIDA, Red Umbrella Fund, UHAI ESHRAI, and Urgent Action Fund Asia and Pacific.[31] The new fund also draws on the experience in Sierra Leone by Purposeful, a participatory Africa-based feminist hub for girls' activism that works all around the world, as well as the With and For Girls Fund, another Africa-based fund that supports girl activists, their allies, and girls' resistance around the globe.[32]

It takes time to build these kinds of relationships—those based on trust and accountability—and the processes to guide them. Like all movements, the climate justice movement is ever changing. As a result, participatory grantmaking models need to continually monitor their processes to ensure that they are accountable to their own principles and the social movements they support. When accountable systems are created, these models de-incentivize self-centered views and the abuse of power from anyone participating in them. The decisions of who is participating, the criteria for involving participants, and the arguments behind the decisions on funding priorities and grantees all require an important degree of transparency and accountability.

CONCLUSION

Many participatory grantmaking funders hold dear the values of trust, equity, justice, diversity, and representation and could potentially guide other funders in a process to strengthen or adjust their grantmaking models. In doing so, they would need to pay particular attention to issues of colonialist practices and funder biases—all the intersecting forms of oppression and power. Existing participatory grantmaking models could be strengthened to reflect not only the constant evolution of the specific movements they support but also the evolution and creative thinking of other movements, groups, and trends in flux. After all, funders—especially intermediary funders, because of their position within philanthropy—have an enormous capacity to connect money with opportunities, issues (through activists), and experts of all kinds (including those with traditional knowledge).

The three funds we have highlighted in this chapter emerged from similar processes where needs and resource gaps were identified in varied social movements. Today, their participatory grantmaking has reached thousands of grassroots organizations, many of which would have never been connected to this funding if it had not been for peers recommending and supporting their causes. The knowledge gained from participating in funding decisions is useful for strengthening agendas, collaborating, and advocating for grassroots-led solutions. FCAM, FRIDA, and Global Greengrants—and other participatory grantmakers around the world—have accumulated experience and capacity that could be valuable for each other as well as mainstream funders interested in climate, grassroots grantmaking, and movement building.

Participatory processes are embedded with diverse and often conflicting or antagonistic approaches and views. But conflict is essential for a vibrant civil society and democratic processes, and participatory grantmaking processes should seek to create the structures and processes to navigate conflict in a healthy, deliberative way. Combining collaboration with confrontation allows social systems to expand and sharpen collective thinking to coproduce new knowledge. Being open to persuasion from others, listening actively, and learning while making decisions are all components of participatory grantmaking, which are also essential to generate the collective understanding needed to tackle the climate crisis.

Although the three featured funds have been supporting global grassroots climate justice movements through different and unique participatory models, they all prioritize turning the decisions over to those directly affected by these issues. They are also supporting climate justice agendas through an intersectional approach in their grantmaking, through which organizations of BIPOC and LGBTQIA2S+ communities, Indigenous Peoples, women, people with disabilities, and youth are at the center of their funding.

And though there is a need for further research on participatory grantmaking internationally, mainstream and other funders can learn from the knowledge that has remained invisible in the hegemonic worldview. The dilemma of what to prioritize can become a productive tension. All participants in a collective dialogue—funders as well as activists—can learn and grow from the process. Participatory grantmaking connects communities of people so that they can imagine social change together and discuss complex issues of fairness, representation, justice, and transparency in funding.

The creation of additional participatory funds around the world has strengthened collaboration and learning within the participatory grantmaking ecosystem. However, there is a need for a comprehensive mapping of global participatory grantmaking funds and those from majority countries because they hold an enormous wealth of information and knowledge from which other funders could learn.

Shifting power and democratizing philanthropy is an urgent demand because without it, we will not be able to support solutions to the climate crisis. Therefore, participatory grantmaking is not only a practice to help funders strengthen their agendas. It is also an essential component for reshaping philanthropy to be able to respond better to today's gravest problems.

ACKNOWLEDGMENTS

The authors are extremely grateful to Megan Barickman at Greengrants, as well as the feminist consulting collective Sukuamis, including Perla Vazquez and Laura Vergara, for their collaboration and work on this project.[33] They conducted interviews, were thought partners, read, critiqued and edited drafts, as well as checked citations and obtained permission to use quotations. In particular, the members of Sukuamis offered their knowledge from mapping different participatory approaches of grantmakers, based especially in majority countries, as shown in table 10.1. We also thank those interviewed for their time and perceptive reasoning. For our parts, we are the current and former CEOs of the Global Greengrants Fund. We acknowledge that our view is predominantly through the lens of Greengrants, while confirming how much we each admire the work of the other funds featured here.

NOTES

1. Interviewed by Megan Barickman, 2022.
2. Jonathan Moore, ed., *Hard Choices: Moral Dilemmas in Humanitarian Intervention* (Lanham, MD: Rowman & Littlefield, 1998); Jonathan Moore, *A Practical Guide to International Philanthropy* (New York: Cambridge University Press, 2014).
3. Anand Giridharadas, *Winners Take All: The Elite Charade of Changing the World* (Harlow, UK: Penguin Books, 2020); Teresa Odendahl, *Charity Begins at Home: Generosity and Self-Interest Among the Philanthropic Elite* (New York: Basic Books, 1990); Robert Reich, *The Common Good* (New York: Alfred A. Knopf, 2018); Robert Reich, *Just Giving: Why Philanthropy Is Failing Democracy and How It Can Do It Better* (Princeton, NJ: Princeton University Press, 2020).
4. Titilope Ajayi, "In Defense of Traditional Philanthropy as 'Effective Altruism' Looms," *Nonprofit Quarterly*, September 22, 2015, https://nonprofitquarterly.org/in-defense-of-traditional-philanthropy-as-effective-altruism-looms/.
5. FRIDA, the Young Feminist Fund, is moving away from the term *Global South* and is instead using the phrase *majority countries*. This is a politically conscious decision to subvert colonial terminologies and to reorient accepted jargon in the philanthropic and development sector. The terms *majority countries* or *majority world* question what is inaccurately perceived as the majority of the world and inverts the thinking that Europe and North America literally and imaginatively sit on the top. FRIDA uses *majority countries* as an umbrella term to refer to countries with varying levels of socioeconomic, cultural, and political status. This includes countries in these regions: South, Southeast, East Asia and the Pacific nations; Latin America and the Caribbean; Africa and the Middle East; Central and Eastern Europe; and the Caucasus and central and northern Asia. The authors commend and support FRIDA's approach. We have had some difficulty with finding an equally adequate substitute for the term *Global North*, and so continue to use it in this chapter while inviting others to rethink and reflect on the "Global North/South" narrative.
6. Edgar Villanueva, *Decolonizing Wealth: Indigenous Wisdom to Heal Divides and Restore Balance* (Oakland: Berrett-Koehler, 2018).
7. Carmen Aliaga, "Justice from the Territories," ep. 1 of "La Bola de Cristal," FCAM podcast, April 5, 2022, Instagram video, https://www.instagram.com/p/Cb-ajIQL485/.
8. Kimberlé Crenshaw, *On Intersectionality: Essential Writings* (New York: New Press, 2017).
9. BIPOC—a term used in the United States to refer to Black, Indigenous, and People of Color—recognizes that these groups are subject to systemic racism. LGBTQIA2S+ refers to Lesbian, Gay, Bisexual, Transgender, Queer and/or Questioning, Intersex, Asexual, Two-Spirit, and the countless affirmative ways in which people choose to self-identify.
10. Crenshaw, *On Intersectionality*.
11. California Environmental Associates, *Soil to Sky: Climate Solutions That Work* (San Francisco: CLIMA Fund, 2019), https://climasolutions.org/wp-content/uploads/2019/09/Soil-to-Sky-1.pdf.
12. Ford Foundation, "Governments and Private Funders Announce Historic US $1 Billion Pledge at COP26 in Support of Indigenous Peoples and Local Communities,"

news release, November 1, 2021, www.fordfoundation.org/news-and-stories/news-and-press/news/governments-and-private-funders-announce-historic-us-17-billion-pledge-at-cop26-in-support-of-indigenous-peoples-and-local-communities/.
13. Global Greengrants Fund and Prospera International Network of Women's Funds, "Our Voices, Our Environment: The State of Funding for Women's Environmental Action," www.greengrants.org/wp-content/uploads/2018/03/GGF_Mapping-Report_Executive-Summary_HighRes-FINAL.pdf.
14. Maria Alejandra Rodriguez Acha, "FRIDA's 10th Anniversary Intergenerational Dialogue," Facebook video, November 30, 2020, https://www.facebook.com/FRIDAFund/videos/fridas-10th-anniversary-intergenerational-dialogue/419704712497216/.
15. Ayana Elizabeth Johnson and Katharine K. Wilkinson, eds., *All We Can Save: Truth, Courage, and Solutions for the Climate Crisis* (New York: One World, 2020).
16. Cynthia Gibson, *Participatory Grantmaking: Has Its Time Come?* (New York: Ford Foundation, 2017), https://www.fordfoundation.org/media/3599/participatory_grantmaking-lmv7.pdf.
17. E.g., the Intergovernmental Panel on Climate Change (IPCC) report released in 2022 states that "climate-resilient development is advanced when actors work in equitable, just and enabling ways to reconcile divergent interests, values and worldviews, toward equitable and just outcomes. These practices build on diverse knowledges about climate risk and chosen development pathways account for local, regional and global climate impacts, risks, barriers and opportunities. Structural vulnerabilities to climate change can be reduced through carefully designed and implemented legal, policy, and process interventions from the local to global that address inequities based on gender, ethnicity, disability, age, location and income. This includes rights-based approaches that focus on capacity-building, meaningful participation of the most vulnerable groups, and their access to key resources, including financing, to reduce risk and adapt. Evidence shows that climate resilient development processes link scientific, Indigenous, local, practitioner and other forms of knowledge, and are more effective and sustainable because they are locally appropriate and lead to more legitimate, relevant and effective actions." IPCC, "Climate Change 2022: Impacts, Adaptation and Vulnerability. Working Group II Contribution to the IPCC Sixth Assessment Report," p. 31, https://www.ipcc.ch/report/ar6/wg2/downloads/report/IPCC_AR6_WGII_SummaryForPolicymakers.pdf.
18. Ford Foundation, "Governments and Private Funders Announce Historic US $1 Billion Pledge."
19. California Environmental Associates, *Soil to Sky*. For more information, see CLIMA Fund's website, https://climasolutions.org/.
20. Alex Aylett, "Participatory Planning, Justice, and Climate Change in Durban, South Africa," *Environment and Planning* 42, no. 1 (2010): 104.
21. Interviewed by Laura Vergara, 2022.
22. Interviewed by Megan Barickman, 2022.
23. Chet Tchozewski, "Chet Tchozewski, Executive Director, Global Greengrants Fund: Empowering the Grassroots," interview by Mitch Nauffts, *Philanthropy News Digest*, September 29, 2004, https://philanthropynewsdigest.org/features/newsmakers/chet-tchozewski-executive-director-global-greengrants-fund-empowering-the-grassroots.
24. Interviewed by Perla Vazquez, 2022.
25. Amina Doherty, FRIDA's 10th Anniversary Intergenerational Dialogue.

26. Global Greengrants Fund, "How Funders Can Address Ableism in the Environmental Justice Movement," August 8, 2021, https://www.greengrants.org/2021/08/09/ableism/.
27. Interviewed by Teresa Odendahl and Laura García, 2022.
28. Personal communication with Perla Vásquez and Laura Vergara, October 13, 2022.
29. Interview with Peter Kostishack, April 6, 2022.
30. See www.theglobalresiliencefund.org/.
31. See https://uhai-eashri.org/.
32. While this chapter has highlighted a few feminist participatory grantmaking efforts, there are many other new funds and models. The Rawa Fund is an example of a bold and innovative participatory grantmaker in a conflict region. "Rawa's participatory funding model supports creative Palestinian community development and inspires a new culture of international aid and local resource mobilization." The fund's vision and values are based on collective problem solving, dignity, equitable power dynamics, trust and transparency, as well as agility and hope. Under development since 2014, Rawa's pilot grantmaking period was 2019 to 2021. Rawa has supported 23 small and medium-sized Palestinian organizations and unregistered groups. They provided additional resources and analysis of the Palestinian context during the COVID-19 pandemic. Rawa is a leader in a global conversation around "changing the culture of development aid and empowering grassroots communities." See www.rawafund.org.
33. See www.sukuamis.org.

CHAPTER 8

Participatory Grantmaking and Giving Traditions in Communities of Color
The CLLCTIVLY Case

Stephanie Clintonia Boddie and Tracy R. Rone

This chapter describes five American philanthropic traditions that exist in the shadow of established philanthropic institutions' history of systematically ignoring or undervaluing giving traditions in communities of color, which is part of a broader disinvestment in those communities. Communal giving programs help fill this gap in institutional support. Such programs have several features in common with participatory grantmaking, such as collective decision-making, emphasizing relationships over transactions, and connecting giving with larger cultural practices. To highlight these common features, this chapter presents a case study on CLLCTIVLY, an evolving ecosystem and participatory grantmaking program for Black-led organizations and communities in Greater Baltimore. The study documents how the value and relevance of giving traditions in communities of color align with the growing interest in participatory grantmaking.

> Philanthropy is commendable, but it must not cause the philanthropist to overlook the circumstances of economic injustice which make philanthropy necessary.
> —Martin Luther King Jr., *Strength to Love*

INTRODUCTION

The social act of giving is considered a human universal. While contemporary philanthropy in the United States is most often associated with wealthy, white private donors and white-led foundations, the tradition of giving is as varied and as ancient as the oldest societies. The word "philanthropy" is derived from *philanthropia*, a Greek phrase meaning "to love people." Attributed to the playwright Aeschylus, philanthropy refers to the voluntary giving of monetary gifts or other resources, such as time through service and grantmaking.[1] In the wake of the coronavirus pandemic, civil unrest, and protests for Black lives, it is important to recognize alternative forms of philanthropy, including those emerging from communities of color.

Over time, philanthropy has evolved from community-focused generosity and has cultivated connections in society. Building on ideas from leaders of the southern nonprofit MDC and others, Lynn and Wisely offer five categories of philanthropic traditions that reflect these varied connections: relief, improvement, social reform, civic engagement, and repair (see table 11.1).[2] Philanthropy as relief values compassion and aims to alleviate urgent and critical needs. Philanthropy as improvement values progress, maximizes human potential, and promotes self-efficacy. Philanthropy as social reform values justice and aims to address the root causes of social problems. Philanthropy as civic engagement values participation and seeks to build community and recognize local assets. Philanthropy as repair values reconciliation and strives to amend past harms.

The dominant form of philanthropy has long been and continues to be professionalized and elite giving that focuses primarily on relief and improvement. This form of philanthropy also tends to promote charity and generosity over dignity and justice.[3] And it has systematically underinvested in communities of color. According to Dorsey, Bradrach, and Kim, Black and Latinx nonprofit leaders receive about 4 percent of funding, even though they make up about 10 percent of nonprofit leaders.[4] Between 2010 and 2014, only 11 percent of large contributions to facilitate social change went to organizations led by people of color.[5]

More recently, some organizations and communities have begun to challenge the professionalized and elite forms of giving and move toward more democratized, civically engaged, and participatory philanthropic approaches—including participatory grantmaking—which embody social reform, civic engagement, and repair.[6]

In challenging the philanthropic status quo, proponents of participatory approaches would do well to understand the commonalities such approaches have with giving traditions in communities of color. Given institutional foundations' systematic underinvestment in Black communities as part of a broader disinvestment in communities of color, African American giving traditions in particular help fill the gap in institutional support. These traditions draw on cultural pillars such as the Black Church, the seven principles of Kwanzaa, the cooperative movement, and the participatory democracy approach of Ella Baker. All share participatory grantmaking's emphasis on collective decision-making, valuing relationships over transactions, and connecting giving with prominent cultural practices.

The chapter begins by describing Lynn and Wisely's five traditions of American philanthropy and the ways African American communities have practiced them. It then lays out four cultural pillars through which African Americans practice philanthropy on their own terms and identifies the pillars' commonalities with participatory grantmaking.

Building upon the five traditions of American philanthropy and four pillars of the African American practice of philanthropy, the chapter then provides a detailed case study of CLLCTIVLY, an evolving ecosystem and multifaceted participatory grantmaking program for Black-led organizations and communities in Greater Baltimore. Drawing on four interviews with its founder, Jamye Wooten, data from the organization's website and internal documents, and the history of Baltimore, the case study shows how Wooten's founding of CLLCTIVLY in 2019 can be properly understood as a continuation of a long-standing tradition of Black cultural self-assertion in the face of disinvestment. Also described is the iterative approach that Wooten takes to developing CLLCTIVLY's grantmaking strategies, which are grounded in the African American cultural traditions identified above and embody the close relationship between these traditions and contemporary participatory grantmaking practices. The evolution of CLLCTIVLY's strategies between 2019 and 2022 is traced, documenting how they relate to Lynn and Wisely's five traditions of American philanthropy, the four cultural pillars of African American giving, and the spectrum of participatory grantmaking laid out in the introduction to this book. The chapter's conclusion invites readers to consider more deeply the relationship between participatory grantmaking and giving traditions in communities of color.

THE FIVE TRADITIONS FOR CULTIVATING CONNECTIONS IN PHILANTHROPY

The African American philanthropic traditions, from which CLLCTIVLY and other organizations that use participatory philanthropic approaches emerged, are deeply rooted and historical. While each has its own sources and origins, they share many of the overall traditions associated with American philanthropy.

According to Lynn and Wisely, philanthropy seeks to facilitate connections between members of society, such as family, community, and congregations.[7] This is particularly true for African Americans.[8] The breadth, depth, and goals of these connections, however, vary depending on the philanthropic tradition in which they are based.[9] The five traditions are philanthropy as relief, as improvement, as social reform, as civic engagement. and as repair.

Philanthropy as Relief

The impulse to give in response to human need or suffering is the most basic form of philanthropy, and is commonly referred to as relief or charity. Derived from the Latin root *caritas*, *charity* means love for humanity. This tradition, which is often associated with a religious worldview to care for those with the greatest need, recognizes that "we are all connected to one another as a part of God's creation."[10]

This philanthropic tradition's focus on expressing care and empathy for others by meeting urgent and specific needs is indisputably honorable. However, it is often limited to reacting to crises or current conditions (e.g., poverty, food insecurity, social inequality), rather than to understanding and connecting with society's deeper needs.

Nevertheless, because those giving these resources within the dominant society often wield significant power, this philanthropic tradition continues to serve as the status quo. Sometimes referred to as "status quo giving," it continues to play a dominant role among the other philanthropic traditions.[11]

This relief tradition takes a different form within African American communities, however. As W. E. B. Du Bois notes, it is less focused on reacting to time-limited crises than on meeting the everyday survival needs of African Americans, especially those living in poverty or struggling with problems that require long-term support.[12] This ethos is widely shared among African Americans, who, despite low wealth and challenging circumstances, give to help others in need.

Philanthropy as Improvement

The impulse for "progress" or "improvement" drives the second tradition of philanthropy, and this goes beyond simply maximizing individuals' potential to meet their own needs.[13] Perhaps the best-known example of this tradition is Andrew Carnegie, who, based on a philosophy of helping people help themselves, funded libraries aimed at educating people. Lesser-known

African American philanthropists in this tradition include Colonel John McKee, the founder of schools for colored boys; Bridget "Biddy" Mason, a midwife, entrepreneur, and founder of the First African Methodist Episcopal (AME) Church in Los Angeles; and Oseola McCarty, a washerwoman and major donor to the University of South Mississippi.[14]

This approach goes beyond immediate relief to creating more lasting efforts, and also cultivates assets, such as the ability to read, that can last a lifetime. At the same time, it does not consider the impact of structural inequities on people's possibilities for improvement. In accord with the maxim of "not giving a man a fish, but teaching him how to fish," what if there is a fence around the pond? While this tradition does provide individuals with opportunities to "improve," it tends to benefit primarily those individuals with the skills and capacity to take advantage of them.[15]

Philanthropy as Social Reform

Justice and social reform are the primary drivers of the third philanthropic tradition.[16] Recognizing the limitations of the improvement tradition, philanthropists in this category focus their giving on social change and the quest for innovative solutions. The philosophy animating their work is to address the root causes of injustice.

The advantages of this approach are that, if successful, it can offer a more lasting and comprehensive impact. The challenges are that such lasting change can take many years and carries greater risk of failure.

Examples of social reform in African American communities include the antislavery work of Harriet Tubman and Frederick Douglass, which involved raising funds to support abolitionist organizing; the prison reform work and establishment of schools for homeless young people by Frances Joseph-Gaudet; the civil rights efforts of Georgia Gilmore, who supported the Alabama bus boycott by selling food to raise funds; and A. G. Gaston, who used his financial resources to pay the legal fees and bail for civil rights activists.[17]

Philanthropy as Civic Engagement

Philanthropy is currently shifting to greater participation and to thus advancing civic engagement, which requires investments in relationship and network building while nurturing community conversations.[18] The impulse behind this approach is to build community by creating new institutions and systems that promote solidarity and provide alternatives to the status quo.

In African American communities, examples of such alternative systems are institutions created through the Black Church and Black-led entrepreneurship. For example, Richard Allen, the founder of the first AME church in the early eighteenth century, urged his followers to consider giving as a Christian duty toward family, friend, or foe.[19] Madam C. J. Walker was an entrepreneur who built a fortune by developing and marketing cosmetics and hair care products to Black women around the turn of the twentieth century. Embracing the AME Church's gospel of giving, she used her network of sales agents to develop "benevolence clubs" that performed charitable acts in local communities.[20] Frederick Patterson was a veterinary doctor in the mid–twentieth century who encouraged giving to historic Black colleges by establishing the United Negro College Fund.[21]

Philanthropy as Repair

The philanthropic impulse to reconcile drives repair.[22] Philanthropy that emphasizes repair recognizes that building wealth can benefit or harm society, and seeks a redistribution of resources and power to those communities most affected by structural inequality.[23] It also seeks to build trust across racial and class lines, change the narrative about who is deserving of success, and mobilize new stakeholders as partners.[24] This may require donors to ask themselves what they will need to give up instead of what they need to give.[25] This kind of giving requires acknowledging and addressing past wrongs, such as exploitative and extractive practices like stealing land from Native Americans and enslaving people of African descent.[26]

A common misconception is that the work of repair lies solely with either the dominant or the marginalized group. The current system of inequality affects everyone, and so all communities have work to do toward repair, even if that works looks different for each.[27] Many leaders of color acknowledge the social and psychological harm of existing systems, particularly the economic system.[28] Hence, there is a need for Black-led organizations to engage in their own trust building, mutual learning, and the formation of deep relationships across organizations. Ultimately, giving as repair seeks to heal communities and benefit everyone.[29]

The giving of the nineteenth-century abolitionists and entrepreneurs James Forten and Thomy LaFon is an example of how repair can play out in a community.[30] Forten and LaFon supported Black-owned newspapers that would be central to the narrative-changing work needed to end slavery.[31] They gave generously to institutions ranging from asylums for orphan boys to old folks' homes to universities and other charities, which supported both Black communities and the broader society. LaFon was so revered for his contributions by the citizens of New Orleans that the state legislature commissioned a bust in his honor. Similarly, Forten was recognized for his contributions beyond the Black community. Generally, such "reparative efforts preserve dignity and fight for justice for all, while recognizing the differential effects that structural inequality has on communities."[32]

All these examples promote collective forms of giving through which individuals undertake charitable acts together. The civic engagement and repair approaches most closely align with participatory grantmaking.

AFRICAN AMERICAN PHILANTHROPY ON THEIR TERMS

Table 8.1 highlights African American giving traditions as they relate to mainstream philanthropy and provides specific examples of African American philanthropists who embody those traditions—a connection that is often underappreciated. But African American giving also has its own distinct cultural roots.

While philanthropy has often overlooked the distinct cultural practices and perspectives on giving by leaders of color, few races in the United States are as instinctively philanthropic as African Americans.[33] The context of Black philanthropy is love for freedom and each other.[34] Black philanthropy is "rooted in the ideals of mutual aid, self-help, and social solidarity"; was "essential to the survival and well-being of Black slaves and freed Blacks alike"; and demonstrated Black agency in the face of limited wealth-building opportunities.[35] As James Baldwin put it, "If we had not loved each other, none of us would have survived."[36]

For these reasons, this chapter uses a more inclusive definition of philanthropy that moves beyond giving large sums of cash to other forms of "gifting," which includes small to mid-size giving.[37] This has been described as the giving of time, talent, treasures, testimony, and ties.[38]

There are four historical components of African American culture that complement the five traditions of American philanthropy, and together provide a matrix from which participatory philanthropic efforts like CLLCTIVLY emerge: the Black church tradition, Nguzo Saba (the seven principles of Kwanzaa), a history of cooperative movements, and the tradition of participatory democracy embodied in the work of Ella Baker.

Table 8.1: Five Traditions of Philanthropy as Expressed in African American Communities

	Giving as relief (compassion)	Giving as improvement (progress)	Giving as social reform (justice)	Giving as civic engagement (participation)	Giving as repair (reconciliation)
Principles					
Examples:	• Catherine Ferguson • Everyday people	• Col. John McKee • Bridget "Biddy" Mason • Oseola McCarthy	• Harriet Tubman • Frederick Douglass • Frances Joseph-Gaudet • Georgia Gilmore • A. G. Gaston	• Richard Allen and the AME Church • Madam C. J. Walker and her agents • Frederick Patterson and the United Negro College Fund • Judge George W. White and the United Black Fund	• James Forten • Thomy LaFon • Valaida Fullwood
Impulse:	Alleviate human suffering	Maximize human potential	Solve social problems	Build community	Mend past harms
Philosophy:	Help those in need	Equip those to help themselves	Address causes of injustice and inequities	Promote solidarity and create alternate systems to challenge the problem	Shift power and builds infrastructure for large-scale resourcing that benefits all

Advantages:	• Draws attention to key social issues • Alleviates urgent and critical needs • Responds quickly to unforeseen events • Offers simple and accessible ways to relieve donors' urge to "do something"	• More lasting efforts • Builds people's assets to become more effective in directing their life and meeting their own needs • Encourages self-responsibility rather than dependency	• Deals with root causes of problems • Most lasting and comprehensive impact if successful • Highest leverage of philanthropic dollars • Innovative because it experiments with alternative solutions to social problems	• Fosters collaboration through conferences, networking, and coalition-building • Empowers organizations and communities • Builds trust • Builds more reflective and resourceful local communities • Recognizes local assets	• Restores what has been lost • Operates from a mindset of abundance • Recognizes the need for systemic changes • Maximizes the charitable contribution • Views inclusiveness as a pre-condition for effective giving • Asks why challenges like poverty and inequities in education, health, and wealth persist
Challenges:	• Need is limitless • Fails to address root causes • Focuses on symptoms • Typically short-lived • Can disempower people through dependence	• What if there is a fence around the pond? • Often benefits the well-situated or highly motivated • Receptivity to training varies • Must guard against the we-know-better-than-you attitude	• Who decides what must be reformed? • Highest risk of failure • Hard to identify and implement comprehensive solutions	• Does discourse lead to action? • Difficult to render into measurable outcomes • Takes time to create visible impact	• Requires large and sustained efforts • Takes change in discourse to engage donors in this kind of giving • Receptivity to this kind of giving varies

Sources: Adapted from Elizabeth M. Lynn, and D. Susan Wisely, "Toward a Fourth Philanthropic Response: American Philanthropy and Its Public," in *The Perfect Gift: The Philanthropic Imagination Poetry and Prose*, ed. Amy Kass (Bloomington: Indiana University Press, 2002), 102–12; Elizabeth M. Lynn and Susan Wisely, "Four Traditions of Philanthropy," Lake Institute on Faith & Giving, October 13, 2022, YouTube video, www.youtube.com/watch?v=QC8ohnF_rZI;

The Black Church Tradition

Black-led and Black-owned churches have been the primary institutions for—and Black congregations the leaders in—political, social, and philanthropic work since the eighteenth and nineteenth centuries.[39] As organizations that largely operated independently from white authorities, churches were supported by large numbers of the Black community members and served as a type of "community foundation" able to receive individual donations to meet community needs.[40] Black businesses, community, and faith leaders—including Harriet Tubman, Frederick Douglass, James Forten, Richard Allen, Thomy LaFon, Biddy Mason, Madam C. J. Walker, Georgia Gilmore, A. G. Gaston, Frederick Patterson, Oseola McCarty, and Martin Luther King Jr.—have also sacrificed and given their time, talent, and treasure to advance Black people's progress in ways that reflect the five traditions of American philanthropy (see table 8.1).

Within Black communities, churches are among the first places children are taught about giving and fundraising. Tithes and offerings are a central part of this giving—appeals that are bolstered by the full "force of authority and legitimacy."[41] According to Lincoln and Mamiya's 1990 study of the cultural traditions undergirding the Black Church, "the tradition of mutual aid lay deep in the African heritage, which stresses a greater communalism and social solidarity than either European or American customs allowed."[42] The mutual aid tradition of the Black Church, through which individuals pool resources to help meet the larger needs of the community, is the foundation for the kind of community-based, participatory grantmaking often found in Black communities.[43]

Black Church giving also serves the function of racial uplift and creates a financial base necessary for supporting burial societies, schools, colleges, credit unions, and other collective efforts to sustain the liberation of Black people.[44] As W. E. B. Du Bois documents, Black churches have important assets such as salaried employees, charities, and property.[45] As one of the first to document the philanthropic efforts of the Black Church, Du Bois found that by 1900, Baptist churches were supporting some 980 schools and 18 academies and colleges.[46] Between 1884 and 1900, the AME Church raised over $1 million for educational purposes and supported twenty-two institutions providing postelementary education. The AME Zion Church was supporting eight colleges. The Colored Methodist Episcopal Church had established seven schools.[47]

Black Church giving also supported the long struggle for civil rights and racial equality beyond simply financing activism.[48] According to Morris, "the Black church functioned as the institutional center of the modern civil rights movement, [providing it] with an organized mass base; a leadership of clergymen ... skilled in the art of managing people and resources; an institutionalized financial base ... and meeting places where the masses planned tactics and strategies and collectively committed themselves to the struggle."[49] Motivated by faith, giving during this era was a means to confront and combat racial injustices. Contributions were often used to pay for bail bonds and lawyers' fees for those arrested for civil disobedience.[50] While entrepreneurs like A. G. Gaston significantly contributed to such causes, working people (predominantly women) gave more informally through Black churches by "passing the hat" or selling dinners.[51]

Today, Black Church members continue to give out of an obligation to serve God and their community by supporting issues and organizations that reflect their values and where they invest their time.[52] Black churches—such as those affiliated with the Church of God in Christ—also continue to emphasize tithing. Baptist denominations tend to have the most generous members.[53] Among Black churches, the AME Zion, Presbyterian, and United Methodist denominations have higher church incomes and donation levels for church missions.[54] Black households continue to be more religious than other US households and are more likely to give to religiously affiliated organizations.[55]

Nguzo Saba: The Seven Principles of Kwanzaa

In addition to these faith-based practices, there are also secular traditions that are distinctly African American and provide a backdrop for Black giving. One of these is the seven principles of Kwanzaa—known as Nguzo Saba—an annual week-long celebration that honors Black history and culture. Kwanzaa was created in 1966 by Dr. Maulana Karenga (previously known as Ronald Karenga) in response to increasing Black nationalism and to the mainstream visibility of Black unrest, as exemplified by the 1965 Watts riots. Kwanzaa, which takes place during the last week of the calendar year, was meant to be a specifically African American alternative to Christmas and other year-end holidays. In designing it, Karenga drew upon African language and tradition, deriving the name and the seven principles from Swahili, a language spoken in multiple African countries.[56]

Kwanzaa's foundation rests on seven principles (Nguzo Saba) identified by Karenga as central to Black family life, community, and racial heritage. The principles and their Swahili names are: Unity (*Umoja*), Self-Determination (*Kujichagulia*), Collective Responsibility (*Ujima*), Cooperative Economics (*Ujaama*), Purpose (*Nia*), Creativity (*Kuumba*), and Faith (*Imani*). In Karenga's view, these principles reflect the "celebration, solidarity and continued struggle for a shared good in the world."[57] Together, they promote a collective, communal worldview that runs counter to the individualistic, every-man-for-himself approach of mainstream American society and culture. Nguzo Saba, which are tied to a holiday but intended to be more encompassing, can be seen as a foundation for an Afrocentric value system that decolonizes giving and gifting practices within the Black community and for building mutually accountable relationships.[58] This collective approach has a cultural affinity with participatory grantmaking, in which power is distributed rather than concentrated and decisions are made collectively.

Cooperative Movements

Another tradition undergirding African American giving is alluded to in the Nguzo Saba: Cooperative Economics (*Ujaama*). African Americans have a long history of collective economic advancement and group solidarity that serve as a basis for pooling resources, increasing economic benefits, and sharing profits.[59] Examples of these kinds of cooperative efforts include pooling resources to purchase the freedom of enslaved family members, mutual aid societies that assisted with costs incurred due to illness or death, and the African revolving community funds, known as *esu, susu, esusu,* or *sou sou*.[60]

Many of these efforts were born out of the legalized discrimination, segregation, and exploitation that dominated the lives of Black people before the civil rights era and new forms of Jim Crow that emerged later, prompting many Black leaders—such as William Hooper Councill, Booker T. Washington, W. E. B. Du Bois, and Marcus Garvey Jr.—to argue that Black self-determination was essential for Black people to create alternate economic solutions and gain economic control.[61] Recognizing the buying power of the Black consumer, Du Bois believed that by working together across institutions (e.g., churches, schools, and newspapers), Black people could create an alternative economy that would lead to group self-sufficiency.[62] Any surplus income would be reinvested to purchase land and advance Black businesses.

Black farmers were among the first to establish formal cooperatives, such as the Colored Farmers' Alliance and Cooperative Union in 1886.[63] At its peak, this cooperative had more than 1 million members who shared agricultural techniques and innovations, secured loans, and purchased goods. Early stock ownership companies and mutual insurance companies were other examples of cooperatives noted by Du Bois.[64] The most prolific era of Black cooperatives was the Great Depression, when hard economic times inspired mutual aid and creative forms of economic survival.[65] During the

1960s, civil rights leaders like Fannie Lou Hamer sought to leverage cooperative economics in service of Black advancement through the Freedom Farm Cooperative.[66] Community members did their part through grassroots efforts like the Freedom Quilting Bee, which brought together Black quilters in the South, and sold their wares to fund civil rights activism.[67]

Participatory Democracy

Participatory democracy is another major foundation on which Black philanthropy rests and is most significantly expressed in the work of Ella Baker. As a civil rights pioneer, activist, cofounder of the Southern Christian Leadership Conference, and founder of the Student Nonviolent Coordinating Committee (known as SNCC), Baker was critical of the patriarchal, hierarchical, and messianic leadership style of civil rights leaders such as Martin Luther King Jr.[68] Instead, Baker believed that "what is needed is the development of people who are interested not in being leaders as much as in developing leadership among other peoples."[69] This is what she called "group-based leadership" and what some scholars refer to as "collective leadership."[70] These collective models "exercise influence as part of a community of equals in which every person contributes a distinctive, indispensable voice to the whole, while also standing strong with others in support of mutually agreed goals."[71]

Ultimately, Baker believed people "have to be made to understand that they cannot look for salvation anywhere but to themselves."[72] Baker was known by some as Fundi, "a Swahili word meaning a person who masters a craft with the help of community, practices it, then teaches it to the next generation."[73]

Connecting the Five Traditions, the Four Pillars, and Participatory Grantmaking

So far, we have reviewed five traditions of American philanthropy, highlighting African Americans' distinctive contributions to them. And we have identified four pillars of African American cultural practice that undergird Black giving. These two frameworks are closely interconnected. The Black Church practices philanthropy as relief, the Nguzo Saba principles enact philanthropy as improvement, cooperative economics represent philanthropy as social reform, participatory democracy is a form of philanthropy as civic engagement, and all four pillars, by providing cultural self-determination that resists ongoing structural discrimination, exemplify philanthropy as repair.

Given the theme of this book, it is worth noting that two of the four pillars also demonstrate a strong connection to participatory grantmaking. By distributing power through shared resources and shared decision-making, the cooperative movement is rooted in a practice that centers the common good over the needs of one individual, much like participatory grantmaking. And Ella Baker's work reflected three themes that participatory grantmaking shares: (1) active participation by local people in the decisions affecting their lives, (2) the minimization of hierarchy and professionalization in social change organizations, and (3) direct action to address the sources of injustice.[74]

The deep connections among the five traditions, the four pillars, and participatory grantmaking are illustrated in the case study of Baltimore's CLLCTIVLY that comprises the remainder of this chapter. CLLCTIVLY's approach combines elements of the five traditions of American philanthropy: it provides direct relief, it offers opportunities for individual improvement, it advances social reform by strengthening access to funding for Black business and nonprofits, it promotes civic engagement through collective events and participatory models of decision-making, and it emphasizes repair through its narrative campaigns and no-strings-attached grantmaking. And it does these in a distinctly African American vein, drawing on the cultural traditions represented by the four pillars.

CLLCTIVLY: BUILDING BLACK FUTURES TOGETHER

In 2019, Jamye Wooten, a Baltimore native, launched CLLCTIVLY to mobilize resources that would serve Black-led organizations and help overcome the city's history of discrimination and racial exclusion. Today, CLLCTIVLY operates with the mission of building "place-based social change centering Black genius, narrative power, social networks, and resource mobilization."[75]

Wooten founded CLLCTIVLY after he lost his sister Sherri, an entrepreneur and owner of two pizza delivery stores in West Baltimore, to cancer at age fifty-three. "I watched her build her businesses from the ground up with little to no funding," he said. A second-generation entrepreneur himself, Wooten began looking for ways to help Black business peers and landed on establishing an organization that would be a hub for Black-led businesses to "learn from and about each other and be a resource for the Greater Baltimore community that seeks to find, fund, and partner with Black social change organizations."[76] This vision was based on the premise that community organizations often work in silos that lead to fragmentation, duplication, and wasted resources of time, talent, and treasure. As a result, marginalized populations struggle to meet their needs.

For Wooten, CLLCTIVLY primarily builds upon African American giving, particularly the seven principles of Kwanzaa, the more than four hundred years of the Black Church tradition of giving, and cooperative asset building.[77] It continues in the long history of cooperative movements within the Black community.[78] In the present day, as Black communities face new challenges and new entities emerge, CLLCTIVLY has positioned itself to mobilize Black-led organizations to address a range of social and economic concerns. CLLCTIVLY ushers in a new form of cooperative economics using new technology to promote greater self-sufficiency among Black-led organizations in Greater Baltimore. Wooten provides a nonhierarchical, collective leadership style for CLLCTIVLY.

Growing up in the church, Wooten began giving as a child and watched the ways church members pooled resources to meet the needs of the community. While formerly serving as the director of the Collective Banking Group, Wooten observed the ways its founder, the Reverend Dr. Jonathan Weaver, mobilized over two hundred congregations in Prince George's County, Maryland, and brought business sophistication to the traditions, rituals, and technology of the Black Church to pool resources and meet the needs of its members and the broader community.[79]

Like the Black Church and Black American cooperative movements, CLLCTIVLY uses an asset-based framework. Wooten draws upon the strengths and local assets of Black-led organizations as the primary building blocks for sustainable giving and community building. Kwanzaa and the Nguzo Saba are also foundational to the framing and design of the participatory grantmaking practiced by CLLCTIVLY.

Baltimore: The Context of CLLCTIVLY

Such a multifaceted approach is a reflection not only of Wooten's design and the cultural traditions on which he draws but also of the social, cultural, and political environment in which CLLCTIVLY emerged. The organization's history, philosophy, and strategies cannot be fully appreciated without an understanding of the historical context and geographical location in which it operates: Baltimore.

Founded in 1730, Baltimore City has a legacy of nearly three hundred years of racialized policies and practices, including an initial economy that relied on the slave trade of Africans for labor.[80] In the nineteenth century, the *Baltimore Sun* circulated advertisements for the commercialization of the enslaved and shaped racialized narratives, using terms like "cash for Negroes," "Negro domination," and "Negro invasion"—narratives that fueled discriminatory policies and other exclusionary realities experienced by thousands of Black people and their communities.[81] Fear of slave insurrections fueled other restrictions on Black Marylanders.

Alongside this oppression, a tradition of Black-led resistance emerged. By 1820, Baltimore had one of the largest free Black communities of any North American city.[82] In 1861, as the Civil War began, it was home to about 26,000 free Blacks and 2,000 enslaved Africans.[83] Two Black Marylanders, Harriet Tubman and Frederick Douglass, escaped slavery and used their resources to help other enslaved people gain their freedom.[84]

After the 1863 Emancipation Proclamation, Baltimore became a stronger manufacturing center that was home to more millionaire philanthropists than any other American city, including Johns Hopkins, Enoch Pratt, Moses Shepherd, and George Peabody.[85] The traditions of American philanthropy were very much in evidence in Baltimore—as were the pillars of African American giving. With the passage of the Fourteenth and Fifteenth amendments to the Constitution, which extended the rights of Black people, a group of Black leaders affiliated with the religious community emerged. Churches such as Sharp Street and Bethel AME provided education and civic meetings, as well as sites for political action.[86] By the 1860s, Baltimore had sixteen Black congregations.[87]

As Baltimore's Black community grew, it unified around mutual aid and racial progress, even as race relations continued to be a politically and socially divisive issue.[88] In 1911, Baltimore City became the first city in the United States to enact a restrictive, race-based housing covenant, which limited residence based upon where residents lived, worshipped, or went to school.[89] The city also formed its Committee on Segregation to enforce racially restrictive covenants, which prohibited the sale of homes to Black buyers, and it continued to engage in predatory lending, redlining, and other housing discrimination and segregationist practices in subsequent years. The legacy of these historical practices endures; in the past decade, Massey and Tannen identified Baltimore as one of eight "category five" hypersegregated and devastated cities.[90] In a recent review of $670 million in funding for capital projects, predominantly white neighborhoods were expected to receive twice as much funding as predominantly African American neighborhoods.[91]

According to Brown, such racialized practices have fostered inequitable access to high-quality housing, food, employment, transportation, public safety, education, and health care that is still pervasive in chronically underinvested communities in Baltimore.[92] This is hardly the "city of the future" that many of Baltimore's leaders claim it to be. Historical policies designed to "quarantine Blacks," as Baltimore's mayor put it in 1911, continue to cripple a large segment of the city's population to this day.[93] Race and zip code are still the primary determinants of people's life outcomes. And there is an ongoing legacy of discrimination and inequality that is marbled into Baltimore's housing, education, and health systems, along with its philanthropic patterns, especially the relatively small number of investments in Black communities. While Baltimore's legacy of discrimination and inequities gained greater attention with the 2015 Uprising in response to the death of Freddie Gray in police custody, the coronavirus pandemic, and the 2020 protest after the police killing of George Floyd, Black leaders are still "working hard for half as much."[94]

This racial climate, which extends across the United States, has shaped the course of Black philanthropy in Baltimore and pushed it in directions far different from white philanthropy.[95] It is also an important backdrop for CLLCTIVLY's inspiration, formation, and launch.

Origin

CLLCTIVLY emerged in part as a reaction to the social unrest that began on April 25, 2015, with the tragic death of Freddie Gray while in police custody.[96] As the world watched the dramatic footage of protesters breaking windows, setting buildings on fire, and marching in the streets, some discerned the voices of young people demanding more from their city. Many local residents refer to these events as "the Uprising" or "the Awakening," because the protest awakened the city's privileged and wealthy white population to the causes and severity of consequences of the social, economic, educational, and health inequities many of the city's Black and low-income residents experienced daily.

Just three days after Freddie Gray's arrest, grassroots activists, faith-based leaders, and concerned citizens came together to establish Baltimore United for Change (BUC), a coalition working for justice in Baltimore City.[97] The local Black social entrepreneur Jamye Wooten was among this group of Black leaders who brought vision to the 2015 Uprising and voice to the protesters' demands in ways that embodied several of the five traditions of American philanthropy described earlier in this chapter.

In the weeks and months after the Uprising, BUC raised over $100,000 for jail support for those arrested during the Uprising and bailed out nearly 100 individuals with amounts ranging from $50,000 to $500,000—an example of philanthropy as relief. BUC provided safe spaces and fed thousands of students and families throughout the city while Baltimore schools were closed. It also hosted nonviolent civil disobedience training sessions and other workshops to educate citizens about their rights (philanthropy as civic engagement). Only a few days after the Uprising, Wooten began calling leaders to establish a skills bank for community members looking for ways to serve their city (philanthropy as improvement). From mental health professionals to graphic designers, more than 260 individuals and organizations joined this skills bank.[98]

In the aftermath of the 2015 Uprising, despite the excessive wealth located in Baltimore's wide network of predominantly white family philanthropic organizations and an infusion of small, state, and federal revitalization zone funding, very little changed for the better in Baltimore—at least, not for low-income and African American residents. Crime and the opioid epidemic spiraled out of control. Maryland's governor canceled planned transportation initiatives that were critical to providing employment opportunities for Baltimore's mostly Black and low-income population.[99] Store closures in already resource-challenged Baltimore communities left many residents with even less access to food and medication. Baltimore agencies reported increased levels of trauma in schools as families continued to struggle with inequity in economic, health, educational, and transportation resources.[100]

By late 2018, Wooten realized that Baltimore was even more racially inequitable than it had been after the 2015 Uprising. In January 2019, he launched CLLCTIVLY with the goal of closing the triangle between human needs in health, employment, and housing across the available network of resources.

Mission and Programming

CLLCTIVLY's mission is to amplify Black genius by helping individuals who have a vision but lack adequate funding. It advances this mission by providing networking, visibility, and funding to these individuals, and to the community organizations and businesses of which they are a part. Through in-person events, online crowdfunding, and partnerships with institutional donors, CLLCTIVLY mobilizes philanthropic dollars and mutual aid for the betterment of Baltimore's Black communities.

The organization creates an ecosystem to foster "collaboration, increase social impact and amplify voices of Black-led organizations."[101] CLLCTIVLY has a membership of more than 150 organizations that have joined its platform and share its guiding principles. Its membership requirements are that the organization must be Black-led or have a leadership team or board that is 51 percent Black, and that the organization must be based in and serve constituents in Baltimore City or Baltimore County. A web-based asset directory (CLLCTIV ASSET) allows people to easily search for these organizations by service topic and target neighborhood. Like time banking, whereby community members exchange time spent working instead of money, such as bartering auto repairs for a haircut, Wooten envisioned community leaders with limited financial resources giving of their skills to support Black-led organizations throughout the city.[102]

Such connections are further reinforced through a series of in-person, community-based events, such as the giving day during August, which is Black Philanthropy Month. While these events were interrupted during the COVID-19 pandemic, the connections built during the launch year of 2019 have been maintained. The fact that CLLCTIVLY has always had a combination of online and offline programming has allowed it to adapt to the realities of virtual and hybrid programming.

The intent of this design was that, over time, iterations and the launch of new strategies would strengthen the ecosystem, and the different components would begin to reinforce each other. As described above, an asset directory of Black-led organizations, originally labeled CLLCTIV ASSET, was the first component Wooten developed as part of BUC in 2015. As he launched CLLCTIVLY as its own effort in 2019, the Amplify online platform was the next component to emerge. Amplify offers spotlights and mobilizes resources for Black-led organizations serving Greater Baltimore.

An example of the types of organizations that are featured on Amplify is Baltimore Ceasefire. Founded in 2017 by Erricka Bridgeford, who lost her older brother to gun violence, Baltimore Ceasefire asks people to honor life, to celebrate life, to be peaceful, and to have a different reaction when people are murdered in the city. Declaring a three-day armistice for the weekend of August 4–6, 2017—dubbed the first "Ceasefire Weekend," when no murders would be committed—Bridgeford and her colleagues handed out flyers, posted signs, and promoted the armistice on social media. The group invited people to participate in the fifty life-affirming community events held that weekend. At that time, there was estimated to be a murder in Baltimore every 19 hours. Over this initial three-day weekend, Baltimore

Ceasefire's efforts resulted in sixty-seven of the seventy-two hours passing by without a murder. And the city unified in love and support to celebrate the two young men's lives that were lost in Baltimore that first Ceasefire Weekend.

The next component of CLLCTIVLY's work to emerge was grantmaking. After identifying Black-led business and nonprofits through CLLCTIV ASSET and increasing their visibility through Amplify, Wooten began to channel dollars to these efforts through funding strategies. These have taken several forms: a micro-grant program, a giving circle, and partnerships with local and national institutional donors. In developing grantmaking strategies, CLLCTIVLY has intentionally sought to combine individual funds from within the community and institutional dollars from outside it. In this way, it seeks to bridge some of the historic divides that have led to systemic underinvestment in Black communities. While CLLCTIVLY has continued to iterate on its strategies, as described in the next subsections, its core activities of networking, visibility, and funding have remained.

Approach to Participatory Grantmaking and Decision-Making

CLLCTIVLY is characterized by an entrepreneurial spirit and a holistic approach. Rather than start from a fixed grantmaking strategy, as many institutional foundations do, CLLCTIVLY develops, tests, and iterates multiple strategies that respond to the particular circumstances, needs, and expressed interests of Black communities in Baltimore. And it does so in a way designed to build power in these communities.

This iterative approach is grounded in a fundamental belief that philanthropy is best practiced in close collaboration with the community, listening to what its members need, and developing new strategies that respond to these needs. Not all such strategies may end up lasting beyond a few iterations, but the point is to continue listening, reflecting, networking, and developing to ensure CLLCTIVLY's continued relevance.

Four strategies enable an iterative approach:

Relational
- Connect people.
- Convene people to network virtually or in person.
- Build trust.

Intentional
- Focus on opportunities, challenges, and issues.
- Check biases and assumptions that get in the way of trust.
- Engage people to develop strategies and/or actions to strengthen the network, build trust, and increase power.

Support-based
- Set up communication systems and platforms to increase networking and collaboration.
- Reconstruct resources to support networks and collaboration.
- Incorporate reflection and evaluation.
- Support other network weavers.

Action-oriented
- Encourage people to take initiative.
- Cluster people interested in the same projects or issues.
- Support mutual learning.
- Foster collaboration across the network.
- Define success and outline effects that are important for their work and their community.

Prioritizing this kind of work helps CLLCTIVLY, as a new grantmaker, remain transparent and focused on supporting Black-led organizations rather than on employing traditional philanthropic practices that seek to direct and control grantees.[103]

A key component that ensures CLLCTIVLY's relevance is the use of participatory approaches throughout its grantmaking strategies. These approaches are grounded in the traditions of African American philanthropy described above—the Black Church, the seven principles of Kwanzaa, the cooperative movement, and the participatory democracy principles of Ella Baker. And they similarly draw upon the five traditions of American philanthropy that Lynn and Wisely identified: giving as relief, improvement, social reform, civic engagement, and repair.[104] The iterative stance CLLCTIVLY takes allows it to undertake activities that exemplify all these different approaches.

The participatory democracy model shows up in this way through CLLCTIVLY: Wooten implements a decentralized model of leadership much like Ella Baker's participatory democracy model. Using the hashtag #MLK2BAKER, Wooten brings together social media, traditional media, and social justice organizing to mobilize Black-led organizations for sustainable change.[105] Wooten's goal is to engage ordinary people in the decision-making that ranges from asking for input ("thin participation") to planning, implementing, and assessing new programs ("thick participation").[106]

To enable this, CLLCTIVLY has devoted its first three years to base building, trust building, network weaving, and power building with Black-led organizations that are engaged in the community and are affected by community challenges. Microgrants have been one way to advance this base-building work. Microgrants provide much-needed financial support to Black-led organizations while also strengthening relationships and building trust to foster collaboration and solidarity. The hashtag #MLK2BAKER is about building a network based on shared values and the Nguzo Saba principles to move member organizations #beyondreactivism and to organize for power.

To build power, most of CLLCTIVLY's philanthropic grantmaking strategies allow the decision-making to be concentrated or distributed among individuals from the community or community groups (see table 8.2). CLLCTIVLY's funding model reflects a commitment to gathering support both from institutional foundations and from members of the community, thereby bridging the historic gap between mainstream institutions and Black communities that exercise more agency. In general, 50 percent of CLLCTIVLY's funding comes from foundations (of these foundation funders, 90 percent have Black professionals in senior positions). The remaining funding comes from individuals.

The funding CLLCTIVLY provides comes with no strings attached, offering the ultimate flexibility in grantmaking.[107] This approach allows "money to be used as a tool for love, to facilitate relationships" to help its members thrive, rather than to hurt and divide the community.[108] To date, CLLCTIVLY has distributed over $1 million in grants ranging from $500 to $25,000. CLLCTIVLY uses electronic transfers to disburse all funds within a two-week period. This is an added advantage of its grantmaking strategies. For the largest awards, CLLCTIVLY's advisory board, funding advisers, or institutional funders typically make the final decisions with input from community members through a vote or crowdfunding process.

As table 8.2 demonstrates, CLLCTIVLY's iterative approach has allowed it to develop strategies that fit across the spectrum of participation that appears in this book's introduction. This holistic, culturally grounded approach to philanthropy is an example of how the principles of participatory grantmaking can be expressed in communities of color, a topic worthy of further consideration and research.

Table 8.2: CLLCTIVLY's Spectrum of Participation in Philanthropy by Decision-Maker and Power

		Decision-maker	
		Individual	Institution
Power	Concentrated	28 Days of Black Future Crowdfunding	Business Quest We Got Your Back
	Distributed	Giving Circles CLLCTIVGIVE CLLCTIV SOUP Micro-grants Adaptive Village We Give Black Fest	Black Solidarity Fund Adaptive Village

Source: CLLCTIVLY's conceptualization.

The Evolution of CLLCTIVLY's Participatory Grantmaking Strategies

CLLCTIVLY's participatory grantmaking strategies have not been static but have continually evolved over time in response to seismic social changes that require nimble and strategic responses. In 2019, building atop an ecosystem of interlinked programs focused on networking and visibility, CLLCTIVLY launched the first of its ten participatory grantmaking strategies. As table 8.3 illustrates, each strategy targets particular Black-led communities—from businesses and nonprofits to specific service needs throughout Greater Baltimore—and uses a decision-making strategy that is participatory in some way.

These ten strategies are described in greater detail below. They are divided into two sections: before the COVID-19 pandemic and the murder of George Floyd in 2020, and after those seismic events. Before the pandemic, CLLCTIVLY launched Black Futures microgrants, the CLLCTIVGIVE Annual Day of Giving, and the Black Futures giving circle. These established a set of relationships, knowledge, and experiences as a baseline. When the events of 2020 hit, CLLCTIVLY was able to draw on this experience, as well as the four pillars of African American giving, to continue iterating new strategies, including the Black Solidarity Fund, the We Got Your Back campaign, Business Quest, #28 Days of Black Futures, Adaptive Village, We Give Black Fest, and CLLCTIV SOUP.

Some of the strategies complement each other in specific ways. For example, CLLCTIVGIVE was launched in 2019 as an annual Day of Giving

Table 8.3: The Evolution of CLLCTIVLY's Grantmaking Strategies

Fund Black Futures strategy and date founded	Funding sources	Number of grants awarded	Range of grant award	Decision-making process	Decision-makers
Black Futures micro-grants January 2019	3 foundations	50	$500–$5,000	Online community; public tally	Community vote only
Black Futures 360 Giving Circle January 2019	Giving Circle members or anonymous donors		$30,000 range	40% divided by grantmaking review committee; 40% members themselves; 20% operational	Giving Circle members and community advisory board
CLLCTIVGIVE, August 2019	Individual donors, foundations, and 24 hours of crowdfunding $5,600, $56,000, $102,000 / 50 organization	100	$400–$18,000	Online crowdfunding	Donors support organizations of their choice
Black Solidarity Fund, March 2020	316 donors, crowdfunding; 4 foundations; 1 HBCU	200	$500–$10,000 3 awards of $10,000	Advisory board and community nomination	Advisory board and community nomination
We Got Your Back, April 2021	1 donor giving $600/month); 128 donors via crowdfunding	1	$24,000 or $2,000/month stipend for a year	Advisory review committee of all Black women	Advisory board made up of all Black women

Business Quest August 2021	Foundations	8 awards: 4 for organizations and 4 for individuals	$1,000, $3,000–$5,000 (organizations); $1,000 random drawing; $1,000, $500, $250 for individuals and $100 gift card	50+ nonprofit organizations and 30 businesses participating in the scavenger hunt	Organizations that receive the most points
28 Days of Black Futures February 2022	Crowdfunding	28; $51,000 raised	$1,806 for each organization	Founder and a few advisory board members	Founder and a few advisory board members
Adaptive Village April 2022	1 HBCU and a local nonprofit	5 grants available at $25,000 2 grants available at $10,000 4 grants available at $5,000 5 grants available at $2,000	$2,000–$25,000	Community voting and panel of HBCU and partnering nonprofit; community members	Community voting and review panel; community members
We Give Black Fest August 2022	Individuals and institutional partners	$235,000			
CLLCTIV SOUP Planned for 2023	Individuals	$10 donation	All funds raised for the evening	Attendees vote	Community voting

Source: CLLCTIVLY.

in August during Black Philanthropy Month. In 2021, the Black Business Quest emerged as a distinct component of CLLCTIVGIVE, consisting of a scavenger hunt encouraging community members to visit different Black-led businesses in Baltimore and learn about local history. In 2022, CLLCTIVLY introduced We Give Black Fest as a three-day festival in August, encompassing CLLCTIVGIVE day, the Black Business Quest, and other activities. For each of the strategies includedin table 8.3, the month and year of its founding are listed, along with the form of funding its mobilizes through participatory approaches.

The Black Futures video contest and no-strings-attached microgrant, started in 2019 and funded by foundations, is a monthly participatory grantmaking event that identifies winners through a community decision-making process. Each month, Black-led organizations are invited to submit a 3-minute video to feature its work in ways that connect to the Nguzo Saba principles, after which community voting opens for a ten-day period. Participants are encouraged to share the video link with their networks to increase their chances of winning, further disseminating these stories of Black genius and Black giving. The selection criteria for the Black Futures awards are informed by need and location. The first-place winner receives $1,000 and the runner-up receives $500. All participants gain visibility, as each video typically attracts new opportunities and resources, like speaking engagements, new clients, and volunteers. To date, $75,000 has been awarded to over fifty grantees. One example is the 2022 Women's Month Herstory winner, KRS Smoothies.[109] Its founder, Kamri Moses, started her smoothie business at fourteen years old. Her Nguzo Saba principle is Purpose (Nia). Winning this award has allowed her to teach entrepreneurship to fellow youth, through making smoothies. She is now a freshman at Spelman College with plans to make a difference in her hometown.

The Black Futures 360 Giving Circle, founded in 2019 and funded by individual donors, connects people with common causes to pool their time, talent, and money to support Black-led organizations with $360 each year. Currently, there are about sixty members in Giving Circles, which acknowledge the history of racial capitalism and the ways it has harmed African Americans. Giving Circle members also explore ways they can address the harm, pursue common interests, set giving priorities, and pool resources to make a greater impact. In the spirit of Ujima (Cooperative Economics), these individuals learn to support one another, dream together, and work together to advance their work.

Established in 2019 and funded by foundations and individual donors, CLLCTIVGIVE is an annual Day of Giving held in August during Black

Philanthropy Month, to raise funds for Black Futures projects, which are also supported through the giving circle described below. By participating in this global celebration of giving by people of African descent, CLLCTIVLY is elevating and supporting Black-led organizations in way that shifts the narrative from Black people as beneficiaries to those who are benefactors. In 2019, CLLCTIVLY raised $5,000 in 24 hours; in 2020, $56,000 was raised; in 2021, $102,000; and in 2022, $235,000. In the tradition of helping promoted through the Black Church, CLLCTIVGIVE is an opportunity to pass the plate and invite everyone to give to support organizations of one's choice. Over the last three years, two hundred organizations have been awarded funds through this participatory grantmaking strategy.

Participatory Grantmaking in 2020–2021: Responding to Seismic Social Events

At the onset of the coronavirus pandemic and the racial unrest after the murder of George Floyd in 2020, CLLCTIVLY was well positioned as a source for those seeking to fund Black-led organizations. As these groups responded to emerging needs, they became financially vulnerable themselves as they scrambled to cover the cost of expanding their services or were forced to suspend programs and events that generated revenue.

With a database of over 150 Black-led organizations, Wooten launched five new Black Futures grantmaking strategies: the Black Solidarity Fund, We Got Your Back, #28 Days of Black Futures, Adaptive Village, and We Give Black Fest. CLLCTIV SOUP is a forthcoming program.

The Black Solidarity Fund, founded in March 2020, was sparked by the disproportionate impact Black communities in Baltimore experienced during the pandemic. CLLCTIVLY's founder built upon the Black Futures microgrants, the Black Futures 360 Giving Circle, and CLLCTIVGIVE to create the Black Solidarity Fund.[110] In the spirit of *Ujima* (Collective Work and Responsibility), the fund was first established with crowdfunding. It was later continued with funding from individual donors and foundations to support Black-led organizations in need during the pandemic. Baltimore Ravens defensive end Calais Campbell and the Rockefeller Foundation supported CLLCTIVLY to expand economic opportunities for Baltimore's Black-led organizations during the pandemic. Campbell's gift leveraged the support of a foundation and unleashed the untapped giving potential among individual donors. This project allowed members of the Black community to see themselves as philanthropists. Black businesses owners like Terence

Dickson of Terra Café that faced barriers to receiving the federal government's Paycheck Protection Program loan were supported by the Black Solidarity Fund.[111] Wooten initially anticipated securing $1,600 from foundations and $1,600 from individual donors to help fund 50 grants at $500. However, funding exceeded his expectation, and CLLCTIVLY distributed 100 grants for $500 and 3 awards of $10,000.

Founded in 2020 and funded by individual donors, We Got Your Back is a campaign to support Black women changemakers in Baltimore. In partnership with a community of established women changemakers and entrepreneurs, an individual is integrated into this new community and supported with a no-strings-attached stipend of $2,000 per month. This grant can cover her living expenses or finance whatever brings her joy for one year. The *Global Entrepreneurship Monitor 2015 United States Report* indicated that 61 percent of women self-fund their startup capital, compared with 50 percent of men.[112] In talking about the motivation for starting We Got Your Back, Wooten recalled his own sister, Sherri: "She was not only committed to being a successful businesswoman, but she was also equally committed to giving back to the community. While we celebrate the resiliency of our community, we also know the grind and stress of entrepreneurship can take you out." The We Got Your Back campaign seeks to address this reality. Most philanthropy invests in projects and programs; instead, CLLCTIVLY invests in people to make sure they are whole and trusts them to use the funds to obtain what they need to pursue their dreams. CLLCTIVLY started this initiative with one donor pledging $600 a month; through crowdfunding, $11,729 of the $17,000 requested was raised from 132 individual donors.

Black Business Quest, founded in 2021 and supported by Black businesses and nonprofits, is a scavenger hunt that leads up to a fundraising event. To boost the visibility and resources of Black-led organizations, participants move around the city visiting various businesses, purchasing goods, and answering trivia questions. The businesses range from coffee shops to clothing stores. The participants who complete the tasks and gain the most points have a chance to win cash prizes while supporting Black-owned businesses. These Black-led organizations also compete for prizes. This event takes place in August during the 24-hour Day of Giving, CLLCTIVGIVE. In the spirit of philanthropy as repair, this activity places everyone in a community of equals as each person plays the game and has an opportunity to give. As with Ella Baker's vision, those that participate in this quest advance with the help of the community.

Established in 2022 and supported by individuals, #28 Days of Black Futures is a crowdfunding and narrative-power campaign that mobilizes resources and promotes the Black genius of Black-led organizations serving Greater Baltimore. In addition to amplifying the voices of twenty-eight Black leaders, the grantmaking goal is to raise $100,000 to support organizations that have historically been underfunded. All funds donated through this crowdfunding campaign are divided equally among the twenty-eight Black leaders. In 2022, the Reverend Dr. Heber Brown III and the Black Church Food Security Network received a share of the funds to continue to grow a network of Black churches and Black farmers to gain control over their food supply.[113] The Black Church Food Security Network reflects the future of Black people as it promotes "health, wealth, and power" in neglected communities by tackling one of the most basic human necessities: nutritious food. It also hearkens to the work of Fannie Lou Hamer and the Freedom Farmers, part of the cooperative movement in the 1960s and a pillar of Black giving that seeks to repair the economic imbalances in communities of color.[114]

The Adaptive Village small grants program is the most recent philanthropic program offered through CLLCTIVLY. Created in 2022 by Morgan State University's School of Community Health and Policy in partnership with the Family League of Baltimore, it is funded by individuals and institutional partners. Adaptive Village supports leaders in Baltimore communities who promote health equity and the creation of healthy spaces for children and the community. This new program acknowledges the need to support Black-led leaders holistically in wealth building. Each leader shares their story and project purpose and mission through a short video. There are four award categories for winners: $2,000, $5,000, $10,000, and $25,000. Organizations like the John Newman Honeybee Company received over 1,500 votes to help other Black people return to the ancestral tradition of beekeeping as well as claim economic empowerment and food sovereignty.[115] Other entries ranged from after-school and mental health programs to festivals and cultural programs. CLLCTIVLY awarded $220,000 to twenty-one organizations, five of them at $25,000. A total of 39,000 votes were cast.

We Give Black Fest is a three-day festival dedicated to resource mobilization for Black-owned businesses as well as social change and "celebration of culture as the foundation of community-driven wealth."[116] Founded in 2022 and funded by individuals and institutional partners, the festival includes engaging presentations, demonstrations, music, food, and prizes, and it hosts other events, such as CLLCTIVGIVE, Black Business Quest, and the Changemaker Awards. This festival is sponsored in partnership with the Vegan SoulFest and is held in August during Black Philanthropy Month. During the first We Give Black Fest, $235,000 was raised. The festival had eleven partners, including Kaiser Permanente, the Rockefeller Foundation, T. Rowe Price, South Baltimore Gateway Partnership, PNC Bank, Double Zero Baltimore, Liora, Good Neighbor, Dr. Bronner's All-in-One, and WJZ-TV. Ultimately, this festival builds upon the existing ways of giving, magnifies the power of Black giving, and amplifies the stories of Black genius.

CLLCTIV SOUP is a microgranting dinner series to celebrate and support Black-led social change organizations. Attendees give a $10 donation and receive soup, salad, bread, and a vote for one of four leaders sharing a 4-minute presentation. The winners take home half the funds raised. All presenters have an opportunity to network and share resources with attendees from across the city. This combination of food, fellowship, and cooperation reflects the influence of the Black church tradition and the cooperative movement. The launch of this program was postponed due to COVID-19, but CLLCTIVLY planned to offer it in 2023.

An Example of the Ecosystem Approach in Practice

One of the projects funded through the We Got Your Back campaign illustrates how CLLCTIVLY's multiple strategies reinforce one another. At one time, the Baltimore entrepreneur Dominiece Clifton had a dream to create a business that would provide holistic wellness services while increasing BIPOC representation in the wellness industry—but lacked funding to make it come true.

With funding support from We Got Your Back, Clifton officially launched her wellness company, Move And Still, in January 2022, in addition to pursuing certifications in yoga, meditation, and breathwork. Move And Still helps businesses and organizations promote emotional well-being and alignment for their employees through rest, stress management, and trauma recovery services using body-centered approaches to healing. To date, the organization has provided wellness services and stress education to over 360 beneficiaries, including PIVOT, the Community Assistance Network, Baltimore City Parks and Recreation, Sister's Circle, and Ballet After Dark.

In addition to providing funding, CLLCTIVLY has formed partnerships with the nonprofit organization The WELL (The Women Entrepreneur Leadership Lab) to support Clifton's business.

As a result of funding support, Clifton has been able to manage her own stress as an individual entrepreneur by resting, assured that critical living expenses, such as her mortgage, have been paid on time this year, as well as by investing in key business components like coaching and marketing support. Businesses like Clifton's—those without a proven track record—would not be supported by traditional grantmakers. Typically, access to grants requires organizations to prove that they are worthy.[117] According to Wooten, Clifton is "a sister making a huge impact in our city." Wooten hopes the success of projects like this one will help change the way elite donors consider the goals of philanthropy.

SUMMARIZING THE RELATIONSHIP BETWEEN CLLCTIVLY'S STRATEGIES AND PARTICIPATORY GRANTMAKING

CLLCTIVLY's efforts are important in light of the history of disinvestment in the Black community. Wooten implemented the tools used by his ancestors for resistance and cooperation to establish an evolving ecosystem and 100 percent participatory grantmaking model for Black-led organizations and Black communities in Greater Baltimore.[118] CLLCTIVLY primarily leverages the technology of social media to build its network of over 30,000 subscribers and fundraisers.

CLLCTIVLY's iterative approach to strategy allows it to stay in close relationship with the communities it serves and develop programs and campaigns that are directly relevant to them. Using its website and presence on Facebook, Instagram, and Twitter, CLLCTIVLY mobilizes resources through crowdfunding and crowdsourcing information to share the stories, new ideas, services, and goods generated by Baltimore's Black-led organizations and their leaders. Storytelling campaigns help change the narrative regarding Black-led organizations. Wooten prioritizes the relational work to provide the time and space to foster healing and build the opportunities for regular engagement for Black solidarity and community ownership of this work.

All of CLLCTIVLY's work reflect the four pillars of African American giving and address the five traditions of American philanthropy, providing relief, improvement, social reform, civic engagement, and repair. Since its launch in 2019, CLLCTIVLY has mobilized more than $1 million for about four hundred grants to Black-led organizations. Its primary funding strategy is participatory, trust-based, no-strings-attached grantmaking. This enables CLLCTIVLY to shift power by providing flexible grants, with the community driving the decision-making. This kind of philanthropy is disrupting traditional practices and the existing power base from which they are drawn. Wooten notes that local funders are beginning to follow in his footsteps. He has been asked to consult with funders to consider ways to better engage the community. However, he would prefer to see foundations fund CLLCTIVLY as an intermediary rather than establish their own, Black-led fund that could have a short-term life of three to five years. CLLCTIVLY is distinct in the local ecosystem as a place-based intermediary that is on the ground and knows the community.

In the same way that the ancient Greek word *philanthropia* connotes "to love," CLLCTIVLY prioritizes "love for people" and relationships over projects, programs, and profits. "Often funders invest in projects and programs, but we wanted to develop a fund that invests in people first and fosters a culture of health," CLLCTIVLY's founder, Jamye Wooten, says. "I know my sister would be proud."

CONCLUSION

Color-blind approaches to philanthropy are now being challenged as part of a broader reconsideration of how foundations can best contribute to social betterment. Their future will require exploring the often-neglected philanthropic traditions of people of color, as well as considering alternative philanthropic models such as participatory grantmaking. These include an emphasis on proximity and on "those who are closest to the problems [being] the best positioned to offer solutions to them."[119] This type of grantmaking often uses money as well as time, skill, effort, creativity, and networking to "heal what hurts ... and begin to heal ourselves, using money as medicine."[120]

The dominant grantmaking model remains a hierarchical, data-driven, and evidence-based process. It largely remains a rich-giving-to-the-poor model that comes with conditions. Given limited funding by traditional philanthropic organizations of Black communities, these culturally specific forms of giving are essential. However, Wooten's participatory grantmaking model invites elite foundations to invest in Black-led organizations with insights like "they want us to win" and "they really believe in the work that we're doing."[121] CLLCTIVLY builds on the philanthropic tradition of social reform, civic engagement, and repair to disrupt the structural racism and implicit racial bias found in traditional philanthropic practices.

After three years of operation, other cities like Atlanta, Chicago, Durham, and Philadelphia are already calling Wooten to bring CLLCTIVLY to their city. He is hopeful that the ecosystem in which participatory grantmaking strategies are embedded will sustain a system of shared community power and decentralized decision-making processes. He believes this kind of place-based giving will move the field of philanthropy much closer to the kind of racial equity that prevents harm, improves opportunities, and redistributes benefits.[122] A restorative justice lens for this work emphasizes power shifting from traditional philanthropists to community leaders engaged in education, change making, and social transformation.[123]

"As funders, we need to reject the impulse to put grantmaking rather than change making at the center of our worldview," Ford Foundation president Darren Walker stated in 2020. "Listening, learning, and lifting up voices who are most proximate and most essential to unlocking solutions is critical to the type of change making that we seek."[124] In the case of CLLCTIVLY, Wooten's model amplifies the voices and work of Black-led organizations and their leaders. This kind of participatory grantmaking helps to liberate our imaginations in ways that free us to listen, learn, unlearn, and lift up the genius of those often excluded from traditional philanthropy. CLLCTIVLY offers new ways to determine who sits at the funding tables, who receives the funds, and how we might see new philanthropists at these tables. Wooten, through CLLCTIVLY, challenges the old patterns of looking for what is best for big investors and traditional philanthropists and instead promotes new narratives that create opportunity for everyone to be philanthropists and for those with more resources to engage with the communities creating their own solutions.[125]

ACKNOWLEDGMENTS

We gratefully acknowledge Jayme Wooten for devoting several hours of his time to interviews and for providing organizational data. For their research support, we also thank the Baylor University librarian and director of digital scholarship, Joshua Been, and our research assistant, Miracle I. Chukwula-Eze. We also thank Chrissy Baker, Sabrina Carter, and Kelly Porter for research assistance managing the bibliographic database and support to identify resources. We are grateful for the review of and feedback on various chapter versions from Sandy Williams, Toni Fitzgerald, Dr. Becca Cassidy, Dr. Elizabeth Lynn, Dr. Una Osili, Dr. Trina Shanks, and Dr. Mia Moody-Ramirez.

NOTES

1. Marty Sulek, "On the Classical Meaning of Philanthrôpía," *Nonprofit and Voluntary Sector Quarterly* 39, no. 3 (2009): 385–408, https://doi.org/10.1177/0899764009333050.
2. Elizabeth M. Lynn and Susan Wisely, "Four Traditions of Philanthropy," Lake Institute on Faith & Giving, October 13, 2022, YouTube video, https://www.youtube.com/watch?v=QC8ohnF_rZI.
3. Darren Walker, "From Generosity to Justice: A New Gospel of Wealth," UTHSA Center for Medical Humanities and Ethics, September 11, 2020, YouTube video, https://youtu.be/b75SSxAH61I.
4. Cheryl Dorsey, Jeff Bradach, and Peter Kim, *Racial Equity and Philanthropy: Disparities in Funding for Leaders of Color Leave Impact on the Table* (Boston: Bridgespan Group, 2020), https://www.bridgespan.org/bridgespan/Images/articles/racial-equity-and-philanthropy/racial-equity-and-philanthropy.pdf.
5. William Foster, Gail Perreault, and Bradley Seeman, "Becoming Big Bettable," *Stanford Social Innovation Review* 17, no. 2 (Spring 2019), https://ssir.org/articles/entry/becoming_big_bettable.
6. Cynthia Gibson, *Participatory Grantmaking: Has Its Time Come?* (New York: Ford Foundation, 2017), https://www.fordfoundation.org/media/3599/participatory_grantmaking-lmv7.pdf.
7. Elizabeth M. Lynn and D. Susan Wisely, "Toward a Fourth Philanthropic Response: American Philanthropy and Its Public," in *The Perfect Gift: The Philanthropic Imagination in Poetry and Prose*, ed. Amy Kass (Bloomington: Indiana University Press, 2002), 102–12; Lynn and Wisely, "Four Traditions."
8. Emmett Devon Carson, *A Hand Up: Black Philanthropy and Self-Help in America* (Washington, DC: Joint Center for Political and Economic Studies Press, 1993); Emmett Devon Carson, "Giving Strength: Understanding Philanthropy in the Black Community," *Philanthropy Matters* 2, no. 4 (2001): 2–4.
9. Lynn and Wisely, "Toward a Fourth Philanthropic Response," 102–12.
10. Lynn and Wisely, 102.
11. Michael Remaley, "The State of American Philanthropy: Philanthropy, Social Justice and Shifting Power," *Inside Philanthropy*, 15, www.insidephilanthropy.com/state-of-american-philanthropy-pdfs/philanthropy-social-justice-and-shifting-power.
12. W. E. B. Du Bois, ed., *Efforts for Social Betterment among Negro Americans* (Atlanta: Atlanta University Press, 1909).
13. Lynn and Wisely, "Toward a Fourth Philanthropic Response," 102–12; Lynn and Wisely, "Four Traditions."
14. Dwayne Ashley, Tashion Macon, and Jennifer Jiles, "Cultural Icons for Social Change: 12 Top Pioneers of Black Philanthropy," Bridge Philanthropic Consulting, February 26, 2021, https://bridgephilanthropicconsulting.com/wp-content/uploads/2021/02/Pioneers-of-Black-Philanthropy-compressedv2.pdf; Marne Campbell, "African American Women, Wealth Accumulation, and Social Welfare Activism in 19th-Century Los Angeles," *Journal of African American History* 97, no. 4 (Fall 2012): 376–400, https://doi.org/10.5323/jafriamerhist.97.4.0376.
15. Lynn and Wisely, "Toward a Fourth Philanthropic Response," 102–12.
16. Lynn and Wisely, "Toward a Fourth Philanthropic Response"; Lynn and Wisely, "Four Traditions."

17. Emmett Devon Carson, "Black Philanthropy's Past, Present, and Future," *New Directions for Philanthropic Fundraising* 48 (May 12, 2005): 5–12, https://doi.org/10.1002/pf.100; Violet Harrington Bryan, "Frances Joseph-Gaudet: Black Philanthropist," *Sage Open* 3, no. 1 (Spring 1986): 46; Bernice McNair Barnett, "Invisible Southern Black Women Leaders in the Civil Rights Movement: The Triple Constraints of Gender, Race, and Class," *Gender & Society* 7, no. 2 (1993): 162–82, https://doi.org/10.1177/089124393007002002; Ashley, Macon, and Jiles, "Cultural Icons."
18. Lynn and Wisely, "Toward a Fourth Philanthropic Response," 102–12.
19. Dennis Dickerson, *The African Methodist Episcopal Church: A History* (Cambridge: Cambridge University Press, 2020); Tyrone McKinley Freeman, *Madam C. J. Walker's Gospel of Giving: Black Women's Philanthropy during Jim Crow* (Champaign: University of Illinois Press, 2020); Richard Newman, *Freedom's Prophet: Bishop Richard Allen, the AME Church, and the Black Founding Fathers* (New York: New York University Press, 2008).
20. Freeman, *Madam C. J. Walker's Gospel*.
21. Marybeth Gasman, "Rhetoric vs. Reality: The Fundraising Messages of the United Negro College Fund in the Immediate Aftermath of the Brown Decision," *History of Education Quarterly* 44, no. 1 (2004): 70–94, www.jstor.org/stable/3218111.
22. Lynn and Wisely, "Four Traditions."
23. Walker, "From Generosity to Justice."
24. Aria Florant and Venneikia Williams, "Reimaging Philanthropy to Build a Culture of Repair," *Nonprofit Quarterly*, November 21, 2022, https://nonprofitquarterly.org/reimagining-philanthropy-to-build-a-culture-of-repair/; Remaley, "State of American Philanthropy."
25. Walker, "From Generosity to Justice."
26. Miki Akimoto, "The Work of a Lifetime: Reparative Philanthropy, Relationships, Healing, and Joy," Family Giving News blog, National Center for Family Philanthropy, November 16, 2022, www.ncfp.org/2022/11/16/the-work-of-a-lifetime-reparative-philanthropy-relationships-healing-and-joy/; Edgar Villanueva, *Decolonizing Wealth: Indigenous Wisdom to Heal Divides and Restore Balance* (Oakland: Berrett-Koehler, 2018).
27. Akimoto, "Work of a Lifetime."
28. Villanueva, *Decolonizing Wealth*.
29. Akimoto, "Work of a Lifetime"; Florant and Williams, "Reimaging Philanthropy."
30. J. M. Murphy, "Thomy LaFon," *Negro History Bulletin* 7, no. 1 (1943): 6–20; Ray Allen Billington, "James Forten: Forgotten Abolitionist," *Negro History Bulletin* 13, no. 2 (November 1949): 31–45.
31. Murphy, "Thomy LaFon," 6–20; Billington, "James Forten," 31–45.
32. Valaida Fullwood, personal communication, November 28, 2022.
33. Dorsey, Bradach, and Kim, *Racial Equity*; Du Bois, *Efforts for Social Betterment*; and Freeman, *Madam C. J. Walker's Gospel*.
34. Tyrone McKinley Freeman, "'If We Had Not Loved Each Other . . .': An In-Person Book Talk at the Gantt with Author Tyrone McKinley Freeman, PhD," September 15, 2022, YouTube video, www.youtube.com/watch?v=7zK1bMYmyF0.
35. Halima Leak and Chera Reid, "'Making Something of Themselves': Black Self-Determination, the Church, and Higher Education Philanthropy," *International Journal of Educational Advancement* 10 (2010): 236, https://doi.org/10.1057/ijea.2010.20; Freeman, *Madam C. J. Walker's Gospel*; Freeman, "'If We Had Not Loved Each Other.'"

36. James Baldwin, "My Dungeon Shook: Letter to My Nephew on the One Hundredth Anniversary of the Emancipation," in *The Fire Next Time* (New York: Dial Press, 1963), 21. In "'If We Had Not Loved Each Other,'" Freeman explained the context of philanthropy as love and used Baldwin's "Letter to My Nephew on the One Hundredth Anniversary of the Emancipation" to emphasize that love has sustained and energized Black generosity.
37. Alan Fowler and Jacob Mwathi Mati, "African Gifting: Pluralising the Concept of Philanthropy," *Voluntas: International Journal of Voluntary and Nonprofit Organizations* 30 (2019): 727–29, https://doi.org/10.1007/s11266-018-00079-z.
38. Rodney Jackson, *A Philanthropic Covenant with Black America* (Hoboken, NJ: John Wiley & Sons, 2009); Freeman, *Madam C. J. Walker's Gospel*; Valaida Fullwood, *Giving Back: A Tribute to Generations of African American Philanthropists* (Charlotte: Foundation for the Carolinas, 2012).
39. Carson, *Hand Up*; Henry Louis Gates Jr., *The Black Church: This Is Our Story, This Is Our Song* (New York: Penguin Press, 2021); C. Eric Lincoln and Lawrence Mamiya, *The Black Church in the African American Experience* (Durham, NC: Duke University Press, 1990).
40. James Joseph, "Black Philanthropy: The Potential and Limits of Private Generosity in a Civil Society" (lecture, National Portrait Gallery, Smithsonian Institution, Washington, 1991), 5.
41. Carson, "Giving Strength," 4.
42. Lincoln and Mamiya, *Black Church*, 242.
43. Stephanie Clintonia Boddie and Prema Thirupathy, *Way to Give: A Guide to Connecting, Giving and Asset-Building* (Baltimore: Annie E. Casey Foundation, 2005); Alice Burnette, "Giving Strength: Understanding Philanthropy in the Black Community," *Philanthropy Matters* 11, no. 1 (2001): 3–5.
44. Stephanie Clintonia Boddie, "Ways to Give: Black Churches Giving During the Pandemic," paper presented at Annual Meeting of Society for the Scientific Study of Religion, Baltimore, November 11–13, 2022; Emmett Devon Carson, *Black Volunteers and Givers and Fundraisers* (New York: Center for the Study of Philanthropy, 1990); Carson, "Black Philanthropy's Past," 5–12; Darryl B. Holloman, Marybeth Gasman, and Sibby Anderson-Thompkins, "Motivations for Philanthropic Giving in the African American Church: Implications for Black College Fundraising," *Journal of Research on Christian Education* 12, no. 2 (2003): 137–69, https://doi.org/10.1080/10656210309484949; Leak and Reid, "'Making Something of Themselves,'" 235–44.
45. W. E. B. Du Bois, *The Philadelphia Negro: A Social Study* (Philadelphia: University of Pennsylvania Press, 1899); W. E. B. Du Bois, ed., *The Negro Church* (Atlanta: Atlanta University Press, 1903).
46. Du Bois, *Negro Church*.
47. Joseph C. Hartzell, "Methodism and the Negro in the United States," *Journal of Negro History* 8, no. 3 (July 1923): 301–15.
48. David J. Garrow, "A Circle of Trust: Remembering SNCC," *Journal of American History* 85, no. 4 (March 1999): 1672–73, https://doi.org/10.2307/2568404; Gates, *Black Church*; Joseph, "Black Philanthropy"; Harold Trulear, "Philanthropy and Religion," in *A Philanthropic Covenant with Black America*, ed. Rodney Jackson (Hoboken, NJ: John Wiley and Sons, 2009), 19–47; Lincoln and Mamiya, *Black Church*.

49. Aldon D. Morris, *Origins of the Civil Rights Movement: Black Communities Organizing for Change* (New York: Free Press, 1984), 4.
50. Carol Jenkins and Elizabeth Gardner Hines, *Black Titan: A. G. Gaston and the Making of a Black American Millionaire* (New York: One World, 2005).
51. Jenkins and Hines, *Black Titan*; Morris, *Origins*, 25; Evelyn M. Simien and Danielle L. McGuire, "A Tribute to the Women: Rewriting History, Retelling Herstory in Civil Rights," *Politics & Gender* 10, no. 3 (2014): 413–31, https://doi.org/10.1017/S1743923X14000245.
52. Sandra L. Barnes, "Black Church Giving: An Analysis of Ideological, Programmatic, and Denominational Effects," *Sage Open* 3, no. 2 (April–June 2013): 2158–440, https://journals.sagepub.com/doi/10.1177/2158244013490706; Boddie and Thirupathy, *Way to Give*.
53. Barnes, "Black Church Giving," 2158–440.
54. Barnes.
55. Besheer Mohamed, Kiana Cox, Jeff Diamant, and Claire Gecewicz, *Faith Among Black Americans* (Washington, DC: Pew Research Center, 2021), www.pewresearch.org/religion/2021/02/16/faith-among-black-americans/; Una Osili, Patricia Banks, Sarah King Bhetaria, and Stephanie Boddie, "Everyday Donors of Color: Diverse Philanthropy during Times of Change," working paper, Indiana University Lilly Family School of Philanthropy, August 2021, https://scholarworks.iupui.edu/handle/1805/26496.
56. Maulana Karenga, "Annual Founder's Kwanzaa Message: Practicing Kwanzaa and the Seven Principles; Ensuring the Well-Being of the World," *Los Angeles Sentinel*, December 23, 2021, https://lasentinel.net/annual-founders-kwanzaa-message.html; Vanessa D. Johnson, "The Nguzo Saba as a Foundation for African American College Student Development Theory," *Journal of Black Studies* 31, no. 4 (2001): 406–22, https://doi.org/10.1177/002193470103100402.
57. Karenga, "Annual Founder's Kwanzaa Message," 1.
58. Vanessa D. Johnson, "The Nguzo Saba as a Foundation for African American College Student Development Theory," *Journal of Black Studies* 31, no. 4 (2001): 406–22.
59. Jessica Gordon Nembhard, *Collective Courage: A History of African American Cooperative Economic Thought and Practice* (University Park: Pennsylvania State University Press, 2014).
60. Nembhard, *Collective Courage*.
61. Michelle Alexander, *The New Jim Crow: Mass Incarceration in the Age of Colorblindness* (London: Penguin Books, 2012); William Hooper Councill, *The Negro Laborer: A Word to Him* (Huntsville, AL: R. F. Dickson, 1887); Booker T. Washington, "Up From Slavery," in *Three Negro Classics: 1856–1901* (New York: Avon Books), 23–206; W. E. B. Du Bois, "The Economics of Negro Emancipation in the United States," *Sociological Review*, no. 4 (1911): 303–13, https://doi.org/10.1111/j.1467-954X.1911.tb02169.x; Marcus Garvey, *Selected Writings and Speeches of Marcus Garvey* (Mineola, NY: Dover, 2004).
62. W. E. B. Du Bois, ed., *Economic Co-Operation among Negro Americans* (Atlanta: Atlanta University Press, 1907); Sigmund C. Shipp, "The Road Not Taken: Alternative Strategies for Black Economic Development in the United States," *Journal of Economic Issues* 30, no. 1 (1996): 79–95, https://doi.org/10.1080/00213624.1996.11505767.

63. Nembhard, *Collective Courage*; Monica M. White, *Freedom Farmers: Agricultural Resistance and the Black Freedom Movement* (Chapel Hill: University of North Carolina Press, 2018).
64. Du Bois, *Economic Co-Operation*.
65. Nembhard, *Collective Courage*.
66. Karen Crozier, *Fannie Lou Hamer's Revolutionary Practical Theology: Racial and Environmental Justice Concerns*, Theology in Practice series, vol. 9 (Boston: Brill, 2020); Priscilla McCutcheon, "Fannie Lou Hamer's Freedom Farms and Black Agrarian Geographies," *Antipode* 51, no. 1 (January 2019), https://doi.org/10.1111/anti.12500; SNCC Digital Gateway, "Fannie Lou Hamer Founds Freedom Farm Cooperative," https://snccdigital.org/events/fannie-lou-hamer-founds-freedom-farm-cooperative/; White, *Freedom Farmers*.
67. Nancy Callahan, *The Freedom Quilting Bee: Folk Art and the Civil Rights Movement* (Tuscaloosa: University of Alabama Press, 2005); Stella Hendricks, "A Timeline of the Freedom Quilting Bee," BMA Stories blog, Baltimore Museum of Art, March 8, 2021, https://stories.artbma.org/timeline-the-freedom-quilting-bee.
68. Joshua H. Miller, "Empowering Communities: Ella Baker's Decentralized Leadership Style and Conversational Eloquence," *Southern Communication Journal* 81, no. 3 (April 25, 2016): 156–67, https://doi.org/10.1080/1041794X.2016.1149613; Charles Payne, "Ella Baker and Models of Social Change." *Signs* 14, no. 4 (1989): 885–99, https://doi.org/10.1086/494549.
69. Ella Baker, "Developing Community Leadership," interview by Gerda Lerner, December 1970, 4, https://americanstudies.yale.edu/sites/default/files/files/baker_leadership.pdf.
70. Ellen Cantarow, Susan Gushee O'Malley, and Sharon Hartman Strom, *Moving the Mountain: Women Working for Social Change* (New York: Feminist Press at City University of New York, 1980), 55; Edna R. Comedy, "Reconceptualizing Leadership through the Prism of the Modern Civil Rights Movement: A Grounded Theory Case Study on Ella Baker" (PhD diss., University of St. Thomas, 2015), 135–37, https://ir.stthomas.edu/cgi/viewcontent.cgi?article=1057&context=caps_ed_lead_docdiss; Carol Mueller, "Ella Baker and the Origins of 'Participatory Democracy,'" in *The Black Studies Reader*, ed. Jacqueline Bobo, Cynthia Hudley, and Claudine Michel (New York: Routledge, 2004), 85, 89.
71. Stephen Preskill and Stephen D. Brookfield, *Learning as a Way of Leading: Lessons from the Struggle for Social Justice* (San Francisco: John Wiley & Sons, 2008), 95.
72. Mueller, "Ella Baker," 83.
73. *Fundi: The Story of Ella Baker*, directed by Joanne Grant (Brooklyn: Icarus Films, 1981).
74. Mueller, "Ella Baker," 79–91.
75. CLLCTIVLY, "CLLCTIVLY: Building Black Futures Together," https://cllctivly.org.
76. CLLCTIVLY; Cori Lucas, "Healing the City by Giving People a Space to Openly Celebrate Life and Love," CLLCTIVLY, February 23, 2022, https://cllctivly.org/healing-the-city-by-giving-people-a-space-to-openly-celebrate-life-and-love/.
77. Carson, *Hand Up*; Gates, *Black Church*; Karenga, "Annual Founder's Kwanzaa Message;" Lincoln and Mamiya, *Black Church*; Trina Williams Shanks, Stephanie Clintonia Boddie, and Robert Wynn, "Wealth Building in Communities of Color," in *Race and*

Social Problems: Restructuring Inequality, ed. Ralph Bangs and Larry Davis (New York: Springer, 2014), 63–78, https://doi.org/10.1007/978-1-4939-0863-9_4.
78. Nembhard, *Collective Courage*.
79. Shanks, Boddie, and Wynn, "Wealth Building," 63–78, https://doi.org/10.1007/978-1-4939-0863-9_4.
80. City of Baltimore, "Comprehensive Master Plan," draft, https://planning.baltimorecity.gov/sites/default/files/History%20of%20Baltimore_1.pdf; Felipe González, Guillermo Marshall, and Suresh Naidu, "Start-Up Nation? Slave Wealth and Entrepreneurship in Civil War Maryland," *Journal of Economic History* 77, no. 2 (2017): 373–405, https://doi.org/10.1017/S0022050717000493.
81. Lawrence T. Brown, *The Black Butterfly: The Harmful Politics of Race and Space in America* (Baltimore: Johns Hopkins University Press, 2021).
82. Christopher Phillips, *Freedom's Port: The African American Community of Baltimore, 1790–1860* (Champaign: University of Illinois Press, 1997); Garrett Power, "Apartheid Baltimore Style: The Residential Segregation Ordinances of 1910–1913," *Maryland Law Review* 42, no. 2 (1983): 289–328, http://digitalcommons.law.umaryland.edu/mlr/vol42/iss2/4.
83. Phillips, *Freedom's Port*.
84. L. P. Maxwell, "Harriet Tubman," in *Encyclopedia of African-American Culture and History: The Black Experience in the Americas*, ed. Colin A. Palmer, 2nd edition, vol. 5 (New York: Macmillan Reference USA, 2006), 2210–12; Frederick Douglass, *Narrative of the Life of Frederick Douglass, an American Slave* (Boston: Anti-Slavery Office, 1851).
85. City of Baltimore, "Comprehensive Master Plan."
86. Carter Godwin Woodson, *The History of the Negro Church* (Washington, DC: Associated Publishers, 1921).
87. Marion Orr, *Black Social Capital: The Politics of School Reform in Baltimore, 1986–1998* (Lawrence: University Press of Kansas, 1999).
88. Phillips, *Freedom's Port*.
89. *New York Times*, "Baltimore Tries Drastic Plan of Race Segregation; Strange Situation Which Led the Oriole City to Adopt the Most Pronounced 'Jim Crow' Measure on Record. Baltimore Tries Drastic Plan of Race Segregation," December 25, 1910; Power, "Apartheid Baltimore Style," 289–328.
90. Douglas Massey and Jonathan Tannen, "A Research Note on Trends in Black Hypersegregation," *Demography* 52, no. 3 (June 2015): 1025–34, https://doi.org/10.1007/s13524-015-0381-6.
91. Luke Broadwater and Talia Richman, "Are City Services Worse in Black Baltimore Neighborhoods? Racial Equity Bill Would Require Answers," *Baltimore Sun*, August 1, 2018, www.baltimoresun.com/maryland/baltimore-city/bs-md-ci-racial-equity-charter-20180731-story.html.
92. Lawrence T. Brown, "Make Black Neighborhoods Matter," in *Urbanite: Truth, Reconciliation, and Baltimore*, issue 100 (November 2015): 74–75; Brown, *Black Butterfly*.
93. Richard Rothstein, "From Ferguson to Baltimore: The Fruits of Government-Sponsored Segregation," Working Economics blog, Economic Policy Institute, April 29, 2015, www.epi.org/blog/from-ferguson-to-baltimore-the-fruits-of-government-sponsored-segregation/.

CHAPTER 8

94. Erin Weber-Johnson, "Philanthropic Redlining: Working Twice as Hard for Half as Much," in *Crisis and Care: Meditations on Faith and Philanthropy*, ed. Dustin Benac and Erin Weber-Johnson (Eugene, OR: Cascade, 2021), chap. 10, Kindle.
95. Carson, *Black Volunteers*.
96. Jamye Wooten, "#BlackDeath: Can Pain Be Transformed into Power?" *HuffPost*, July 13, 2016, www.huffpost.com/entry/on-the-anniversary-of-san_b_10973856.
97. Baltimore United for Change, "About: We Demand Justice for Freddie Gray and Police Accountability," December 9, 2014, http://bmoreunited.org/about.
98. Sheilah Kast and Melissa Gerr, "CLLCTIVLY: A Network to Grow Black Genius," interview with Jamye Wooten, April 29, 2022, *On the Record*, National Public Radio, www.wypr.org/show/on-the-record/2022-04-29/cllctivly-a-network-to-grow-black-genius.
99. Ovetta Wiggins and Bill Turque, "NAACP to Challenge Cancellation of Baltimore Red Line Rail Project," *Washington Post*, December 21, 2015, www.washingtonpost.com/local/md-politics/naacp-to-challenge-cancellation-of-baltimore-red-line-rail-project/2015/12/21/6cdb45aa-a7fc-11e5-8058-480b572b4aae_story.html.
100. Danielle Underferth, "New Report Finds Stark Transit Inequity in Baltimore City," Johns Hopkins University, Bloomberg School of Public Health, October 7, 2021, https://publichealth.jhu.edu/2021/new-report-finds-stark-transit-inequity-in-baltimore-city.
101. Kast and Gerr, "CLLCTIVLY"; Lucas, "Healing the City."
102. Edgar S. Cahn and Christine Gray, "The Time Bank Solution," *Stanford Social Innovation Review* 13, no. 3 (Summer 2015): 41–45, https://doi.org/10.48558/T7DT-5794.
103. Remaley, "State of American Philanthropy."
104. Lynn and Wisely, "Toward a Fourth Philanthropic Response," 102–12; Lynn and Wisely, "Four Traditions."
105. Kast and Gerr, "CLLCLTIVLY"; Jamye Wooten, "#BeyondREactivism: The Use of Multimedia for Movement Building," presented at the 15th Anniversary of the Samuel DeWitt Proctor Conference, Memphis, February 11, 2018, https://btpbase.org/wp-content/uploads/2018/02/BeyondReActivism.-MULTIMEDIA-FOR-MOVEMENT-BUILDING.pdf.
106. Emily Finchum-Mason, Kelly Husted, and David Suárez, "Institutional Change or Shooting Star? The Landscape of Stakeholder Participation among Large Foundations in the United States," in *Participatory Grantmaking Research Collection*, ed. Cynthia Gibson, Chris Cardona, Jasmine Johnson, and David Suárez (Washington, DC: Georgetown University Press, forthcoming).
107. Remaley, "State of American Philanthropy."
108. Villanueva, *Decolonizing Wealth*, 22.
109. Kamri Moses, "BmoreHERstory Micro Futures Grant," March 16, 2022, YouTube video, www.youtube.com/watch?v=30I_xpActEc.
110. Black News, "New Fund in Baltimore Launches to Provide $500 Micro-Grants for Black-Led Organizations Impacted by COVID-19," May 22, 2020, https://blacknews.com/news/baltimore-fund-500-micro-grants-for-black-led-organizations-impacted-by-covid-19.
111. Ben Popken, "Why Are So Many Black-Owned Small Businesses Shut Out of PPP Loans?" NBC News, April 29, 2020, www.nbcnews.com/business/business-news/why-are-so-many-black-owned-small-businesses-shut-out-n1195291.

112. Donna J. Kelley, Abdul Ali, Candida Brush, Andrew C. Corbett, Caroline Daniels, Phillip H. Kim, Thomas S. Lyons, Mahdi Majbouri, and Edward G. Rogoff, *Global Entrepreneurship Monitor 2015 United States Report* (New York: Babson College and Baruch College, 2016), 43, www.gemconsortium.org/file/open?fileId=49562.
113. Cision PR Newswire, "CLLCTIVLY Asked 28 Black-Led Organizations, 'What Would a Fully Funded Black Futures Look Like?'" CLLCTIVLY, February 3, 2022, www.prnewswire.com/news-releases/cllctivly-asked-28-black-led-organizations-what-would-a-fully-funded-black-futures-look-like-301475204.html.
114. Crozier, *Fannie Lou Hamer's Revolutionary Practical Theology*; McCutcheon, "Fannie Lou Hamer's Freedom Farms and Black Agrarian Geographies;" SNCC Digital Gateway, "Fannie Lou Hamer Founds Freedom Farm Cooperative"; White, *Freedom Farmers*.
115. John Newman Honeybee Co., "John Newman Honeybee for Adaptive Village Grant," May 10, 2022, YouTube video, www.youtube.com/watch?v=YC86Mjh68yU.
116. Kast and Gerr, "CLLCTIVLY."
117. Villanueva, *Decolonizing Wealth*.
118. Gibson, *Participatory Grantmaking*.
119. Remaley, "State of American Philanthropy," 18.
120. Villanueva, *Decolonizing Wealth*, 2.
121. Osili et al., "Everyday Donors," 33.
122. Remaley, "State of American Philanthropy."
123. Remaley.
124. Dorsey, Bradach, and Kim, *Racial Equity*, 10.
125. Pablo Fuentenebro, "Will Philanthropy Save Us All? Rethinking Urban Philanthropy in a Time of Crisis," *Geoforum* 117 (December 2020): 304–7, https://doi.org/10.1016/j.geoforum.2020.07.005; Remaley, "The State of American Philanthropy."

PART III

The Challenges for and Limits of Participatory Grantmaking

This part of the book comprises four chapters that identify challenges for participatory grantmaking (PGM) or represent cases where an organization decided it was not the right practice at the right moment. Taken together, they provide a counterpoint to the examples of successful over-time adoption of PGM identified in part II. The examples in both sections also include significant amounts of self-reflection, identification of contextual factors that contribute to or make more difficult the adoption of PGM, and a commitment to practicing philanthropy in a way that aligns with the values of the respective organization or donor.

In chapter 9, Dale and Carter, an academic and a practitioner, respectively, collaborate to describe the experience of the Pride Foundation, a Seattle-based LGBTQ+ public foundation, as it considered whether to adopt PGM as a practice. The backdrop of the COVID-19 pandemic and the racial justice uprising of 2020 had a powerful influence on the Pride Foundation's deliberations. Given the extraordinary and novel context these societal trends created for the foundation and its nonprofit partners, the foundation ultimately decided not to adopt PGM in favor of a trust-based philanthropy approach that put less emphasis on sharing power for making decisions on grants and more on mitigating the power dynamics inherent in the funder–nonprofit relationship. For Pride, nonadoption is not a simple "yes/no," but rather a search for a set of philanthropic tools that fit the organization's purpose and values, as well as the societal moment in which it operates.

In chapter 10, MacLean, Merenda, and Bartel, from the perspective of the community-foundation network CFLeads, examine how community foundations have chosen to embrace—or not—PGM under the rubric "community leadership." While much of what falls within CFLeads's community leadership frame is participatory, it crucially does not always include affording nonprofit partners the opportunity to make decisions on grants. In this respect, community foundations operating under a community leadership frame do not usually "go all the way" toward PGM (understood as sharing power over decision-making about grants). And yet they practice an approach to participation that is related to, but distinct from, PGM.

In chapter 11, Hartmann and Schambra introduce further nuances from a conservative perspective. They question whether PGM is exclusively a progressive construct or whether conservative donors can and should engage in it. They identify elements of "participatoriness" that they argue are inherent in many conservative causes, such as support for school vouchers. They also suggest that rather than invent a new PGM process to understand what the community wants, funders can look to the organizations that communities already trust and invest in those. The authors conclude by wondering why more conservative donors do not practice PGM, given the affinity of certain elements of the conservative tradition with PGM's emphasis on localized, community-driven decision-making.

In chapter 12, Katahira and Jackson broaden the frame to consider the perspectives of megadonors alongside traditional foundations. They examine a set of funders that chose to experiment with PGM as a way of advancing racial equity and making their funding practices more inclusive. They identify internal and external factors that shaped the results of these experiments. And crucially, they observe that most of the funders had originally planned to continue or expand their PGM experiments, but ultimately chose not to.

These four chapters offer contrasting perspectives on the question of whether and in what circumstances it makes sense for traditional foundations and megadonors to adopt PGM. In doing so, they complicate and deepen the insights gleaned from the case studies of adoption presented in part II. In the conclusion, the four coeditors consider how the book's twelve chapters have informed and helped sharpen the analysis and frame presented in the introduction.

CHAPTER 9

Community Representation, COVID-19, and the Challenges of Shifting Grantmaking Power
How a Public LGBTQ+ Foundation Weighed the Options

Elizabeth J. Dale and Katie Carter

This chapter discusses how the Pride Foundation, a public foundation serving the LGBTQ+ community, rethought its Community Grants Program as part of making a broader institutional commitment to racial equity. It details what the transition away from a traditional, application-based grantmaking model looked like in real time during the height of the COVID-19 pandemic, and it raises important questions for other foundations to answer when aligning their grantmaking with an equity lens. One of these questions is: Under what circumstances should established foundations explore and adopt alternative approaches to grantmaking, such as participatory grantmaking and trust-based philanthropy? This chapter discusses how the Pride Foundation ultimately adopted a trust-based philanthropy approach, which centers mutually accountable relationships between funders and grantees and shifts power away from funders to consider grantees' needs.

INTRODUCTION

When COVID-19 swept across the United States in March 2020, businesses, the government, and nonprofits quickly shut down their in-person operations. But as people lost income and then jobs, and others became ill, the individuals and communities that already faced systemic and institutional barriers—like racism, sexism, and homophobia—experienced even greater insecurity and loss. For a community foundation like the Pride Foundation, marshaling and moving its resources to the lesbian, gay, bisexual, transgender, and queer (LGBTQ+) organizations it supports became its immediate focus. While all individuals and organizations grappled with the uncertainty of the weeks and months ahead, for the Pride Foundation, the pandemic's call to action would leave a lasting imprint on its approach to grantmaking.

As a public foundation with a thirty-seven-year history in the LGBTQ+ community, the Pride Foundation was already several years into deep antiracism and culture change work when the COVID-19 pandemic began. The foundation recognized that while all LGBTQ+ people confront discrimination, LGBTQ+ people of color face systemic and structural racism that creates significant barriers to opportunities throughout their lives and also lowers the commitments of philanthropic funding.[1] In 2017, the Pride Foundation adopted a racial equity action plan that addressed remedying injustice throughout all aspects of the organization. A critical part of this work was revising the foundation's grantmaking strategy and decision-making processes to center racial equity as a core commitment across the organization.

Because the participatory grantmaking model is aligned with a justice and equity focus, the Pride Foundation seriously considered adopting participatory grantmaking as a way to operationalize its racial equity commitment.[2] When it began this work in 2019, there was (and still is) little information available to established foundations interested in making the transition to a participatory approach. While the foundation decided to forgo immediately moving to a comprehensive participatory grantmaking model, it used the transition process as an opportunity to carefully examine whether and to what extent a participatory grantmaking approach would be feasible and the factors that influenced that decision—information that could also be helpful to the larger field of institutional and individual donors.

This chapter not only details what the Pride Foundation's grantmaking transition looked like but also raises important questions to consider for other foundations that are committed to aligning their grantmaking with an equity lens. One of these questions is: Under what circumstances should established foundations explore alternative approaches to participatory grantmaking, such as trust-based philanthropy? The trust-based approach was ultimately adopted by the Pride Foundation, showing that there is more than one path to implementing equitable grantmaking.

THE IMPETUS FOR THIS WORK

A confluence of factors led the Pride Foundation to begin evaluating its grantmaking process and structure in 2019. First, the foundation had adopted a racial equity action plan in 2017 under the leadership of past CEO Kris Hermanns, the goal of which was to "fundamentally transform our work to center racial equity throughout our mission, structure, internal culture, programs, practices, and investments."[3] This culture change work grew out of the recognition that LGBTQ+ people of color face systemic and structural racism, along with a lack of philanthropic investment in addressing these barriers.

Working with a racial equity consultant from 2016 to 2019, the Pride Foundation's staff and board members went through training sessions, began race-based caucusing, and started analyzing every aspect of the organization's operations, both internally and externally. Ultimately, the Pride Foundation created a racial equity action plan that detailed specific steps for each department and the board to take to center racial equity throughout the organization. With expansive goals, the level and scope of commitment of the plan were well ahead of those of many peer foundations and included:

- centering racial equity in the organization's structure and culture;
- elevating the leadership opportunities for people of color among board, staff, and volunteers;
- ensuring that donors, volunteers, and supporters were engaged in and committed to racial equity and reflective of the organization's full community;
- integrating racial equity learning and education opportunities across the organization;
- revising policies to incorporate a racial equity lens; and
- prioritizing racial equity in all funding decisions and resource allocation, as well as creating authentic and reciprocal relationships with stakeholders and community partners.

Next, the foundation experienced a leadership transition in 2019, appointing the fifth CEO in its history and hiring a new director of programs. With new leadership, the racial equity plan, and a new strategic plan in place for 2019–21, the Pride Foundation was ready to examine, reflect on, and make changes to its core Community Grants Program to align it with the organization's racial equity goals.

As the foundation began examining its centerpiece grantmaking program, it realized that the knowledge and experience gained from the transition it was experiencing might be useful to share with other established foundations interested in adopting participatory models. While there has been significant research and writing about foundations engaged in participatory grantmaking and the core tenets of the practice, there has been relatively little research dedicated to studying foundations during a period of grantmaking transition.[4] We believed that to encourage more funders, including public and private foundations, to adopt participatory and power-sharing grantmaking models, it was essential to understand how a foundation that currently used a more traditional, application-focused funding process could shift its work and address the potential challenges that a new model of grantmaking presented.

While the paper by Dale and Plastino provides a description of the full case study, this chapter takes a retrospective look back and charts a path forward—both for the Pride Foundation and other foundations interested in equitable grantmaking.[5] We use three core questions to chronicle the foundation's work and then pose those same questions for funders interested in these efforts. These core questions are:

1. Why should established foundations consider participatory grantmaking? What other models shift or share power?
2. Who would make grant decisions in a participatory funding approach? What specific changes to the grantmaking process would best accomplish the foundation's goals?
3. What opportunities and challenges might be expected in implementing a different grantmaking structure, especially one that is focused on shifting power?

We believe that by asking, discussing, and answering each question, foundations, including the Pride Foundation, will have a better understanding of the tenets of participatory grantmaking, the range of ways to shift power and broaden participation in philanthropic funding, and the challenges of transforming grantmaking practice.

RESEARCH METHODS

Given that the Pride Foundation was already on a racial equity path to undertake culture change work to align its grantmaking, we conceived the research process as a single, embedded case study, whereby the researcher (Elizabeth Dale) and a graduate assistant provided ongoing consultation, research, and facilitation to support the grantmaking transition. They also created reflective space for the organization to discuss the transition process.[6] Recognizing that documenting the Pride Foundation's thought processes as well as the challenges that arose and how the foundation navigated these challenges could offer deeper insight to the foundation field, we conducted our research over a fifteen-month period from December 2019 through April 2021. Data gathering included individual interviews with the Pride Foundation's five regional program officers, its director of programs, and CEO; monthly meetings with the researchers, director of programs, and CEO; an audit of the Community Grants Program from 2011–19; an analysis of the Pride Foundation's and other participatory grantmaking foundations' grant applications; and a survey of grantee and applicant organizations to the foundation from the prior three years. These research materials aided the Pride Foundation in its transition, and they informed the retrospective conversation that is discussed below.

EVOLUTION OF THE PRIDE FOUNDATION'S GRANTMAKING

Founded in 1985 in response to the HIV/AIDS crisis, the Pride Foundation was established by and for the LGBTQ+ community. As of 2022, the foundation manages over $47 million in restricted and unrestricted assets, which include donor-advised funds, an extensive scholarship program for LGBTQ+ students, and the Community Grants Program (CGP). Since its inception, the Pride Foundation has made over $80 million in grants in the Pacific Northwest states of Alaska, Idaho, Montana, Oregon, and Washington. Beginning largely as a volunteer effort, the public foundation began hiring staff in the late 1980s, and it has grown substantially over the past three decades, increasing its staff, growing its programmatic offerings, and increasing the amount of money raised and awarded. Over the course of this time, different models of grantmaking have been utilized, and they have shifted with the practices of the time and the size of the foundation. Its staff and board continue to be broadly reflective of the LGBTQ+ community. As a public foundation, the Pride Foundation's assets have come from hundreds of donors, and the foundation continues to raise new money from donors each year to expand its grantmaking and scholarship programs.

Beginning in 1987, the CGP was one of the first programs that the Pride Foundation established, which has awarded more than $12 million in grants since its inception. When the foundation began to reexamine its grantmaking in 2019, the CGP was awarding more than $550,000 in each annual grantmaking cycle (see table 9.1). Over the course of the past three-plus decades, the Pride Foundation had used a variety of decision-making models to administer its community grants, continually evolving with the larger grantmaking field in determining ways to best serve LGBTQ+ communities. For example, earlier iterations of the foundation's grantmaking utilized giving circle models, whereby local communities raised resources and dispersed them to groups based on narrow geographic locations. Later, the CGP moved to using state-based committees of reviewers to evaluate grant applications from each state and make grant award decisions. This model became more formalized in the 2010s through the hiring of state-based, regional program officers and engaging a cadre of volunteer reviewers who each read and scored a small portion of the grant applications. In the most recent iteration of its community grantmaking, volunteers provided input during the application review but did not make final grant decisions; those rested with the staff and, ultimately, the organization's board.

In the initial round of project interviews conducted in early 2020 with the Pride Foundation's five regional program officers, director of programs, and CEO, staff members identified several key challenges for the CGP:

- *The effort that applicant organizations spent completing grant proposals was not consummate with grant awards.* The current grants program required applicants to complete a lengthy written application, yet the average grant award was only $5,000.
- *Input from nonstaff volunteers was inconsistent, and volunteers were not decision-makers.* While volunteers provided input, they did not necessarily read all the applications or have knowledge of specific organizations or broader ecosystems. Also, although the Pride Foundation had an open call for grant review volunteers, participation across its five-state region was uneven and did not necessarily reflect the grantee community.
- *The process was lengthy and slow in getting funds out the door.* The time from application deadline to decision could last as long as six months, which seemed too long, given the number of smaller organizations that applied for grants and needed funding more quickly.

To address these issues, leadership and program staff initially expressed interest in adopting a participatory grantmaking model, whereby members

Table 9.1: Timeline of Key Events in the Pride Foundation's Grantmaking Transition

2017	Racial Equity Action Plan adopted
	Katie Carter named CEO
	Jeremiah Allen named director of programs
	Research engagement begins
2019	Review of Community Grants Program begins
	COVID-19 pandemic forces organization to close in-person operations
	Crisis Community Care Fund launched
	Community Grants Program application simplified and decision-making cycle shortened
2020	Program staff begin a learning community around participatory grantmaking and trust-based philanthropy
	Kim Sogge promoted to director of programs
2021	Reimagined Community Grants Program begins, featuring a proactive and trust-based funding model with two-year grants

Source: Author data.

of the grantee community would be involved in setting grantmaking priorities and making grant decisions. However, before this model could be fully considered and developed, the COVID-19 pandemic ushered in a new kind of grantmaking. This approach stemmed from a need to rapidly respond to organizations' pandemic-related needs and the emergence of a new organization—the Trust-Based Philanthropy Project—that advocated an equity-based grantmaking philosophy that placed the onus of culture change on funders: "At its core, trust-based philanthropy is rooted in a set of values that help advance equity, shift power, and build mutually accountable relationships."[7] While trust-based philanthropy still leaves grant decision-making with the funder, its approach incorporates greater power awareness, mutual trust and partnership with nonprofits, and a commitment to ask for and act on feedback from grantee organizations, among others—attributes that traditional approaches to institutional philanthropy do not necessarily embody.

In March 2020, the Pride Foundation created a new funding stream in response to the pandemic (the Crisis Community Care Fund), and made proactive grants to groups without requiring a formal application or request. Table 9.1 provides a timeline of key events.

Table 9.2: The Pride Foundation's Community Grants Program Transition

Grantmaking practice	Past practices, 2015–19	Transition year: 2020	Trust-based philanthropy, starting in 2021
Grantee application	Online application required tailored information and a program or organizational budget	Online application reduced to three questions; allowed applicant organizations to repurpose material from other applications; no longer required a detailed budget	Shift to proactive grantmaking, relying on program staff to build relationships with grantee organizations; no application or grant proposal required
Review process	Applications reviewed by two staff members and at least two volunteer community reviewers	Applications reviewed by six staff members; no community volunteers involved	Materials, notes, and past applications reviewed by three program staff members
Decision-making	Volunteers provided input, but regional staff made final grant recommendations to Board of Directors	Program staff met weekly to review applications and used a consensus-based model to make recommendations to Board of Directors	Program staff met over several meetings to review all organizations and make recommendations to Board of Directors
Length of time from application to decision	5–6 months	3 months	3 months
Type and amount of awards	Annual funding, with an average award of $5,000	Annual funding, with an average award of $7,000	Multiyear funding, with an average annual award of $8,733

Source: Dale and Plastino, "Giving with Pride," 7–20. Reprinted with permission from *The Foundation Review*.

The experience of making proactive grants to current and previous grantee partners was a catalyst for the foundation to minimize long-standing barriers to organizations seeking funding, ensure that grantmaking dollars could most effectively help organizations deliver on their mission, and center racial justice in the Pride Foundation's work. While some of these changes—such as more clearly defined grantmaking priorities that prioritized BIPOC-led and serving LGBTQ+ organizations and a simplified application—were instituted in 2020 to ease the burden on applicants as well as being part of the overall transition process, the reimagined CGP began in 2021, when the Pride Foundation decided to move to making proactive, multiyear general operating support grants that were not based on receiving a written application as its standard grantmaking practice. Table 9.2 provides a summary of the grantmaking transition.

The next section features interviews by Elizabeth Dale, the principal researcher, with Katie Carter, CEO of the Pride Foundation, and Kim Sogge, director of programs. Using the three core questions given above, they discuss how the foundation implemented the transition as well as the lessons learned from the self-study and case study research. Carter has worked at the foundation since 2014, starting as the regional officer in Oregon, then serving as the director of strategic priorities, and becoming CEO in 2019. Sogge has worked at the foundation since 2015, first as a Momentum Fellow, then as the regional officer in Oregon. In 2021, Sogge was promoted to senior grants program officer, and she became director of programs in late 2021. Both were integral in shaping the Pride Foundation's grantmaking during the time of this study.

Why Consider Participatory Grantmaking? What Other Models Shift or Share Power?

ELIZABETH DALE: While there is no singular definition of participatory grantmaking, Gibson highlights the way participatory grantmaking shifts power to community members who are typically grant recipients, not funders. She writes, "Participatory grantmaking cedes decision-making power about funding—including the strategy and criteria behind those decisions—to the very communities that funders aim to serve."[8] Participatory grantmaking emphasizes the idea of "nothing about us without us," acknowledges the inherent power imbalance between funders and grantees, and breaks down the barriers to accessing power for the people most affected by the issues.

KATIE CARTER: One of the reasons the Pride Foundation, which used a variety of grantmaking models throughout its existence, considered participatory grantmaking, was because our program staff had recently begun to be influenced by peer foundations like the Third Wave Fund and Trans Justice Funding Project, both of which had been using participatory grantmaking for years and were founded with an explicit model of participatory grantmaking in place. The Pride Foundation had also used giving circle models and community-led decision-making processes to make grants in the past, both of which we identify as part of the participatory philanthropy spectrum.

When I assumed the role of CEO in 2019, the Pride Foundation used a responsive, or application-based, funding model and the traditional grant decision-making process. However, this model was also one where the individuals in program officer-type roles built deep community relationships, strong connections to organizations, and developed an in-depth understanding of local and regional landscapes. We incorporated volunteers into the process who provided feedback on the applications but ultimately were not the decision-makers. While the existing form of grantmaking was relational in nature, the Pride Foundation was drawn to participatory grantmaking for the ways it shifted power to the communities directly affected by grant decision-making. We wanted to make this transition thoughtfully and also wanted any new approach to grantmaking to reflect the learning emanating from our internal assessment of the Community Grants Program and racial equity processes, which we were still in the midst of.

KIM SOGGE: I think that the broad and not singularly defined way that participatory grantmaking works was also appealing to the Pride Foundation. As Katie mentioned, our grantmaking model and mechanisms have evolved over time—from giving circle models and other iterations of grantmaking when we had a considerably smaller amount of discretionary resources but still needed to balance representation and participation from communities most impacted in shaping our strategy and process, which can take time and resources. As the resources available for grantmaking have grown, more options for how we could make grants have opened up.

DALE: Recently, both scholars and practitioners have written extensively about the historic inequities and racialized barriers within traditional philanthropy.[9] Participatory grantmaking (PGM) recognizes and works to break down those barriers in four distinct ways:

- By involving affected communities in grantmaking, which respects their dignity and agency, PGM can avoid adopting the "savior" ideology inherent in traditional philanthropy.

- By recognizing that equity and equality are not the same, PGM can be designed to maximize accessibility and inclusion.
- By requiring funders to model vulnerability as a strength, PGM cedes the "expert" position to those most affected by systemic problems and inequality and acknowledges that funders do not have or know all the answers.
- By seeing participation is an important outcome, PGM increases participants' knowledge, leadership, and self-determination, ultimately strengthening civil society and even democracy at large.

DALE: How did the Pride Foundation's racial equity work inform the evolution of its grantmaking?

CARTER: As the Pride Foundation's work centering racial equity grew and deepened, we wanted to go beyond prioritizing and allocating most of our resources to BIPOC-led and serving LGBTQ+ organizations. Recognizing that decision-making was key to this process, we had to evaluate and figure out how to more fully shift power back to our community with respect to grant decisions. As participatory grantmaking rethinks the role of the community in foundation work, participation not only increases agency and can build leadership among more marginalized people but also can bring justice and equity into a process that is too often guided by the priorities of wealthy, white funders.

DALE: While the Pride Foundation's program team spent much of 2020 learning about and reflecting on participatory grantmaking, the onset of the COVID-19 pandemic ushered in a very different grantmaking landscape. It also revealed some competing priorities in terms of best practices in the field and what grantees needed. How did the pandemic impact the work that was already in motion at the Pride Foundation and the direction you ultimately chose to take?

CARTER: There was a call in 2020 for funders to move resources quickly, with few strings attached, to groups on the ground. A participatory process, and especially a *new* participatory process, would have required significant time and energy to set up and likely would have taken many months to get resources out the door. We had to weigh a set of priorities. Staff—of both the Pride Foundation and grantee organizations—were dealing with personal and organizational challenges during the pandemic that made the prospect of such a significant change in grantmaking more difficult. Those competing priorities were in stark relief during the pandemic but are something funders need to be prepared to contend with, even outside that context.

DALE: At the same time, the Pride Foundation was learning about participatory grantmaking approaches, the program's team was also learning about trust-based philanthropy. Ultimately, the Pride Foundation opted not to adopt participatory grantmaking as its ultimate strategy for the CGP, instead favoring an approach rooted in trust-based philanthropy. What informed this decision?

CARTER: Because we undertook the grantmaking transition at the beginning of 2020, so many of our original plans had to be adapted and changed as the realities of the pandemic, the racial justice uprisings, and massive changes in our lives, work, and field, unfolded. So, our story in many ways is one that was contingent upon the circumstances we were in. The decisions we made likely would have been different if we were making them in 2019 or even now in 2022, for example.

Our program team had begun really digging into the framework offered by the Trust-Based Philanthropy Project because we saw it as compatible with and foundational for the shift we were making to a participatory approach.[10] It also was reflective of so much of our philosophy and approach to grantmaking already, and this offered a contextual framework in which to ground that work, as well as additional guidance for how we could lean more deeply into it.

For example, we already had a culture of "doing the homework" [one of the key trust-based philanthropy principles[11]] within our existing model, where our programs staff was intimately connected with and aware of not only the work of individual organizations and groups, but also the broader landscape in which they were operating. This also enabled us to "offer support beyond the check" to our partners and to show up with our organization's capacity and team in partnership with organizations on the ground.[12]

These principles guided much of how we responded to community organizations during the pandemic, specifically with the creation and implementation of our Crisis Community Care Fund, which we launched in March 2020. We knew LGBTQ+ groups and organizations were going to be hard hit by the pandemic, and even though we didn't know all the nuances of what that would mean when we started the fund, during the crisis we leaned even harder into the trust-based principles of grantmaking.

In particular, we focused our energy on researching and tracking all the work our current grantee partners were undertaking, starting with publicly available sources like newsletters and social media. We also examined the different circumstances affecting communities in our five-state region: in urban versus rural communities, and in different states based on what local governments were implementing. We sent a brief survey to organizations or offered quick meetings to understand what their needs were and how we could best support them, especially because in the early days of the pandemic, organizations' needs weren't purely financial; they also included technology equipment, Zoom accounts, and the like.

One of the key decisions we made for the Crisis Community Care Fund was to not create an application that organizations needed to fill out or have any reporting requirements for current or future grants. Simplifying and streamlining paperwork is, in fact, another of the key principles of the trust-based approach.

Much of the feedback we received in our initial conversations were how people were stretched thin for time and capacity, especially as the needs of communities continued to grow, meaning that filling out additional paperwork could and should not be a priority for groups to receive grants. Moreover, we had extensive notes about grantees from the surveys we sent them and in-person meetings asking about their needs. Together, this information—and our familiarity with the work of many of the groups, because they had been grantee partners for years—was more than enough to cover what was requested in our standard application.

We decided instead to award proactive grants and developed a set of principles and priorities for our funding decisions that were based on the conversations and survey feedback we had received. Using this information, the grants team made a decision to prioritize funding for groups that were aligning their programming with COVID-19 realities, and/or those that were struggling to stay afloat because of the hit their revenue streams were taking because of the pandemic. As we fundraised among our community of donors and supporters, we moved resources out to more groups and, in some cases, provided multiple funding to groups that were rapidly expanding programming to support communities in response to the pandemic or racial justice uprisings.

We received extensive feedback from our grantee partners that this model of grantmaking was extraordinarily effective. They appreciated how little administrative hoops we had, that we deeply understood what they were facing, and that we were "in it with them" in the best way we could be—by trusting them implicitly. Some of the responses we received from organizations included these:

- We want to thank you for the award and say how impressed/grateful we are with the low barrier requirements and how Pride Foundation is addressing social injustices in access to public health services (and social injustice in every other area as well). Thank you for all the great work that you do and the financial assistance that you so generously provide us.
- Thank you and the rest of Pride Foundation for funding the healing spaces we are creating for and with Black trans and queer folks during these traumatic times.
- I cannot even begin to express what a *relief* this is, and the way that this will impact our community (though I will try as it occurs). Thank you *so much* for the work that you do, and [for] making sure that we get the resources we need to serve our community! I am truly breathing deep sigh of relief and smiling.
- I'm speechless. (You know as well as anybody, that almost never happens!) My coworkers have expressed so well our shock and gratitude for this extraordinary gift. I can only add how deep our appreciation for you specifically, runs through [our organization]. You have been an amazing champion for [us], and from our very first conversation, you have been someone who genuinely understands the work we're doing, and the impact we're having. In addition to the financial generosity you've spearheaded over the year, on our behalf, I think of the time you've spent, sitting on planning committees, and connecting us to people and resources.

DALE: What I hear you both saying is that grantmaking needs to follow and be responsive to the current context that organizations are facing. I also want to draw out your comment that participatory grantmaking and trust-based philanthropy principles both attend to power dynamics in philanthropy and share common values to increase equity and build relationships. What do you see as the relationship between these two grantmaking approaches?

CARTER: I understand trust-based philanthropy to be a broader framework or approach to how a foundation can think about the way it wants to do grantmaking and be in relationships with partner organizations and communities that shift and share power. Implementing a participatory grantmaking model is one key trust-based approach to grantmaking. At the Pride Foundation, we have really been focusing on honing our trust-based approach as foundational to our grantmaking, which then opens up a number of different ways to move resources, with power sharing and shifting at the center.

Who Would Make Grant Decisions? What Specific Changes to the Grantmaking Process Would Best Accomplish the Pride Foundation's Goals?

DALE: One of the central tenets of participatory grantmaking is that individuals in the communities most affected by the problems that foundations aim to solve are the ones setting priorities and making grant decisions—instead of foundation staff, board members, and/or founders, who often have more positional power and more privileged identities, be they wealthy, white, highly educated, and so on. How did being an LGBTQ+-community foundation and an organization that has intentionally diversified its board and staff factor into the decision to adopt the trust-based philanthropy approach to grantmaking?

CARTER: This, for me, is always one of the hardest questions in participatory grantmaking. When we think about community members participating in the grantmaking process, how are they selected? Who is considered "the community" that is charged with grantmaking decisions? Who decides who the deciders are? This decision is still imbued with significant power!

The other component is that many community members who are closest to the issues and pain of injustice are also the ones most often tapped for roles like this. While of course offering stipends and monetary compensation is critical, as well as creating an understanding and flexible environment where this work happens, this work still requires a commitment on top of many other commitments that participants may have. This was in especially sharp focus during

2020–21, when folks had no capacity to take on additional work while they were also trying to survive and support the community directly.

One of the aspects of the Pride Foundation that I'm proudest about is that we have a staff and board that are deeply representative of and connected to the communities we're serving. While we have always valued and prioritized diversity among our staff team and made sure we are led by the communities we are supporting, we acknowledge and understand that sitting in these roles is often far removed from the day-to-day realities that communities are facing, and we likely are not best positioned to make these decisions.

One of the questions we encountered in considering participatory grantmaking is who would we want to be on such a grant making panel or committee? This is an existential question: Should we pay people to participate in a grantmaking panel as sort of a one-off, or at least a time-limited involvement, versus employing and recruiting those same people for our board and staff? We are also seeing more and more queer, trans, Black, Indigenous, and people of color (QTBIPOC) who have been staff members at community-based organizations coming into philanthropy. How does this change the thinking about and approach to participatory grantmaking, especially when we think about the initial reasoning behind participatory grantmaking?

SOGGE: I think this question cannot be answered in isolation from the priorities or strategies of the grantmaking mechanism, because these things should inform where decision-making lies. In response to some of Katie's reflective questions, I wonder what it would look like to move beyond asking community members to be part of grantmaking panels and involve them in shaping some of those solutions, allowing our community the agency and flexibility to define for themselves what those solutions might look like in their community. Representation is so important, and yet it is also only one piece of the direction we'd like to be moving in at the Pride Foundation.

I don't think participatory grantmaking and implementing trust-based principles are mutually exclusive. In 2021, we didn't choose to implement trust-based principles over or instead of participatory grantmaking. As mentioned previously in the chapter, there is no singular definition of participatory grantmaking, and I think one of the constant complexities of our work at the Pride Foundation is that our mission is to fuel movements, which, as we know, don't look one particular way or utilize one particular strategy.

What Opportunities and Challenges Might Foundations Expect in Implementing a Different Grantmaking Structure?

DALE: While the Pride Foundation couldn't have anticipated the pandemic or racial justice uprisings that occurred in 2020, you could control how you responded to them with respect to the pace and direction of your shifting grantmaking process. Based on your experience, what are your cautions or critiques for funders interested in undertaking a participatory process?

CARTER: A question I often ask myself and discuss on our team is whether we would have implemented a participatory process had the pandemic not happened. Considering this question makes me realize how dependent on circumstances using a participatory grantmaking process can be. If we had already had PGM in place, I think we could have continued it in 2020, but the creation of such a process was so beyond our—and our community's—capacity to begin in 2020 with everything else that was happening.

I think the intentionality with which we made this decision is worth noting because implementing a participatory process requires intentionality in spades. It also requires significant community input, trust building, and connection with grantees. Asking more of our community during an extended crisis felt like it would erode trust and could potentially be ineffective. Additionally, we know that the people who are most affected by injustice are those who we would want to be in the decision-making roles in our participatory process. But these same people are often the ones most engaged in responsive efforts during a crisis and are already at capacity.

This was also a big change within the existing staff and board structure of our foundation, so shifting roles from a program-officer-type model to one where grants staff would spend more time as facilitators, community connectors, and builders also took time, capacity, and energy that was not feasible during those early months of the pandemic. Ultimately, this led us to a full restructuring of the organization and significant changes in many (and really, all) staff roles that took the better part of a year to implement. These changes were necessary to set us up structurally so we could even begin to consider implementing and visioning how we could best create a participatory process, which we are only now, halfway through 2022, better poised to do.

DALE: As your model was changing in real time, what did you learn along the way about how best to communicate proactively and transparently with grantees and your broader community?

CARTER: In the midst of awarding our Crisis Community Care Fund grants in response to the pandemic, we had our usual annual grantmaking funds to award—funds we'd intended to award using a participatory model. We had learned so much from using the proactive, trust-based model in the rapid response grants and had received resoundingly clear feedback from our grantee partners that this model of funding was better for them, not only because it created more time to focus on their work versus securing funding but also because it better positioned us as a partner in their work. Opening an application to ask the questions we already knew the answers to after so much engagement and feedback in response to the pandemic seemed not only unnecessary and laborious, but that it could be detrimental and actually erode so much of the trust we had built.

After extensive internal conversations, we took the pool of resources we had for the Community Grants Program and awarded them using the priorities we'd outlined for the Crisis Community Care Fund. In 2021, we were in the same situation where prioritizing trust and reducing the burden on organizations felt more pressing than implementing a participatory grantmaking model which, to be honest, we weren't sure how to do this without an application and with the funding circumstances we had for this main pool of funds (namely, that there were many donor restrictions on the funds earmarked together for our broader CGP). So, we took the feedback we had received from a survey we sent to grantee partners and refined our priorities once again. Then, for the first time in our history, we awarded two-year grants in 2021, using the same trust-based, proactive model.

One learning we had from this, which we only realized in later 2021, was that we did not communicate to grantee organizations that all the resources we were moving out through the Crisis Community Care Fund were new funds we had raised in response to the crisis of the pandemic. In many instances, we awarded significantly larger grants than we had in the past, and most groups did not realize the circumstances that had enabled us to do this—namely, new but temporary resources. However, many of these were one-time grants or gifts made to the Pride Foundation in 2020, and not all of them were renewed in 2021, so we were not able to continue providing funding at the same level we had in 2020, which was an unfortunate surprise for many groups whose members were hoping, and even expecting, a comparable renewal of funding in 2021. The trust-based lesson here is to communicate more thoroughly where our resources come from and, especially as a public fundraising foundation, to share with our partners our own limitations and the realities we are grappling with.

DALE: One of the constituencies we haven't discussed is the Pride Foundation's donors and the fundraising that you all do. How have you communicated this shift to your donors, and what, if any, feedback have you received?

CARTER: We share a lot with our donors about our processes—maybe more than they are interested in knowing sometimes! Honestly, one of the most incredible things I experience is that so many of our donors tell us time and time again how important they know the work is that we're doing, how much they appreciate that we're doing it, and that they really trust us. They show us this with their giving and generosity, but also by expressing their appreciation for our efforts to build relationships with community members thoughtfully and intentionally. To be offered this kind of support and the resources to just do our work I think is a big part of why deepening our commitment to the trust-based approach with community-based organizations felt so values-aligned for us. In both literal (in the sense of unrestricted gifts) and figurative ways, our experience with donors has enabled us to pay this trust forward in our approach to our grantmaking. I've always thought that "trust begets trust," and this seems to be some evidence for that.

DALE: Even though the Pride Foundation didn't adopt a grantee-led participatory grantmaking model, do you see participatory grantmaking being part of your grantmaking in the future?

CARTER: One of the very real factors that gave us pause in pursuing participatory grantmaking—in addition to our staff structure and the capacity issue previously mentioned—is that the funding pool for our CGP, where we had been planning to implement a participatory approach, was cobbled together from "area of interest" funds (many of which are from deceased donors) that have restrictions as to where funding can go; nearly half these funds, in fact, have some kind of funding restriction. As we considered participatory grantmaking, we felt that these restrictions would not only be too complicated for external application reviewers but would also limit their ability to make truly participatory funding decisions.

For a public fundraising foundation, this has been a real consideration for how we can best approach participatory grantmaking. We want to have unrestricted dollars that would be able to be offered to a participatory panel that would fully allow for their decision-making to be final. One of the ways we have tried to address this over the past few years has been to diversify our fundraising sources, which allows us more room for creating unique initiatives to do this work. Many of the endowed funds we draw on for grantmaking are donor-restricted funds or designated for particular areas of interest, thus limiting who they can be awarded to. Diversifying our funding (e.g., getting more foundation grants) allows us more flexibility to create grantmaking programs that are responsive to what we're hearing from communities. We are considering several options around our existing funding streams in addition to new money raised and how we can utilize a participatory model that is grounded in our trust-based approach to award funds. One of the outstanding questions we still have is whether and how to use an application within this process.

DALE: What advice do you have for other funders that may be interested in adopting more power-shifting grant processes?

SOGGE: Make sure you have genuine relationships with the communities you are hoping to serve. Know where the limitations of your foundations' existing infrastructure are. (E.g., how long does it take you to issue grant payments? What are your existing reporting requirements? How does your board or executive team view participatory models?) Thinking through some of that existing infrastructure can allow you to be more open and transparent with the broader community about what you are actually able to shift and do.

As Katie mentioned, we set ourselves up in 2020 to implement a handful of the larger changes we made to our grantmaking, and this learning was incredibly powerful in shaping future strategies. The learnings from our 2021 strategy and process will also be utilized to continue to evolve.

CARTER: For other funders, I would say, think about your "why" for this shift, and what is at the core of your motivation to make these kinds of shifts. Take the time you, your team, and your board need to really think through why you're exploring this model of grantmaking that is, in fact, much more than a model. It really must align with the organization's internal culture. It can be easy to get caught up in the mechanics (and they are incredibly important to get right!), but centering the purpose and what you hope to make different will be even more important as you move through what really will become a significant change management process.

The work that the Pride Foundation did before even entering the exploration phase helped keep us grounded on the outcome we were seeking—namely, centering communities most affected in our grantmaking decisions and shifting power to them. It also enabled us to be less prescriptive or tied to the path that we as a foundation needed to take to get there. And it gave us the space to be adaptive within a clearly articulated set of boundaries and values that kept us focused on our "why," even as crises and unexpected twists and turns could have meant that we lost our ultimate purpose and motivation for making these shifts. This early commitment also meant that, even amid the unexpected context of the COVID-19 pandemic, we were still committed to changing our process in meaningful ways that made an impact.

Next, I would encourage funders to think about and plan for what it will actually take in terms of structural changes and staff role shifts and build in time for this to move at a reasonable pace (especially if your team is part of the community you are serving). What pieces of your structure can you keep? What will need to change? Who should be involved? What are the sticking points or situations you are going to come across? What are the administrative considerations? Do you have the capacity and skill sets among current staff that you need in this new model?

While it might seem obvious to say "plan for it," the magnitude of this undertaking is significant. It is, fundamentally, about doing our work in philanthropy differently, and that is a big change. It might also not take nearly as long as it has taken us; it just all depends on where your organization is in terms of internal culture and external relationships. In the spirit of being able to hold two somewhat contradictory truths at the same time, it's also critical to be willing to learn, be adaptive, and be creative as you go.

Most importantly, my advice would be to talk with and really listen to the community that you are set up to serve. At the end of the day, that is who this entire endeavor is about. If those relationships are not there yet, take the time to build them. As has often been said, move at the pace of trust. Be willing to center those perspectives and experiences, and to change direction if that is what is being asked—even if it is not what your organization had hoped or planned for. Our plans are not what are most important.

While, of course, our original intention was to implement a participatory model in 2020, we did not ultimately do that—yet. But what we ended up doing instead I am incredibly proud of because it was rooted in what LGBTQ+ community organizations needed and asked for from us, and we were able to meet them in the moment—even though it wasn't what we planned for.

CONCLUSION

As the experiences of the Pride Foundation show, the process of undertaking a grantmaking transition rooted in the values of racial equity and shared power with community members and grantee partners not only involved structural and programmatic changes but also required deep reflection by the individuals working in the organization. While the Pride Foundation initially thought it would adopt a participatory grantmaking model for its CGP, implementing that approach during the COVID-19 pandemic would have likely been ineffective, because the process would have taken considerable time and resources, both of which grantees had little of in 2020. It also could have risked the trust the foundation held and continued to build with its grantee partners by ignoring the feedback and requests those organizations had shared with the foundation.

Instead, the rapid response funding model adopted soon after the pandemic began moved the Pride Foundation toward a trust-based philanthropy approach that shares many of the same values and tenets of participatory grantmaking—advancing equity, building mutual relationships, following the lead of communities, asking for and acting on grantee feedback, and engaging in ongoing reflection—but leaves decisions about strategies and funding to foundation staff and board members. While the two approaches are "neither identical, nor mutually exclusive," they are both part of grantmaking practices that champion equity and justice.[13] In conversations with Pride Foundation staff, they reflected the idea that trust-based philanthropy is a framework—one that supports, but does not require, a participatory grantmaking process. Engaging in trust-based philanthropy also means that the work of designing and implementing more equitable grantmaking is an ongoing process, and that co-creating new initiatives with grantee partner organizations occurs over time and should not be rushed. The Pride Foundation also decided to maintain an open application for its Community Care Fund to allow new and unfunded organizations the opportunity to apply for first-time funding.

For foundations looking to adopt participatory and/or trust-based grantmaking frameworks, the experiences of the Pride Foundation demonstrate that first, rather than foundations being one-sided drivers of change, listening to what partner (grantee) organizations needs is crucial. Second, foundations need to be realistic about the many challenges inherent in shifting power: What is the foundation's capacity for change? Where is the foundation in its own racial equity and power-shifting/sharing journeys, especially when wealth has been generated from deeply unjust systems over many generations? Has the foundation dedicated the time needed to clarify its organizational values and build an internal culture that supports frank conversations about power imbalances and bias? Third, foundations need to consider whether and to what extent they currently hold relationships with community leaders and key stakeholders. What will it take to build or strengthen these? For example, is there a history of harm that will require a reparative process? Has the foundation operationalized, in staff time and prioritization, what it will take to build and sustain authentic relationships, conduct independent research to reduce burdens on grantees, and receive and respond to feedback from partners? Answering these questions honestly is the true first step foundations must take before grantmaking processes change. Only then can grantmakers map out a strategy in concert with their intended beneficiaries.

Finally, we believe that it is important for foundations to understand that a participatory grantmaking approach is not the only way for grantmakers to shift power to the communities they serve. Whether grant decisions take the form of community members allocating funds or of proactive, unrestricted, multiyear support, what is most important is that foundations build reciprocal, respectful, and trust-based relationships in partnership with the communities at the very heart of their mission.

NOTES

1. Funders for LGBTQ Issues, "2019–2020 Resource Tracking Report: LGBTQ Grantmaking by US Foundations," https://lgbtfunders.org/wp-content/uploads/2022/06/2019-2020-Tracking-Report.pdf.
2. Michael H. Remaley, "The State of American Philanthropy: Philanthropy, Social Justice and Shifting Power," *Inside Philanthropy*, 2022, www.insidephilanthropy.com/state-of-american-philanthropy-pdfs/philanthropy-social-justice-and-shifting-power.
3. Pride Foundation, "Transforming the Future: Our Racial Equity Core," https://pridefoundation.org/about-us/racial-equity-core/.
4. Cynthia Gibson, *Participatory Grantmaking: Has Its Time Come?* (New York: Ford Foundation, 2017), www.fordfoundation.org/media/3599/participatory_grantmaking-lmv7.pdf; Cynthia Gibson, *Deciding Together: Shifting Power and Resources through Participatory Grantmaking* (New York: Foundation Center, 2018), https://learningforfunders.candid.org/content/guides/deciding-together/.
5. Elizabeth J. Dale and Nicole Plastino, "Giving with Pride: Considering Participatory Grantmaking in an Anti-Racist, LGBTQ+ Community Foundation," *Foundation Review* 14, no. 1 (2022): 7–20.
6. Robert E. Stake, *The Art of Case Study Research* (Thousand Oaks, CA: Sage, 1995); Robert K. Yin, *Case Study Research: Design and Method*, 4th edition (Thousand Oaks, CA: Sage, 2009).
7. Trust-Based Philanthropy Project, www.trustbasedphilanthropy.org/.
8. Gibson, *Deciding Together*, 7.
9. E.g., see Will Cordery, "Dear Philanthropy: These Are the Fires of Anti-Black Racism," *Nonprofit Quarterly*, 2020, https://nonprofitquarterly.org/dear-philanthropy-these-are-the-fires-of-anti-black-racism/; Vu Le, "How Donor-Centrism Perpetuates Inequity, and Why We Must Move toward Community-Centric Fundraising," Nonprofit AF blog, May 15, 2017, https://nonprofitaf.com/2017/05/how-donor-centrism-perpetuates-inequity-and-why-we-must-move-toward-community-centric-fundraising/; and Edgar Villanueva, *Decolonizing Wealth: Indigenous Wisdom to Heal Divides and Restore Balance* (Oakland: Berrett-Koehler, 2018).
10. The Trust-Based Philanthropy Project is a five-year, peer-to-peer funder initiative established by three foundations that began in January 2020. See www.trustbasedphilanthropy.org/.
11. Trust-Based Philanthropy Project, *The 6 Grantmaking Practices of Trust-Based Philanthropy*, March 3, 2021, www.trustbasedphilanthropy.org/resources-articles/grantmaking-practices.
12. Trust-Based Philanthropy Project.
13. Trust-Based Philanthropy Project, "Participatory Grantmaking and Trust-Based Philanthropy," www.trustbasedphilanthropy.org/resources-articles/2022-1-25-cei-tbp-learning-evaluation-8lz2r-6x4rp.

CHAPTER 10

Community Foundations and Community Leadership
An Approach to Participatory Philanthropy

Melody MacLean, Caroline Merenda, and Len Bartel

As place-based grantmakers, community foundations are well positioned to adopt participatory practices, including—but not limited to—grantmaking. In this chapter, staff members of CFLeads, a community-foundation network, explore the connections between participatory philanthropy and community leadership, an approach a growing number of community foundations are embracing across the country. The chapter explores the history of the community foundation field and its participatory nature, building momentum for community leadership, and the importance of amplifying and integrating residents' voices in community philanthropy.

INTRODUCTION

During the past decade, community foundations have been buffeted by the same dramatic changes that have affected other organizations in our society. People have become more distrustful of established institutions; they want more transparency and collaborative approaches to problem-solving, as well as more voice in political processes.[1] Racial disparities, which are deeply engrained in our systems and our institutions, have become increasingly apparent due to the COVID-19 pandemic and calls for racial justice in communities across the country.

As charitable organizations that provide support for the needs of a geographic community or region, community foundations are particularly well positioned to respond to these issues compared with most philanthropic organizations. In recent decades, however, community foundations have been under pressure to distinguish themselves in this regard, due to competition from both for-profit companies (e.g., Fidelity, Schwab, Vanguard) and other nonprofit organizations (e.g., United Way agencies, giving circles). Donors seeking more control over—and impact from—their philanthropy now have a number of these kinds of philanthropic vehicles from which to choose.

In 2005, a seminal report by the Monitor Institute, *On the Brink of New Promise: The Future of US Community Foundations*, urged community foundations to reexamine their missions, their activities, and the ways in which they operate within and with communities.[2] The report noted that community foundations' claim that their strategic advantage was community knowledge, relationships, and leadership was still "largely rhetoric[al]," and that to capitalize on their unique advantage, community foundations needed to refocus on why they exist and whom they ultimately serve. Specifically, if community foundations were to remain relevant, they needed to undertake three key shifts. The first is from institution to community.

On the Brink explored the competitive landscape of the field and emphasized the danger of community foundations staying focused on operational efficiency and institutional preservation. The report recommended that community foundations shift their efforts outward to stay relevant and to reexamine their role in the context of rapidly changing communities.

The second key shift is from financial assets to long-term leadership. *On the Brink* advised community foundations against being focused on the size and growth of their assets. The report argued that in the future, community foundations' role must be to mobilize a community and its resources to "recognize the community's collective aspirations, engage its own toughest challenges, and embrace its most inspiring opportunities."[3] This requires community foundations to take on a long-term leadership role in the community.

The third key shift is from competitive independence to coordinated impact. Ultimately, *On the Brink* argued that a fundamental mind-set shift must occur in the community foundation field, from independent value to coordinated impact. The report emphasized the importance of community foundations working in collaboration with others: with donors, with the community, and with other organizations.

This call to action—to be by, of, and for the community rather than to serve as a charitable bank that merely collects and distributes funds—was a challenge that a trailblazing group of community foundations was eager to take on.

Specifically, they wanted to champion a new approach to philanthropy known as "community leadership." Through this approach, community foundations would not only provide grants but also form partnerships with community stakeholders to identify important issues, commission research, convene decision-makers, engage in advocacy, and help marshal needed resources.

In 2007, CFLeads was formed to respond to this call to action and to champion this approach. As a small coalition of the willing, the community foundations that joined CFLeads' network set out to define and develop what it means to engage in "community leadership"—an approach that has evolved to embrace and advocate for participatory practices.

What follows is a description of how participation, as a value and practice, has been an integral part of the history of community foundations. It also describes community leadership's commonalities with participatory philanthropy and the important distinctions between the two.

COMMUNITY FOUNDATIONS' DEEP PARTICIPATORY ROOTS

No discussion of community leadership would be complete without understanding community foundations' deep historic roots, public purpose, and mission. During the past century, this emphasis has waxed and waned, depending on the external environments in which community foundations have operated. At times, they have been powerful advocates, conveners, and leaders in supporting community engagement with serious issues. There have also been periods during which their focus narrowed to collecting and leveraging local donors' philanthropic contributions (i.e., serving as "charity banks" more concerned with asset size than public purpose). And some community foundations were founded on—and remain committed to— one or the other of these goals.

In fact, the first community foundation was created in Cleveland in 1914 with a dual purpose: to pool the financial resources of local donors to encourage philanthropic giving and to leverage these resources in ways that would benefit the local community. The foundation's governance structure reflected this dual purpose, by splitting responsibility among local banks, which managed its funds, and a local "citizen board" that distributed those funds. Its activities were also externally focused. For example, the foundation used community-wide surveys to identify critical community needs, particularly those "causing misfortune and social dysfunction."[4] These first "community maps" helped residents and other local institutions document the need for reform efforts and to initiate them—advocacy that was then relatively unheard of among foundations.[5]

From 1914 to 1929, this community engagement model spread across the country until the Great Depression, which hampered community foundations' ability to increase their financial resources.[6] In response, community foundations shifted to a different, private charity model focused on building local community chests separate from government. The need for resources after World War II made fundraising to create these assets a major activity for community foundations,[7] and by 1960, they and their community chests were seen as "central elements in the framework of private agencies for the control of community life."[8]

During the 1970s, social unrest and the civil rights movement sparked renewed interest among community foundations to encourage and support community action and "enlarg[e] the sense of public—and government—responsibility" for communities.[9] This focus continued during the 1980s, when reductions in publicly funded community development and social service programs led to calls for community foundations to fill the gap.[10]

During the economic boom of the 1990s, community foundations grew rapidly, but so did other forms of philanthropy. There was also a growing realization that philanthropy was a business and, potentially, a "profitable market or product extension for financial service firms."[11] The turning point came with the establishment of the Fidelity Charitable Gift Fund, a new offshoot of the giant financial service corporation formed to help community-level donors with their philanthropic investments. To community foundations, this was a shot across the bow, putting them on notice that there was now competition for their core business model, which centered on providing giving options and services for donors.[12] More commercial philanthropic enterprises soon followed, leading to concerns that this competition had the potential to eclipse community foundations' traditional role as the primary philanthropic brokers at the local level.[13]

This sea change in the philanthropic landscape had the effect of prompting many community foundations, which were worried about commercial funds' ability to attract individual and new donors, to adopt asset size as a proxy measure of success. As a result, a significant number of community foundations began devoting considerable time and energy to building their asset base and using it to suggest impact. Community foundations' public purpose, in short, shifted more toward the back burner.[14]

This changed in 2005, with the publication of reports such as *On the Brink of New Promise*, which incited renewed attention to the public purpose of community foundations and the unique role they could play in strengthening communities across the country. As noted earlier in the chapter, a new network of community foundations committed to community leadership called CFLeads emerged as the result of this attention.

CFLEADS: COMMUNITY FOUNDATIONS LEADING CHANGE

CFLeads was established in 2007 by a board made up of community foundation CEOs to respond to the challenges outlined in *On the Brink of New Promise*. Recognizing that community foundations would need support to embrace this new way of thinking and working, CFLeads began its work by forming the National Task Force on Community Leadership, which was charged with developing the then-new community leadership approach.

Working in partnership with the Aspen Institute Community Strategies Group and the Council on Foundations' Community Foundations Leadership Team, the task force designed and developed its *Framework for Community Leadership by a Community Foundation*, which defined the concept and outlined building blocks of practices that community foundations could adopt to integrate community leadership as a core competency.[15] It also underscored community foundations' role in serving as trusted and valued community institutions, noting their unique attributes:

- independence (not beholden to electoral and business cycles);
- permanence (endowments);
- local orientation (local relationships and knowledge);
- broad community betterment mission; and
- 501(c)(3) nonprofit, tax-exempt status (and thus able to lobby for public policy change).

The unique structure of a community foundation presented an opportunity to go beyond traditional asset-building and grantmaking roles and adopt additional roles that could help produce positive outcomes for the communities they serve.

One of the first activities to emerge from CFLeads was a pilot of two community leadership networks. These networks were made up of community foundations of different sizes, shapes, and cultures, which were located in different places and had unique community leadership challenges and approaches. The objectives of these networks were to (1) increase the understanding of community leadership more broadly, (2) develop an inventory of approaches that community foundations have used and issues they have addressed in their community leadership efforts, and (3) provide opportunities for community foundation leaders to learn from their peers about their experience navigating critical community leadership challenges.

In 2011, CFLeads launched its Executive Leadership Institute (ELI) to help small groups of community foundation leaders improve their community leadership practice. Originally created for CEOs, the ELI quickly expanded to include cohorts of vice presidents interested in embedding the practice of community leadership more deeply in and across their organizations, including program, donor services, financial, and community impact departments and activities.

While these and other activities generated by the *Framework* helped to advance the community leadership model among individual community foundations, it was still far from a field-wide norm—and the approach was not perfect. As more and more community foundations were introduced to the *Framework* and the community leadership approach, they wrestled with their role in engaging the community and how to do it in an authentic way.

In 2012, CFLeads brought together a group of philanthropic leaders, scholars, practitioners, and people from community groups to form the national Cultivating Community Engagement Panel. The focus of the panel was to explore the meaning of community engagement, identify why it might be an appropriate role for community foundations, and uncover and document what it looked like "on the ground." The group also discussed how community foundations could align their organizations differently, given their expanding roles in community-based engagement efforts.

During these convenings, some community foundations that had been using a community leadership approach suggested that there was still a gap in the practice—specifically, in *resident* engagement. This was defined as the active participation by the people who live in the neighborhoods where change is occurring and whose lives are most affected by the policies, systems, and structures that are targeted for change. In reality, residents were still not necessarily involved in or represented in community engagement efforts—including those led by or involving community foundations—as full partners, unless change agents made a deliberate effort to include them.

Fortuitously, a small number of community foundations that had begun to organize and support these kinds of resident-driven community engagement projects were on hand to provide insight to the larger panel about their experiences. A key learning for these practitioners—which continues to be regularly emphasized by residents affected by the work of the philanthropic sector—was the importance of distinguishing between simply asking people for input or mobilizing them to advocate for a particular cause; to working with residents as equal partners to identify the issues most important to them; and then, together, creating plans to address those issues. This concept of "nothing about us without us" is a vital component of authentic participatory philanthropy.

In 2013, the panel issued *Engaging Residents: A New Call to Action for Community Foundations*, which encouraged community foundations to "reach beyond the traditional leaders and experts" who were usually the most involved in community decision-making and include more diverse and representative voices in those efforts.[16] As the report noted, "There is growing awareness among some community foundation leaders who are experimenting with or have adopted community leadership approaches that an essential... element of that approach is the proactive, intensive engagement of ordinary people in all aspects of community building and civic life.... It is intentionally focused on seeing residents—representing diverse parts of the population—as actors in all facets of planning, implementing, assessing and developing efforts to strengthen communities. It is an approach that melds 'top down' and 'bottom up' strategies for decision-making. And it is inherently democratic."[17]

Specifically, the Cultivating Community Engagement Panel agreed that:

- Residents are a crucial part of community engagement and must be at the core of community foundations' community engagement work.
- Community foundations are well positioned to play an important role in engaging residents and communities, and they can contribute resources to that effort that go beyond money.
- Community foundations can and should do more than they currently do to engage with residents. This will require interacting with a broader range of people in the community, beyond the traditional community leaders and constituency groups.
- Effective community engagement on the part of community foundations should be expanded to involve significant resident engagement principles and practices, and these should be included in an updated *Framework for Community Leadership by a Community Foundation*.

To help community foundations operationalize the call to action, CFLeads produced several tools and publications that emerged from its nationwide peer-to-peer learning exchanges among community foundations experimenting with this model.[18] Figure 10.1 depicts the mutually beneficial relationship community foundations should seek to build with the communities they serve.

CFLeads also updated its *Framework for Community Leadership* to incorporate building blocks that focused on resident engagement principles and practices.

In 2013, CFLeads deepened its commitment to this approach by creating the resident engagement Community Leadership Network to help community foundations incorporate authentic resident engagement as a core part of their efforts. The Community Leadership Network structure eventually morphed into what CFLeads now calls "issue networks," whereby a cohort of community foundation teams come together on a specific issue (e.g., gun violence or economic mobility) and take a community leadership approach to address the challenge.

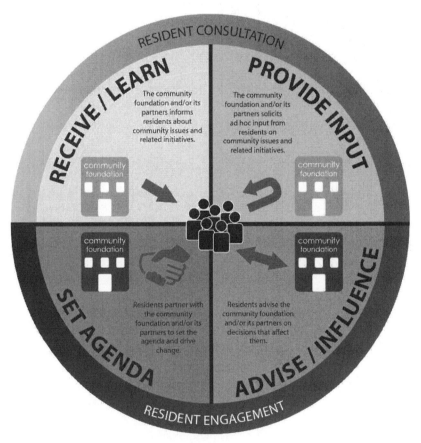

Figure 10.1 Resident Engagement Spectrum
Sources: Aspen Institute Community Strategies Group; CFLeads, *Resident Engagement Guidebook*, 2014.

Today, engaging residents has become one of the five core competencies of community leadership that CFLeads integrates into all its community foundation programming, including its ELI and issue networks. Most recently, in light of the racial reckoning that is occurring across the country, community foundations are taking this work one step further by ensuring that their resident engagement efforts include sufficient representation of residents from underserved communities whose voices are often absent from these discussions.

PARTICIPATORY PHILANTHROPY AS COMMUNITY LEADERSHIP

The "nothing about us without us" principle is at the heart of community leadership, resident engagement, and participatory philanthropy. While involving residents in grantmaking is one way to engage in participatory philanthropy and community leadership, it is not the only option. Even with vast assets, grantmaking by community foundations alone cannot solve a community's most pressing issues. Engaging residents in systems change work that affects government spending at all levels is critical for moving the needle on most local challenges.

That is why CFLeads advocates for a community leadership approach, through which community foundations move *beyond* the grantmaking process and act as valuable partners in driving positive change in the area(s) they serve. In short, involving communities in making decisions about important resource allocations (which includes deciding on funding priorities, strategy development, grant decisions, and other parts of that process) is essential, but decisions about how those resources are ultimately implemented "on the ground" in pursuit of overall community change is an equally important and fundamental component of community leadership.

Another distinction between participatory grantmaking and community leadership is that many participatory grantmakers operate with fewer restrictions than community foundations, which are still viewed as more formal, established institutions. As such, they have a responsibility to be accountable to the entire community in all its diversity, and this includes donors, residents, public officials, educators, businesspeople, and myriad others. Decisions about how community foundations will engage with their communities and on what issues depend on what partners and constituencies agree will be most beneficial. Sometimes, this may include participatory grantmaking; but other times, it may involve participatory strategies that fall under the community leadership rubric.

CFLeads views a community foundation that is engaging in community leadership as one that is pursuing the community's greatest opportunities and addressing its most critical challenges; is inclusively uniting people, institutions, and resources from throughout the community; and is producing significant, widely shared, and lasting results. Through its tools, resources, and programs, CFLeads encourages community foundations to employ several participatory methods of meaningfully engaging the community in their work:

- having processes that engage community members in the foundation's work, especially those that foster a sense of shared ownership;
- proactively seeking the voices of underserved communities to influence organizational decision-making;
- selecting foundation board, staff, and committee members who represent a broad cross-section of the community;
- having mechanisms to receive ongoing feedback and accept criticism, admit mistakes, and take proactive and timely steps to improve the foundation's practices; and
- identifying community leadership priorities in consultation with community stakeholders and pertinent research on community needs.

A Compass for Community Leadership

CFLeads has designed the Community Leadership Compass as a visualization of how its different community leadership resources work together.[19] The participatory nature of community leadership is evident in each ring of the compass, with the importance of *relationships* emphasized in the *Framework for Community Leadership*, *engaging residents* as a core competency, and *amplifying community voice* as a key area of momentum in the community foundation field (figure 10.2). Each resource is summarized in table 10.1, with the participatory components highlighted.

COMMUNITY FOUNDATIONS AND COMMUNITY LEADERSHIP   295

Figure 10.2 Community Leadership Compass
Source: CFLeads, *Community Leadership Field Guide for Community Foundations*, 2021.

Framework for Community Leadership

The latest version of this landmark resource for community foundations integrates the focus on resident engagement, as advised by the Cultivating Community Engagement Panel. It also includes metrics for community foundations to track their community leadership progress using the new Community Leadership Assessment Tool.

Table 10.1: Community Leadership by a Community Foundation

DEFINITION AND OUTCOME

The community foundation is a community partner that creates a better future for all by pursuing the community's greatest opportunities and addressing the most critical challenges, inclusively uniting people, institutions, and resources from throughout the community, and producing significant, widely shared and lasting results.

FIRST-LEVEL BUILDING BLOCKS

A	B	C	D
Values, culture, and will	*Relationships*	*Resources*	*Understanding and skills*
The community foundation manifests the values, culture and will to exercise community leadership.	The community foundation continuously builds the relationships to exercise community leadership.	The community foundation accesses and develops the resources necessary to exercise community leadership.	The community foundation accesses and develops the understanding and skills to exercise community leadership.

SECOND-LEVEL BUILDING BLOCKS

The community foundation is committed to effecting change that advances the *common good*.	The community foundation is an *engaged* and *trusted* community partner.	The community foundation serves as *a place for residents and other stakeholders to connect* with intellectual, political, social and financial capital.	The community foundation actively *learns* about, *with* and *for* the community.
The community foundation is *of, by and for* the community it serves.	The community foundation is positioned to *join with or convene* those involved in, affected by or concerned about an issue.	The community foundation's *internal information and implementation systems* maximize its ability to influence community change.	The community foundation has the *skills to help* residents and other *stakeholders* be involved in and drive community improvement efforts.

Table 10.1: (*continued*)

SECOND-LEVEL BUILDING BLOCKS			
The community foundation is a *results-driven learning organization*.	The community foundation *engages* and *supports* other community leaders.	The community foundation has the *human resources* to exercise community leadership.	The community foundation stimulates *dialogue*, promotes understanding and builds consensus.
The community foundation is *humble, respectful, and transparent*.		The community foundation's *business model* provides flexible financial resources to support community leadership efforts.	The community foundation *strategically crafts and acts* on community leadership opportunities.
			The community foundation engages in *public policy* to advance the common good.
			The community foundation *evaluates* the impact of its community leadership work.

Source: CFLeads, *Community Leadership Field Guide for Community Foundations*, 2021.

Community Leadership Assessment Tool

Created in 2021 in partnership with Candid—the largest source of information about global philanthropy and US nonprofits—this tool emerged out of conversations with community foundation staff members who wanted a more structured mechanism for assessing specific community leadership activities and communicating the impact of this work beyond financial metrics.

The tool has five sections. The first pertains to community leadership activities. Items in this section ask foundation staff whether or not they engage in seven distinct community leadership activities, including the five competencies of community leadership outlined in figure 10.3.

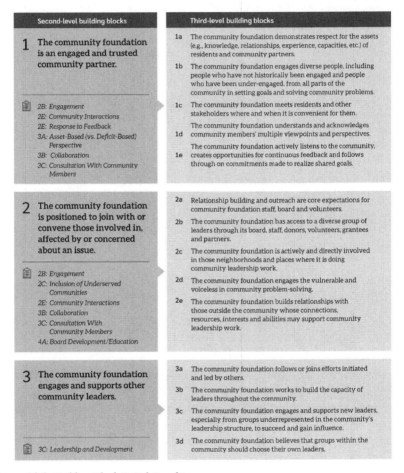

Figure 10.3 Building Block B: Relationships
Source: CFLeads, *Framework for Community Leadership*, 2021.

Community foundations are encouraged to assess their community leadership efforts using this tool, which connects directly with the building blocks of CFLeads' Framework for Community Leadership. For example, Building Block B: Relationships is all about the community foundation engaging in participatory philanthropy as a community partner. In sections 2–5, foundations are asked to rate their level of engagement in several dimensions of community leadership on a scale from one to seven, with one being "minimal" and seven being "strong." Descriptions accompany the rating scale to tangibly define what "minimal," "basic," "intermediate," or "strong" engagement looks like in each of these dimensions. Space is also available in each section for respondents to provide clarifying comments.

The second section is about organizational culture. This section taps into organizational culture, policies, and practices that support community leadership work, including mission and values; community voice; a commitment to diversity, equity, and inclusion; learning; and integrity.

The third section is about relationships. This section focuses on how foundations engage with community stakeholders and includes items related to community trust, convening and collaboration, and shared leadership.

The fourth section is about resources. This section focuses on the extent to which the foundation has the resources and capacity to support community leadership activities through human capital, donor engagement, and business model.

The fifth section is about understanding and skills. These questions focus on foundation practices in these areas as they relate to their community leadership efforts: community knowledge, community change processes, communications, strategic orientation, public policy, and evaluation. The organization also places an emphasis on peer learning, thereby creating opportunities for community foundations that are taking a community leadership approach to share their successes, failures, and lessons with others in the field so as to learn and adapt.

Under each second-level building block in the *Framework* are the relevant metrics in the Community Leadership Assessment Tool that the community foundation can use to measure its community leadership process. The example below, 2C: Inclusion of Underserved Communities, can be found under Section 2B: Community Voice of the assessment tool, in figure 10.4, which shows how to assess the level to which the voices of underserved communities are included in a community foundation's decision-making.[20]

Another participatory metric that appears under Building Block B in the *Framework* and Section 2B of the assessment tool is Engagement, where the highest ranking (5) means that the community foundation "has established processes in place to engage community members in its work that fosters a sense of shared ownership."

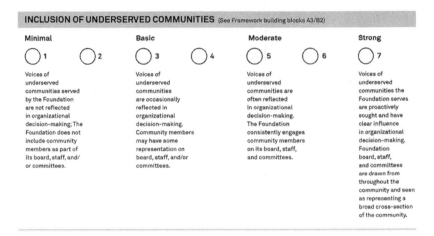

Figure 10.4 Using the Community Leadership Assessment Tool for Discerning the Inclusion of Underserved Communities
Source: Candid, *CF Insights Community Leadership Assessment Tool*, 2021.

Community foundations can also measure their ability to build trust with the community under Section 3B: Community Trust of the assessment tool, which connects to a number of building blocks in the *Framework*. This section measures the community foundation's practice in consulting with community members and whether it takes an asset-based, as opposed to a deficit-based, approach to consultation. The highest ranking (5) means that the foundation "values and leverages the range of assets (knowledge, relationships, capacities) that community members offer."

Section 3C: Shared Leadership asks community foundations to assess how their community leadership priorities are derived. This shows how to assess the level to which a community foundation engages with community members in the course of its work (figure 10.5).

The *Framework* and the Community Leadership Assessment Tool are both free resources, available online for any community foundation to use. They are also thoughtfully integrated into CFLeads' ELI, which helps community foundation leaders develop the skills and strategies needed to take a community leadership approach to their work.

At the first in-person meeting of an ELI, participants complete a "dot exercise" with the *Framework*. This exercise invites each participant to assess their organization's community leadership practice by giving themselves a green, yellow, or red dot on each second-level building block of the

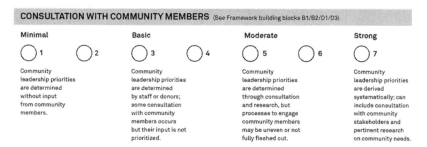

Figure 10.5 Using the Community Leadership Assessment Tool to Consult with Community Members
Source: Candid, *CF Insights Community Leadership Assessment Tool*, 2021.

Framework. Green indicates they feel they are doing something very well, yellow is not well enough, and red indicates they are not doing something well. Participants then describe why they rated their work this way, which generates a rich conversation with their peers about how and where they can improve their community leadership practice.

At the second in-person meeting of an ELI, the Community Leadership Assessment Tool is introduced. Participants independently assess the forty-one measures of the assessment tool, which provides a more nuanced understanding of where the institution is in its community leadership practice. ELI participants are encouraged to invite their staff and board to complete the assessment tool as well, to determine whether everyone is in alignment with how they would assess the organization. Some participants have also used the assessment tool to help frame strategic planning conversations.

Five Competencies of Community Leadership

The middle ring of the Community Leadership Compass includes the five competencies of community leadership. In an effort to document the work of community foundations using a community leadership approach and to articulate the nongrantmaking roles that community foundations could embrace, CFLeads identified five competencies critical to effective practice. When done well, the community foundation should take a participatory approach to all five competencies to ensure that residents are engaged and heard when engaging in community leadership.

Table 10.2: Community Leadership Activities

Our foundation has engaged in these activities in the past 12 months:	Yes	No	No, but has done so in the past	No, but plans to do so in the future
Commissioned and disseminated local data and research to help understand the nuances of community challenges and provide information to help solve problems				
Engaged residents to actively listen to their concerns and engage them in community problem-solving				
Worked across sectors, recognizing that community challenges cannot be solved by any one entity or sector				
Engaged in public conversations and other activities intended to influence the development of public policy, recognizing that government systems have a significant impact on community challenges				
Marshalled resources beyond the foundation's own grants—from private foundations as well as from local, state, and federal government—to address community needs				

Source: Candid, *CF Insights Community Leadership Assessment Tool*, 2021.

The competencies are:

- engaging residents to hear their concerns, lift up their ambitions, and harness their talents;
- commissioning and disseminating local data and research to help understand the nuances of community challenges and provide information to help solve problems;
- working across sectors, because the challenges facing communities are multifaceted and interconnected and cannot be solved by any one entity or sector;
- shaping public policy, recognizing that government systems have a significant impact on the lives of every resident; and

- marshaling resources beyond the foundation's own grants—from private foundations as well as from local, state, and federal governments—to address community needs.

These five competencies are introduced in all CFLeads programming, including its issue networks. They also show up in the Community Leadership Assessment Tool, allowing both CFLeads and individual community foundations to track how much these competencies are being used (table 10.2).

The Going All In *Study*

At the center of the Community Leadership Compass are the three areas of momentum identified through *Going All In*, a major research study that CFLeads commissioned in 2019 aimed at understanding the environment in which community foundations were working and where they could add further value. Of particular interest was assessing community foundations' nongrantmaking roles, which served as a proxy measure of community leadership. It was guided by an advisory committee made up of fifteen community foundation CEOs, who met six times to guide its progress.

The project was informed by a survey conducted by Candid in late 2019, which provided insights from 152 community foundation leaders plus dozens of interviews conducted by CFLeads. Survey ideas and input were collected and incorporated into subsequent interviews and then refined through an iterative process that took into account changing circumstances and perspectives (e.g., COVID-19, racial protests, and the economic downturn).

The survey sample was distributed across several cohorts by asset size, staff size, and geography, indicating that the survey findings were reasonably representative of the field as a whole. Each of the standard community foundation asset size cohorts (in millions: $0–25, $25–50, $50–100, $100–250, $250–500, and $500+) made up at least 12 percent of the survey respondents. The largest cohort in the survey sample, 29 percent, represented the largest number of community foundations in the field: those managing less than $25 million in assets.

As seen in figure 10.6, the key finding of the study was clear: 98 percent of community foundation leaders plan to deepen or expand their community leadership over the next few years. This finding confirmed CFLeads'

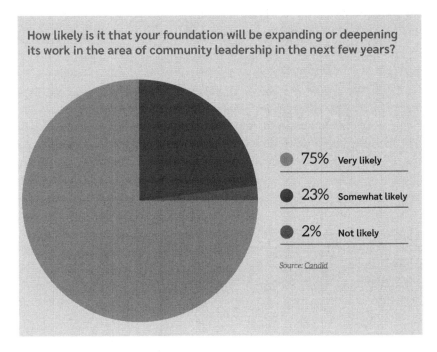

Figure 10.6 The Study's Key Findings
Source: CFLeads, "Going All In" portal, https://cfleads.org/going-all-in/.

belief that community leadership is not limited to those community foundations with greater assets; the interest in taking a community leadership approach is evident throughout the sector.

The research also showed that community leadership is not a side project for community foundations. Nearly all survey respondents (91 percent) sustain their community leadership work using their operating budget, and 70 percent maintain two or more sources of funding to support their work. Some have even launched funds to support their community leadership efforts.

The research also identified three areas of momentum that show great promise and potential for the field. These areas, which were illuminated by survey findings and interviews and were reinforced by the historic events that have taken place since the project began, are (1) insisting on racial equity, (2) amplifying community voice, and (3) influencing public policy and systems.

The emergence of "amplifying community voice" as a key area of momentum demonstrates the growing commitment by community foundations to engage residents in various aspects of their work, including helping to inform their priorities, grantmaking, and activities. The research found that the majority of community foundation respondents plan to increase their staff allocation for hosting convenings on issues, engaging donors in community problem-solving, and participating in resident engagement/visioning activities. It also identified skills that were emerging in the field, with only 18 percent of respondents rating their relationship with "emerging community leaders" as excellent. (Comparatively, 58 percent rated their relationship with individual donors as excellent.)

Going All In also highlighted how important it is for a community foundation's staff, board, and leadership to reflect the diversity of the community it serves. Eighty-nine percent of respondents said they learned about community aspirations and needs from staff participation in civic life, and as one community foundation leader noted, "If we get more of our information from staff, and they are not diverse, who are we in touch with?" However, respondents also identified a number of other participatory approaches to learning about community needs, including community forums, community representation on the board, site visits, and community participation advisory committees. While participatory grantmaking was also mentioned, it was one of the lower-ranked approaches to learning about community aspirations and needs.

To capture this momentum, CFLeads created the *Going All In* portal on its website, which highlights the current direction of the field and lifts up emerging themes and promising illustrations to help inform and inspire community foundations during this time of national tumult and reexamination and beyond.[21] This research has helped inform CFLeads' strategic plan, as the organization explores new ways to support the community foundation field on racial equity, community voice, and participatory public policy.

COMMUNITY LEADERSHIP ON THE GROUND

CFLeads recognizes that each community foundation is at a different stage of its community leadership journey and may be further along in one action area than another. It also recognizes that because community leadership is often collaborative, community foundations work closely with donors, residents, neighborhood leaders, businesses, government agencies, and other nonprofits to create lasting change in their communities.

For these reasons, there is no single or "correct" way for community foundations to do community leadership work. Each community foundation is unique, as are the communities they serve, which means that their approaches to this work will differ. What they have in common is a commitment to a more participatory, community-minded way of working.

The way this commitment shows up in the organization varies, but it can include changes to the foundation's mission statements, values, and job descriptions. The skill sets needed to properly infuse resident engagement into the work of a community foundation are significantly different from the skills needed if a foundation is primarily focused on serving its donors. The next subsections give a few examples of how residents participate in the work of community foundations across the country.

Advocating for Community Needs

Community foundations benefit from the participation of community members in many ways, including informing the foundation about community needs. This is a particularly helpful approach for community foundations serving a broad geographic region with diverse communities and needs.

The *Oregon Community Foundation* works with more than 1,800 local volunteers who provide the foundation with personal, in-depth knowledge of community needs across the state. The volunteers serve on the foundation's board and on its advisory and leadership councils, and they evaluate grant proposals and scholarship applications.

Inspired by the Oregon Community Foundation's leadership councils, the *Innovia Foundation*, which serves Eastern Washington and North Idaho, has established local leadership councils representing a diverse demographic to advise its work. Council members are trusted local leaders who are best equipped to diagnose and solve community problems. In 2019, Innovia staff spent 205 workdays outside Spokane County, racking up more than 16,500 miles in efforts aimed at strengthening community engagement.

Providing Foundation Leadership

Having community members serve on the board of the community foundation is another example of participatory philanthropy and is one of the community leadership metrics tracked in the Community Leadership Assessment Tool. In 2021, the *Kalamazoo Community Foundation* opened its board of trustees application process to the entire community for the first time in its nearly one-hundred-year history. Through this community-centric process, Kalamazoo sought to intentionally include trustees whose identities and communities are most systematically affected by injustice.

Informing Local Initiatives

Community foundations are also deeply engaging community members in local initiatives. The *San Francisco Foundation*, for example, has been engaged in a community-driven strategic planning process to assess and understand how wealth-building policies and strategies can lead to economic advancement for isolated public housing communities that are transforming into mixed-income communities.

The foundation's community leadership work was bolstered by its participation in one of CFLeads' issue networks, the *Economic Mobility Action Network*. Through the network, the San Francisco Foundation and HOPE SF—a large-scale community development initiative focused on public housing—explored how their partnership could evolve from a vision of repairing and redressing systematic racial oppression toward a vision of wealth building. In this new approach, trust building and power sharing with residents are central objectives. The Partnership for HOPE SF put together a planning and design team that includes ten HOPE SF residents as paid consultants, and the group is committed to having HOPE SF residents continue to make up at least half of the table throughout the planning process.

All six community foundations that participated in CFLeads' Economic Mobility Action Network saw resident engagement as a vital part of their mission to develop and implement economic mobility agendas that use a racial equity lens in their communities. An evaluation of the network found that one of the biggest equity practice increases over time was "engaging residents' voices to inform or identify needs."

Another example of residents informing local initiatives is the *Greater Milwaukee Foundation*, which has formed partnerships with a private medical college and a leading innovator in urban development in a unique collaboration called ThriveOn. This partnership is dedicated to eliminating racial, health, economic and social disparities in Milwaukee by making generational investments in the well-being of its community, starting with the restoration and redevelopment of an old department store. Based on resident input, the collaboration has designated the 40,000-square-foot first floor of the building, now called ThriveOn King, for community use. The design of the first floor was curated by visioning sessions hosted by ThriveOn and the Community Advisory Council, made up of residents, which serves as an active partner on many levels, from the representation of art and history throughout the first floor to an active grantmaking body.

Engaging in Trust-Based Philanthropy

The *San Antonio Area Foundation* is one community foundation that has embraced the practice of trust-based philanthropy by focusing on general operating support, making multiyear grants and loosening reporting requirements for its grantees. As the name suggests, trust-based philanthropy seeks to address the power imbalances in philanthropy between foundations and nonprofits, believing that the nonprofit is knowledgeable and capable of knowing how the funding can best benefit the community it serves. Almost all of the San Antonio Area Foundation's $8 million in discretionary grants are disbursed to local nonprofits as general operating support. Its 2023–25 Responsive Grant Process calls for the continuation of this approach and for soliciting feedback from Community Advisory Committees to inform grantmaking decisions.[22]

Hosting Giving Circles

Another approach to philanthropy that is growing in popularity is giving circles, where a group of people with shared values come together to collectively discuss and decide where to make a pooled gift. This collective giving model puts grantmaking into the hands of residents, but community foundations can play a valuable role as "hosts." Giving circle hosts offer a range of support services to giving circles, including training local leaders to enable long-term sustainability. Dozens of community foundations have gone through Philanthropy Together's Launchpad for Hosts training, a virtual incubator to launch giving circles within the institution.

Making Community Grants

Other foundations have fully integrated participatory grantmaking into their strategic plans. At the Brooklyn Org (formerly the Brooklyn Community Foundation), all its strategic grantmaking—over $4 million annually—uses the participatory model. The foundation started small, engaging nearly two dozen young people to develop a minigrant program to fund community projects led by youth. It also developed a neighborhood-focused fund in Crown Heights, where the foundation is based, to award $100,000 a year for three years through a community consensus. Now, all the foundation's strategic grantmaking programs are conducted in partnership with community members. Community advisory council members are trained and compensated for their work.

WHAT IS NEXT FOR THIS APPROACH?

CFLeads' *Going All In* research makes it clear that this community leadership approach is growing in popularity among community foundations. Virtually all community foundations that participated in the survey were planning to deepen or expand their community leadership over the next few years, and many were willing to invest more resources in community leadership practices, including resident engagement and public policy work.

However, this momentum does come with challenges, and the path to community leadership is not always an easy one. For community foundations with long histories of serving as transactional grantmakers, it will take time, commitment, and resources to transition to transformational changemakers—ones that share power with the communities they serve. In order to do community leadership well, community foundation staff need unique skills and capacities that will enable them to build trust with the community, form partnerships with them in an authentic way, and ultimately advance co-created and community-led solutions to challenges that the foundation has identified together with the community.

As noted above, in discussing the *Going All In* research, most community foundations doing community leadership are funding it through their operating budgets. While this is positive, creating a business model that can sustainably support this vital work remains an ongoing challenge for many community foundations. Another challenge that the field continuously faces is turnover. In recent years, a significant number of leadership transitions have taken place at community foundations, with many longtime CEOs retiring and others leaving to take other roles in or outside the philanthropic sector. These transitions can affect an institution's continued commitment to community leadership and its participatory practices, and there is a risk that it will revert back to the role of traditional grantmaker and a focus on assets.

With community foundations of all sizes across the country undergoing this shift, there is a tremendous opportunity in the field for community foundations to support and learn from each other. CFLeads believes the most effective way for community foundations to develop their community leadership skills is to learn from peers. Virtually all its offerings incorporate a peer learning element, creating opportunities for community foundations to connect with one another across sizes and geographies. CFLeads also highlights "promising illustrations" in the field, from which community foundations can learn and from which they can be inspired through in-person events, online webinars, case studies, blog posts, and research projects like *Going All In*.

Believing that the community leadership approach requires all hands on deck, CFLeads continues to expand its peer learning offerings and to create more opportunities for a broader range of community foundation staff members to engage in community leadership. CFLeads' ELI is now available to CEOs, VPs, CFOs, and CEO and board pairs, and its introductory course on community leadership, Setting the Table, is open to all community foundation staff.

CFLeads also supports community foundations taking a community leadership approach to a specific issue. Through a well-established peer learning model, community foundations come together to learn from each other and from content experts about the most critical issues facing their communities, and they work with CFLeads to create an action plan to address them—one that incorporates the five competencies of community leadership. Recently completed issue networks from CFLeads include the Racial Equity Network, the Economic Mobility Action Network, and the Gun Violence Prevention Network. Through all its programming, CFLeads will continue to emphasize the importance of participatory practices in community leadership and to lift up examples of community foundations that are doing the important work of engaging residents and amplifying their voices as they seek to lead community-driven change.

NOTES

1. Matt Leighninger, *The Next Form of Democracy: How Expert Rule Is Giving Way to Shared Governance . . . and Why Politics Will Never Be the Same* (Nashville: Vanderbilt University Press, 2006); Cynthia Gibson, *Citizens at the Center: A New Approach to Civic Engagement* (Washington, DC: Case Foundation, 2007).
2. Lucy Bernholz, Katherine Fulton, and Gabriel Kasper, *On the Brink of New Promise: The Future of US Community Foundations* (San Francisco: Blueprint Research & Design and Monitor Institute, 2005), 7.
3. Bernholz et al., *On the Brink*, 38.
4. D. C. Hammack, "Community Foundations: The Delicate Question of Purpose," in *An Agile Servant: Community Leadership by Community Foundations*, ed. Richard Magat (New York: Foundation Center, 1989), 27–28.
5. Hammack.
6. Hammack, 29.

7. Hammack, 33.
8. Hammack, 34.
9. Hammack, 39.
10. Hammack.
11. Hammack.
12. Peter de Courcy Hero and Peter Walkenhorst, *Local Mission—Global Vision: Community Foundations in the 21st Century* (New York: Foundation Center, 2008); Bernholz et al., *On the Brink*.
13. Alex Daniels and Drew Lindsay, "Donor-Advised Funds Reshape the Philanthropy Landscape," *Chronicle of Philanthropy*, October 27, 2016, www.philanthropy.com/article/donor-advised-funds-reshape-the-philanthropy-landscape/.
14. Elizabeth Graddy and Donald Morgan, "Community Foundations, Organizational Strategy, and Public Policy," *Nonprofit and Voluntary Sector Quarterly* 35, no. 4 (2006).
15. CFLeads, *Framework for Community Leadership by a Community Foundation* (Kansas City: CFLeads, 2019), https://cfleads.org/wp-content/uploads/2023/01/Framework-One-Pager.pdf.
16. CFLeads, *Engaging Residents: A New Call to Action for Community Foundations* (Kansas City: CFLeads, 2013), https://cfleads.org/wp-content/uploads/2019/12/CFLeads-Call-to-Action.pdf.
17. CFLeads, 4.
18. Lella Flester and Deborah Ellwood, *Powerful Partners: Lessons from Community Foundations about Resident Engagement* (Kansas City: CFLeads, 2014), https://cfleads.org/wp-content/uploads/2019/11/CFLeads-Powerful-Partners.pdf; Aspen Institute Community Strategies Group, *Resident Engagement Guidebook: Exploring Readiness and Options* (Kansas City: CFLeads, 2014), https://cfleads.org/wp-content/uploads/2019/11/CFLeads-AspenInstitue-Resident-Engagement-Guidebook.pdf.
19. CFLeads, "Community Leadership Field Guide for Community Foundations," July 2021, https://cfleads.org/wp-content/uploads/2022/05/Community-Leadership-Guide-Long-Version.pdf.
20. Candid, "CF Insights Community Leadership Assessment Tool," June 2021, www.issuelab.org/resources/36380/36380.pdf.
21. CFLeads, "Going All In" portal, https://cfleads.org/going-all-in/.
22. Mike Scutari, "This Community Foundation Went All In on Trust-Based Philanthropy; Here's What It Has Learned," *Inside Philanthropy*, February 14, 2023.

CHAPTER 11

"Participatoriness" in Philanthropy
A Conservative Perspective

Michael E. Hartmann and William A. Schambra

Participatory philanthropy could benefit greatly from drawing on the long tradition of conservatism that underlies conservative philanthropy. Participatory philanthropy continues to evolve as a model, and "conservative philanthropy," as a general category of grantmaking, is still relatively undefined, making it difficult for participatory practitioners to see connections between the two. Conservative philanthropy, however, has several traditions, values, and practices that dovetail with philanthropic "participatoriness." The authors provide an overview of these areas of alignment, discuss how they have been applied in conservative philanthropic practice, and explore some of the reasons for conservatives' caution about incorporating a full spectrum of power sharing in all aspects of the grantmaking process.

INTRODUCTION

Most studies of participatory philanthropy involve organizations associated with progressive causes, but we argue that participation might align with some traditions, values, and practices in conservative philanthropy. We begin by describing conservative philanthropy, positing that this label encompasses two distinct perspectives or streams of thought. We then focus on the Burkean or Tocquevillean perspective, which emphasizes "mediating structures" and empowering people to be active participants in solving the problems they confront. We conclude by considering why conservative philanthropists might be reluctant to practice participatory grantmaking as it is currently conceived.

WHAT IS "CONSERVATIVE PHILANTHROPY," ANYWAY?

While there is no formal definition of "conservative philanthropy," those who have attempted to describe it usually point to specific foundations with a conservative philosophy or political tradition, using their principles and practices as indicators to make a general characterization. These usually include the John M. Olin Foundation, Smith Richardson Foundation, Lynde and Harry Bradley Foundation, and Scaife Foundations.

Risking oversimplification, these foundations use approaches that, to varying degrees, have generally reflected a respect for history, tradition, religion, the market, and localism, and an aversion if not outright hostility to "bigness," centralization, professionalization, and elitism. This conservative view also looks proudly askance at well-credentialed experts from institutions afar and, instead, prefers weighing the wisdom of real people, such as responsible businesspeople, from a family neighborhood around the corner, which may even have a church or synagogue on it.

In the eyes of conservative grantmakers, this respect and these aversions stand in stark contrast to what they have seen as the progressivism of establishment philanthropy in America. To the degree that participatory philanthropy similarly stands against powerful credentialed experts making decisions about communities and residents with which they have little contact, there might be opportunities for some of these conservatives and participatory philanthropy advocates to explore listening to and learning from each other.

Two Traditions

Those who have studied conservative philanthropy—including former Olin Foundation executive director and trustee James Piereson, now the president of the William E. Simon Foundation—suggest there are two traditions undergirding its paradigm, which first emerged around the time of the French Revolution.[1] These two traditions are distinguished by whether they believe that market capitalism can function on its own or requires external support from societal structures like law and civil society. This matters when it comes to their views about nonprofits and philanthropy, which are seen either as essential for the functioning of market capitalism or as superfluous.

First is the tradition originating with the eighteenth-century political philosopher Edmund Burke, who employs the language of prudence and tradition to defend representative government, the rule of law, and the nongovernmental units of civil society—what political philosophy would label classically "liberal institutions," according to Pierson. "Conservatism brings something from outside liberal thought to the defense of these liberal institutions."[2] Note that "liberal" is used here as a political philosophy, rather than in the contemporary sense of being associated with a particular ideology or even political party within a democratic system.

Alexis de Tocqueville and others in the nineteenth century consonantly argued, Piereson notes, "that it is necessary to preserve" these institutions, "namely church, family, local governments, and voluntary associations as a foundation for markets and representative government. . . . Liberal institutions cannot stand entirely on their own and require support from the outside as it were."[3]

Second is another, newer tradition: the one undergirding market capitalism. This tradition, Piereson notes, "suggests that market capitalism can stand on its own foundations without external support from the kinds of institutions discussed before." In such a tradition, nonprofits and philanthropy are not viewed as essential to support the effective functioning of a capitalist society.

The Burkean and Tocquevillian tradition of conservatism, therefore, offers more of a grounding for a conservative approach to participatory philanthropy. In such an approach, grantmakers would pay special attention to how the institutions of civil society—including nonprofits, but also less formal volunteer efforts (particularly at the local grassroots level), serve to moderate, supplement, or bolster the function of market capitalism in society. Such an approach would eschew the centralized, planned efforts of a top-down progressivism—in government policy or establishment philanthropy—and instead focus on a smaller-scale, more locally driven version of giving that values the unique contributions of grassroots leaders.

Mediating Structures and Grantee-Orientedness

To the degree that there has been and is a conservative interest in this form of grantee-oriented philanthropy, it has been and is rooted in the first tradition's perceived necessity of preserving Tocquevillean civil society. More contemporarily, it can be found in the work done by the sociologist Peter Berger and the theologian Richard John Neuhaus at the American Enterprise Institute in the 1970s. Their monograph *To Empower People: The Role of Mediating Structures in Public Policy* argued that American public policy had become deadlocked between two diametrically opposed approaches: (1) the championing of a powerful central government, and (2) the emphasizing of the centrality of the individual in public affairs. The deadlock basically resulted from deemphasizing—if not missing—the first, older conservative tradition.[4]

Echoing Burke and Tocqueville, Berger and Neuhaus argued that there is a very important approach nestled between the individual and the centralized state: a vast array of mediating structures such as families, neighborhoods, houses of worship, and voluntary and ethnic associations. All these mediating structures are used by everyday Americans seeking to solve their own problems according to their own values and based on their own lived experiences, rather than relying on experts or other outsiders for answers. Essentially, these structures have always been and remain participatory. It would be in this framework of conservative philanthropy that participatory philanthropy could be well received.

This framework has been best exemplified by the work of Robert Woodson Sr., a former Urban League official who had been recruited by the American Enterprise Institute, considered a conservative and business-friendly think tank, to apply the mediating-structures framework to issues of urban poverty.[5]

To do so, Woodson developed what he called the "zip code test." He argued that every neighborhood—no matter how seemingly distressed—has community leaders who are living day-to-day with difficult problems and who are, despite these challenges, developing insightful, if often idiosyncratic, ways to address those problems. The most effective poverty programs, Woodson maintained, are rooted in the experience, wisdom, and authority of local leaders living in the same zip code as the problems needing resolution.

Woodson went one step further, however, suggesting that this approach could and should be used to distinguish conservative philanthropy, because it emphasized what Tocqueville described as the "everyday institutions of American civil society" to solve public problems, rather than relying on large, remote, intrusive, centralized institutions like government and other more top-down institutions.[6] As later inspiringly described by Woodson in his 1998 book *The Triumphs of Joseph: How Today's Community Healers*

Are Reviving Our Streets and Neighborhoods, by seeing community residents as actors in their own lives, this approach had the added benefit of providing opportunities for them to engage more fully and authentically in civic life, which strengthens democracy.[7] In short, Woodson argued, it does little good for conservatives to merely talk about the virtues of civil society while employing the same top-down, expert-driven approaches that they believed progressive philanthropy had been increasingly employing and, in his view, substituting for local democracy.

Woodson was both a MacArthur Foundation fellow (the so-called genius grants) and a recipient of the Bradley Prize—prestigious awards conferred annually by their respective progressive and conservative foundations. His work has since been supported by some conservative foundations that practice what could easily and should be considered participatory philanthropy, though they might not recognize the term as such. One of these is the Bradley Foundation, which awards the Bradley Prizes. In addition to its embrace of participatory approaches like those described by Woodson, Bradley has also helped to lay the foundation for a demonstration project supporting parent-driven educational choice (first in Milwaukee, and then nationally)—something that we believe was and remains a fundamentally participatory endeavor.

In a healthy democracy, conservatives with a Woodson-like inclination assume that regular, everyday citizens can and should be trusted at least as much as or even more than well-credentialed professionals in ivory towers and/or their allied government bureaucracies to contribute meaningful and actionable "expertise" to—or, again, to participate in—the way we go about living with each other. This is in direct (and ironic) contrast to progressive foundations, which these conservatives note have relied on those (fellow) elites since the Progressive Era and through the failed War on Poverty.

Elitism and Progressive Philanthropy

More than a century ago—led by one of its intellectual godfathers, Herbert Croly—the modern Progressive movement came to view local communities and their Tocquevillean mediating institutions—as well as libertarian-touted individual rights, for that matter—as backward, parochial, and irrational. As explained by Croly in his 1909 book *The Promise of American Life*, they only gummed up the works of the smoothly humming machinery of public affairs, which had been crafted according to the new sciences of sociology, psychology, and public administration.[8]

The aim of these sciences was to organize and engineer human affairs in a rational, objective, coherent fashion. Progress required removing authority from local communities and placing it in the hands of professional elites trained in these sciences.

Applying the thinking of Croly, these purely public-spirited social engineers would be devoted heart and soul to a grand vision of national purpose or national community—a vision all too likely to elude ordinary citizens, trapped as they were in shabby local communities, still clinging to antiquated, parochial moral and religious myths.

The first large American foundations—Carnegie, Rockefeller, and Russell Sage—were enthusiastic supporters of these social engineers and this vision. Their early grantmaking thus focused on reforming and rationalizing the elite leadership professions of American public life: medicine, the law, education, and public administration. They also established research universities and policy institutions to provide the nonpartisan, objective research necessary to expand the scientific management of public affairs by rationalized, centralized social service bureaucracies.[9]

Today, this philanthropically funded vision heavily influences American politics, policymaking, and culture, making it challenging for everyday citizens to question the authority invoked to inflict the social engineering behind it. Participatory philanthropy is, and might be more of, a good and effective way to check this authority, because it is an implied and potential actual threat to establishment philanthropy. While there has been more receptivity to participatory philanthropy from progressive foundations—especially small or community-based organizations—a limited but growing number of conservatives are either applying similar anti-"elite" thinking in their philanthropic efforts or are becoming more receptive to it.

WHAT DO CONSERVATIVES CONSIDER TO BE PARTICIPATORY PHILANTHROPY?

As introduced by Cynthia Gibson in her important, path-breaking 2017 paper—*Participatory Grantmaking: Has Its Time Come?*—participatory philanthropy "covers a wide range of institutional and individual activities, such as incorporating grantee feedback into grant guidelines and strategy development, inviting nongrantmakers to sit on foundation boards, crowdfunding, and giving circles."[10]

In that paper and in the introduction to this volume, the term *participatory grantmaking* is distinguished from *participatory philanthropy* to describe a process that narrows the focus to how, by, and for whom grant decisions are made. Some see participatory grantmaking as one of many types of participatory philanthropy. Others think it is distinctive because it moves decision-making about money—seen by them as the epitome of power—to the people most affected by the issues donors are trying to address.

The conceptual refinement of participatoriness in philanthropy overall to grantmaking in particular would be—and in some cases, is—a monumental shift from how philanthropy traditionally has allocated funds. It is a disruption that may explain why participatory grantmaking is for the most part still relatively rare, particularly when compared with other forms of participatory philanthropy. It also gives rise to real, genuine, and perhaps justified skittishness among conservative givers who might otherwise be receptive to participatoriness.

In both Gibson'spaper and in this volume, one need not really stretch too far to see the anti-elitist impulses from which both participatory philanthropy and grantmaking spring. "Long-lasting change within foundations will only occur when the field fully embraces participation's transformative potential and when . . . people are willing to cede control and power," Gibson writes in her published paper. During recent years, some conservatives have issued similar calls for cessions of control and power from establishment progressive philanthropies that they see as having forgotten about the average American and/or condescending to them.

The Heart of the Matter, Left and Right

At the heart of the participatory approaches is the notion of trust, as many of its proponents have written (and, indeed, as participatory philanthropy/grantmaking was gaining visibility, a new framework, "Trust-Based Philanthropy," emerged, echoing the centrality of trust in "addressing the inherent power imbalances between foundations and nonprofits"[11]). Gibson, for example, notes that "for participatory practices to take hold in philanthropy, foundations have to trust the community of nongrantmakers. Foundations also have to value the lived experience and wisdom that nongrantmakers bring to the table in important decisions about how resources—including money and more—are distributed."[12]

Like some progressives, some conservatives think and hope that participatoriness should include a bit of healthy self-abnegation on the part of establishment philanthropy. Although conservatives like to assume that their trust has always resided in non-elite (and maybe even anti-elite) institutions and structures, still relatively few conservative foundations have incorporated participatory approaches that share or cede power about resource allocation. And while progressive foundations like to proclaim their allegiance to helping underserved or "disempowered" constituencies, in our opinion, their funding tends to rest on strategies developed in large, bureaucratic, and expert-driven think tanks, universities, and/or consulting firms.

On the Right, at Least Some Familiarity

The First Components

The framework for philanthropic participatoriness put forward in Gibson's paper—helpfully created as a "baseline," on which the larger field would be asked to iterate with comments and suggestions—has four components. The first two are "informing" and "consulting." The third component, "involving," can have something to do with the actual awarding of a grant, or not. The fourth component, "deciding," seems to have to do directly with which groups get a grant, and for how much. Some have since added a fifth component, in which funders explicitly cede *all* decision-making to nonfunders.[13]

Gibson's paper and this book also provide examples of activities and processes for each component. Almost all the examples are from liberal or left-leaning organizations. Given the expressed desire for a "common language" and a "consensus" behind the cause, there should also perhaps be a right-leaning example or two.

We think it easy to find examples of conservative foundations "informing" and "consulting" with existing or would-be grantees about program issues and aims, no differently from liberal foundations. Grantmakers and nongrantmakers alike find similar tools in their toolboxes: these include public relations and public education campaigns; websites; officials' appearances on conference panels; published papers, articles, and op-eds; site visits; meetings with board and program staff members; and the like. Fewer, but still many, conservative foundations could be considered to involve nongrantees, especially if that is considered to include extensively consulting with them and relying on their input.

Indeed, some conservative foundations are clearly cognizant of being too top-down in their thinking and know that humility is a prerequisite for ultimate success in the exercise of the grantmaking power. But humility is a challenge for any human being or human enterprise. At the board level, humility represents an effective, professional stewardship of resources. At the staff level, it is just good program officer practice, part of the obligation owed to board and donor alike.

At the Bradley Foundation, for example, the program staff knew quite well that we did not know which schools in which parts of central Milwaukee were preferred by parents living in the community, so we attentively listened to—and were genuinely instructed by—them in putting together grant recommendations for our board. We knew we did not know the challenges facing human services case workers in the state's welfare system, so we asked them what they would do as we tried to put together a welfare reform grant program in Wisconsin. We knew we did not know how to run a community-based residential facility—or an Ivy League political science department, for that matter, or a publishing house, or a symphony, or a museum.

We were not stupid, let us please say, but we were generalists, trying to apply common sense, in line with the foundation's founding intent and directors' directives. For Bradley, success followed, we believe, including in the contexts of school choice, welfare reform, neighborhood revitalization, higher education, public discourse, and others.

School Choice as Participatory Philanthropy

We believe that privately funded school choice could easily have been and still could be considered participatory philanthropy, in that it devolved decisions on the best use of grant dollars not to foundation officials but to community members—namely, to the parents of school-age children.

In 1990, the State of Wisconsin began to fund vouchers that poor parents in Milwaukee could use to send their own children to whichever participating private K–12 school they themselves chose. Before the program was expanded to include religious schools in 1995, Bradley substantially supported a charitable organization that offered parents the option to send their children to a participating religious school. The donated money was given directly to parents, who funneled it to any participating religious school that they themselves deemed the most worthy recipient. They decided where the money went, which is an important component of participatory grantmaking.

Neither Bradley nor any other donor picked which parents got the empowering largesse, which schools were on the list, or which religions they taught or the tenets in which they believed. The grant support was premised upon trusting participating parents to make the decision.

It is worth noting that, unlike many conservatives, Bradley did not frame its support for school choice in the libertarian language of markets, through which schools would be improved by competing for vouchers wielded by parents. Rather, Bradley understood school choice as an essential device for undergirding the mediating structures (e.g., churches and community centers) necessary for a healthy local democracy. Families were strengthened by enabling parents—too often infantilized by public programs—to make the critical decision about their children's education on their own and according to their own values. And the schools thus supported through vouchers were often themselves vital centers of Tocquevillean community life, reflecting the full range of moral, spiritual, and cultural principles of local neighborhoods.

Although there was cross-ideological (and bipartisan) support for the system-transforming school choice effort, however, we recall it being quite harshly attacked by many prominent progressive philanthropies and their grantees, which included many (well-funded) lawsuits. When the prominent parent choice activist Howard Fuller was named to the board of directors of Chicago's Joyce Foundation and Brother Bob Smith was on the Bradley Foundation board, moreover, no one lauded it as properly "participatory" or anything similar.

While it may not fit the definition of participatory grantmaking advanced by its proponents, including those in this volume, we offer the example of a foundation funding school choice as a meaningful alternative in the sector's understanding of what counts as participation in philanthropy. The essence of this example—that these programs gave parents the ultimate choice for how to allocate foundation dollars, and that this was the explicit intention of the funding—to us shares something fundamental with the spirit of participatory grantmaking. And this is an intriguing area of commonality between conservative efforts in the Burkean/Tocquevillean mediating-structures tradition and the progressive efforts described elsewhere in this volume. They both explicitly seek to devolve decision-making power over philanthropic dollars from credentialed foundation officials to everyday community members.

One could argue that school choice is different because the decisions made by parents are fundamentally individual ones, while participatory grantmaking tends to be done in an intentionally collective manner. In our opinion, an openness to individual participants in participatory philanthropy by its proponents might get them more conservative allies. And conservative funders could also consider pursuing efforts that promote collective participation in participatory philanthropy. We turn now to some of the considerations—and concerns—of conservatives vis-à-vis participatory philanthropy.

CONSERVATIVES' CONCERNS AND CAVEATS

There are really no examples, at least about which we are aware, of a conservative philanthropist consciously, systematically, and procedurally ceding or delegating grantmaking authority to an external decision-maker. To the degree that one has even been presented with the idea by a trusted partner, they would have concerns and caveats about doing so—perhaps some, though not necessarily, borne of their underlying conservatism. For example, because foundations are still fiscally and legally responsible for their operations, they would be remiss in ceding all control over the decisions they make.

Another potential risk that both conservative and progressive foundations face in participatory grantmaking are conflicts of interest among participants who are actual or would-be grantees. Conflicts could also occur when participants are working in, on the board or staff of, and/or have professional or personal relationships with an organization being considered for funding. As we understand it, these topics come up regularly in discussions of participatory grantmaking, and various techniques for addressing them have been developed.

Donor Intent

There are additional issues, however, that conservative foundations would be particularly concerned about when deciding whether to wade into participatory-philanthropic waters. At the top of this list is donor intent, which is not sufficiently addressed in the current participatory grantmaking literature, and to which conservative philanthropists and "philanthropoids" have historically and traditionally accorded great value.

Obviously, if the donor is alive and seeks participatoriness, this is not a problem. But it could be a case of an absent donor who did not approve or even know about participatory grantmaking before their departure. External participants will very likely not be as concerned about donor intent as the board and staff of a donor's philanthropic legacy whose stated role is to safeguard that legacy.

Advisory Roles

Another concern that arguably may have more resonance with conservative foundations is the role of philanthropic advisers when it comes to participatory grantmaking. An analogy using the financial services industry may be helpful here. Within the financial services industry, there has been an ongoing debate for years about the legal, moral, and ethical standards to which certain types of advisers should be held. Historically, investment advisers who work directly for the client investor have been held to a fiduciary standard (i.e., they must place the client's interests ahead of their own) by law, regulation, and licensors. Investment brokers, by contrast, also make recommendations to a client investor, but they are employed by broker-dealers, meaning they need only believe that their recommendations are suitable for the client, which is a lower standard than the advisers' fiduciary one. To some, that is not good enough.

While it is unlikely that grantmakers will ever be governed in the same way as financial advisers (and they should not be), the debate about the standard to which financial advisers should be held offers insights into how givers and their advisers should think about these questions. Conceptually, to what sort of standard or standards, if any, should giving advisers or external participants of various sorts be held, by whom, and how? To the degree that internal program staffers may compromise their ability to meet whichever standard, intentionally or not, the board and executive should internally hold them accountable—up to and including severing the employment relationship.

Such a duty is certainly breached if there is an actual outright undisclosed conflict of interest, financial or otherwise, of course. Short of that, however, a wide spectrum of more nebulous factors could risk a breach, and there should pretty much always be a carefully tuned sensitivity to it—ranging from serving formal roles at or with a grant recipient or applicant organizations to allowing themselves to be seen as "playing favorites" in making recommendations or evaluating performance.

Program officers should internally hold themselves to the same standard, too, with the necessary, but unfortunately uncommon, humility and discipline to do so. If there were an imaginary fiduciary standard for program officers in big American philanthropy, it would currently be often outright breached, and more often—too often—seriously compromised.

For more nebulosity, widen the spectrum to include "independent" advisory board members, outside reviewers, and consultants. In most cases, for their wisdom and advice, they will have been retained by the foundation or grantmaker, to which they thus owe something. And in most cases, they will be employed by another entity to which they also owe something in return (not unlike investment brokers, in our analogy).

That which they owe to the client, and separately to the employer, might conflict—or at least be in tension, skillful as they will likely be at rationalizing away or reconciling any such dissonance. When considering already-existing professional and personal connections, for example, an adviser might plausibly think that these are why they were asked to participate in the first place, after all. Or maybe the firm's other clients fully share this one's goals and worldview—or, at least, they largely overlap—so tailoring guidance to other donors' interests is not wrong or anything. As always, a moral and ethical compromise is awfully tempting.

Potential Pawnmaking

Finally—perhaps less charitably, if not outright cynically—there is another serious risk that participatory grantmaking could become a mechanism by which to invoke—then misuse—the moral authority of real-life, everyday participants in ways that give a foundation some street cred. In other words, if this brand of grantmaking acquires enough popularity, foundations may simply give lip service to "participatory grantmaking," inviting grantees or outside participants whom they believe will endorse whatever program they already want to fund.

For instance, if it turns out that all or most grants made through the participatory process just happen to flow into conspicuously progressive or conservative causes, then one might become suspicious that *behind* the process there had been careful, ideologically tainted prescreening of those engaged *in* the process. If participatory grantmakers overwhelmingly support, say, nonprofits devoted to defunding the police or making abortion illegal, then a possibly uncharitable (but not incomprehensible) reading could lead one to conclude that a great deal of prescreening had indeed been involved (e.g., in the case of defunding the police, most opinion surveys suggest that low-income BIPOC communities are more interested in an increased, if more culturally attuned, police presence).

On some parts of the left, a well-established doctrine exists for explaining this sort of discrepancy between what "the masses" *should* want and what they in fact *do* want: namely, "false consciousness." In Marxist theory, false consciousness is a way of thinking that prevents people from properly perceiving the true nature of their social or economic situation. This doctrine soon leads to the certainty that only an enlightened vanguard can be trusted to make the appropriate decisions for the masses, who are otherwise too immured in petty, everyday concerns to see their true interests.

Ironically, if participatory grantmaking were to be misused in this way—letting the outcome justify the decision—it would perversely resemble the intellectual errors whereby certain foundations used powerfully credentialed academics or "experts" to justify what they were going to do in the first place. This seems, to us, a plausible risk.

The Woodson approach to participation, by contrast, assumes and validates the authenticity of what emerges—without implicit, expert-designed ideological filters—from the grassroots. Whatever filtering occurs when grantmakers seek out those whom the local community has already validated—which can be discovered by, say, the level of activity and energy present in a nonprofit, and by word-of-mouth among everyday community citizens, who can point out quickly and precisely where they go when they are in need of assistance, advice, and support.

This may not fit together into a rational and orderly pattern in the program officer's mind or in the foundation's strategic plan. Why, for instance, is Milwaukee's Cordelia Taylor—the founder of the community-based senior care center called Family House—also dispensing advice to low-income mothers about how to make nutritious meals from the canned goods she gives them? It is because Mother Taylor is the first person to whom the neighborhood turns when a problem—even one not related to senior care—arises. The Woodson approach would say: support her generously, and in turn ask her who else in the circle of community leaders she would advise one to support.

Democratic participation, in this sense, is always already present, in whom the local community has informally but clearly elevated to positions of authority. It does not need to be reconstructed through a formal institutional process, as some participatory grantmaking may seek to do, and indeed may well lose something in the effort to do so. But seeking out and funding grassroots groups that have already come to embody the community's spirit is subtle, difficult—and, of course, also subject to abuses, as are all human institutions and behaviors.

To pursue this approach, a foundation's board and program staff must put aside all ideological preconceptions about what people should want and remain humbly open to whatever the community has already indicated that it does want, by the sorts of nonprofits to which they have given rise and which they support by their presence, their voluntary energies, and their own giving. To our way of thinking, this Woodsonian approach in the Burkean/Tocquevillean tradition of conservatism would be a genuine alternative to the current practice of participatory grantmaking, and one that holds promise worth exploring in practice.

IFS, BUTS, AND LET US

If proponents of participatory philanthropy are looking to attract receptive conservatives to their cause, it will be difficult for them to do so if the standard of participatoriness means conceding the principle of donor intent (if and when applicable), and breaching a properly perceived, fiduciary-like duty of loyalty to a grantmaker. It may be impossible if participatoriness comes to be—or even to seem—just another mechanism to rationalize tax-incentivized philanthropy in furtherance of one particular ideological or partisan political end.

If conservative philanthropy is honestly and self-critically looking to exemplify anti-elitism in and improve its grantmaking, however, it would more aggressively explore options to humbly check what might be its own elitism and increase participatoriness in that grantmaking—maybe even potentially riskily including, if and when appropriate, "deciding" about it. The caveats we have raised here are genuine, and, we believe, surmountable. As in so many other contexts, we believe we could and should trust and—with respect and good nature—try learning more from each other.

NOTES

1. James Piereson, remarks made during the event "What Is Conservative Philanthropy?" held at the Hudson Institute's Bradley Center for Philanthropy and Civic Renewal, New York, September 2012.
2. Piereson.
3. Piereson.
4. Peter L. Berger and Richard John Neuhaus, *To Empower People: The Role of Mediating Structures in Public Policy* (Washington, DC: American Enterprise Institute Press, 1976).
5. For examples of Robert Woodson Sr.'s work, see Robert Woodson, *A Summons to Life: Mediating Structures and the Prevention of Youth Crime* (Pensacola, FL: Ballinger, 1981); Robert Woodson, *Youth Crime and Urban Policy: A View from the Inner City* (Washington, DC: American Enterprise Institute Press, 1981); Robert Woodson, *On the Road to Economic Freedom: An Agenda for Black Progress* (Chicago: Regnery

Gateway, 1987); and Robert Woodson, *The Triumphs of Joseph: How Today's Community Healers Are Reviving Our Streets and Neighborhoods* (New York: Free Press, 1998).
6. Tocqueville, *Democracy in America* (New York: G. Dearborn & Co., 1838).
7. Woodson, *Triumphs*.
8. Herbert Croly, *The Promise of American Life* (New York: Macmillan, 1909).
9. See William A. Schambra, "Charity, Progressive Philanthropy, and Eugenics," October 8, 2005, https://phillysoc.org/schambra-charity-progressive-philanthropy-and-eugenics/.
10. Cynthia Gibson, *Participatory Grantmaking: Has Its Time Come?* (New York: Ford Foundation, 2017), 11, www.fordfoundation.org/media/3599/participatory_grantmaking-lmv7.pdf.
11. Trust-Based Philanthropy Project, "Principles," www.trustbasedphilanthropy.org/principles-1.
12. Gibson, *Participatory Grantmaking*, 42.
13. Nwamaka Agbo, *Powershift Philanthropy: Strategies for Impactful Participatory Grantmaking* (Los Angeles: California Endowment, 2021).

CHAPTER 12

What Will It Take to Change?
Traditional Foundations and Megadonors Experiment with Participatory Grantmaking

Anne Katahira with Marissa Jackson

Since 2020, more traditional foundations and megadonors have begun experimenting with participatory grantmaking (PGM). For many of them, this has been explicitly motivated by a new or renewed commitment to racial equity. On the basis of interviews with these grantmakers, this chapter explores how conditions inside organizations (e.g., internal culture and how power moves) and conditions outside organizations (e.g., trust, track records, and transparency) shape whether and to what extent participatory grantmaking can take root and grow. It also explores how interviewees see the connections between PGM and racial equity. This project was conducted by practitioners with practitioners as a readership in mind.

INTRODUCTION

In 2020, the global COVID-19 pandemic, national uprisings against anti-Black racism and police brutality, economic collapse, and numerous climate crises forced our collective eyes open to the fact that the policies and systems governing our society—from health care to public safety, education, and beyond—do not serve the needs of most of our communities. It became much more difficult to dispute or ignore the fact that Black, Indigenous, Latinx, Asian, and Native Hawaiian / Pacific Islander communities, and those with intersecting identities in the LGBTQIA+ and disabled communities, are not only the least served but also often the most harmed by these crises and systems.

Auspiciously, funders took immediate action to support racial equity, COVID-19 relief, and related efforts at record levels. Working as consultants to philanthropies through the Giving Practice at Philanthropy Northwest, a national philanthropic consulting firm, we observed many of our clients, including traditional foundations and megadonors, make new or renewed commitments to racial equity as a primary focus and often a core value.[1]

While some funders continued to use traditional grantmaking systems and practices to deliver new support, we also saw funders question some of these typical ways of working. Often, these involved rigid processes, inflexible criteria, restricting funding to specific programs, and decision-making about funding by the donor, trustee, or program staff after a review and evaluation of applications and proposals by grant-seeking nonprofits. We heard stories of letting go of many of these practices and shifting decision-making power to communities. We saw the practice of participatory grantmaking gain momentum across the sector, alongside an increased commitment to racial equity.

It struck us that these two practices—participatory grantmaking and racial equity—could and should be connected and potentially reinforce each other. According to Cynthia Gibson, "Participatory grantmaking cedes decision-making power about funding—including the strategy and criteria behind those decisions—to the very communities that funders aim to serve."[2] It is grounded in the central belief that communities are experts in their own lives, know what they need, and should hold the power to make decisions affecting their lives.

Some of the practices ingrained in participatory grantmaking include these:

- The people most affected by the issues at hand are involved in decision-making about how to address them.
- There is inclusive and equitable participation by diverse people and voices.
- There is reciprocal communication that leads to shared decision-making.
- Problem-solving is collaborative.
- There is transparency about decision-making processes.
- Practices are values-based.

Participatory grantmaking can be a powerful tool for grantmakers to align their values, practices, and funding. It not only encourages shifts in grantmaking practices and structures but also inspires an ethos—or guiding principles—to embody across all our work, holding grantmakers accountable to the communities they serve.

Participatory grantmaking practices overlap with these commonly held values and practices underlying racial equity:[3]

- The voices, experiences, and perspectives of Black, Indigenous, Latinx, and Asian and Native Hawaiian / Pacific Islanders are centered.
- Honor and build power with and for those pushed to the margins.[4]
- Thinking and acting are collective and collaborative.[5]
- There is transparency to hold tensions and navigate challenges.[6]
- There is accountability to principles and people.[7]

Against the backdrop of participatory grantmaking as a way of being and doing, we realized that this approach could be an effective tool for advancing racial equity because it encourages funders to make structural and behavioral changes, which we believed are necessary for racial equity. We were eager to test this theory and, hopefully, move it into practice. There was no shortage of pressure as the outside world continued to demand changes to the sector and its practices, so we looked inward. We became curious about the internal and external conditions required for participatory grantmaking to take root and grow in an organization. We had our own observations from our work with our clients, many of which were traditional foundations and some megadonors, but a question kept nagging at us: What is in the way? We needed to dig deeper.

RESEARCH QUESTIONS

In 2021, Marissa Jackson, a former consultant with the Giving Practice, and I conducted a study to explore the factors preventing philanthropies from fully embracing participatory grantmaking. Having worked with a number of funders along the spectrum of PGM—from those who were just curious to those who were already ceding all decision-making power to participants from communities the funders wanted to affect and learn from—we decided to interview them to learn more.

The key questions we sought to answer were:
- What internal or external conditions affect organizational readiness to take on PGM?
- How do grantmakers seek to overcome obstacles to adopting PGM?
- Do grantmakers see a relationship between PGM and racial equity?

METHODOLOGY

We selected interviewees from a pool of the Giving Practice's past and current clients, and members of Philanthropy Northwest, the six-state regional philanthropy network that houses the Giving Practice. We opted to interview people with whom we had existing relationships or who were, at a minimum, connected to our organization, and thus familiar with our values, our general approach, and our backgrounds as practitioners. We believed we would be most successful if we drew on the fuel that drives participatory grantmaking: trusting relationships.

Twelve people from eight different philanthropic organizations were interviewed. Two were CEOs / executive directors, and ten were in program officer–equivalent or director-equivalent roles. The interviewees' philanthropic organizations represented a range of philanthropies, including two traditional foundations, three megadonors, an identity-based community foundation, a federated fund (whose participatory grantmaking work is funded by one of the three megadonors), and a health conversion foundation.[8]

As of 2019 and 2020, the assets of these eight organizations ranged from $66 million to more than $1 billion, with a mean of $103.3 million and a median of $111 million (excluding the largest one). The mean of traditional foundations and megadonors was $122.1 million, and the median was $115.8 million (excluding the largest one).[9]

The traditional foundations and megadonors with which we spoke were founded between 1991 and 2015. The average age of traditional foundations and megadonors' institutions was 18.8 years. At the time of the interview, the oldest had been in operation for 33 years, and the two most recently established were 6 years old.

We also included inputs from our direct observations, which were taken while supporting two traditional foundations in exploring or piloting participatory grantmaking programs. (We did not interview either of these two former clients for this project, as internal staff transitions meant we no longer had relationships with the program team.) For reference, one foundation had assets of about $240 million and the other had more than $1 billion.

As practitioner consultants who believe in including the voices and perspectives of community members in participatory grantmaking programs, we were unable to do so because we did not have the funds to compensate them for their time and engagement (something in which we strongly believe). Also, when we began this project, we thought that, at a minimum, we would be able to elicit information and perspectives about community partners through our work with funders either planning or piloting participatory grantmaking programs. However, these opportunities did not materialize; those funders either changed course and did not implement their initial plans to adopt PGM, or they ended their pilot programs.

RESULTS

Across the eight philanthropies we interviewed, we found a range of PGM activities (see table 12.1). In the cluster of traditional foundations and mega donors (rows 1 through 5 of table 12.1), four of the five were implementing or funding implementation of participatory grantmaking programs. Of the four, three were implementing participatory grantmaking programs, and one was funding an intermediary (also an interviewee) to implement a participatory grantmaking program. Finally, one expressed early interest among program staff in exploring participatory practices. Of the four active PGM programs, all were relatively new. One had been operating since 2018, one was in the second year of a pilot program, and two had completed the first cycle of funding.

In the cluster of other funders (rows 6 through 8 of table 12.1), one had a long history of participatory grantmaking practices but was working to refine and align participatory grantmaking with organizational values, including racial justice. Another had completed a cycle of participatory grantmaking in one portfolio funded by the above-mentioned megadonor but had also piloted two other participatory grantmaking programs in two different portfolios. One of these focused on Indigenous communities and the other on Black communities—all three of which centered racial equity.

The last of this cluster of other funders expressed skepticism about participatory grantmaking because they had seen it play out, pointing to how training community members in traditional program officer roles can replicate and perpetuate the pitfalls of grantmaking, such as power imbalances and gatekeeping, none of which advance racial equity. As a result, they were practicing and refining a trust-based approach to their philanthropy, which explicitly focuses on "advancing equity, shifting power, and building mutually accountable relationships" and shares many overlapping values with participatory grantmaking and racial equity.[10]

Table 12.1: Uptake of Participatory Grantmaking by Organization Type and Asset Size

Row	Organization type	Asset size in dollars	Participatory grantmaking (PGM) activity
1	Traditional foundation	190.7M	Curious about PGM
2	Traditional foundation	115.0M	Implementing PGM program
3	Megadonor	66.0M	Curious; funding an intermediary to implement PGM
4	Megadonor	1.0B+	Piloting PGM program
5	Megadonor	116.7M	Implementing PGM program
6	Health conversion foundation	111.0M	Wary that PGM replicates power imbalances inherent in traditional grantmaking; practicing trust-based philanthropy
7	Identity-based community foundation	48.0M	Transforming internal culture to adopt PGM
8	Federated fund	76.0M	Implementing multiple PGM programs

Source: Author data.

This variation in uptake led us to explore the internal and external conditions that contribute to readiness for PGM. In doing so, we also identified obstacles to PGM and how grantmakers sought to overcome them, along with respondents' views on the relationship between PGM and racial equity. In the spirit of practitioners addressing practitioners, these patterns are framed in the style of recommendations, which is part of how we as philanthropic advisers think and talk.

Laying the Foundation for Participatory Grantmaking: Internal Conditions Supporting Readiness

Internal organizational conditions and operations that influence readiness for participatory efforts include norms and culture, how organizational values are lived and operationalized, power dynamics, communication, decision-making, staff capacity, hiring practices, leadership support, and more.

There are seven themes about internal conditions that support organizational readiness.

Understand where you are starting from: know your own internal organizational conditions. When organizations are starting to explore participatory grantmaking, it is important that they have a clear and shared understanding of their internal conditions, including clarity about staff capacity, leadership support, and more. Interviewees cited two additional elements necessary for assessing readiness: an understanding of the organization's values and key elements of its culture. As one person noted, "The first thing for me is asking what are your institution's values? What are the top three values you use as the lens for decisions? The first thing that needs to be in place is a set of values aligned with the *why* of participatory grantmaking."

The above reflected our previous work piloting a participatory program, which concluded that any organization seeking to try PGM needs to understand the *why* for doing this work. PGM requires thoughtful development for organizations because each is different and has its own culture, structure, and values—all of which need to be assessed as to their alignment (or not) with participatory approaches. Because participatory grantmaking also includes many decision points—such as the program's structure and how systems can be changed or built—having a clear and shared understanding of why an organization wants to experiment with PGM is essential. Without a clear understanding of this "why," aligning funders' approach, structure, and investment priorities with participatory grantmaking will be nearly impossible.

One interviewee encouraged funders to do the introspective work of understanding what PGM is, what they hoped it could help them accomplish, and why they would be willing to make shifts to this approach: "The strong value of and philosophical commitment to including community in the decision-making process has to come first.... For us, it's about racial equity and racial justice.... Our team is trying to shift power back to community."

As key elements of culture, curiosity and flexibility—particularly at the leadership level—were also identified as supporting factors. One interviewee explained, "I don't know if you call it openness or curiosity. There has to be some flexibility in the people who are part of the power structure of the organization to say, 'We might not be doing it right,' and 'What might be an alternative model?' If you don't have that open curiosity to explore, then it's hard to shift."

Most funders acknowledged the importance of assessing internal organizational conditions before beginning PGM. Yet, in practice, none indicated that they had done so at an organization-wide level, but only on a smaller scale, within their respective teams. Further, they noted that a formal assessment tool does not exist, prompting them to point to the need for one. Short of a tool, those who did look closely at internal conditions then asked questions, such as:

- What are our vision, mission, and values?
- Is there shared understanding among our team, other departments, and leadership about how we understand our values and how we are practicing them? If not, what do we need to do to create more alignment?
- How do we understand power and how power moves in our organization? Who holds power now, and how is it being used?
- Can we develop an internal practice of accountability with each other inside our organization to prepare us to practice accountability and repair in our relationships with the community?
- What characteristics of our organizational culture align with PGM's values and ethos?

Aligning internal organizational conditions with participatory grantmaking's ethos sets the stage for adopting PGM. All respondents who were exploring or practicing participatory grantmaking spoke to the importance of developing a clear understanding of participatory grantmaking's ethos and its underlying principles before introducing, testing, and adopting PGM. These principles include trust, inclusion, equity, diverse people, centering community voices at the table, reciprocal communication, collaboration, transparency, and values-driven decision-making.

These terms are often used, but the meanings behind them can vary. Some identified the need to develop shared language and meaning within organizations to effectively talk about and begin participatory grantmaking.

Mapping an organization's values to these principles was recommended to determine whether some principles are missing and to identify what might be in the way. These conversations can help create shared meaning vis-à-vis concepts of participatory grantmaking while also making the internal conditions of an organization explicit. This creates more transparency and brings multiple voices into the conversation, both of which are key participatory grantmaking values.

Expansive staff roles with fewer constraints can drive the work. The exploration and development of each PGM program was driven by staff interest and commitment to centering the voices of those from the communities the funding aimed to affect. Each of these organization's internal cultures fostered staff and role autonomy to pursue those interests. An interviewee running a program that began in 2018 spoke to the changing roles of the program officer at their foundation, sharing that staff have "autonomy to work on things that interest us with the foundation.... If you have this and an organizational culture that views roles expansively, staff are more likely to bring their own interests and expertise to their work benefiting the whole."

The importance of revisiting traditional roles extends to those of trustees and board members, who are often the final decision-makers when it comes to organizations' core strategies and grant decisions. As a result, these "job descriptions" and structures have reinforced practices of centralizing and hoarding power, and they can and do thwart efforts to advance more participatory cultures and practices, including PGM.

Staff interests and expertise are further aligned with PGM when hiring practices prioritize employees who come from the communities that funders seek to serve, which narrows the gap between funders and grantees. The power of staff members who have intimate knowledge of and trust in the community is even more evident in participatory grantmaking. This subject is not without its own tensions, given that once they become "a philanthropy professional," the very definition of who is "still part of the community" is not straightforward. But the power of proximity came across clearly.

Deeply held racial equity commitments can propel participatory grantmaking. Every funder with whom we spoke has a mission or values grounded in equity in some respect, though not always racial equity. Interviewees reflected on the relationship between racial equity and participatory grantmaking, as well as whether or how their organizational equity journeys affect readiness for participatory grantmaking. Their responses reflected a range of approaches.

Some find participatory grantmaking and its ethos perfectly aligned with advancing racial equity:

> As part of our racial equity practice, we want to listen to and be guided by community. Community is asking us how we are deepening our community-centric practices. We know that during the Trump presidency and especially after the murder of George Floyd, community folks are tired of being brought to the table to tell staff, to tell boards what to do. They'd get invited to two or three tables and get a few minutes on an agenda, but it didn't move anything. Participatory grantmaking gives us the ability to push decision-making to the community and this is what community wants. This is how we center community. We can ask, How are you centering community? What are your practices? How are you [putting these values into] practice every day?

Another pointed out that "participatory grantmaking is tied to populist movements and is not, therefore, inherently about racial equity." That, others said, could perhaps be addressed by using a definition of community that includes those who are most oppressed or are historically and systemically disenfranchised: "When we say community means those who are most oppressed, we can then center Black, Indigenous, trans, and disabled people in our participatory grantmaking to help shift where money goes."

Another theme that surfaced is that participatory grantmaking can be a tool that helps program staff members advance their institution's racial equity commitments beyond where leadership may be willing to go, at least initially. It allows for money and power to move back to the community as a restorative practice, which is often not yet the language of leadership.

As one respondent noted, "Our team has a strong value and philosophical commitment to including the community in decision-making processes, first as part of racial equity and racial justice." Further, their team believes that because philanthropic dollars belong to the community, not the donor, the community should have decision-making power over how funds are distributed.[11] At the staff level, they see the practice of participatory grantmaking as "a restorative, regenerative process," and that the best way for them to help their organization meet their mission is to use their roles to shift power back to the community.[12]

One interviewee used simple logic to illustrate how participatory grantmaking aligns with racial equity, asking, "Why would a community member impacted by all the issues we're trying to impact not be at the table? Inclusion is equity. Centering racial equity is our first principle."

One funder with whom we spoke supports an annual place-based responsive grantmaking program that seeks to benefit communities most affected by structural racism and inequities. The team is committed to hiring staff who reflect the communities they seek to serve, where over 60 percent of the population are people of color, nearly 35 percent are foreign born, and over 20 percent are Spanish speaking.

To ensure that the community's voice is represented in grantmaking, the interviewee led a small team that launched a participatory grantmaking pilot. They explained how a team member brought their keen understanding of and personal passion for language justice to the work.[13] They worried about their capacity to add this element from the standpoint of budgetary and staff capacity. However, in aligning their commitments to racial equity and justice with participatory grantmaking's practice of centering the voices of the communities they seek to serve, their choice was clear:

We asked, How can you not have this if we want participation? It's *literally* community voice.... There's a lot you won't have capacity for in a participatory grantmaking program, but with our demographics and team members who are themselves Spanish-speaking Latinx and personally committed to language justice, we came together to push for this. If the goal of this new program was inclusion and true participation, then it made sense that language justice be a central commitment.

Staff capacity and internal systems need to shift, and staff teams need to be brought along. Staff capacity, in terms of both individual readiness and availability, is a factor that affects the scope and scale of participatory grantmaking programs, which are time intensive. One interviewee's approach was to accept this and work to change the scarcity mind-set that can exist when changes that may counter the often-held value of efficiency are suggested: "It's a fact. Participatory grantmaking takes more time. We remind people and we say, 'the process is the outcome' again and again."

It is not only program staff that participatory grantmaking affects. Doing participatory grantmaking often requires shifting from a grantmaking model that can be rife with existing and time-consuming processes along with timelines that are, as one interviewee said, "designed for what we are told is efficiency." Thus, supervisors, grant administrators, and accounting and evaluation teams are also affected. One interviewee emphasized the need for staff in all positions to "be upfront with each other on what deadlines and constraints are real," which they characterized as being "kinder to everyone involved in the long run."

One interviewee encouraged those considering PGM to begin by clarifying staff roles and responsibilities and then working with staff members to envision new ways of working that relax rigid deadlines and payment cycles. They emphasized the importance of ensuring that everyone involved understands why things are shifting and how these shifts align with the values of the work and the larger organization to help bring everyone along.

For another interviewee whose foundation focuses on individuals living with a disability, accessibility design was a critical element in developing a participatory grantmaking program: "The majority of our time in the beginning was focused on translating grant systems designed for program officers to something that can be accessible to everyone with different abilities. It was a challenge but a hugely important piece of our work."

Developing shared clarity on power is foundational. Clarity on how your organization understands power—what it is, where it sits, and how it moves—is foundational to advancing participatory grantmaking. In the context of the racial justice movement, power has been defined as "the ability to change the rules. Sometimes the rules are written—like the written rules of policy—and sometimes they're the unwritten rules of culture."[14] Philanthropic organizations have long operated within a structure of concentrated power that extends to their staff and board. Grantmaking jobs, in fact, are often largely about decision-making regarding new policies, procedures, and practices; how data are collected and understood; strategy development and refinement; who sits at the table and has a voice in the process; deadlines to which applicants must adhere; how program staff recommend or do not recommend an organization for funding; and perhaps most important, how staff engage with community.

Some of the interviewees with whom we spoke described the importance of making power visible. One pointed to their practice of looking closely at each decision to shine a light on where power lives in everyday practices, systems, and structures: "People think of strategic focus areas. That's exercising power." Their team created a framework to support asset building and power building, which necessitates that "people need things and people need voice." They explained that their strategy "is about giving up power rather than exercising our own observations and confidence." Simply put, "Our theory of change is literally to trust the community's theory of change."

One funder described a power-mapping activity they undertook with their board members as groundwork for their participatory program. The goal was to understand where power lives and how it moves inside the organization. Speaking specifically about some white male members, the funder said, "It was so illuminating to me that the folks with the power had the hardest time understanding what we were doing." Power, it seemed, elicited discomfort and fear, which got in the way. The interviewee wondered if it might be helpful to begin the conversation with the more familiar (and perhaps less threatening) concept of privilege, the idea being that those with privilege are more used to seeing themselves within that frame. Scaffolding learning around topics that seek to shift how people see themselves can be helpful in bringing people along. Another interviewee reflected on their own blind spots and practices tied to power and control, which they viewed as a manifestation of white supremacy culture that they needed to unlearn to do this work.[15]

Other interviewees emphasized individual accountability. One interviewee consistently asks themself, "'What is my role?' When I see it is power hoarding and gatekeeping and how those continue to maintain what has been, I need to shift." This awareness and responsibility were shared among multiple interviewees. Another stated in no uncertain terms that accountability *is* the role: "We need to be accountable internally for the ways that power shows up." Another summarized, "Name the power differentials and then do something about it."

One interviewee reflected on how power manifests in family foundations, which can differ from traditional foundations: "I wonder about family foundations and power because there is so much ownership of the dollars. How can we best cede power with the board in a way that feels right? Family legacy is tied to this foundation. How do trustees have ownership and have pride for the work and also make space for other voices to be included?"

Interviewees showed us how an awareness of what power is and how it moves within philanthropic systems is an opportunity to choose how we wield it and to what end. Interviewees reminded us that every decision we make is exercising our power or, by extension, that of our institutions. With this awareness, we can practice self-reflection day to day, decision to decision, to consider whether our actions maintain power over or move us closer to power with communities.[16]

One cautioned, "You have to understand the concept and develop a deep grounding in power and privilege on your team. I had to be real with myself and to be able to confront myself to see my limitations. This is a skill set, and having that expertise has to be part of the process. Issues around power and privilege will come up. When they do, we have staff with this awareness. Without it, you can create a violent space and not know it."

Program staff have the power to be key drivers of—and lay the groundwork for—internal culture change. Ten of the twelve interviewees with whom we spoke were program staff members—primarily program directors, officers, or managers—and it was these people, not leaders, who were doing the internal work in their organizations to shift the conditions required for participatory grantmaking to be introduced, take root, and grow. Program staff members actively worked to change the culture by embodying a participatory grantmaking ethos as individuals and as team members, while often taking tangible steps to embed progress in a way that demonstrated the value of their approach and created internal and external accountability to advance it.

The program staff of four of the five active participatory programs, for example, carefully documented their efforts and shared their learning with peers through published works. They intentionally and effectively built support for the ongoing utilization of PGM with staff in their organizations and with the larger community, generating internal and external pressure on leadership to continue the work. There was a clear an element of "it's easier to ask for forgiveness than permission" here, as well as a deep commitment to advancing participatory grantmaking inside their own organizations and the broader field.

This practice of documenting learning made a case for success and impact, while also normalizing mistakes and learning. These funders were avoiding a pitfall we heard about from others: a fear of failure or need for perfection, which can be paralyzing and get in the way. They are also seen by some as characteristics of white supremacy culture. Instead, they were learning by doing and modeling making mistakes and sharing them publicly—all of which create permission for others to do the same. It reinforced that among all interviewees, the concept of participatory grantmaking is seeded by programmatic staff, who can work to create the conditions for the program to grow and to prepare leadership to buy into the approach and the approve its continued operation.

Laying the Foundation for Participatory Grantmaking: External Conditions Supporting Readiness

External conditions include characteristics like trust; transparency; a track record; who serves; as the public face of the foundation, and how an organization lives its values in public, invests time to build authentic relationships, and demonstrates follow-through. All these send a message to grantee partners and the larger community about who a funder is and what they care about.

There are also six top themes for external conditions that support organizational readiness. *Participatory grantmaking done right moves at the speed of trust.* We consistently heard from interviewees that external trust building cannot be separated from centering trust as an organizational value and living it on the inside. Interviewees talked about the time it takes to build authentic trusting relationships externally, which ties back to having space in their roles to work in new and different ways. They also told us that only from this orientation and commitment can trust with external community be built.

Neglecting this step can be costly. In one case, a traditional foundation skipped over building relationships with community members invited to serve as decision-makers in a participatory grantmaking process. Instead, they outsourced that process to consultants, one of whom had lived expertise and personal connections to the geographic communities the foundation sought to serve but had no capacity to influence the foundation's internal culture. While the consultant was able to develop trust with participants, the funder did not do the same, and the opportunity to move away from transactional exchanges to authentic relationships was missed.

Assess and repair to demonstrate accountability from the start. Some respondents emphasized the importance of understanding and assessing how a community perceives the funder and its historical and current approach to engagement, especially any types of harm that may have occurred as a result of the institution's past work and actions. They highlighted the opportunity to demonstrate accountability, break old patterns, and improve the relationship. Two program leaders with the affinity-based social justice funder working to align their participatory grantmaking with racial justice shared their experience: "If we're going to do racial justice work, we can't do it without acknowledging and naming the harm that's been done. How are we acknowledging the harm that the foundation has done and acknowledging that hurt has happened? If we cannot name that harm and engage with communities of color, then we are not doing racial justice work." Most interviewees explicitly named following through on commitments, including living out organizational values, as an essential step in building trusting relationships with community.

Building a track record of listening to and trusting community is key. To understand the true nature of issues that communities face, interviewees emphasized two critical elements. First, staff need to be humble and seeking to grow while listening to and trusting community. One interviewee explained, "We start by focusing on relationships and listening and learning. Our foundation hires people who love to learn and listen and recognize that there is always room for growth. We understand that we don't know everything."

Second, developing a solid track record of listening to and trusting community as experts on the issues in their own lives is essential. As one funder notes: "Our founders prioritize equity and listening to those from impacted populations, which are two of our five public equity statements. They have a track record of being in community and listening to these populations. The fact that they are highly engaged listeners in direct relationship with communities we work with, supports me being able to do this work because it's consistent."

Expect to make mistakes, and value them as opportunities to deepen relationships. A frequent suggestion was for funders to be up front internally and externally about how mistakes are inevitable when organizations step into PGM. Mistakes can offer opportunities to address barriers to carrying out a robust participatory grantmaking program, which, in turn, creates space for deepening relationships. Across our conversations, interviewees noted, "You're going to stumble. It's inevitable. It's what you do with it—you learn and grow from it."

Several interviewees named discomfort, perfectionism, and defensiveness as frequent responses to mistakes. These characteristics, which some pointed to as part of white supremacy culture, often get in the way of learning and making needed changes as they can come with feelings of shame and sometimes paralysis. To counter this, some reframed mistakes specifically as opportunities for developing accountability: "Treat mistakes as learning opportunities and be transparent about it. Own it and talk about it.... When you do have conflict or there is a misstep, part of the biggest barrier is being OK ... that we did something wrong. If we truly care, we have an opportunity to do better. Even with the best intentions, folks are going to mess up. If participatory grantmaking was easy to do, then everyone would do it. Change is constant, and as the world changes and as community changes, what we're doing today might not be right tomorrow."

Participation should start early and often through the cycle of design to implementation. Some interviewees noted that since, in their view, participatory grantmaking is an ethos with participation at its core, community members should ideally be engaged throughout the grant cycle from start to finish. One noted that true transformation could best happen if program staff learned from participants early in the design phase to ensure participation and community voice can be baked into how the entire program works. Another continued this thread of learning from participants and suggested "building in feedback loops to the process so participants can provide feedback before, during and after a grant cycle." Most, however, noted that they had decided that rather than getting it all right, which would have taken more time or required more permission, they would engage community participants where they were able to do so with greatest ease (or least resistance) first, and work toward more participation across the cycle over time.

Be clear and transparent about what decision-making power you are ceding. Interviewees considered how they communicate to participants about the boundaries and limits of what they were and were not letting go of. Those already operating participatory grantmaking programs emphasized the importance of being up front with participants and community, including those seeking funding through these processes, about what decision-making power was ceded to participants or retained by the funder. Three of the five active participatory grantmaking programs have completely ceded decision-making authority to community participants. In two, participants make funding recommendations to staff, who can approve or modify recommendations before seeking final approval through typical channels (board, executive leadership, et al.).

A program officer at a traditional foundation shared a common mistake rooted in internal philanthropic cultures that shows up externally: a lack of transparency about how much power participants truly have. "A misstep that we took early on was when we weren't as clear as we could have been." They explained how in early work testing a participatory process, "we received feedback from [participants] who said, 'We told you that we didn't like this proposal and now you're going to fund it!' Now, when we work with the group, we are more explicit about [participants'] roles and [expectations]."

Summary of Results

When we step back and look at all that we heard from our twelve interviewees about the internal and external conditions required to lay the groundwork from which participatory grantmaking can take root and grow, several high-level themes are evident. First, whether this was named or implied, nearly everyone emphasized the importance of starting the work of creating the conditions for participatory grantmaking as an individual in their own roles inside their own organizations. They spoke to the need to reflect on how they, as individuals with powerful roles, had fulfilled their roles in the past and how they had or might need to shift elements of their roles and internal systems to successfully launch or run a participatory grantmaking program. They discussed the opportunity to "just start" changing internal culture by recognizing that their own work could seed new ideas and ways of working together on teams while demonstrating value to leadership. And many spoke to the shared values of participatory grantmaking and racial equity and the opportunity to use the former to advance the latter.

Finally, their primary pieces of advice to grantmakers considering PGM were a mix of leading with trust, prioritizing transparency around what power is ceded to community, and that while preparation and care are critical for launching a participatory program, mistakes are inevitable and can be opportunities for deep learning and transformative change with the right mind-set.

DISCUSSION

Having directly engaged with these topics over the past twenty years, I (Anne) wanted to discuss the results of this study through the lens of my experience as a practitioner. In important ways, it mirrors the experiences of several of the interview subjects.

Before becoming a consultant to philanthropies, I worked in nonprofits running programs, engaging volunteers, and raising money. I was thrilled to get my first job in philanthropy as a program officer with the local community foundation. I loved making connections between people, ideas, and resources, and the opportunity to move money back into communities I was part of or connected to was thrilling. I envisioned the role largely as translation—one in which I, with my own lived experience and authentic relationships in many of the communities that had historically received less funding, would be able to help create openings, remove barriers, flatten hierarchies, and help the foundation's grantmaking committee develop a clear understanding of the phenomenal work people were doing in their own communities each day. Was I naive? Of course. But, while I did not have the language we use today, my philosophy was simply to trust people and trust community. As Curtis Yancy of the Chan Zuckerberg Initiative says, "Community knows what community needs." This remains one of my core beliefs, instilled in me when I was a beneficiary of my family's neighborhood babysitting co-op sometime around 1974. It has stayed with me since when I first entered philanthropy twenty years ago and every day since.

I was, however, also wary of occupying a decision-making/influencing role in philanthropy. I became familiar with the power imbalances inherent to the job, thanks to the grounding of my excellent supervisor, and promised myself that my practice would resist them. Over the years in my role, I witnessed multiple trends in the philanthropic sector, including one to provide unrestricted operating support, which I championed. As time went by, there was more attention to prioritizing donors and becoming more strategic, which focused on metrics and donor-defined frameworks. Listening to community members was important, but only if they had a clear theory of change or a five- to ten-year strategic plan. Throughout, what nagged at me most was the feeling as if I had been duped. I had understood philanthropy to be the root of its word—love of humanity—and a community foundation to be just that in service to its community. Yet hierarchies at the staff and board levels prevailed; and rules, spoken and unspoken, that determined to whom money flowed centered the interests of high-net-worth donors and board members or were rooted in what professional staff deemed evidence-based best practice.

To survive, I learned the new ways we were expected to work, and, for a time, I put my head down and tried to move as much money as I could to communities, especially communities of color. I chose to trust community-based grantseekers, to check my own biases against applications that were not beautiful reads, and budgets that were not a sure bet. I also translated the incredible value of what happened on the ground in Seattle's neighborhoods—the Central District, the Chinatown–International District, or Rainier Valley—through their work to a grants committee that included members who employed their own lens of wealth and privilege and were encouraged to do so by the structure that awarded them decision-making authority in the first place.

While helping to move money—which, arguably, would not have returned to some communities of color, or at least not at the scale or frequency that it once did—was satisfying to a degree, ultimately, I knew I could not do my job as I had defined it: in service to the communities from which I came and to others unseen, without a voice or even a seat at the table. I had too little power to influence substantive change and was horribly frustrated by the chasm between "deciders" and community. So I moved on.

I later returned to philanthropy in corporate grantmaking, staffing private family foundations and megadonors. Over the last six years, I have served as a consultant to a broad range of philanthropies. When I initially returned, I observed that some of the distressing trends I had seen take root in the late 2000s to early 2010s—namely, that further professionalization of the field, individualism, disconnection, distrust, and division—were more entrenched. It was disheartening. The field felt so far from its stated purpose.

Yet in 2020, the world changed, and the field responded in some exciting ways. Again, my colleagues and I observed an increasing interest in new approaches in philanthropy and were thrilled specifically by the growing interest in participatory grantmaking—and the appetite for more information about it, which we supplied through conference sessions and blog posts, in addition to directing curious funders to the Participatory Grantmaking Community of Practice and a growing number of experts in the field.

We had worked with a range of philanthropies that shared this increased interest in participatory grantmaking falling along the spectrum of curiosity to implementation. While this was exciting to see and support, we noticed exploration did not often lead to implementation. When it did, in most cases with those running pilot programs or utilizing the approach in one small portfolio, PGM was not having an impact inside the philanthropies beyond being the latest new trend. Based on this experience, we wanted to know what was preventing funders from adoption and implementation. We were curious about what was in the way of this practice taking root inside and growing. Further, if uptake was increased because foundations were increasingly committing to racial equity as a core value and recognized the complimentary nature of participatory grantmaking, then why was it not sticking or spreading?

Before the research, we had some hunches. One was simply that the field of philanthropy is entrenched in old systems, structures, and habits that are hard to break. Participatory grantmaking necessitates structural and behavioral change by the funder, so perhaps it was the sector's notoriously glacial pace of change, which is maintained by old systems and practices. Another hunch was that there was a reluctance to invest the time needed to build and run grantmaking in a different way (which is, again, systems and structural change). Or, most cynically, perhaps PGM was just window dressing: low-hanging fruit to demonstrate new efforts in community engagement but with no follow-through to match. Another possibility was that those in decision-making roles fundamentally believe they are best equipped to decide how to solve a community's challenges and where to invest resources to do so. We hoped we would learn what it takes to truly shift power.

What we found confirmed some hunches and brought me full circle. In our small sample, and among others we were watching or supporting through our consulting work, we noticed these:

- Progressive program staff were nearly always the ones seeding the concept of PGM in their organizations and taking the lead in exploring and developing programs.
- Most program staff leading the work were people of color (eight of ten in a small sample).
- All staff at this level identified participatory grantmaking as a tool to advance racial equity.
- Those who had more autonomous roles moved farther faster, and their programs were less siloed and more built into their institutions than counterparts with less freedom in their roles.
- Where staff leading the work had supportive peers to form partnerships with to troubleshoot questions on program development, programs were more established, and staff were more willing to speak freely about their work in interviews.
- Staff members, who documented work and wrote about their work for publication, are still utilizing participatory grantmaking beyond pilot phases and have generated external interest that applies pressure

- to leadership to appreciate and support the work, which certainly helps sustain it.
- The role of trustee and board member has not itself been examined or changed on any meaningful scale, a clear and entrenched barrier to shifting power.
- Findings did not show any clear differences in how traditional foundations or megadonors experience these dynamics related to internal and external conditions. Aligning organizational values with participatory grantmaking values will almost always help a foundation meet its mission. Further, when racial equity is a core value, participatory grantmaking's overlapping values can advance it.

Guidance from staff in the interview findings offers an approach that is fundamentally about redistributing power from those who currently hold it to those who have the expertise to address the issues philanthropies seek to solve. They offer advice on organizational values, culture, and a specific grantmaking tool to help meet a mission. They, too, offer insights into what leadership needs to look like in our times.

When reflecting on the findings of this research, I am left with the fundamental question: What will it take to shift power to the people who are experts in their own lives? What might happen if trustees, including traditional foundation trustees and megadonors, followed the guidance from their own staff who are, often carefully and quietly, asking them to do just that? They are, in fact, the very seat of power. And thus far, after the upheaval of the early 2020s, which pushed foundations to broadly shift their practices and take up new approaches, foundations and nonprofits have also been more open to adopting new leadership structures, like codirectorships. Still, the role of the foundation trustee has remained intact and is still relatively unexamined. As mentioned above, there are cases of family foundation boards adding nonfamily members altering composition, which can bring new and more diverse perspectives, including "community representation," but this does not fundamentally address the role itself.

The conversation about legacy is happening in some corners, as some are exploring employing privilege to build power for others. And in these circles, there is an awareness that the wealth that trustees steward is not their own and was often gained through extractive, harmful practices. However, that is a small segment of traditional foundations; and, again, the role of trustee has not itself been changed. This clearly seems to one be of the most enduring barriers to shifting power.

There is, however, good news. Even with trustee roles, there are precedents for change. While trustees are fiduciaries legally required to act for the sole benefit of a foundation, when they do not have the expertise or capacity to fulfill a duty, such as managing foundation investments, they are responsible for finding a partner like an investment adviser or manager with such expertise. Adopting participatory grantmaking, grounded in the central belief that communities are experts in their own lives, presents a case that fiduciary duty must also apply, and decision-making must be ceded to those who know what they need. Should communities not also hold the power to make decisions affecting their lives?

This research focused on staff efforts to explore, seed, and implement participatory grantmaking within their organizations. It found that barriers exist between exploration and adoption of this approach. The largest barrier of all may be the role of the trustee or donor and its misalignment with values of participatory grantmaking. Practitioners should call the question and future research should explore this question further.

CONCLUSION

In May 2022, Aya Tsuruta of the Giving Practice and I presented a session, "Let's Talk about Power: Making Meaningful Change through Participatory Grantmaking," for the Grantmakers for Effective Organizations national conference in Chicago. The session featured a conversation between Paul Bocanegra, cofounder of the nonprofit ReEvolution Group, and Curtis Yancy, senior manager of community at the Chan Zuckerberg Initiative. In a wide-ranging discussion, the two demonstrated for an audience of funders how the traditional roles of funder and grantee can change through a participatory grantmaking process. They explained how sharing power with and ceding power to community worked in their process and that trust, partnership, and transparency were required.

The session asked participants to discuss power inequities that surface in their own organization's grantmaking processes and to look at their own role in maintaining or disrupting these inequities. After the session, a program officer from a traditional foundation asked how she could get her board to let go of power, particularly decision-making power in grantmaking. She noted how the principles of participatory grantmaking align with their values, but decision-making is just "what they do."

There it was. Why do people hold onto power and resist ceding it? While there can be many reasons, including those described above, the one that surfaced in this moment was so simple. The traditional role of the trustee at a grantmaking institution, and in philanthropy more broadly, *is* the center of power. Trustees understand their role to *be* decision-makers, arbiters of funding, and stewards of resources. For traditional foundations and megadonors whose families, names, and faces are often attached to the funding, they are also typically builders and keepers of legacy, often their own family's legacy.

What became clear after all this research and discussion, when asked in real life by someone in the funder role, grappling with these questions for actual application, was this: The entrenched role of the trustee and board member (along with the program staff) can (and, many argue, must) change and be redefined. These "job descriptions" and structures have reinforced practices of centralizing and hoarding power, and they have stood in the way.

It struck me that what is happening field-wide is a failure of our collective imagination: an inability to see beyond what has been and is now, ahead to what might be, to what we can create together.

Resistance to ceding decision-making power is grounded in the fear that if the role *is* decision-making and holding tight to power, then perhaps there will be no role at all without it. Without this traditional role, what would the trustee and the board member do? How would they contribute? What value might they bring? How could they steward their family's legacy?

As these thoughts swirled in my head in that conference room in Chicago, our conversation with the program officer continued. "Yes!" she exclaimed, in response to the idea that trustees should give up decision-making power. "Oh. What can they do instead?"

But what if, instead, ceding power could be the role present-day decision-makers play? What if those decision-makers could become partners in learning and translating and giving permission by example to other trustees in other philanthropies, particularly other traditional foundation trustees and megadonors? What if collectively, we could redefine legacy as leading a significant change that aligns us with our values and moves us toward our missions? And what if ceding power to the community and leading this change could also be a way to embody racial equity and transformation through action?

Ultimately there is a clear opportunity to redefine what it means to be a leader within a philanthropic organization of any type. Can we redefine leadership to align with the overlapping values and practices of participatory grantmaking and racial equity? Can leadership become about influencing a shift in to whom power flows, of letting go and giving it back to the community? What might a world infused with a participatory ethos look like? Can we imagine it?

Many of the people we interviewed can and are already creating it. Sometimes, it is small shifts in perspective that clear the way for us to change our behavior and our systems and take needed and promising risks. One of our interviewees excitedly shared one such powerful reminder: "Power is a renewable energy! By sharing power, we all get more power!"

APPENDIX: AN INTERVIEW PROTOCOL

The semistructured interviews utilized a protocol focused on organizational readiness to take up participatory grantmaking.

Readiness/Internal Work

1. Describe the internal conditions (internal culture, staff capacity, leadership, commitment to equity, etc.) in your organization when you started thinking about participatory grantmaking. What conditions were conducive to participatory grantmaking? What needed/needs to change? What was/is in the way?
2. Tell me more about your organization's understanding of power and what you are willing to let go of.
3. Describe any relationship you see between participatory grantmaking and racial equity?

Readiness/External Work

1. What kind of orientation to trust and relationships with community are required to begin participatory grantmaking? How do you understand and assess how community perceives your organization?
2. Tell me about your process of designing and implementing a participatory grantmaking program. How did you identify participants? Did you work with participants throughout the duration of the process? What did you learn from participants in the design phase? In what ways could participants provide feedback about the process before, during and after a grant cycle? Did you build in feedback loops to your process?
3. How did you communicate to participants about the boundaries and limits of what you were letting go of and what you were not?

Advice

We also asked interviewees to share advice with peers considering participatory grantmaking in two ways:

1. What is one piece of advice you would have for an organization starting this work?
2. What is one piece of advice for anyone who has made a mistake in this work, which is inevitable?

NOTES

1. We use the traditional foundation and megadonor labels adopted in this collection. In this chapter, *traditional foundation* refers to family foundations that use a traditional operating structure of professional staff, governing board of directors, and financial endowment that allows them to exist in perpetuity and make grants to charitable nonprofit organizations. *Megadonors* refers to philanthropic entities led by individual donors with assets above $30 million that may or may not have a structure similar to a traditional foundation but operate in a way in which power is consolidated at the top and decisions are made by the donors themselves, not a governing board.
2. Cynthia Gibson, *Deciding Together: Shifting Power and Resources through Participatory Grantmaking* (New York: Foundation Center, 2018), https://learningforfunders.candid.org/content/guides/deciding-together/.
3. Racial Equity Tools, MP Associates, Center for Assessment and Policy Development, and World Trust Educational Services, "Glossary," July 2022, https://www.racialequitytools.org/glossary. Racial Equity Tools defines *racial equity* as "the condition that would be achieved if one's racial identity no longer predicted, in a statistical sense, how one fares." Racial Equity Tools thinks about racial equity "as one part of racial justice, and thus [also] include[s] work to address root causes of inequities, not just their manifestation. This includes elimination of policies, practices, attitudes, and cultural messages that reinforce differential outcomes by race or fail to eliminate them." These racial equity principles were developed by the Dismantling Racism Works collaborative after a decade of experience working with and for community based leaders and organizations living into their racial justice commitment.
4. Racial Equity Tools et al., "Glossary." In terms of power sharing, we define *power* as "the ability to make decisions that impact others, to make rules about those decisions and to impose one's beliefs." This definition, as described by Racial Equity Tools, reflects the concept that all power is relational.
5. White Supremacy Culture, "Racial Equity Principles," https://www.whitesupremacyculture.info/racial-equity-principles.html.
6. White Supremacy Culture,
7. White Supremacy Culture.
8. An identity-based community foundation raises and distributes funds to benefit a particular identity group (e.g., women, and immigrants, BIPOC) in a defined geographic

region. A federated fund is a campaign that raises money in the workplace to distribute to a variety of nonprofits. A health conversion foundation is formed by the sale of a nonprofit hospital to a for-profit entity where proceeds from the sale are used to create an endowment charged with supporting the original mission of the sold hospital.

9. The end-of-year book value was obtained from available 2019 or 2020 IRS Form 990s on Candid's GuideStar database, https://www.guidestar.org/.
10. Trust-Based Philanthropy Project, "Overview," https://www.trustbasedphilanthropy.org/overview; Trust-Based Philanthropy Project, "Values," https://www.trustbasedphilanthropy.org/values.
11. It is a widely held and debated notion that because philanthropic endowments are tax-deductible to the donor, those funds should be considered at least partially public, because they would otherwise go into tax coffers. For an example of debate on this topic, see Aaron Dorfman, "NCRP Statement Regarding the Philanthropy Roundtable's 'How Public Is Private Philanthropy: Separating Myth from Reality,'" June 30, 2009, https://www.nonprofitpro.com/article/ncrp-statement-regarding-philanthropy-roundtables-how-public-private-philanthropy-separating-myth-reality-409705/all/.
12. Justice Funders, "Resonance: A Framework for Philanthropic Transformation," https://justicefunders.org/resonance/.
13. Casey Payton, Joann Lee, Ana Paula Noguez Mercado, and Alena Uliasz, "Language Justice During COVID-19," https://www.americanbar.org/groups/young_lawyers/projects/disaster-legal-services/language-justice-during-covid-19/. *Language justice* is defined as a framework respective of "every individual's fundamental language rights—to be able to communicate, understand, and be understood in the language in which they prefer and feel most articulate and powerful."
14. Adele Peters, "'Power Is the Ability to Change the Rules': How Rashad Robinson Holds Companies Accountable," *Fast Company*, October 25, 2017, https://www.fastcompany.com/40474488/power-is-the-ability-to-change-the-rules-how-rashad-robinson-holds-companies-accountable.
15. White Supremacy Culture, home page, https://www.whitesupremacyculture.info/. Coined by Tema Okun, "white supremacy culture" is "the widespread ideology baked into the beliefs, values, norms, and standards of our groups (many, if not most of them), our communities, our towns, our states, our nation, teaching us both overtly and covertly that whiteness holds value, whiteness is value." Okun says, "We are all swimming in the waters of white supremacy culture," and our collective immersion makes the characteristics difficult to recognize.
16. One resource to support self-reflection in the field of philanthropy is from the Giving Practice: "Philanthropy's Reflective Practices: Build What You Bring to the Work," June 2018, https://philanthropynw.org/resources/philanthropys-reflective-practices.

CONCLUSION

Future Directions for Participatory Grantmaking Research and Implementation

Chris Cardona, Cynthia M. Gibson, Jasmine McGinnis Johnson, and David Suárez

The purpose of this collection on participatory grantmaking (PGM) has been twofold. For those working in the philanthropy industry, we have sought to build the evidence base for PGM so that participatory grantmakers, traditional foundations, and megadonors might better understand the ethos and process of authentic participation and make more informed choices about whether and how to implement this approach. For those interested in understanding contemporary expressions of the practice of democratic participation, we have sought to illuminate a dimension of this practice that receives relatively little attention: how it shows up in the world of institutional philanthropy, where increasing inequality and a growing interest in greater inclusion coexist tensely.

In the four years since the original research that inspired this collection was commissioned, the field of philanthropy has changed significantly in its attitudes toward power and inclusion, which are the domain of PGM. How the research studies have played out during this time has reflected these changes and can help us make sense of them.

Across these studies, PGM rarely operates on its own; it tends to be a critical element of a broader strategy for achieving a philanthropic mission or social goal. For the members of Women's Funding Network (chapter 3), it is part of advancing gender equity and gender justice. For the Disability Rights Fund and the Disability Rights Advocacy Fund (chapter 4), it is an expression of disability rights and the principle "nothing about us without us." For the Haymarket People's Fund (chapter 5), it is part of an antiracist grantmaking model. For the New England Grassroots Environment Fund (chapter 6) and the Global Greengrants Fund (chapter 7), it is a necessary component of climate justice. For CLLCTIVLY (chapter 8), it is a contemporary expression of ancestral giving traditions in African American communities. And for the traditional-foundation and megadonor staff members experimenting with PGM who were interviewed by Anne Katahira and Marissa Jackson (chapter 12), it is part of their commitment to practicing racial equity in response to the seismic events of 2020.

None of these practitioners saw PGM as something to be done in isolation or as a free-standing practice without a broader purpose. And it was always part of a larger conversation about power and responsibility in philanthropy. Who is authorized to decide how philanthropic resources—not just money but also other forms of support—should be allocated? What should be the roles of foundation and megadonor staff, and of trustees or donors? What does building nonprofit and community capacity to make philanthropic decisions through PGM mean? How does PGM relate to other practices of inclusion, such as trust-based philanthropy, antiracism, community leadership, and racial equity? Are some forms of PGM (or participation, more broadly) "more authentic" or "deeper/thicker" than others? As documented in this collection's studies, these are important questions that those studying participatory approaches—in philanthropy and more broadly—continue to explore. In the introduction to this collection, the editors offered our views on some of them, but they are not necessarily shared by all the contributors to this volume, let alone the philanthropy sector more broadly. To us, this is an accurate reflection of the state of play with regard to participation in philanthropy.

Reflecting this creative ferment, the authors also identify challenges or uncertainty in the practice of PGM. Finchum-Mason, Husted, and Suárez (chapter 1), for example, document through original survey research that large foundations are embracing greater stakeholder participation—but not necessarily when it comes to grant decisions. This pattern suggests that foundations are amenable to democratizing philanthropy by incorporating community voice in certain activities, but power sharing is limited to those that do not threaten donor control. This chapter helps us conceptualize that the majority of foundations are on the lower rungs of Arnstein's ladder of participation, where stakeholders do not have any power to affect decisions.[1] Power and authenticity are the themes of this chapter, and also of many others; this one helps us begin to understand the challenges of large foundations engaging in authentic participation.

McGinnis Johnson (chapter 2) homes in on a nuance about how the form of participation may affect the associated grant outcomes. When foundation staff members cede power entirely to grant committees, these committees are more likely to identify newer grant recipients but not necessarily smaller ones. However, when foundation staff share power with a committee and sit at the table alongside nongrantmakers, they do better at choosing smaller and less established organizations for funding, thereby achieving the goal of wider outreach. Both outcomes may be desirable, which poses an interesting quandary for those designing PGM processes: Is it enough to engage in any form of participation to change outcomes, or does the latter require more "authentic" participation? Dale and Carter (chapter 5) surface additional challenges by documenting how the Pride Foundation sought to adopt a PGM model but ultimately adopted a less radical approach: trust-based-philanthropy. They describe their decision-making process, which was strongly influenced by the COVID-19 pandemic and the racial justice uprising of 2020, and they pose a series of tough questions they believe any foundation considering a PGM model must consider. To wit, they suggest that effectively adopting PGM requires a more significant organizational review and restructure than they, and perhaps others, had been expecting. What they share with PGM is a belief that donors considering PGM need to first focus on developing reciprocal and trusting relationships with the communities they wish to support. This informs a greater understanding of participation frameworks, where participation does not just occur in an isolated unit of an organization but requires the entire organization to get on board.

Also, in the vein of other challenges, Hartmann and Schambra (chapter 9) argue from a conservative perspective that forms of democratic decision-making already exist in grassroots communities, as manifested in their support for and willingness to engage with nonprofit leaders they trust and who reflect their values. Hartmann and Schambra suggest that rather than seeking to create a process of identifying community leadership through PGM, funders should listen to what communities are already saying they want through the organizations that they trust. This echoes Dale and Carter's assertion that donors considering PGM should focus first on developing reciprocal and trusting relationships with the communities they wish to support. These chapters further inform theories and frameworks of participation and how we can learn from PGM to determine how community leadership and trust play an integral part in authentic participation.

Despite their diversity, what emerges from the studies in this collection are two key insights: PGM is best practiced in conjunction with other forms of inclusion in philanthropy, and PGM is most successful when it is grounded in deep relationships with—and trusted by—the communities from which it seeks to draw participation.

For national foundations and megadonors, it may be tempting to think that PGM is a practice that can be adopted atop an existing structure of strategy, grantmaking, and evaluation. But as the studies in this collection demonstrate, this view overlooksone of PGM's greatest benefits. When done well, it is an expression of an organizational value—inclusion—that can genuinely shift power to communities by democratizing the decision-making process about how foundations allocate their resources. And it is most effective when it is accompanied, and even preceded, by a deeper process of organizational transformation toward less concentration of power in the hands of foundation or megadonor staff.

ISSUES AND QUESTIONS

Democracy and Social Justice

Although power sharing has been at PGM's core since its beginnings, there are still questions as to what it would mean to diminish—and even relinquish—the power of foundation boards or megadonors themselves. This question of redistributing power in philanthropy has been considered for many years by numerous practitioners under the rubrics of social justice philanthropy and racial equity in philanthropy. This tradition is reflected in figure I.4 in this collection's introduction, which maps participation in philanthropy by how much it is structured at the individual versus organizational level and whether it is concentrated or distributed. The more organizational and distributed power sharing occurs in the figure's lower-right quadrant: PGM and social justice philanthropy.

Some argue, however, that although the history of participatory grantmaking is linked directly to social justice philanthropy, participatory grantmaking has expanded without grappling with the implications of this legacy. Groups like the Philanthropic Initiative for Racial Equity, CHANGE Philanthropy, Justice Funders, Decolonizing Wealth Project, and other advocates of social justice have presented fundamental critiques of traditional foundations that in some cases recommend their dissolution. In this view, philanthropy in the form of traditional foundations and megadonors is emblematic of wealth inequality and social injustice. As such, a greater redistribution of power and wealth in society would necessarily entail fewer traditional foundations and megadonors. There are many other variants of this argument, most of which critique institutional philanthropy as the product of a capitalist system built on exploitation and fueled by racism, colonialism, ableism, and slavery.

Participatory grantmaking emerged in this context as a practice closely aligned with the political aims of social justice philanthropy, but as documented in this collection, it does not necessarily challenge the very enterprise of traditional foundations and megadonors. Various authors of the chapters that make up this collection hint at such connections to social justice, whether García and Odendahl on the links between participatory grantmaking and climate justice or Westdijk and Huang on how the entrenched philanthropy industry is in some ways at odds with the aspirations of the environmental justice movement. The contemporary practice of participatory grantmaking, then, is at the very least adjacent to and connected with the contemporary practice of social justice philanthropy.

Does this mean that participatory grantmaking is inextricably tied to a normative political project or is an innovative practice that philanthropic foundations and megadonors can embrace regardless of their political orientation? And if a foundation commits to sharing grantmaking power—and does so by empowering a mix of local stakeholders that is representative of its community—is the fact of using such a process what makes it PGM or does it matter that the grants go to different organizations as a result? Does the label "participatory grantmaking" apply, for instance, to the work of a foundation if stakeholders ultimately support nonprofits that reinforce socially constructed gender roles, or promote restrictions on reproductive health rights for women, or expand funding for gun rights? If not, what is the appropriate label for something that resembles participatory grantmaking in design and implementation but does not privilege social justice? Conversely, does participatory grantmaking—or any kind of democratic participation, for that matter—have to only be seen as a means to an end (whether normative or not), or can it also seen as a means to whatever end the process elicits because that process may be valuable in itself—for example, strengthening participants' capacity, voice, and agency in whatever collective activity in which they wish to engage? The question also arises in other sectors; for example, are efforts to increase civic engagement a means to the end of achieving social justice and/or a political agenda? Or the process of engaging itself of value for trust, network building, and learning about democratic processes?

Chapter 11 in this volume, which outlines a conservative perspective, suggests that participatory approaches are not necessarily predicated on a social justice foundation. In fact, the chapter's authors believe that "participatoriness" among foundations, which they see as largely progressive, is questionable in light of their history of "elitist and technocratic" practices. And, like other chapter authors, they offer full-throated support for empowering local stakeholders, rather than traditional institutions, to develop solutions to community problems. Clearly, the issue of whether participatory grantmaking is an innovative practice in the giving processes of institutional philanthropy or a fundamental and inextricable component of the social justice movement remains unsettled.

Elites and Expertise

We would be remiss to overlook another factor that has contributed to the upsurge of philanthropic critiques during the past decade: the antiestablishment backlash occurring in politics, higher education, the media, the law, and other fields where elite interests are perceived to have drowned out the concerns of ordinary people. Americans of all stripes and political persuasions have come to believe they have little say in guiding public decisions and improving the health and well-being of their communities.

Although there are varying definitions of "elites," in recent years, they have come to be seen as highly educated, professional people living mainly in US coastal cities. While some of these individuals may be wealthy, their power lies less in financial affluence than their overrepresentation in the decision-making positions of powerful institutions such as universities, government, the media, the law, technology, think tanks, professional associations, and, yes, philanthropy. Critics contend that philanthropists tend to view social change as the purview of professional and credentialed experts who rely on technocratic, top-down decision-making and large-scale interventions, rather than on the collective experiences, assets, and wisdom of communities and residents to solve social problems.

Philanthropy, especially larger foundations, are a part of this mix. For decades, foundations have been fixated on developing uniform models of best practices that can be supported by empirical data, "scaled up," and replicated. The voices and views of the people to whom these interventions were targeted have been rarely consulted, and the smaller-scaled, local, and community-based efforts they were undertaking were (and continue to be) underfunded and seen as "band-aids" rather than real-world solutions for resolving difficult issues.

Some of the most vocal proponents of this perspective have been populist conservatives, including those in philanthropy. A common question about PGM, in fact, is whether there are examples of this approach being used by foundations that are not rooted in progressivism. In chapter 11, Schambra and Hartmann argue that conservative philanthropy has several traditions, values, and practices that dovetail with PGM: a respect for local wisdom and practical experience, an aversion to elitism and professionalization, and a skepticism about "well-credentialed experts from institutions afar." In practice, the authors maintain, this is reflected in their support for efforts that seek out, consult with, and involve people who "live in the same zip code" as the problem being addressed. They concede, however, that much of their participatory approach is still largely limited to consulting with residents, rather than engaging them as equal partners in decisions about strategy or funding—something they share with many of their mainstream and some progressive foundations. Whether this will change remains to be seen, but it raises interesting questions as to how foundations and megadonors of differing political perspectives can employ PGM approaches.

Levels of Participation

As noted in the introduction and several chapters, the issue of defining PGM is still one that has yet to be decided, especially the debate between those who see that involving nonfunders in any part(s) of the grantmaking process is equally valuable in shifting power and others who believe that participation is on a continuum based on the degree to which nongrantmakers are part of decision-making. This debate has also been part of other participatory fields, including deliberative democracy, which characterizes participation as "thin" or "thick"; and other typologies, such as the International Association for Public Participation's Spectrum of Participation, which starts with "informing the public" and then moves to consulting, involving, collaborating, and, ultimately, "empowering" it.

The initial participatory framework put forward in the 2017 Ford Foundation monograph that helped lay the groundwork for the research initiative offered similar categories to those cited above, suggesting different types or levels of PGM but stopping short of claiming them as a hierarchy. Recently, this framework was challenged by Justice Funders, a group of social justice funders who do see PGM as being situated on a hierarchy, the highest level of which is removing donors altogether from the decision-making process and ceding that power to communities. Citing Rosa Gonzalez's *The Spectrum of Community Engagement to Ownership* tool, these practitioners maintain that collaborative decision-making, though important, still fails to acknowledge the role that philanthropy has played in wealth accumulation that has fueled economic inequality.[2]

Thus, they advocate for movement organizations to self-organize, identify their funding needs, and then activate their network of funders to organize and mobilize other funders to meet those budget needs. This process is different from most PGM efforts because the latter still depends on foundations to identify a dedicated pool of resources and then reach out to a set of community leaders and/or organizations to help determine which organizations should be funded according to particular processes and criteria. Examples include Bay Rising, which proactively meets its movement needs and goals first, rather than reactively responding to requests from funders; the Equity Fund's new "noncompetitive approach to grantmaking"; and the Southern Partners Fund's blend of community problem-solving and participatory grantmaking/resource allocation.

Practical Questions for PGM Implementation

In addition to the foregoing theoretical questions, myriad practical questions emerge from the studies in this collection about the implementation of PGM for those who do choose to practice it:

- How does stakeholder participation change as participatory practices become institutionalized in traditional foundations?
- Are there specific organizational attributes that make foundations more or less likely to engage stakeholders, such as a social justice ethos, a diverse staff and leadership, or an expansive peer network?
- How do foundations upend existing practices to incorporate stakeholder participation into their repertoire, and what kinds of support do they need to do so?
- Do some practices of community member recruitment designed to support the needs of donors and board members impede the intentions of centering those most affected by the issues and their ability to advance social justice and democratizing principles by introducing bias into who is recruited?

- How are philanthropic institutions integrating participatory values and approaches in their *internal* operations, such as staff hiring/promotions, financial/asset management, and community representation?
- What would a comprehensive mapping of global PGM funds reveal?
- How can PGM evaluation be designed and implemented in ways that reflect the participatory approaches and values undergirding it? What are some of the new and different theories about and models for evaluating PGM?
- How is PGM redefining traditional "conflict of interest" policies and procedures, which assume that personal experience, knowledge, and networks have no place in funding decisions?
- What does a PGM approach to strengthening movements and organizations (commonly referred to as "capacity building") look like, and how does it differ from traditional approaches?
- How can—or should—PGM be defined in ways that distinguish it from—or relate it to—other forms of inclusion, such as trust-based philanthropy, antiracism, community leadership, and racial equity? Is there value in further clarification; and if so, what is it?
- Does the level of participation that nonfunders have in the process make a difference in who gets funding? If the participation of nonfunders in any or all of the components of a participatory grantmaking process leads to similar outcomes, it calls into question whether such participation is hierarchical. If not, is that variance dependent on the degree to which participants are involved?
- For traditional foundations and megadonors that are not ready to adopt participation as a full-blown ethos, how can they experiment with PGM in a responsible and effective fashion? And do such efforts provide an incentive to adopt participation as an organizational ethos?

It is important to emphasize that most of the contributors to this volume are PGM pioneers; they work with or for organizations dedicated to empowering stakeholders and minimizing philanthropic paternalism. These practitioners have developed their expertise in PGM over time, yet they too are still learning, which they demonstrate by experimenting with novel practices that might strengthen their effectiveness in initiating, implementing, and managing PGM initiatives. For the foundations and megadonors that have experimented with PGM and seek to deepen their commitment, the chapters in this collection might provide motivation and guidance. And for traditional foundations and megadonors that support PGM in theory but do not know where to begin in practice, the chapters in this volume might serve as a road map—with multiple routes or entry points—for undertaking a PGM journey. Some foundations understandably will be cautious about making an unwavering commitment to PGM, but a critical lesson from this edited volume is that even modest PGM initiatives can make important contributions to the public good.

The Future of PGM

Where does PGM go next? What will PGM look like in the next five to ten years? We expect that the growth of mutual aid and social justice organizations will demand an increased democratization of philanthropy and that participatory grantmakers deepen their practice—for example, by addressing a wider range of implicit biases in their processes. We have seen similar patterns in the public's demanding participation in local government budget decisions and regulations, although not without a backlash. We expect tensions to come from both the stakeholder/community and philanthropic organizations. From a stakeholder/community perspective, we can imagine challenges similar to what we see in deliberative democracy and participation, such as how much decision-making power community members actually have, along with disillusionment over time with the process of participation if it does not lead to broader shifts in power. From the side of traditional foundations and megadonors, we can expect challenges related to taking on the ethos of participation and ways to include stakeholders in more just feedback processes but truly engaging them in deeper or more authentic participation. We might see issues with community trust in large traditional organizations. For PGM, we may see a growth in the process of PGM but struggles with its ethos. Will there be more competition for funds with the growth of mutual aid and social justice organizations? Will the public better understand PGM, with the growth of participation on college campuses through experiential philanthropy? If so, will the public and communities have greater expectations for PGM through their own experiences of learning how to do participatory philanthropy on college campuses? There are questions for future research in PGM as well as areas of investigation for participation and deliberative democracy.

In closing, it is important to underscore that the studies in this collection capture this field in a moment of flux. From the time when the initial set of research projects was commissioned by the Ford Foundation in 2019 to when the book's manuscript was completed in 2023, awareness and adoption of PGM have burgeoned, as have other practices aimed at increasing inclusion and power-sharing in philanthropy. How PGM will situate itself among these practices, and how they will all continue to evolve beyond the present moment, remain to be seen. But what is beyond doubt, as documented in this collection, is that the robust body of practice and evidence on PGM bears further attention, discussion, and advancement. Untangling the threads of PGM is one of the more meaningful tasks for the philanthropic sector in the years to come. The editors and authors of this collection hope to have contributed to this shared enterprise, as well as to the broader effort to theorize and study the many forms of democratic participation.

NOTES

1. Sherry Arnstein, "A Ladder of Citizen Participation," *Journal of the American Institute of Planners* 35, no. 4 (1969): 216–24.
2. Rosa Gonzalez, *The Spectrum of Community Engagement to Ownership* (Salinas, CA: Facilitating Power, 2020), https://d3n8a8pro7vhmx.cloudfront.net/facilitatingpower/pages/53/attachments/original/1596746165/CE2O_SPECTRUM_2020.pdf?1596746165.

Editors' and Contributors' Affiliations

COEDITORS

Chris Cardona, PhD, formerly of Ford Foundation
Cynthia M. Gibson, MSW, PhD, Cynthesis Consulting
Jasmine McGinnis Johnson, PhD, George Washington University
David Suárez, PhD, University of Washington

CONTRIBUTORS

Elizabeth Barajas-Román, EdM, Women's Funding Network
Len Bartel, MPA, CFLeads
Stephanie Clintonia Boddie, PhD, Baylor University / University of South Africa
Jen Bokoff, Disability Rights Fund / Disability Rights Advocacy Fund
Katie Carter, MA, Pride Foundation
Elizabeth J. Dale, PhD, Seattle University
Kathryn Destin, MA, Boston College
Emily Finchum-Mason, PhD, University of Washington
Laura García, Global Greengrants
Michael E. Hartmann, Capital Research Center
Sarah Huang, PhD, New England Grassroots Environment Fund
Kelly Husted, PhD, US Government Accountability Office
Marissa Jackson, MPH, formerly with Philanthropy Northwest, now with Seattle Foundation
Anne Katahira, formerly with Philanthropy Northwest, now with Anne Katahira Advising
Melanie Kawano-Chiu, Disability Rights Fund / Disability Rights Advocacy Fund

Eva King, MSW, Boston College
Melody MacLean, MA, CFLeads
Mirenda Meghelli, JD, Women's Funding Network
Caroline Merenda, CFLeads
Teresa Odendahl, Global Greengrants
Tracy R. Rone, PhD, Morgan State University
William A. Schambra, Hudson Institute
Jaime Smith, Haymarket People's Fund
Bart Westdijk, New England Grassroots Environment Fund

INDEX

Note: The letter *f* following a page number denotes a figure. The letter *t* following a page number denotes a table.

ableism, 191, 207, 358
Acha, M. A. R., 193
Adaptive Village, 245
advisory roles, 323–24
Aeschylus, 218
African American philanthropy, 223–30; The Black Church Tradition, 226–27; cooperative movements, 228–29; Nguzo Saba, 227–28; participatory democracy, 229
agroforestry, 192
Ajayi, T., 188, 214n4
Al Ghaib, O. A., 118
Aliaga, C., 190
Allen, R., 222, 226
Alliance Mobilize Our Resistance, 155
altruism, 16, 17, 36
AME Church, 226; gospel of giving, 222
American Enterprise Institute, 315
AME Zion Church, 226
Amirkhanyan, A., 40
Andrew, P., 197
Angula, H., 198
Annie E. Casey Foundation: Make It Your Own, 8; Making Connections, 8
anti-Black racism, 328
antiracism, 97, 98, 128, 129, 131, 132, 134, 140–43, 145, 146, 149–53, 155–56, 158–59, 161, 262, 355, 362. *See also* racism

antiracist grantmaking model, 127–61
Ariyani, D., 117–18
Arnstein, S.: ladder of participation, 19, 39, 355
Aspen Institute Community Strategies Group, 289; Resident Engagement Spectrum, 292*f*
Association for Women's Rights, 201
autonomy, 199, 200, 335, 336
Aylett, A., 195

Baker, E., 219, 230
Baldwin, J., 223
Baltimore: CLLCTIVLY, 231–33; Committee on Segregation, 232
Baltimore Sun, 232
Baltimore United for Change (BUC), 233
Barkan, J., 2
barriers to philanthropy, 207
Berger, P., 315
Bethel AME Church, 232
#beyondreactivism, 238
Bill & Melinda Gates Foundation, 36; investments in public education, 9
biodiversity conservation, 192
BIPOC, 140, 191, 210, 213, 214n9, 246, 268, 271, 324
Black Business Quest, 242, 244–45

Black Church Food Security Network, 245
Black Futures 360 Giving Circle, 242, 243
Black Futures microgrants, 239, 243
Black philanthropy, 223, 229, 233
Black Philanthropy Month, 235, 242–43, 245
Black self-determination, 97, 228
Black solidarity, 247
Black Solidarity Fund, 243, 244
Bocanegra, P., 349
Bourns, C., 67
Bradley Foundation, 316, 320, 321
Bradley Prize, 316
Brashier, N., 138
Brazil, 203
Bridgeford, E., 235
Brooklyn Org (formerly the Brooklyn Community Foundation), 308
Brown, L. T., 233
Brown III, H., 245
BUC. *See* Baltimore United for Change (BUC)
Burke, E., 314–15

Campbell, C., 243
Canada, 8
capitalism, 190; market capitalism, 313–14; philanthrocapitalism, 36; racial capitalism, 242
Carnegie, A., 35, 220
CASA Socio Environmental Fund, 203
CDC. *See* Centers for Disease Control and Prevention (CDC)
CDC Foundation, 68
Centers for Disease Control and Prevention (CDC), 68
Central American Women's Fund, 22, 98
CFLeads, 24, 260, 285, 287, 289–95, 298, 300–301, 303, 305, 309–10; Cultivating Community Engagement Panel, 290, 291; Economic Mobility Action Network, 307, 310; Executive Leadership Institute (ELI), 290, 293, 301, 310; Gun Violence Prevention Network, 310; issue networks, 292–93; Racial Equity Network, 310
Changemaker Awards, 245
CHANGE Philanthropy, 357
ChangeWorks, 128
Chan Zuckerberg Initiative, 36
Charles Stewart Mott Foundation: Community Foundations and Neighborhood Small Grants Program, 7–8
Chicago's Joyce Foundation, 321
China, 203
civic engagement, philanthropy as, 218, 220–21, 223–24*t*
civil rights, 221, 226–28; activism, 229; movement, 288
classism, 155, 191
Clifton, D., 246–47
CLIMA Fund, 194
climate change, 187, 189, 197, 199, 206; extreme, 191; impacts of, 195; mitigation, 190; policy development, 192; structural vulnerabilities to, 215n17
climate crisis, 187, 190–96, 200, 210–13, 328; global, 188
climate justice, 355, 358; feminist, 192; global participatory grantmaking through, 187–213; movements, 98, 189–94, 206, 211, 212; participatory approaches to, 191–93; philanthropy, 189; power imbalances and, 193–96 power inequities and, 193–95; value intersectionality, 191–93
climate resilience, 172, 192
CLLCTIVGIVE Annual Day of Giving, 239

CLLCTIVLY, 23, 98–99, 217, 219, 223, 230–49; approach to participatory grantmaking, 236–38; Baltimore, 231–33; decision-making, 236–38, 239t; ecosystem approach, 246–47; mission, 234–36; origin of, 233–34; participatory grantmaking strategies, evolution of, 239–43, 240–41t; programming, 234–36; responding to seismic social events, 243–46; strategies and participatory grantmaking, relationship between, 247–48
CLLCTIV SOUP, 239, 243, 246
collective giving, 1, 308
Colored Farmers' Alliance and Cooperative Union, 228
Colored Methodist Episcopal Church, 226
communities of color, 22, 23, 37, 38, 99, 155, 217–19, 238, 245, 342, 346
community advisory boards, 40
Community Advisory Committees, 308
Community Advisory Council, 307
community-centric analysis of participatory grantmaking, 208t
community development, 216n32, 288, 307
community foundations, 285–310; community leadership by, 295–96t; deep participatory roots, 287–89
community leadership, 24, 89, 166, 260, 285, 287, 289–307, 309–10, 356; activities, 302t; advocating for community needs, 306; by community foundation, 296t; community grants, making, 308; compass for, 294–303, 295f; competencies of, 301–3; engaging in trust-based philanthropy, 308–9; foundation leadership, providing, 306; giving circles, hosting, 308; informing local initiatives, 307; participatory philanthropy as, 293–94
Community Leadership Assessment Tool, 297–301, 300f, 306
community learning, 209–10
community maps, 287
community organizing, 129, 130, 141, 143, 144, 146–48, 150–53, 159
conservative philanthropy, 312–13, 315; advisory roles, 323–24; definition of, 313; donor intent, 322–23; elitism, 316–17; grantee-orientedness, 314–16; mediating structures, 314–16; potential pawnmaking, 324–26; traditions of, 313–14
cooperative movements, 228–29
Council on Foundations; Community Foundations Leadership Team, 289
Courage to Change (Haymarket People's Fund), 146, 150
COVID-19 pandemic, 23, 38, 94, 106, 157, 186n6, 211, 216n32, 239, 246, 259, 261, 262, 267, 271, 273, 281, 282, 285, 328, 329, 356
Crenshaw, K., 191
Crisis Community Care Fund, 267, 272, 273, 279
Croly, H., 316, 317
crowdfunding, 15, 17, 37, 235, 238, 243–45, 247
crowdsourcing, 247
Crown Heights, 308
CRPD. *See* United Nations (UN), Convention on the Rights of Persons with Disabilities (CRPD)
cultural self-determination, 230

decision-making power, 3, 10, 17–19, 24, 34, 363; conservative philanthropy, 321; COVID-19 pandemic and, 271; DRF/DRAF, 108, 111, 120; global participatory

decision-making power (*continued*)
grantmaking through climate justice, 188; Haymarket People's Fund, 128, 146, 156; impact of participation, 62, 63, 68, 69, 74, 75; New England Grassroots Environment Fund, 181; outsiders, 68; stakeholder participation in large foundations, 49, 51, 55; Women's Funding Network, 85, 201

Decolonizing Wealth (Villanueva), 8

Decolonizing Wealth Project, 357

Dedoose, 147

deliberation, 195, 209, 259

deliberative democracy, 6, 9, 19, 63, 64, 360, 363

democracy, 5–6, 357–59; cube, 40; deliberative, 6, 9, 19, 63, 64, 360, 363; participatory, 229, 237

Democracy in America (Tocqueville), 5

Dickson, T., 243–44

disability, prevalence of, 102–4

Disability Rights Advocacy Fund (DRAF), 21, 97, 101–24; 2007–2019, 104–6; accessibility, 110–12; challenges to, 114–16; continued participatory evolution, 121–23; designing processes, 116–17; growth of, 108–10; inclusion, 110–12; intentional efforts to center persons with disabilities, 108–17; methodology, 107–8; recommendations for, 118–21; rights-based grantmaking practices, 101, 102, 113–14; trust, 112–13, 117–18; 2019–2021, 106–8

Disability Rights Fund (DRF), 21, 38, 64, 97, 101–24; 2007–2019, 104–6; 2019–2021, 106–8; accessibility, 110–12; challenges to, 114–16; continued participatory evolution, 121–23; designing processes, 116–17; growth of, 108–10; inclusion, 110–12; intentional efforts to center persons with disabilities, 108–17; methodology, 107–8; recommendations for, 118–21; rights-based grantmaking practices, 101, 102, 113–14; trust, 112–13, 117–18

disabled persons' organizations (DPOs). *See* organizations of persons with disabilities (OPDs)

Doherty, A., 201

donor intent, 322–23

Double Zero Baltimore, 246

Douglass, F., 221, 226, 232

DPOs. *See* disabled persons' organizations (DPOs)

DRAF. *See* Disability Rights Advocacy Fund (DRAF)

Dr. Bronner's All-in-One, 246

DRF. *See* Disability Rights Fund (DRF)

Du Bois, W. E. B., 220, 226, 228

Dundorf, J., 186n7

Earth Island Institute, 202

Ebdon, C., 64

economic empowerment, 188, 245

economic equality, 7

economic inequality, 131, 210, 361

Economic Mobility Action Network, 307, 310

ELI. *See* Executive Leadership Institute (ELI)

elites, 6, 24, 316, 317, 359–60

elitism, 316–17

Emerick, W., 202

Emerson, K., 40

empowerment, 1, 9, 18, 20; economic, 188, 245

ENDS, 200

Engaging Residents: A New Call to Action for Community Foundations (CFLeads), 291

environmental justice, 162, 169, 170, 174, 175, 177, 179, 182, 190, 199,

202; community, 178, 181; elements of, 166; funds, 200; movements, 98, 164, 166, 176, 180, 184, 206, 358; principles, 181
Environmental Protection Agency, 166
equality, 9, 118, 271; economic, 7; racial, 227. *See also* inequality
equitable participation, 193, 194, 329
equity: gender, 21, 80, 82, 88, 90–93, 194, 354; racial, 7, 9, 15, 17, 23, 25, 91, 184, 249, 260–64, 270–72, 283, 304, 307, 328–34, 336, 337, 344, 347, 348, 350, 352n3, 355, 357; social, 53, 54. *See also* inequity
Executive Leadership Institute (ELI), 290, 293, 301, 310
expertise, 3, 64, 81, 88, 93–95, 114, 316, 336, 340, 341, 348, 349, 359–60, 362
expert participation, 194

false consciousness, 325
Family House, 325
Family League of Baltimore, 245
Faulk, L., 69
FCAM. *See* Fondo Centroamericano de Mujeres (FCAM)/Central America Women's Fund
FDO. *See* Foundation Directory Online (FDO)
federated fund, 331, 353n8
Feedback Labs, 9
Fidelity Charitable Gift Fund, 288
Filer Commission, 8
fiscal sponsorship, 125n22
Fondo Centroamericano de Mujeres (FCAM) / Central America Women's Fund, 187, 204, 210; background of, 199–201; methodology, 196; participatory grantmaking process, 203
food system resilience, 172
Food System Resilience Fund, 184

Ford Foundation, 4, 11, 13, 63, 163
Forten, J., 222–23, 226
Foundation Center (now Candid), 297, 303; "GrantCraft Guide," 10
Foundation Directory Online (FDO), 43
Framework for Community Leadership by a Community Foundation (CFLeads), 289–92, 294, 298, 301
Franklin, A., 64
freedom, 200, 209, 223, 228, 232, 347
Freedom Farm Cooperative, 229
Freedom Quilting Bee, 229
French Revolution, 313
FRIDA, 22, 98, 187, 189, 204, 214n5; background of, 201–2; participatory grantmaking process, 204
Friends of the Earth International, 202
Fuller, H., 321
Funders for LGBTQ Issues, 7
Fund for Shared Insight, 9, 82
Funding Exchange, 7, 29n29, 129
Fung, A., 39–40

GAGGA. *See* Global Alliance for Green and Gender Action (GAGGA)
Gaston, A. G., 221, 226, 227
Gates, C., 2
gender equity, 21, 80, 82, 87, 88, 90–93, 194, 354
gender inequality, 210
Gilmore, G., 221, 226
Giridharadas, A., 2,
giving circles, 15, 239, 242, 308
Giving Practice, 329–31
giving projects, 15
Global Alliance for Green and Gender Action (GAGGA), 200, 202
Global Entrepreneurship Monitor 2015 United States Report (Rogoff), 244
Global Fund for Community Foundations, 15
Global Fund for Women, 201

Global Greengrants Fund, 22, 64, 98, 187, 189, 203; background of, 197–99; participatory grantmaking process, 202–3
Global North, 98, 110, 189, 191, 208
Global South, 15, 98, 105, 109, 214n5
Going All In (CFLeads), 303–5, 304f, 309
Good Neighbor, 246
grant decisions, impact of participation on, 62–76; data collection, 69–74, 70t, 72–74t; hypotheses, 68–69; interview protocol questions, 76; power-sharing framework, 64–68, 65t; sample, 69–74, 70t, 72–74t
grantee-orientedness, 314–16
Grantmakers for Effective Organizations, 63
Great Depression, 228, 288
Greater Milwaukee Foundation, 307
Grønbjerg, K., 68–69
group solidarity, 228
Gun Violence Prevention Network, 310

Hamer, F. L., 229
Haymarket People's Fund, 21–22, 38, 98, 127–60; accountability, 152; antiracism and anti-oppression values, 152–53; anti-racism grantee funding criteria, 133, 147; antiracist grantmaking five-year evaluation, 136–57, 137f; antiracist grantmaking process, 135; antiracist plan and timeline, organizing, 154–55; boards, 134–35; coding, 147–48, 148f; data collection tools, 138t; definition of, 129–30; genuine antiracist leadership development, 151; grantees' feedback, 139–42, 142f; grantmaking development, 130–31; grantmaking flowchart, 137f; group interview process, 135; methodology, 136–39; panel and board members' feedback, 142–44; panels, 134–35; peer funders' feedback, 144–45; rating, 149–56, 149t, 150f; research questions, 136; revised grantee criteria, 131–33; systemic antiracist change, organizing for, 153–54

health conversion foundation, 331, 353n8
health inequity, 233
Hermanns, K., 263
He Yi Institute, 203
historic inequity, 270
Hogue, T., 138
homophobia, 191, 262
HOPE SF, 307
Hopkins, J., 232
human rights, 7, 105, 108, 120, 195, 197, 198, 200, 202; culture of, 113; funding, 103; movements, 109, 118, 205
Hyams Foundation, 144

identity-based community foundation, 331, 352–53n8
imperialism, 188, 196
improvement, philanthropy as, 220–21, 224–25t
Indigenous Persons with Disabilities Global Network, 106
individual philanthropy, 16
Indonesia, 203
inequality, 2, 9, 187, 188, 193, 202, 209, 233, 271, 354; economic, 131, 210, 361; gender, 210; social, 220; societal, 20; socioeconomic, 6; structural, 222, 223; wealth, 358. *See also* equality
inequity, 208, 215n17, 234, 352n3; health, 233; historic, 270; power, 93, 193–95, 349; racial, 38, 234; social, 36; structural, 190, 192–93,

221, 337; systemic, 37, 153. *See also* equity
Innovia Foundation, 306
institutional philanthropy, 2, 7, 16, 18, 99, 267, 354, 358, 359; stakeholder participation in large foundations, 35, 40, 42, 42*f*, 43, 49, 53–56
Intergovernmental Panel on Climate Change (IPCC), 215n17
internalized oppression, 143
internal racism, 128
International Association for Public Participation, 40, 41; Spectrum of Participation, 64
International Disability Alliance, 103, 111, 119
International Financial Institutions Advisory Board, 203
International Rivers, 202
intersectionality, in funding strategies, 206–7
IPCC. *See* Intergovernmental Panel on Climate Change (IPCC)

John M. Olin Foundation, 313
John Newman Honeybee Company, 245
Joseph-Gaudet, F., 221
Just Giving (Reich), 8
justice: climate, 98, 187–213, 206, 211, 212, 355, 358; environmental, 98, 162, 164, 166, 169, 170, 175–82, 184, 190, 198, 200, 202, 206, 358; racial, 141, 151, 161, 210, 259, 268, 272, 273, 277, 285, 332, 334, 337, 339, 342, 352n3, 356; restorative, 200, 249; social, 7, 15, 17, 18, 21, 24, 29n29, 30–31n57, 38, 40, 56, 69, 70, 82, 87, 94, 95, 97, 101, 105, 129, 131, 144–46, 159, 160, 174, 196, 198, 206, 237, 342, 357–60, 363
Justice Funders, 9, 63, 357
Just Transition, 15, 165*t*, 168*t*, 169, 183

Kaiser Permanente, 246
Kalamazoo Community Foundation, 306
Karenga, M. (aka Ronald Karenga), 227
King, M. L., Jr., 217, 226
Knight Foundation, 8
knowledge-sharing, 209–10
Kostishack, P., 210–11
KRS Smoothies, 242

LaFon, T., 222–23, 226
Lambright, K., 40
leadership of activists with disabilities, 102–4
Lecy, J., 69
"Let's Talk about Power: Making Meaningful Change through Participatory Grantmaking," 349
levels of participation, 11, 45, 75, 103, 210, 360–61
LGBTQ+, 23, 182, 261–63, 265, 266, 269, 271, 272, 275, 282
LGBTQIA2S+, 191, 213, 214n9
Liberty Hill Foundation, 64
Lincoln, C. E., 226
Liora, 246
Lloyd, C., 138
Lloyd, D., 113
Love, K., 115–16
Lynde and Harry Bradley Foundation, 313
Lynn, E. M., 218, 220, 237

MacArthur Foundation, 316
Mama Cash, 200
Mamiya, L., 226
marginalization, 9, 38, 81–83, 91, 104, 106, 110, 114, 118, 121, 136, 141, 152, 159, 175, 188, 191, 194, 222, 231, 271
market capitalism, 313–14
Martell, L., 68–69
Mason, B. "Biddy," 221, 226

Massey, D., 232
McCarty, O., 221, 226
McGinnis, J., 67–69
McKee, J., 221
megadonors, 8–9, 14, 16, 17, 25, 34, 260, 328–52
Mekonen, M., 138
Mitcham, G., 138
#MLK2BAKER, 237–38
modern critical theory, 191
Mondesir, B., 151
Monitor Institute, 286
Morris, A. D., 226–27
Moses, K., 242
Move And Still, 246
Moy, D., 144
Ms. Foundation for Women, 7
Msitshana, S. A., 118
Muñoz, Y., 206
Murthy, K. B., 120–21
mutual aid, 1, 16, 17, 166, 175, 223, 226, 228, 232, 234, 363; societies, 188, 228

Nabatchi, T., 40
National Black United Fund, 82
National Committee for Responsive Philanthropy, 7, 82
Ndobe, S. N., 188
Neuhaus, R. J., 315
New England Grassroots Environment Fund, 22, 98, 162–86; cohort building, 176; collaboration, leveraging, 176; convenings, 172, 172t; foundation of, 163; grantmaking, 169–72, 171f; grantmaking committee's learning, strengthening, 182–83; Guiding Practices, 164, 166–71, 167–68t; 173, 175, 181–83; Guiding Values, 164, 165t; internal operations, 175; level of collaboration and engagement, 176–79, 178f; mission, 174; participatory process, leveraging, 179–81; process evaluation, baseline for, 168–76 process evaluation, methods and goals for, 173–76, 174f; ripple effects of participatory grantmaking, tracing, 184–86; values, 175
New Hampshire Charitable Foundation, 163
new public participation, 6, 19
News Challenge, 8
Next Generation Youth Climate Advisory Board, 203
Nguzo Saba, 227–28, 242
"nothing about us without us," 9, 10, 21, 101–3, 105, 112, 113, 269, 291, 293, 355

Odaudu, T., 115, 117
Oilwatch International, 202
On the Brink of New Promise: The Future of US Community Foundations (Monitor Institute), 286, 289
OPDs. *See* organizations of persons with disabilities (OPDs)
oppression, 132, 138, 154, 156, 157, 175, 202, 209, 232, 337; forms of, 95n1, 131, 191, 212; internalized, 143; racial, 307; systematic, 191
Oregon Community Foundation, 306
organizational readiness: external conditions for, 341–44; interview protocol, 351–52
organizations of persons with disabilities (OPDs), 102–6, 109, 113, 114, 118

Paarlberg, L., 68–69
participatoriness, 260, 312–26, 359
participatory budgeting model, 64
participatory democracy, 229, 237
participatory grantmaking (PGM): case studies, 21–23, 97–99; challenges

to, 23–25, 259–60; contemporary drivers of, 8–10; definitional ambiguity, 10–14, 12–14*f*; definition of, 3, 63; framework, 13*f*, 13; future of, 363–64; historical roots of, 7–8; limits of, 23–25, 259–60; matrix of participation, 16–17, 16*f*; practical questions, 361–63; practice, mapping, 20–21, 33–34; research and implementation, future directions for, 354–64; research and practice, advancing, 18–20; in Women's Funding Network, 90–93. *See also individual entries*
participatory philanthropy, 11, 17–19, 24, 37–39, 55, 63, 104, 270, 285–310, 312–22, 326, 363; as community leadership, 293–94; school choice as, 320–22
patriarchy, 190, 195
Patterson, F., 222, 226
Paycheck Protection Program loan, 244
Peabody, G., 232
People's Institute for Survival and Beyond, 128, 130, 131, 141, 151, 156; Undoing Racism, 128, 130, 134, 140–43, 146, 159
Pesticide Action Network, 202
PGM. *See* participatory grantmaking (PGM)
philanthrocapitalism, 36
Philanthropic Initiative for Racial Equity, 357
philanthropy: African American, 223–30; as civic engagement, 221–22, 224–25*t*; definition of, 218; as improvement, 220–21, 224–25*t*; as relief, 220, 224–25*t*; as repair, 222–23, 224–25*t*; as social reform, 221, 224–25*t*. *See also individual entries*
Philanthropy Together, Launchpad for Hosts training, 308

Philippines, 203
Piereson, J., 313, 314
Pioneer Valley Workers Center (PVWC), 154
Plastino, N., 264
PNC Bank, 246
police brutality, 153
potential pawnmaking, 324–26
power: definition of, 352n4; imbalances, 193–95, 208; inequity, 93, 193–95, 349; shared clarity on, 338–40
power-sharing framework, 64–66, 65*f*; ceding power, 66; collaboration, 66; consultation, 65; levels of, 66–68
Pratt, E., 232
Presbyterian Church, 227
Pride Foundation, 23, 259–83, 356; Community Grants Program (CGP), 261, 263, 265, 266, 268*t*, 269, 270, 272, 278, 279, 282; Crisis Community Care Fund, 267, 272, 273, 278; goals of, 275–76; grantmaking, evolution of, 265–82; key events, timeline of, 267*t*; research methods, 264–65
program staff, 340–41
progressive philanthropy, 316–17
Promise of American Life, The (Croly), 316
public problem solving, 6
Purposeful's Global Resilience Fund, 106, 211
PVWC. *See* Pioneer Valley Workers Center (PVWC)

QTBIPOC, 276

racial bias, 248
racial capitalism, 242
racial climate, 233
racial disparities, 285
racial equality, 227

racial equity, 7, 9, 15, 23, 25, 82, 87, 91, 184, 249, 260–64, 270–72, 282, 283, 304, 307, 328–34, 336, 337, 344, 347, 348, 350, 352n3, 355, 357
Racial Equity Network, 310
racial exclusion, 230
racial heritage, 227
racial inequities, 38, 234
racial injustice, 227
racial justice, 141, 151, 161, 210, 259, 269, 272, 273, 277, 285, 332, 334, 337, 339, 342, 352n3, 356
racial oppression, 307
racial prejudice, 152
racial unrest, 243
racial uplift, 226
racism, 98, 127, 131, 133, 151–53, 157, 159, 160, 175, 190, 191, 210, 358; anti-Black, 328; internal, 128; reverse, 141; structural, 141, 248, 262, 263, 338; systemic, 130, 154, 214n9, 262, 263. See also antiracism; racial
Rainforest Action Network, 202
Rawa, 216n32
Red Umbrella Fund, 211
Reich, R., 2
relief, philanthropy as, 220, 224–25*t*
repair, philanthropy as, 222–23, 224–25*t*
resilience, 200; climate, 172, 192; food system, 172
Resist, 144
Resource Generation, 144
resource management, 192
restorative justice, 200, 249
reverse racism, 141
Robert Wood Johnson Foundation, 68
Robinson, C., 163, 173, 174, 177, 180–83
Rockefeller, J. D., 35
Rockefeller Foundation, 36, 243, 246
Rourke, B., 2
Rudolph, B., 138

Samarasan, D., 105
Samcam, C., 204
Samdhana Institute, 203
San Antonio Area Foundation, 308
San Francisco Area Foundation, 2023–25 Responsive Grant Process, 308
San Francisco Foundation, 307
Saunders-Hastings, E., 2
Scaife Foundations, 313
school choice, as participatory philanthropy, 320–22
School of Community Health and Policy, Morgan State University, 245
Scott, M., 9
SEJ. *See* Students for Educational Justice (SEJ)
self-determination, 1, 18, 133, 153, 271; Black, 97, 228; cultural, 230
Seller, S., 145
Sharp Street Church, 232
Shepherd, M. 232
#ShiftThePower community philanthropy, 15, 121
Smith, B., 321
Smith Richardson Foundation, 313
social equity, 53, 54
social inequality, 220
social inequity, 36
social justice, 24, 29n29, 87, 94, 97, 105, 129, 197 198, 206, 237, 357–59, 363; ethos, 56, 361; funders, 40, 69, 70, 342, 360; Haymarket, 144–46, 159, 160; movements, 7, 21, 101, 129, 174, 359; philanthropy, 15, 17, 18, 31n57, 38, 82, 95, 357, 358
Social Justice Funders Network, 144
social reform, philanthropy as, 221, 224–25*t*
social solidarity, 223, 226
societal inequality, 20
socioeconomic inequality, 6
Sogge, K., 269–70, 276, 280

Soil to Sky: Climate Solutions That Work (California Environmental Associates), 194
solidarity, 132, 166, 185, 200, 205, 222, 238; Black, 247; group, 228; social, 223, 226
South Baltimore Gateway Partnership, 246
staff capacity, 338
stakeholder participation, in large foundations, 34–57; conceptual framework, 39–43, 42f; consulting, 46–48, 47f, 50, 51f, 53–54; deciding, 48–49, 49f, 51, 52f, 54; direct, 41, 46–49, 47–49f, 47t; indirect, 41–42, 49–52, 51f, 52f, 57; involving, 48, 48f, 50–51, 52f, 54; methodology, 43–46; respondent characteristics, 45, 46t; survey weighting methodology, 56
strategic philanthropy, 17, 81
structural inequality, 222, 223
structural inequities, 190, 192–93, 221, 337
structural racism, 141, 248, 262, 263, 337
Students for Educational Justice (SEJ), 151
Sukuamis, 207, 209, 213
sustainability, 115, 140, 197, 200, 308
Sustainable Development Goals, 104, 106
systematic oppression, 191
systemic inequity, 37, 153
systemic racism, 130, 154, 214n9, 262, 263

Tannen, J., 232–33
Taylor, C., 325
Tchozewski, C., 198
Tezel, B., 138
thick participation, 19, 238
Third Wave Fund, 270
ThriveOn, 307
Tides Foundation, 7, 105, 125n22
tithing, 1, 227

Tocqueville, A. de, 314, 315
To Empower People: The Role of Mediating Structures in Public Policy (Berger and Neuhaus), 315
traditional foundations, 3, 8, 11, 18, 25, 34, 67, 68, 260, 328–52
traditional medicine, 192
Trans Justice Funding Project, 270
transphobia, 191
Triumphs of Joseph: How Today's Community Healers Are Reviving Our Streets and Neighborhoods, The (Woodson), 315–16
T. Rowe Price, 246
Truchan, H., 138
trust-based philanthropy, 15, 17, 19, 23, 115, 259, 261, 262, 267, 268t, 272, 274, 275, 282, 308, 356
Trust-Based Philanthropy Project, 9, 267, 272, 318
Tsuruta, A., 349
Tubman, H., 221, 226, 232
Tuckman, B., 169
#28 Days of Black Futures, 244–45

UHAI ESHRAI, 211
Ujima (Collective Work and Responsibility), 242, 243
UN. *See* United Nations (UN)
Undoing Racism, 128, 130, 134, 159; training, 140–43, 146
UN General Assembly, 103
United Methodist Church, 227
United Nations (UN): Commission on the Status of Women, 106; Committee on Economic, Social, and Cultural Rights General Comment on persons with disabilities, 103; Conference of State Parties to the CRPD, 106; Convention on the Rights of Persons with Disabilities (CRPD), 102–6, 108, 112, 113; Decade of Disabled

United Nations (UN) (*continued*)
Persons (1983–92), 103;
Declaration on the Rights of
Disabled Persons, 103; Standard
Rules on the Equalization of
Opportunities for Persons with
Disabilities, 103; Sustainable
Development Goals, 104,
106; World Program of Action
Concerning Disabled Persons, 103
United Nations Climate Change
Conference, Glasgow (2021), 194
United Negro College Fund, 222
United States (US), 8, 81, 94; civil
sector, 9; COVID-19 pandemic, 259;
Environmental Protection Agency,
166; social change movements, 131;
stakeholder participation, 35–57;
Tax Reform Act of 1969, 36
Urgent Action Fund Asia and Pacific,
211
US. *See* United States (US)

value intersectionality, 191–93
Vazquez, P., 209
Vegan SoulFest, 245
venture philanthropy, 17
Vergara, L., 209
Villanueva, E., 284n9
voting, 6, 68, 204, 211, 242

Walker, D., 249
Walker, Madam C. J., 222, 226
wealth inequality, 358
Weaver, J., 231

We Give Black Fest, 242, 245
We Got Your Back, 244, 246
WELL (The Women Entrepreneur
Leadership Lab), 246
WFN. *See* Women's Funding Network
(WFN)
white superiority, 131, 159
white supremacy culture, 339, 341, 343,
353n15
William E. Simon Foundation, 313
Winners Take All (Giridharadas), 8
Wisely, D. S., 218, 220, 237
With and For Girls Fund, 211
WJZ-TV, 246
Women's Funding Network (WFN),
80–95; context, 82–83; cultural
ethos of participation, 90; data
collection, 85–86; ecosystem,
81; participant selection, 85;
participatory grantmaking in, 90–93
Woodson, R., Sr., 315–16, 325
Wooten, J., 219, 230–31, 234, 237–38,
243, 244, 247–49
World Bank, 102
World Economic Forum (2019), 9–10
World Health Organization, 102

xenophobia, 191

Yancy, C., 345, 349
Young Feminist Fund, 22, 98, 187, 196,
201
youth climate movement, 192

zip code test, 315